MICHELIN

THE MOTORCYCLE
YEARBOOK
2003-2004

CHRONOSPORTS
EDITEUR

ISBN 2-84707-050-8
Also available in French under the title of "L'Année Grands Prix Moto 2003" ISBN 2-84707-037-0 and in German under the title of "Das Motorrad-Rennsportjahr 2003" ISBN 2-84707-059-1

© November 2003, Chronosports S.A.
Jordils Park, Chemin des Jordils 40, CH-1025 St-Sulpice, Switzerland.
Tél. : (+41 21) 694 24 44.
Fax : (+41 21) 694 24 46.
E-mail: info@chronosports.com
www.chronosports.com

Printed and bound in France by Partenaires Fabrication

THE MOTORCYCLE

YEARBOOK

2003-2004

Photos

Stan Perec

Thanks to Nello Zoppe
(Nikon France) for his valued
collaboration and to Lukasz
Swiderek and Jaime Olivares who
have provided some of the photos
in this book.

Texts

Jean-Claude Schertenleib

Contents

"Thanks Daijiro..."

"This 2003 season has been the most important of my career, on the sports front, but more importantly from a human perspective.

"First, I would like to talk about everything we went through before the first GP, during testing. There was something unusual going on back then in the way Daijiro Kato and I teamed up. There was a force uniting all of us and an immense will to win.

"At the Japanese GP, having had a problem at the start, I was climbing up through the field, feeling good on the bike and feeling good in my head. Then, Daijiro had his terrible accident. Everything could have ended there.

"As I arrived in South Africa, two weeks later, I didn't think I had the inner strength to deal with the challenge of taking the start. But we thought about Daijiro and his family. It was the most difficult race of my life, but we won. Above all, we realised we had done it because of the strengths we had forged over the winter.

"Then, as the races went by, we still kept Daijiro in our thoughts and this feeling got even stronger, not just for us, but everyone in the championship...

"After the tragedy at the Japanese GP, everyone worked to improve safety. The drivers spoke their mind and the teams supported them. Dorna, the championship promoter and the International Federation also played their part.

All this time, two opposing feelings ran through my mind. There was the joy of winning, of having become one of the best, but there was also the pain of loss, of not having Daijiro by my side...

"With the 2003 season now over, I am very confident about 2004. Confident, because I know I am still learning and that I have not yet exhausted all my potential.

I know it and everything I have learnt, I owe it to Daijiro...

"Enjoy reading the Moto Grands Prix Yearbook 2003-2004!"

Sete Gibernau

15

TRIBUTE

Where there is life...

...so too there is death. A moving phrase which comes out when the pain is too strong and is oh so appropriate for this sport that we love. Yes, life is made up of risks and sometimes those risks can be fatal. So it is true that where there is life, there is always death.

But in 2003, the grim reaper struck with unexpected force. In the grand scheme of things our world is a little one and that is why this year's tragedies saw rage wipe away any element of understanding and provoked the unanswered questions.
Why Yves Jamotte, who until last year was the "Motorcycle Grand Prix Yearbook" photographer? Why Yves? So young, so full of life, so passionate.

Why Barry Sheene, the hero of our youth? Why Barry? So handsome and so kind hearted.
Why Daijiro Kato? The rider who carried Honda's hopes of bringing the supreme title back to Japan. Yes, why Daijiro, who was all smiles on the eve of qualifying for the Japanese GP, while we chatted with his team-mate, Sete Gibernau and he tried to grasp the intricacies of this conversation held in a mixture of French, Catalan and English?

Why David Jefferies, who since the death of Joey Dunlop, had become Mr. Tourist Trophy? Yes, why David? He was so sure of himself when he landed on the Isle of Man with its ever-present dangers, but also its unique attraction.

Why Steve Hislop, the indefatigable regular of the British championship? Yes, why Steve, who was as keen on racing his bikes as he was on getting behind the controls of the helicopter in which he died?

And why all the other less well known riders from championships in Great Britain, Italy and elsewhere, who were nevertheless all stars in someone's eyes, be they a friend, a spouse, a father, a mother or children.

Yes, why?

Because where there is life, so too there is death. And maybe we should hope that in the land of the dead, after a painful 2003, they must be having a rare old time what with the likes of Yves, Barry, Daijiro, David, Steve and all the others, when they get together to talk about bikes.

Jean-Claude Schertenleib

Yves Jamotte the way we liked him: smiling while he worked.

Daijiro's souvenir album

1996

1997

1997

1998

1999

2000

2000

2000

2001

2001

2001

Donington, Autumn 1982. A few months after his terrible accident at Silverstone, Barry Sheene gets back on a bike. For this first test, his mate Steve Parrish is on the pillion seat, just in case he needs to take over if the rider encounters a problem....

The unforgettable number 7

"Barry Sheene, the 500 cc world champion in 1976 and 1997, who had been living for several years in Australia, died yesterday after a courageous battle with cancer. Sheene, aged 52, died in a hospital on the Gold Coast, at around 2 o'clock in the afternoon, Queensland time. He leaves a wife, Stephanie, their daughter Sidonie (18) and their son Freddie (14.) A private family funeral will take place later in the week." **Press release issued by Barry Sheene's family, Monday, 10ᵗʰ March 2003.**

Sheene was the man with two world titles, multiple fractures with 27 screws hidden in his bones, along with metal plates and pins. Whenever he travelled by plane, he would set off the alarms and cause panic at the security checks. Barry was the ultimate playboy with the permanent smile. He was a stylish character, honoured with the Order of the British Empire in 1978, much to the pride of his parents, Iris and Franco and he was always the king of the jokers in the paddock. But now, Barry was dead...

Born on 11th September...

Barry Sheene was born on 11th September 1950, on a Monday evening, a few minutes before nine o'clock in a London clinic. His father, Frank, or "Franco" as he was known in racing circles, was a brilliant bike builder and Barry was soon steeped in the business of racing.

At the age of 19, having convinced some of his father's friends that he was gifted with an amazing talent, he took part in his first race. At the start of 1970, still not 20, he competed in his first GP. At the time, it was very unusual for someone that young to be racing. Barry Sheene's career had just begun, but legendary status was still a long way off.

Last Autumn, a few weeks after he had made public the fact he had cancer, a crowd of 80,000 turned up to see him at Goodwood, where he took his final win on British soil. They were there not just because of his impressive track record, but because Barry Sheene was much more than the sum of his statistics. He had become a hero, whether loved or regarded with envy.

Barry the playboy in 1977. The face of an angel but an impish nature.

To a certain extent, he was also the first rider of the modern era to understand the importance of image and he dragged motor cycle racing out of its specialist arena into the public domain: something which has not escaped Valentino Rossi. It is not surprising that the two men respected and admired one another. "Barry was magic. He was more than a rider, more than a champion," reckons the current big star in the motorcycle racing firmament.

Overnight star

How was this persona created? Those who lived alongside him in the Seventies have the answer: "Barry Sheene became a star overnight."
It is the start of 1975. On the high speed banking at Daytona, the rear tyre on his Suzuki exploded at around 300 km/h. A television crew there to make a documentary about Sheene filmed what happened next and it featured on every news report around the world. Lying on the tarmac at the Florida track, Barry is conscious. One of his legs is bent so far back that he thinks he has lost it. He has multiple fractures to both his upper and lower limbs: the forearms, one wrist, six ribs, one collar bone, several compressed vertebrae, as well as internal bleeding. It is hard to believe that this body belongs to someone who is somehow still alive. But seven weeks later, Barry Sheene is back in the saddle on a racing motorbike! And one year later, he is world champion for the first time.

The Sheene phenomenon was born, as he embarked on a recovery programme with a cigarette clenched permanently between his teeth, while making life hell, or maybe heaven, for the nurses charged with looking after him. He then went on to win the world championship and he is still the last Englishman to have done so. There were other accidents, including the terrible one during practice for the 1982 British Grand Prix. For a second time, it looked as though he had killed himself, only to be racing again a few months later.

The rebel and the Rolls

That was Barry Sheene for you. His name will remain forever in the motorcycle racing record books and not

Le Castellet, 29th May 1977. Sheene wins the French GP.

just for his talent and his incredible comebacks after near fatal accidents, but also because he had a big heart, a very big heart. He will also be remembered for the rebellious side to his nature, which had made him the scourge of the paddock, always ready to fight against the authorities when it came to improving safety and increasing wages for the riders. Sheene may have had a dilettante side to him – he got through his pack of un-tipped cigarettes every day and his first priority after ever race was to light up a fag! Above all though, he was the first ambassador of the modern era. He understood that in order to convince sponsors to invest in a sport which had a rather downmarket image, a rider had to be prepared to wear a dinner jacket now and again and to be seen at swish parties, with the prettiest model girls hanging off his arm. This was no hardship for a man with an eye for the ladies.

With his first big sponsorship paycheque he bought himself a Rolls-Royce. His second pay packet saw the arrival of a mansion not far from London which housed his workshop. There followed a helicopter which was his pride and joy. He was a legend in Great Britain and when he retired, he became one in Australia too. He was persuaded to settle there by one of his famous friends, the Beatle, George Harrison, who reckoned that the Gold Coast climate would be good for his metal-filled bones.

"It's my decision, it's my life"...

It was cancer that got him in the end: cancer of the throat and the oesophagus, which came on with terrifying speed. It was diagnosed the previous year in July and he decided to fight it without the aid of chemotherapy. "To be honest, when you think of the number of accidents I've survived, it must mean there's someone watching over me. I understand what the doctors are telling me but, at the end of the day, it's my decision. It's my life and it's up to me how I choose to live it." Barry Sheene died in early March, surrounded by his family and his best mate, Steve Parrish. The playboy had gone and no doubt, he was keeping the angels well entertained.

Le Mans, 2nd September 1979. Sheene avoids all the obstacles and wins the final GP of the season.

They knew Barry Sheene...

"Barry was a heart on legs. If he had not stopped in the middle of the race to help me, I would not be alive today..."
Phillipe Coulon, whose life Sheene had saved during the 1977 Swedish GP.

"Barry packed more in to his 52 years than most people would do in a hundred..."
Damon Hill, the 1996 Formula 1 world champion.

"Barry left his mark on motorcycle racing. But more than that, he was someone who made a lot of people happy..."
Michael Doohan, five time 500 world champion.

"Even in heaven, where he is resting now, no doubt he will trip up now and again. And the angels who will help him won't be able to stop falling in love with him, as was the case with people on this earth when he was alive..."
Claudio Costa, the GP doctor.

"He did so many crazy things in his life that we all felt he was immune to death..."
Steve Parrish, an old rival on the track and a great friend off it.

"Barry was an immense talent who always had time for everyone. He met every request with a smile..."
Giacomo Agostini, five times world champion.

"I would not have become Kenny Roberts without Barry Sheene. The only thing that got me out of bed on race mornings was telling myself, "go on, go and beat Barry Sheene!"
Kenny Roberts Senior, his great rival who became a friend.

2002 Australian GP. Barry and his son, Freddie had turned up to see some old friends. Two months earlier, he learnt he had cancer.

The style is still perfect. In recent years, Barry Sheene took part in various historic bike races.

BUSINESS CARD

Name:	Sheene
First name:	Barry
Born:	11th September 1950
At:	Holborn (Great Britain)
First race:	1968
First GP:	Spanish GP, 1970 (125)
Number of GP wins:	23 (1/50; 3/125; 19/500)
First GP win:	Belgium GP, 1971 (125)

Track record

1969: 2nd british championship 125 (Suzuki).
1970: 14th World Championship 125, British champion 125 (Suzuki),
       3rd british championship 250 (Bultaco).
1971: 7th World Championship 50 (Kreidler),
       2nd World Championship 125, British champion 125 (Suzuki),
       33rd World Championship 250,
       2nd british championship 250 (Derbi).
1972: 13th World Championship 250 (Yamaha).
1973: European champion 750, British champion 500,
       British superbike champion (Suzuki).
1974: 6th World Championship 500, British champion 500,
       British superbike champion (Suzuki).
1975: 6th World Championship 500, 2nd European championship 750,
       3rd british superbike championship (Suzuki).
1976: World Champion 500, British champion 500,
       British superbike champion (Suzuki).
1977: World Champion 500, British champion 500,
       British superbike champion (Suzuki).
1978: 2nd World Championship 500, British champion 500,
       British superbike champion (Suzuki).
1979: 3rd World Championship 500, 6th British superbike
       championship (Suzuki).
1980: 15th World Championship 500 (Yamaha).
1981: 4th World Championship 500, 6th British superbike
       championship (Yamaha).
1982: 5th World Championship 500, 9th British superbike
       championship (Yamaha).
1983: 13th World Championship 500,
       7th british championship 500,
       12th british championship "Masters" (Suzuki).
1984: 6th World Championship 500, 6th ITV Superbike World
       of Sport (Suzuki).

MOTOGP

Having taken the title with Valentino Rossi, the RC211V which dominated the first year of MotoGP was further developed over the winter, especially in the area of electronics, as it relates to traction and deceleration control, and power management. Seven riders get their hands on the Honda V5, with three of them regarded as works HRC riders: Valentino Rossi of course, with US Superbike champion Nicky Hayden as his team-mate, Tohru Ukawa, running in Camel Pons colours alongside Massimiliano Biaggi and the lamented Daijiro Kato, whose works bike was handed to his Telefonica Movistar team-mate, Sete Gibernau at the first European GP of the season in Jerez. The seventh rider, Makoto Tamada raced under the Pramac banner, with support from Bridgestone. Rossi is always first to get the latest development parts, but it is Gibernau who takes the first win with the short exhausts, in Germany. From Brno onwards, Biaggi also received new parts.

Repsol Honda Team

HEADQUARTERS: Wijngaardveld 1,
9300 Aalst (Belgium).

INTERNET SITE: www.hondaracinginfo.com

TEAM MANAGER: Koij Nakajima.

RIDERS
Valentino Rossi (16.2.1979)
First GP: Malaysia, 1996 (125)
Italian Champion endurance minibike (1992)
Italian Champion 125 Sport-Production (1994)
Italian Champion 125 (1995)
World Champion 125 (1997)

World Champion 250 (1999)
World Champion 500 (2001)
World Champion MotoGP (2002)
World Champion MotoGP (2003)
Number of GP wins: 59 (12/125; 14/250; 13/500; 20/MotoGP)

Nicky Hayden (30.7.1981)
First GP: Japan, 2003 (MotoGP)
Champion US Supersport 600 (1999)
Champion US Superbike (2002)

TEAM STRUCTURE
Sporting director: Carlo Fiorani.
Chief mechanic: Jeremy Burgess (Valentino Rossi) and Trevor Morris (Nicky Hayden)

Massimiliano Biaggi — 3

Tohru Ukawa — 11

Camel Pramac Pons

HEADQUARTERS: Poligono Industrial Sta. Rita,
C/Acustica 16, 08755 Castellbisbal/Barcelone (Spain).

INTERNET SITE: www.hondapons.com

TEAM MANAGER: Sito Pons.

RIDERS
Massimiliano Biaggi (26.6.1971)
First GP: Europe, 1991 (250)
Italian Champion 125 Sport-Production (1990)
European Champion 250 (1991)
European Champion 250 (1994)
European Champion 250 (1995)
European Champion 250 (1996)

European Champion 250 (1997)
Number of GP wins: 41 (29/250; 8/500; 4/MotoGP)

Tohru Ukawa (18.5.1973)
First GP: Japan, 1994 (250)
Japanese Champion 250 «B» (1991)
Japanese Champion 250 (1993)
Japanese Champion 250 (1994)
Number of GP wins: 5 (4/250; 1/MotoGP)

TEAM STRUCTURE
Technical Director: Antonio Cobas.
Chief mechanic: Santi Mulero (Massimiliano Biaggi) and Ramon Forcada (Tohru Ukawa).

Valentino Rossi — 46

Nicky Hayden — 69

Telefonica Movistar Honda

HEADQUARTERS: Via Fra Domenico Paganelli 8, 48018 Faenza/RA (Italy).

INTERNET SITE: www.gresiniracing.com

TEAM MANAGER: Fausto Gresini

RIDERS
Sete Gibernau (15.12.1972)
First GP: Spain, 1992 (250)
Number of GP wins: 5 (1/500; 4/MotoGP)

Ryuichi Kiyonari (19.9.1982)
First GP: France, 2003 (MotoGP)

Daijiro Kato (4.7.1976)
First GP: Japan, 1996 (250)
Japanese Champion minibike (1988)
Japanese Champion minibike (1989)
Japanese Champion minibike (1990)
Japanese Champion minibike (1991)
Japanese Champion 250 (1997)
World Champion 250 (2001)
Number of GP wins: 17 (250)

TEAM STRUCTURE
Chief mechanic: Juan Martinez (Sete Gibernau) and Fabrizio Cecchini (Daijiro Kato, then Ryuichi Kiyonari).

6 Makoto Tamada

15 Sete Gibernau

Pramac Honda

HEADQUARTERS: Frederik Roeskestraat 123, 1076 EE Amsterdam (Netherlands).

INTERNET SITE: www.pramacracing.com

TEAM MANAGER: Gianluca Montiron.

RIDER
Makoto Tamada (4.11.1976)
First GP: Japan, 1998 (250)
Japanese Champion 250 Novice (1994)

TEAM STRUCTURE
Technical Director: Giulio Bernardelle.
Chief mechanic: Hitoshi Kohara (Makoto Tamada).

23 Ryuichi Kiyonari

74 Daijiro Kato

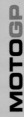

In 2002, thanks to Massimiliano Biaggi, the YZR-M1 was the only machine to interrupt Honda's hegemony. In 2003, Yamaha had done a lot of work on the injection system and in theory at least, should have been a presence to reckon with. Brazil's Alexandre Barros was the transfer of the year and his winter testing results seem to confirm that the M1 will have its say. The 250 world champion, Marco Melandri, is undergoing his apprenticeship in the blue riband category alongside Carlos Checa and Olivier Jacque is Barros' number 2 at Tech 3, while Shinya Nakano has ended up in the Luis D'Antin camp. The riders would spend most of the year complaining about the M1 and recovering from numerous crashes, but the Yamaha MotoGP project leader, Ichiro Yoda is convinced that the gap to the Honda is not so big. "We have a good chassis and the top speed is not bad. However, we are aware that we still have work to do on the way the power is delivered."

Gauloises Yamaha Team

HEADQUARTERS: 635 chemin du Niel, 83230 Bormes-les-Mimosas (France).

INTERNET SITE: www.gauloisesracing.com

TEAM MANAGER: Hervé Poncharal.

RIDERS
Alexandre Barros (18.10.1970)
First GP: Spain, 1986 (80)
Brasilian Champion Cyclo (1979)
Brasilian Champion Cyclo (1980)
Brasilian Champion 50 (1981)
Brasilian Champion 250 (1985)
Number of GP wins: 6 (4/500; 2/MotoGP)

Olivier Jacque (29.8.1973)
First GP: Australia, 1995 (250)
World Champion 250 (2000)
Number of GP wins: 7 (250).

TEAM STRUCTURE
Coordinator: Gérard Valle.
Chief mechanic: Gilles Bigot (Alexandre Barros) and Guy Coulon (Olivier Jacque).

Fortuna Yamaha Team

HEADQUARTERS: Via A. Tinelli 67-69, Gerno di Lesmo, 20050 Milan (Italy).

INTERNET SITE: www.fortunayamaha.com

TEAM MANAGER: Lin Jarvis.

RIDERS
Carlos Checa (15.10.1972)
First GP: Europe, 1993 (125)
Spanish Champion 80 (1991)
Spanish Champion 250 «open» (1995)
Number of GP wins: 2 (500)

Marco Melandri (7.8.1982)
First GP: Czech Republic, 1997 (125)
Italian Champion minibike Junior A (1992)
Italian Champion minibike Junior B (1994)
Italian Champion 125 (1997)
Winner of Honda Italy Trophy 125 (1997)
World Champion 250 (2002)
Number of GP wins: 17 (7/125; 10/250)

TEAM STRUCTURE
Technical Director: Ken Suzuki.
Chief mechanic: Antonio Jimenez (Carlos Checa) and Fiorenzo Fanali (Marco Melandri).

D'Antin Yamaha Team

HEADQUARTERS: Ramon y Cajal 25 (Pol. Ind. Gitesa), 28814 Daganzo de Arriba/Madrid (Spain).

INTERNET SITE: yamahadantin.com

TEAM MANAGER: Luis D'Antin.

RIDER
Shinya Nakano (10.10.1977)

First GP: Japan, 1998 (250)
Champion du Japan 250 (1998)
Number of GP wins: 6 (250).

TEAM STRUCTURE
Technical Director: Naoya Kaneko.
Chief mechanic: Andrea Dosoli (Shinya Nakano).

Gauloises Yamaha

Fortuna Yamaha

D'Antin Yamaha

Of course this was the big news of the second year of the MotoGP era. Ducati landed at Suzuka with its superb Desmosedici, after there had been plenty of positive comment about the red machine. Hitting the headlines, Loris Capirossi set the fastest time in the unofficial dress rehearsal for the series at the Circuit de Catalunya, near Barcelona. Hiding behind this ambitious project is a team of young enthusiasts lead by Claudio Domenicali, its managing director. The Italian marque opted for a 70 degree V4 engine. Ducati Corse's technical supreme, Filippo Preziozi recalls the genesis of the project: "Our approach was based on virtual simulation on computer. We had drawn a rider whom we placed on a bike which did not yet exist. Then the other elements fell into place around this base." Among these elements, the desmodromic engine, the company's signature speciality is just one of the innovative features of this bike, which was quick straight from the crate.

Ducati Marlboro Team

HEADQUARTERS: Via Cavalieri Ducati 3, 40132 Bologne (Italy).

INTERNET SITE: www.ducati.com/racing

TEAM MANAGER: Claudio Domenicali.

RIDERS
Troy Bayliss (30.3.1969)
First GP: Australia, 1997 (250)
British Superbike Champion (1999)
World Champion Superbike (2001)

Loris Capirossi (4.4.1973)
First GP: Japan, 1990 (125)
World Champion 125 (1990)
World Champion 125 (1991)
World Champion 250 (1998)
Number of GP wins: 23 (8/125; 12/250; 2/500; 1/MotoGP)

TEAM STRUCTURE
Director: Livio Suppo.
Technical Director: Corrado Cecchinelli.
Chief mechanic: Bruno Leoni (Troy Bayliss) and Massimo Bracconi (Loris Capirossi).

For its second year in the sport, the Aprilia RS "Cube" not only went on a diet, it also benefited, thanks to Colin Edwards, from a supply of Michelin tyres. The "Cube" is definitely the most extreme prototype in the category, borrowing from advanced F1-derived technology in such areas as the engine, designed by Cosworth. Gigi Dall'Igna, the RSV project leader, knows they have not chosen the easiest way. "This bike is totally revolutionary. That's why we need more time to getting it working properly. We are using technology which comes from F1 and it's not always easy adapting solutions devised for four wheels to a bike. Of course, we could revert to more conventional choices, but that goes against our philosophy." Despite the help provided by Colin Edwards, the RS "Cube" had a difficult season.

Alice Aprilia Racing

HEADQUARTERS: Strada la Ciarulla, 47899 Serravalle (San Marino).

INTERNET SITE: www.racingaprilia.com

TEAM MANAGER: Francesco Guidotti.

RIDERS
Noriyuki Haga (2.3.1975)
First GP: Japan, 1998 (500)
Japanese Champion Superbike (1997)

Colin Edwards (27.2.1974)
First GP: Japan, 2003 (MotoGP)
Champion US 250 (1992)
World Champion Superbike (2000)
World Champion Superbike (2002)

TEAM STRUCTURE
Technical Director: Jan Witteveen.
Chief mechanic: Giacomo Guidotti (Noriyuki Haga) and Adrian Gorst (Colin Edwards).

Ducati Marlboro

Alice Aprilia Racing

The GSV-R should have made its GP debut at the start of 2003, but in fact Suzuki brought its project forward by a year, in order to have a four stroke machine competing in the first year of the MotoGP era. It was a brave decision, especially as Suzuki, which used an in-line four in Superbikes, had opted to go down the V4 route in order to fully embrace the philosophical challenge of the new blue riband category of motorcycle racing. Kenny Roberts was still on parade and he had a new team-mate in the form of John Hopkins. What weapon did they have at their disposal? A bike in a state of constant evolution, but which actually did not work any better than the previous year's machine. Compared to 2002, the V angle had been narrowed from 65 to 60 degrees to try and improve power delivery. Last year's chassis had been an evolution of the RGV500, while this year's was brand new and made of aluminium.

Suzuki Grand Prix Team

HEADQUARTERS: Enterprise Way, Edenbridge, Kent TN8 6HF (Great Britain).

INTERNET SITE: www.suzuki-racing.com

TEAM MANAGER: Garry Taylor.

RIDERS
Kenny Roberts (25.7.1973)
First GP: US, 1993 (250)
World Champion 500 (2000)
Number of GP wins: 8 (500).

John Hopkins (22.5.1983)
First GP: Japan, 2002 (MotoGP)
Champion US Supersport 750 (2000)
Champion US Formule Extreme (2001)

TEAM STRUCTURE
Sporting director: Hiro Iguchi.
Technical Director: Yasuo Kamomiya.
Chief mechanic: Bob Toomey (Kenny Roberts) and Stuart Shenton (John Hopkins).

The ZX-RR, which first saw the light of day at the Pacific GP at the end of 2002, was tackling its first full GP season. Last year, the green team had started off with an engine evolved from its superbike. Over the winter, Kawasaki then developed a brand new 990 cc prototype engine, using aluminium. No one seemed inclined to rethink the rather aggressive lines of the ZX-RR, but the results were catastrophic. A new technical director, Hamish Jamieson, arrived during the year, having started his career in side car racing with multiple world champion, Rolf Biland, before switching to Suzuki. He soon realised what a difficult challenge he faced. "The bike, in terms of its actual structure, still requires a serious amount of work. But we must already start looking at the long term and decide if we would not do better by adopting a different engine configuration." V3? V4? V5? That is the big question.

Kawasaki Racing Team

HEADQUARTERS: Im Gstaudach 6, 92648 Vohenstrauss (Germany).

INTERNET SITE: www.kawasaki-eckl.com

TEAM MANAGER: Harald Eckl.

RIDERS
Garry McCoy (18.4.1972)
First GP: Australia, 1992 (125)
Number of GP wins: 5 (2/125; 3/500).

Andrew Pitt (19.2.1976)
First GP: Malaysia, 2002 (MotoGP)
Australian Champion Supersport (1999)
World Champion Supersport (2001)

TEAM STRUCTURE
Technical Director: Hamish Jamieson.
Chief mechanic: Uwe Weber (Garry McCoy) and Scott Breedin (Andrew Pitt).

Suzuki Grand Prix

Kawasaki Racing

Friday 23rd May 2003, in the paddock at the Bugatti Le Mans circuit. Kenny Roberts Senior's smile is less cocky than usual. In fact, in the fresh morning air, the "King's" face is lit up with pride. In a matter of moments, Jeremy McWilliams is about to give the Proton KR5 four-stroke its first track outing at a Grand Prix, after an intensive series of tests a few days earlier at an airfield track. Once again, Kenny has been true to his word, even if his prototype machine will not appear on a regular basis, because of overheating problems. Along with the KR5, a sprinkling of F1 people have arrived in the paddock. The engine was originally designed by John Magee, but here too is John Barnard, a former McLaren and Ferrari designer, who is deemed to have invented the carbon monocoque and ground effect F1 cars. He had joined the Banbury team in January. His role? To watch and learn about what is a new world for him, before working on the engine which will power the Proton in 2004.

Proton Team KR

HEADQUARTERS: 3 Lombard Way, Banbury, Oxon OX16 4TJ (Great Britain).

INTERNET SITE: www.protonteamkr.com

TEAM MANAGER: Kenny Roberts.

RIDERS
Nobuatsu Aoki (31.8.1971)
First GP: Japan, 1990 (250)
Number of GP wins: 1 (250).

Jeremy McWilliams (4.4.1964)
First GP: Australia, 1993 (500)
Irish Champion 350 Production (1988)
Irish Champion 350 Production (1989)
Irish Champion 250 Short Circuit (1991)
Number of GP wins: 1 (250)

TEAM STRUCTURE
Technical Director: John Barnard.
Chief mechanic: Nick Davis (Nobuatsu Aoki)
and Tom Okane (Jeremy McWilliams).

9
Nobuatsu
Aoki

99
Jeremy
McWilliams

To start with, it played the part of a mystery woman, who was awaited but never appeared. Although Peter Clifford's crew worked day and night during the months leading up to the start of the championship, the bike unveiled at Suzuka did not comply with the MotoGP technical regulations, which bans bikes which are simple evolutions of road-going machines. The Harris WCM was powered by a Yamaha R1 engine, given that the special crankcases and other new parts had not been finished in time. From then on, the WCM season was played out on two levels. On the legal front, WCM appeared for scrutineering only for the bikes to be refused permission to compete by the FIM officials. On the technological front, work continued to produce the home built engine. It finally arrived in Portugal, the eleventh round of the season! From then on, its performance was nothing to be ashamed of, particularly when compared to Suzuki and Kawasaki, especially taking into account the huge difference in available budgets.

WCM

HEADQUARTERS: Parc Industriel des Trois Fontaines, Rue des Trois Fontaines 32A, 1370 Jodoigne (Belgium).

INTERNET SITE: www.harris-wcm.com

TEAM MANAGER: Bob MacLean.

RIDERS
Chris Burns (12.6.1980)
First GP: Great Britain, 1997 (125)

David De Gea (9.12.1977)
First GP: Catalunya, 1995 (125)

TEAM STRUCTURE
Sporting director: Peter Clifford.
Chief mechanic: Malcolm Pitman (Chris Burns) and
Christophe Bourguignon (David De Gea).

52
David
De Gea

35
Chris
Burns

Proton Team KR

WCM

250cc

In the 250 class, Aprilia once again went for quality and quantity. There were four different levels of equipment – maybe five if one considers that Manuel Poggiali's RSW was a bit more of a works bike than the others. The 2003 works bikes were entrusted to Poggiali, the Spaniards Alfonso "Fonsi" Gonzales-Nieto and Toni Elias, as well as France's Randy de Puniet. For his "junior" team, Jorge "Aspar" Martinez stuck with last year's RSW, for Joan Olive and Hector Faubel, while the rest of the pack ran the 2003 RSV250 or the 2002 RS250.

MS Aprilia Team

HEADQUARTERS: Strada la Ciarulla, 47899 Serravalle (San Marino).

INTERNET SITE: www.racingaprilia.com

RIDER
Manuel Poggiali (14.2.1983)
First GP: Imola, 1998 (125)
Italian Champion Minibike (1997)
Italian Champion 125 (1998)
World Champion 125 (2001)
Number of GP wins: 11 (7/125; 4/250)

TEAM STRUCTURE
Technical Director: Jan Witteveen.
Chief mechanic: Rossano Brazzi (Manuel Poggiali).

Repsol Telefonica Movistar

HEADQUARTERS: Poligono Industrial No 2, Avenida de los Deportes, Travesia, 46600 Alzira/Valencia (Spain).

INTERNET SITE: www.teamaspar.com

TEAM MANAGER: Jorge Martinez «Aspar»

RIDERS
Alfonso Gonzales-Nieto (2.12.1978)
First GP: Spain, 1997 (125)
Spanish Champion 125 (1998)
Spanish Champion 250 (1999)
Number of GP wins: 5 (250)

Antonio Elias (26.3.1983)
First GP: Spain, 1999 (125)
Number of GP wins: 8 (2/125; 6/250)

TEAM STRUCTURE
Technical Director: Giovani Sandi.
Chief mechanic: Ivano Mancurti (Alfonso Gonzales-Nieto) and Enrique Peris (Toni Elias).

Safilo Oxydo – LCR

HEADQUARTERS: Gildo Pastor Centre, 7 rue du Gabian, 98000 Monaco.

INTERNET SITE: www.safilooxydolcr.com

TEAM MANAGER: Lucio Cecchinello

RIDER
Randy De Puniet (14.2.1981)
First GP: France, 1998 (125)
French Champion 125 (1998)
Number of GP wins: 3 (250)

Campetella Racing

HEADQUARTERS: Via De Gasperi 74, 62010 Montecassiano (Italy).

INTERNET SITE: www.campetella.it

TEAM MANAGER: Carlo Campetella

RIDERS
Franco Battaini (22.7.1972)
First GP: Italy, 1996 (250)

Sylvain Guintoli (24.6.1982)
First GP: France, 2000 (250)
French Champion 250 (2000)

TEAM STRUCTURE
Technical Director: Eros Braconi.
Chief mechanic: Gianluca Montanari (Franco Battaini) and Christian Boudinot (Sylvain Guintoli).

7 Randy De Puniet

10 Alfonso «Fonsi» Gonzales-Nieto

21 Franco Battaini

24 Antonio «Toni» Elias

50 Sylvain Guintoli

54 Manuel Poggiali

MS Aprilia

Safilo Oxydo LCR

Repsol Telefonica Movistar

Campetella Racing

Aspar Junior Team

HEADQUARTERS: Poligono Industrial No 2, Avenida de los Deportes, Travesia, 46600 Alzira/Valencia (Spain).

INTERNET SITE: www.teamaspar.com

TEAM MANAGER: Jorge Martinez «Aspar»

RIDERS
Joan Olivé (22.11.1984)

First GP: Japan, 2001 (125)
Spanish Champion 50 (1998)
Spanish Champion 125 (2000)

Hector Faubel (10.8.1983)
First GP: Spain, 2000 (125)

TEAM STRUCTURE
Technical Director: Sergio Bonaldo.
Chief mechanic: Agustin Perez (Joan Olivé) and Jorge Gallardo (Hector Faubel).

Zoppini Abruzzo

HEADQUARTERS: Via Alfieri 102, 50013 Campi Bisenzio (Italy).

TEAM MANAGER: Giuliano Cerigioni

RIDERS
Anthony West (17.7.1981)
First GP: Australia, 1998 (125)
Australian Champion 125 (1998)
Australian Champion 250 Production (1998)
Number of GP wins: 1 (250).

Johan Stigefelt (17.3.1976)
First GP: Rio, 1997 (250)
Swedish Champion 125 (1994)
Swedish Champion 125 (1995)
Swedish Champion 250 (1996)

TEAM STRUCTURE
Technical Director: Mauro Noccioli.
Chief mechanic: Carlo Toccafondi (Anthony West) and Adriano Cabras (Johan Stigefelt).

Matteoni Racing

HEADQUARTERS: Via Larga 22, Zona Artigianale, 47843 Misano Adriatico (Italy)

INTERNET SITE: www.matteoniracing.it

TEAM MANAGER: Massimo Matteoni

RIDER
Alex Baldolini (24.1.1985)
First GP: Italy, 2000 (125)

TEAM STRUCTURE
Administration Director: Pietro Gallonetto.
Chief mechanic: Roberto Baglioni (Alex Baldolini)

11 Joan Olivé

14 Anthony West

16 Johan Stigefelt

26 Alex Baldolini

33 Hector Faubel

Équipe de France - Scrab GP

HEADQUARTERS: Avenue des Sports, 32110 Nogaro (France).

INTERNET SITE: www.scrab-competition.com

TEAM MANAGER: Jean-Claude Besse

RIDERS
Hugo Marchand (22.4.1981)
First GP: France, 2000 (125)

Erwan Nigon (27.9.1983)
First GP: France, 2000 (125)
French Champion 125 (2001)

TEAM STRUCTURE
Technical Director: Didier Langouët.
Chief mechanic: Julien Lemaire (Hugo Marchand) and Yannis Maigret (Erwan Nigon).

Aprilia Germany

HEADQUARTERS: SWS Racing AG, P.O. Box 23, 7205 Zizers (Switzerland).

TEAM MANAGER: Dieter Stappert

RIDERS
Dirk Heidolf (14.9.1976)
First GP: Germany, 1997 (125)

Chaz Davies (10.2.1987)
First GP: Japan, 2002 (125)
British Champion Minibike (1996)
British Champion Minibike (1997)
British Champion Minibike (1998)

TEAM STRUCTURE
Technical Director: Robert Reich.
Chief mechanic: Stefan Kurfiss (Dirk Heidolf) and Robert Reich (Chaz Davies).

Équipe de France - Scrab GP

Aprilia Germany

The new "official" version of Honda's 250, code named RS 250RW, made its first appearance at Motegi in the 2002 Pacific Grand Prix. Two riders were entrusted with it: Italy's Roberto Rolfo and the Argentine, Sebastian Oscar Porto. It was outpaced in terms of power by the Aprilias throughout the year, but it was a well balanced machine and from the Czech GP, Rolfo who was in the running for the title, was supplied with new engine and chassis parts. The disparity in performance between the works Aprilias and Hondas was reflected in the standard bikes, as the Japanese RS was no match for the Italian RS.

Fortuna Honda

HEADQUARTERS: Potosi 38, 08030 Barcelone (Spain).

INTERNET SITE:
www.monlaucompeticion.com

TEAM MANAGER: Daniel Amatriain.

RIDER
Roberto Rolfo (23.3.1980)
Number of GP wins: 2 (250)

TEAM STRUCTURE
Coordinator: Jordi Perez.
Chief mechanic: Massimo Capanna
(Roberto Rolfo).

Troll Honda BQR

HEADQUARTERS: Mare Nostrum 26/28,
Urb. San Carlos, 08434 La Roca Del Valles
(Spain).

INTERNET SITE: www.byqueroseno.com

TEAM MANAGER: Joaquin Contreras

RIDERS
Alex Debon (1.3.1976)
First GP: Madrid, 1998 (250)

Eric Bataille (18.4.1981)
First GP: Catalunya, 2000 (125)

TEAM STRUCTURE
Administration Director: Raul Romeo.
Chief mechanic: Josep Oliva (Alex Debon) and
Bartolome Quesada (Eric Bataille).

Telefonica Movistar Junior

HEADQUARTERS: Josep Trueta 4-2,
08970 Sant Joan Despi/Barcelona (Spain).

TEAM MANAGER: Alberto Puig.

RIDER
Sebastian Porto (12.9.1978)
First GP: Argentina, 1994 (125)
Argentinian Champion Minibike (1988)
Argentinian Champion Dirt-Track 50 (1989)
Argentinian Champion Dirt-Track 50 (1991)
Argentinian Champion Dirt-Track 125 (1992)
Argentinian Champion 250 (1994)
European Champion 250 «open» (1996)
Number of GP wins: 1 (250)

TEAM STRUCTURE
Technical Director: Paolo Cordioli.
Chief mechanic: Alex Battle (Sebastian Porto).

Kiefer Castrol Racing

HEADQUARTERS: Zur Rothheck 12,
55743 Idar-Oberstein (Germany).

INTERNET SITE: www.kiefer-mot.de

TEAM MANAGER: Stefan Kiefer.

RIDER
Christian Gemmel (9.6.1980)

TEAM STRUCTURE
Technical Director: Jürgen Lingg.
Chief mechanic: Jochen Kiefer (Christian
Gemmel).

Fortuna Honda

Telefonica Movistar Junior

Troll Honda BQR

Kiefer Castrol Racing

Dark Dog Molenaar

HEADQUARTERS: Panoven 20, 3401 RA Ijsselstein (Netherlands).

INTERNET SITE: www.molenaarracing.nl

TEAM MANAGER: Arie Molenaar.

RIDERS
Henk Van De Lagemaat (13.11.1968)
First GP: Netherlands, 1997 (250)
Dutch Champion 250 (2000)
Dutch Champion 250 (2001)
Dutch Champion 250 (2002)

Katja Poensgen (26.9.1976)
First GP: Japan, 2001 (250)
Champion 125 ADAC Junior Cup (1995)
European Champion Supermono Cup (1998)

TEAM STRUCTURE
Technical Director: Hans Spaan.
Chief mechanic: Robert Dorrestein (Henk Van De Lagemaat) and Koen Van Lierop (Katja Poensgen).

Elit Grand Prix

HEADQUARTERS: Jeremiasova 947, 15500 Prague 5 Stodulky (Czech Republic).

INTERNET SITE: www.paddock.cz

TEAM MANAGER: Daniel M. Epp

RIDER
Jakub Smrz (7.4.1983)
First GP: Czech Republic, 1998 (125)
Czech Republic Champion 125 (1999)

TEAM STRUCTURE
Technical Director: Manfred Wittenborn.
Chief mechanic: Frantisec Lenc (Jakub Smrz).

Henk Van De Lagemaat — 18

Jakub Smrz — 96

Katja Poensgen — 98

Yamaha was no longer officially represented in the 250 world championship, but the Kurz team had the 2003 TZ, fitted with a special kit supplied by the factory. Outclassed in every area by the works Aprilias and the two Honda RS 250RW, the TZ nevertheless managed to pull off the odd surprise thanks to the devilish Naoki Matsudo. He was partnered by two riders: firstly Jaroslav Hules, who ended the season in the Elit team and then, his promising fellow countryman, Lukas Pesek, who had started the year in the European championship.

Yamaha Kurz

HEADQUARTERS: Geiselroter Heidle 1, 73494 Rosenberg (Germany).

INTERNET SITE: www.yamaha-kurz.de

TEAM MANAGER: Josef Liska.

RIDERS
Naoki Matsudo (27.7.1973)
First GP: Japan, 1997 (250)
Japanese Champion 250 (1999)

Jaroslav Hules (2.7.1974)
First GP: Czech Republic, 1993 (125)
Czech Republic Champion 125 (1992)
Czech Republic Champion 125 (1993)
Czech Republic Champion 125 (1994)
Czech Republic Champion 125 (1995)

Lukas Pesek (22.11.1985)
First GP: Czech Republic, 2002 (125)

TEAM STRUCTURE
Technical Director: Tomohiro Saeki.
Chief mechanic: Tomohiro Saeki (Naoki Matsudo) and Gérard Roussel (*) (Jaroslav Hules)
(*): Gerard Roussel left his job at the mid-season.

Dark Dog Molenaar

Elit Grand Prix

Yamaha Kurz

125cc

In the 125 class, Honda employed the same policy it had followed for the past few years by taking on a works rider in the shape of Spain's Daniel Pedrosa, who was the only one to get his hands on an RSW 125, the company's development machine. It evolved throughout the season with new engine parts, chassis, forks and special swing arms etc. Other riders opting to go with the world's biggest bike manufacturer used the RS 125 R, with different engine kits supplied either directly from HRC or from other Japanese tuning companies. The Finnish Ajo Motorsport team was supported by Bridgestone, which delivered one win when Ballerini made a comeback in Australia. The others were all fitted with Dunlop rubber.

Telefonica Movistar Junior

HEADQUARTERS: Josep Trueta 4-2, 08970 Sant Joan Despi/Barcelona (Spain).

INTERNET SITE: www.movistar.com

TEAM MANAGER: Alberto Puig.

RIDER
Daniel Pedrosa (29.9.1985)
First GP: Japan, 2001 (125)
Spanish Champion Minibike (1998)
World Champion 125 (2003)
Number of GP wins: 8 (125)

TEAM STRUCTURE
Technical Director: Paolo Cordioli.
Chief mechanic: Giuseppe Pelosi.

Daniel Pedrosa

Masao Azuma

Elit Grand Prix

HEADQUARTERS: Jeremiasova 947, 15500 Prague 5 Stodulky (Czech Republic).

INTERNET SITE: www.paddock.cz

TEAM MANAGER: Daniel M. Epp

RIDER
Thomas Lüthi (6.9.1986)
First GP: Germany, 2002 (125)
Swiss Champion Pocket-Bike (1999)
Swiss Champion Pocket-Bike (2000)

TEAM STRUCTURE
Technical Director: Manfred Wittenborn.
Chief mechanic: Petr Svatek (Thomas Lüthi).

Thomas Lüthi

Ajo Motorsport

HEADQUARTERS: Erkkilankatu 11, 33100 Tampere (Finland).

INTERNET SITE: www.ajo.fi

TEAM MANAGER: Aki Ajo.

RIDERS
Masao Azuma (24.3.1971)
First GP: Japan, 1996 (125)

Japanese Champion 125 (1995)
Number of GP wins: 10 (125)

Mika Kallio (8.11.1982)
First GP: Germany, 2001 (125)

Andrea Ballerini (2.7.1973)
First GP: Australia, 1995 (125)
Number of GP wins: 1 (125)

TEAM STRUCTURE
Chief mechanic: Johan Luyten (Masao Azuma) and Aki Kajo (Mika Kallio, then Andrea Ballerini).

Mika Kallio

Andrea Ballerini

Telefonica Movistar Junior

Ajo Motorsport

Elit Grand Prix

Metasystem Racing Service

HEADQUARTERS: Via Sacco e Vanzetti 71/73, 41042 Fiorano Modenese (Italy).

INTERNET SITE: www.teamrs.it

TEAM MANAGER: Gabriele Debbia.

RIDERS
Leon Camier (4.8.1986)
First GP: Catalunya, 2002 (125)

Peter Lenart (12.12.1984)
First GP: Japan, 2003 (125)

TEAM STRUCTURE
Reseach and Development: Andrea Oleari.
Chief mechanic: Alberto Iotti (Leon Camier) and Michele Tavolazzi (Peter Lenart).

Team Scot

HEADQUARTERS: Via Brodolini 55/2, 61025 Montelabbate (Italy).

TEAM MANAGER: Giancarlo Cecchini.

RIDERS
Simone Corsi (24.4.1987)
First GP: Italy, 2002 (125)

Andrea Dovizioso (23.3.1986)
First GP: Italy, 2001 (125)
Italian Champion Pocket Bike Junior B (1997)
Italian Champion Pocket Bike Junior B (1998)

TEAM STRUCTURE
Sporting director: Cirano Mularoni.
Chief mechanic: Luciano Furlani (Simone Corsi) and Claudio Eusebi (Andrea Dovizioso).

Road Racing Team Hungary

HEADQUARTERS: 2120 Dunakesi Foti ùt, 055 Hrsz (Hungary).

INTERNET SITE: www.tothimi.com

TEAM MANAGER: Alex Varga.

RIDERS
Imre Toth (6.9.1985)
First GP: Japan, 2002 (125)

TEAM STRUCTURE
Technical Director: Jörg Seel.
Chief mechanic: Ueno Hideaki (Imre Toth).
Chief mechanic: Carlo Toccafondi (Anthony West) and Adriano Cabras (Johan Stigefelt).

Metasystem Racing

Team Scot

Team Hungary

The arrival of a new manufacturer in the 125 class was the big news of the year. The Austrian KTM marque had a great track record in motocross, enduro and rallying and it arrived on the GP scene with clear intentions to succeed. Two world champions were brought on board: reigning champ Arnaud Vincent, who would not see out the season and an older one, Roberto Locatelli. The KTM RRF 125 is the work of engineer Harald Bartol, the father of the Gilera and the Derbi, who left the Piaggio group with a collection of technical baggage which would provoke tensions and threats of legal claims. With the arrival of Mika Kallio, Bartol's favourite rider, the orange Austrian machine suddenly began working properly, after taking a long time to fine tune. This delay was put down to Arnaud Vincent, who was shown the door for having spoken his mind in public.

KTM – Red Bull

HEADQUARTERS: Stallhofnerstrasse 3, 5230 Mattighofen (Austria).

INTERNET SITE: www.ktm.at

TEAM MANAGER: Stefan Pierer.

RIDERS
Arnaud Vincent (10.11.1974)
First GP: France, 1996 (125)
European Champion 125 (1997)
French Champion 125 (1997)
World Champion 125 (2002)
Number of GP wins: 7 (125)

Roberto Locatelli (5.7.1974)
First GP: Italy, 1994 (125)
Italian Champion 125 Sport-Production (1993)
World Champion 125 (2000)
Number of GP wins: 7 (125)

Mika Kallio (8.11.1982)
First GP: Germany, 2001 (125)

TEAM STRUCTURE
Technical Director: Harald Bartol.
Chief mechanic: Harald Bartol (Arnaud Vincent, then Mika Kallio) and Mario Galeotti (Roberto Locatelli).

1 Arnaud Vincent

10 Roberto Locatelli

36 Mika Kallio

Aprilia lost its world champion, Arnaud Vincent, to KTM, although the Frenchman was back on a Noale RSW before the end of the year. In this category, Aprilia did not have a specific works team, but several factory bikes were entrusted to a variety of teams, including that of manager-rider Lucio Cecchinello and that of "Aspar" Martinez, a man who wears many hats on the GP scene. He now ran several teams which operated as a separate autonomous satellite. Also back in the fold was Stefano Perugini, who would provide the biggest threat to Dani Pedrosa in the fight for the world title.

Safilo Oxydo - LCR

HEADQUARTERS: Gildo Pastor Centre, 7 rue du Gabian, 98000 Monaco.

INTERNET SITE: www.safilooxydolcr.com

TEAM MANAGER: Lucio Cecchinello

RIDERS
Lucio Cecchinello (21.10.1969)
First GP: Australia, 1993 (125)

European Champion 125 (1995)
Number of GP wins: 7 (125)

Casey Stoner (16.10.1985)
First GP: Great Britain, 2001 (125)
Number of GP wins: 1 (125)

TEAM STRUCTURE
Technical Director: Massimo Branchini.
Chief mechanic: Roberto Guidi (Lucio Cecchinello) and
Diego Ferrarini (Casey Stoner).

4 Lucio Cecchinello

6 Mirko Giansanti

Matteoni Racing

HEADQUARTERS: Via Larga 22, Zona Artigianale, 47843 Misano Adriatico (Italy)

INTERNET SITE: www.matteoniracing.it

TEAM MANAGER: Massimo Matteoni

RIDERS
Mirko Giansanti (14.9.1976)
First GP: Italy, 1996 (125)

Marco Simoncelli (20.1.1987)
First GP: Czech Republic, 2002 (125)
Italian Champion Minibikes (1999)
European Champion 125 (2002)

TEAM STRUCTURE
Executive Director: Pietro Gallonetto.
Chief mechanic: Claudio Macciotta (Mirko Giansanti) and
Sanzio Raffaelli (Marco Simoncelli).

7 Stefano Perugini

11 Massimiliano Sabbatini

Abruzzo Racing

HEADQUARTERS: Via del Consorzio 10, 60015 Falconara (Italy).

TEAM MANAGER: Giordano Cerigioni

RIDERS
Stefano Perugini (10.9.1974)
First GP: Italy, 1993 (125)
Italian Champion 125 Sport-Production (1992)

European Champion 125 (1993)
Italian Champion 125 (1993)
Number of GP wins: 5 (125)

Massimiliano Sabbatani (4.8.1975)
First GP: Imola, 1998 (125)

TEAM STRUCTURE
Technical Director: Andrea Orlandi.
Chief mechanic: Gabriele Innocenti (Stefano Perugini) and
Alberto Bernardi (Massimiliano Sabbatani).

27 Casey Stoner

58 Marco Simoncelli

Safilo Oxydo - LCR

Matteoni Racing

Abruzzo Racing

Seedof Racing

HEADQUARTERS: C/Fray Juan Gil no 5, 28036 Madrid (Spain).

INTERNET SITE: www.seedorfracing.com

TEAM MANAGER: Susana López Pichot

RIDERS
Chris Martin (24.01.1981)
First GP: Great Britain, 2001 (125)

Álvaro Bautista (21.11.1984)
First GP: Spain, 2002 (125)

TEAM STRUCTURE
Technical Director: Christian Lundberg.
Chief mechanic: Oscar Haro (Chris Martin) and David Galacho (Álvaro Bautista).

14 Chris Martin

15 Alex De Angelis

Globet.com Racing

HEADQUARTERS: Via Beltramina 3, CP 4356, 6904 Lugano Molino Nuovo (Switzerland).

INTERNET SITE: www.globet.com

TEAM MANAGER: Marco Tresoldi

RIDERS
Alex De Angelis (26.2.1984)
First GP: Imola, 1999 (125)

Gino Borsoi (11.3.1974)
First GP: Italy, 1996 (125)

TEAM STRUCTURE
Executive Director: Stefano Bedon.
Chief mechanic: Franco Moro (Alex De Angelis) and Paolo Mancin (Gino Borsoi).

17 Steve Jenkner

19 Álvaro Bautista

Exalt Cycle Red Devil

HEADQUARTERS: 43, route d'Arlon, 8009 Strassen (Luxembourg).

TEAM MANAGER: Fiorenzo Caponera.

RIDERS
Steve Jenkner (31.5.1976)
First GP: Germany, 1996 (125)

German Champion Minibike (1993)
Number of GP wins: 1 (125)

Gabor Talmacsi (28.5.1981)
First GP: Czech Republic, 1997 (125)
Hungarn Champion 125 (1999)

TEAM STRUCTURE
Technical Director: Aligi Deganello.
Chief mechanic: Aligi Deganello (Steve Jenkner) and Tommaso Raponi (Gabor Talmacsi).

23 Gino Borsoi

79 Gabor Talmacsi

Seedorf Racing

Globet.com Racing

Exalt Cycle Red Devil

Master – MX Onda - Aspar

HEADQUARTERS: Poligono Industrial No 2, Avenida de los Deportes, Travesia, 46600 Alzira/Valencia (Spain).

INTERNET SITE: www.teamaspar.com

TEAM MANAGER: Jorge Martinez «Aspar»

RIDERS
Pablo Nieto (4.06.1980)
First GP: Catalunya, 1998 (125)
Number of GP wins: 1 (125)

Hector Barbera (2.11.1986)
First GP: Japan, 2002 (125)
Spanish Champion 125 (2002)
Number of GP wins: 2 (125)

TEAM STRUCTURE
Technical Director: Antonio Alfosea.
Chief mechanic: Angel Perurena (Pablo Nieto) and Enrique Quijal (Hector Barbera)

Sterilgarda Racing

HEADQUARTERS: Via Cavour 33, 46043 Castiglione delle Stiviere (Italy).

INTERNET SITE: www.fontanaracing.com

TEAM MANAGER: Italo Fontana

RIDERS
Youichi Ui (27.11.1972)
First GP: Japan, 1995 (125)
Japanese Champion 125 (1995)
Number of GP wins: 11 (125).

Gioele Pellino (13.8.1983)
First GP: Italy, 2002 (125)

TEAM STRUCTURE
Chief mechanic: Roberto Materassi (Youichi Ui, then Arnaud Vincent) and Daniele Battaglia (Gioele Pellino).

Freesoul Racing

HEADQUARTERS: 30, rue de la Tour, 4458 Fexhe-Slins (Belgium).

TEAM MANAGER: Barbaro Guy Levi.

RIDER
Mike Di Meglio (17.2.1988)
First GP: Japan, 2003 (125)

TEAM STRUCTURE
Technical Director: Mario Martini.
Chief mechanic: Mario Martini (Mike Di Meglio).

Master-MX Onda-Aspar

Sterilgarda Racing

Freesoul Racing

The two Piaggio group marques went through a troubled winter, after Harald Bartol switched to KTM. The project thus fell into the hands of Belgium's Olivier Liegeois, who had made a name for himself preparing some very good Hondas, for the likes of Marco Melandri's GP debut and was behind several wins for Masao Azuma and so forth. Liegeois had no real clear starting point and thus it took quite a while – almost six months – for the bikes which had won world championships a couple of years ago, to fight their way back to the front end. This owed much to one of the revelations of the season, Jorge Lorenzo. As in the recent past, Derbi and Gilera lined up machines bearing their own name.

Caja Madrid Derbi Racing

HEADQUARTERS: La Barca 5/7, 08107 Martorelles (Spain).

INTERNET SITE: www.derbiracing.com

TEAM MANAGER: Giampiero Sacchi

RIDERS
Emilio Alzamora (22.5.1973)
First GP: Malaysia, 1994 (125)
Spanish Champion Supermotard (1993)
Spanish Champion 125 «open» (1995)
World Champion 125 (1999)
Number of GP wins: 4 (125)

Jorge Lorenzo (4.5.1987)
First GP: Spain, 2002 (125)
Number of GP wins: 1 (125)

TEAM STRUCTURE
Technical Director: Olivier Liégeois.
Chief mechanic: Roberto Morelli (Emilio Alzamora) and Juan Llansa (Jorge Lorenzo).

26 Emilio Alzamora

Metis Gilera Racing

HEADQUARTERS: Corse Sempione 43, 20145 Milan (Italy).

INTERNET SITE: www.gilera.com

TEAM MANAGER: Giampiero Sacchi

RIDER
Stefano Bianco (27.10.1985)
First GP: Australia, 2000 (125)

TEAM STRUCTURE
Technical Director: Olivier Liégeois.
Chief mechanic: Stefano Riminucci (Stefano Bianco).

33 Stefano Bianco

48 Jorge Lorenzo

Malaguti's love affair with racing is never ending. The mark is best known for its mopeds which were part of growing up for so many and its scooters. But it has nearly always maintained a competition programme. It's comeback was played out over two acts: last year, under the Engines name, Pierluigi Aldrovani developed a little 125, based on a Honda engine, which saw Fabrizio Lai shine on several occasions in the European and Italian championships, also winning the latter in 2003. It fell to Giorgio Semprucci, entered in GPs for the past decade, to give Malaguti its baptism on the threshold of what looks like being something of a renaissance for the marque.

Semprucci – Angaia Malaguti

HEADQUARTERS: Via Villagrande 228, 61024 Mombaroccio (Italy).

INTERNET SITE: www.teamsemprucci.it

TEAM MANAGER: Giorgio Semprucci

RIDERS
Julian Simon (3.4.1987)
First GP: Spain, 2002 (125)

Fabrizio Lai (14.12.1978)
First GP: Valencia, 2001 (125)
European Champion Minibike (1996)
European Champion Minibike (1997)
Italian Champion 125 (2002)
Italian Champion 125 (2003)

TEAM STRUCTURE
Executive Director: Nicolas Casadei.
Chief mechanic: Romano Fusaro (Julian Simon) and Roberto Bava (Fabrizio Lai).

31 Julian Simon

32 Fabrizio Lai

Semprucci Angaia Malaguti

VALENTINO ROSSI

MANUEL POGGIALI

DANI PEDROSA

Valentino Rossi

Valentino Rossi on title day: a unique media phenomenon.

What a showman!

Valentino, the king who dares

Of course there was the great Giacomo Agostini, who had left MV-Agusta to join the Japanese Yamaha outfit. Of course there was also the astonishing Eddie Lawson, twice 500 world champion with Yamaha, who took his Number 1 to Honda at the end of 1988, only to come back a year later, still with the mantle of the best rider in the blue riband category. Of course we had Freddie Spencer, a brilliant yet ephemeral talent, who appeared to be married for life to the giant Honda organisation and yet tried to bounce back with Yamaha. Yes, okay, there are all these historical precedents from the more or less recent past, but none of them provoked a similar earthquake reaction to the one unleashed by Valentino Rossi: after four years with Honda – 64 GPs, 33 wins, and three consecutive world titles after what was considered an apprenticeship season! – the best rider of the modern era announced on the night after the final GP of the 2003 season, that he needed a new challenge. Would it mean that, in 2004, he would become even more of a giant than he was already?

Valentino, what are your feelings now as you sign the divorce papers?
First, I must say thank you to Honda. To everyone with whom I have worked for these past four years. But unfortunately, we cannot stay together anymore.

What memories will you cherish from this time?
When I moved up to the 500, nobody dared say we were going to win. But for a rider, working with HRC is a dream. At first, the engineers adapted the NSR to my needs and then, the following year, they built a completely different bike. Just for me. It was the last season for the 500 category and this class, this name, is the whole history of racing. When I won the last GP of this historic season, on 3rd November 2001 at Rio, I really think it was the best day of my life.

But then, why not stick with this set up which suited you so well?
Because I feel I have finished my work with the RC211V. I still remember the first time I tried the four stroke prototype. I was angry, convinced that it would be impossible to be as quick on this bike as on a 500 two stroke. Then, with the development work, the results came. And two more titles. Now the time has come to go and look elsewhere.

"I am leaving my most beautiful girlfriend to the enemy"

On a personal note: a divorce is always painful, isn't it?
I am leaving "my" bike, the one which brought me so much satisfaction. She is the nicest girlfriend I have known in my life and leaving her feels a bit like cheating on her with another. It hurts, especially when you know that she will end up in the arms of people, some of whom I do not particularly like.

Why did you hesitate for so long?
Well, because it was the most difficult decision of my career. When I left Aprilia and the 250 for Honda and the 500, I had already dithered for a while, because it would have been quite nice to ride for a season with the Number 1 on my bike. But the attraction of the top class was irresistible and riding that Honda had been a childhood dream.

"Brno was a turning point..."

The day the championship definitely tipped in Rossi's favour. He wins in Brno, ahead of Gibernau and Bayliss.

Let us look back for a moment at the last few months: the turning point in the season had to be your victory in Brno. That's where you felt you had to win...
The joke on the victory lap in the Czech Republic, with the world champion disguised as a convict and carrying his ball and chain onto the podium, was much more significant than the others. I wanted to remind everyone that there were times when things were also difficult for me. Of course, there is no comparison with someone clocking-in at a factory every morning and my difficulties are different to those.

A scenario played out every time Rossi gets on his bike.

What are they?
When you have won so many races, as soon as you make the slightest mistake which drops you to second or third place, people talk about a crisis. Seen from the outside, when you look at my results over the past three years, one can get the impression that it is easy to win a world title. But nothing could be more wrong. To take the supreme prize, you have to pull together all sorts of small elements, including of course, a bit of luck.

"It's true, I was no longer having fun..."

One of these elements has to be enjoyment. Is that always as strong?
I admit that, this year, I went through a spell when I was no longer having fun, when I really felt under pressure. Then, at Brno in fact, I started winning again. And as I have a lot of fun when I win...

Let's change subject. Having won everything on two wheels, having tried your hand at rallying – starting the Rally of Great Britain last year, ending in a crash – there is talk of you switching to Formula 1. There

are even suggestions that Bernie Ecclestone himself will do whatever it takes to get you there.
Of course, I would like to try it, but I cannot say if I can drive that sort of machine. Is it easy? I am not convinced.

If you take on this challenge, it would mean that someone who is a legend on two wheels would have to start all over from scratch, like any other beginner...
For sure, but that is nothing new for me. I have always needed new challenges, difficult and unusual ones. That's why I'd like to give it a go.

"The talent, this need..."

Today, you are one of the only riders, maybe the only rider in the world championship who can "make the difference." How do you interpret this statement?
Making the difference is first of all a case of pulling together a complex alchemy. It requires preparing every element to 100%, never letting a rival get away with anything and naturally, to have the necessary talent. Some have it, others don't. In all modesty, I think I have.

This new title, the second in MotoGP, the fifth of your career, how do you sum it up?
Last year was a transition year. In 2003, we went through a season similar in some ways to the final year of the 500 cc two strokes. There were no excuses and the competition was quite closely matched.

And, as a result, we found there were riders who could beat the master?
The stature and true character of a person is revealed by his behaviour. You have to be able to say: "ok, today, I made a mistake. Today, someone else was stronger." In this environment, anyone who never says that is not speaking the truth.

"I have no relationship with Biaggi"

Is your relationship with Biaggi the way it is described in the media?
I have no relationship with Biaggi. It's

quite simple. We are not great friends. That's it...

24 years old, with five world titles in the bag, have you got everything you want?
Let's say, I've got a lot of it. In fact, it is one thing to win a title once, but it is something completely different to repeat the performance four or five times.

Motorcycle racer in your first life, F1 driver in your second, what will Valentino Rossi do in his third life?
A good question. The truth is that I have not thought about it much. I would like to find something enjoyable and a bit less stressful. On the other hand, I am not at all sure that I would want to stay in this environment. I think it would be too difficult and too sad to be at the track without riding a bike.

How has Valentino Rossi changed in between the first 125 world title and this one?
I am getting old, old and tired. I would like to keep going for another two or three seasons at this level, but I know it will not be easy.

Are you having less fun?
At the start of my career, 90% of what I did was fun and I considered the remaining 10% as work. Then came a time when the split was 50/50 pleasure and work and for me, with the character I have, that was already too much. To survive for a few more years in this environment, I absolutely have to find a balance that suits me. Let's say 70% pleasure.

In Sepang, your mother Stefania was, as always, present when you took the title. Graziano your father no longer likes flying and stays in Italy. How important has he been in your career?
My father helped me a lot. He gave me this passion and it was thanks to his contacts in the sport that I got my first bike, a Cagiva, when I started in the Italian 125 Sport-Production Championship. In the early days, there were plenty of advantages. But after that, I quickly decided that I preferred to handle things myself. You know, it's not advice that makes you ride quickly!

The quiz for the perfect little Rossi fan

1) How much did Aprilia pay in 1995 to get Valentino Rossi under contract?

30 million old lire, equivalent to about 15,000 Euros! It was a three year contract, with a hundred percent increase for 1996. In 1997, the year of Rossi's first world title, the base amount had been increased six fold.

2) Who signed this famous contract?

Carlo Pernat, the then sporting director at Aprilia and Graziano Rossi, Valentino's father. Looking back to that time, Carlo Pernat recalls that: "Vale was a rebel, with no rules. In the morning, we had the devil's own job to wake him up in time for practice. And it was even worse if we had an appointment in a studio to do a commercial."

3) Who said: "For him riding is fun. Something he does for pleasure?"

Rossano Brazzi, who was his chief engineer, when he took his second title in the 250 cc class.

4) And who said: "For him, finishing second means real suffering?"

Luca Cadalora, former triple world champion (once in 125 and twice in 250.) "The great champions all share this characteristic: whatever their discipline they are competitive, even if they are playing cards!"

5) Is Valentino Rossi good at setting up his machine?

Definitely, according to Jan Witteveen, the Dutch engineer, who created and developed the racing Aprilias. "What was fantastic with him, was that he could explain precisely what was wrong, without having the slightest idea how to fix the problem. A lot of riders want to play at being engineers without knowing anything. Valentino let the engineers do their job. And when we could not find the solution, he would change his riding style."

6) Can Valentino Rossi stand comparison with Mick Doohan, his predecessor as Honda's number one rider?

According to Jeremy Burgess, chief engineer to both riders, the answer is no. "They only have one thing in common, they both love winning. Mick was less demanding with us in terms of setting up the bike. For him, it was enough that it worked. He was a lot less precise than Rossi in terms of some set-up requirements. Valentino works a lot on the set-up of his bike and when he joined us, he found it hard to understand that we made do with what we had. He did not know that at Honda, it was the test drivers who did all the development work."

BUSINESS CARD

Name:	Rossi
First name:	Valentino
Born:	16th February 1979
At:	Urbino/Pesaro (Italy)
First race:	1992
First GP:	Malaysian GP, 1996 (125)
Number of GP wins:	59 (12/125; 14/250; 13/500; 20/MotoGP)
First GP win:	Czech Republic GP, 1996 (125)

Track record

1989:	First karting races
1990:	Regional karting championship
1991:	5th Italian junior karting championship, first Minibike win
1992:	Italian Champion endurance Minibike
1993:	12th Italian Championship 125 Sport-Production (Cagiva)
1994:	Italian Champion 125 Sport-Production (Cagiva)
1995:	3th European Championship 125, 11th Spanish championship 125 open, Italian Champion 125 (Aprilia)
1996:	9th World championship 125, 10th European championship 125 (Aprilia)
1997:	World Champion 125 (Aprilia)
1998:	2th World championship 250 (Aprilia)
1999:	World Champion 250 (Aprilia)
2000:	2th World championship 500 (Honda)
2001:	World Champion 500 (Honda)
2002:	World Champion MotoGP (Honda)
2003:	World Champion MotoGP (Honda)

Manuel Poggiali

Manuel Poggiali in action:
world champion in 250 at
his first attempt.

Time for a smile.

Manuel Poggiali, hyperactive man

Imola, early September 1998. A fifteen and a half year old lad is trying his luck for the first time in the world championship. The Italians, whose passion for racing can be overpowering are prone to making shock statements at the drop of a hat. "Better even than Valentino Rossi. You just wait and see." So, who is this adolescent whom everyone is talking about? Manuel Poggiali, born in the Republic of San Marino, Italian minibike champion the previous year and soon to be Italian 125 champion. He is highly talented, but he is also a rough diamond who is injured in qualifying, trying too hard in this his first GP in the world of the big boys. But the talent is plain to see. Five years later, he is a world champion for the second time, in two different categories. He's a hyperactive lad this one; just ask anyone who has travelled on a long-haul flight with him. It's a spectacle on its own! He is capable of making big mistakes on the track, but above all, he is capable of winning. So, who is he really? While everyone knows Manuel Poggiali the rider, not much is known about Poggiali the man. It is true there might be something of Valentino Rossi about him, in terms of talent, but there is very little about him which says "star."

Indeed, the decisive weekend of Manuel Poggiali's 2003 season perfectly summed up his character. Right from Friday afternoon, Poggiali could see that his only rival for the title, Roberto Rolfo, did not have the technical means to beat him and get back the necessary eight points. But Poggiali still had to beat his most feared competitor – himself. As a result of this, on Saturday, at the end of qualifying and on Sunday morning in the warm-up he was involved in two collisions for which he was to blame; the first time with France's Erwan Nigon and the second with Germany's Christian Gemmel.

Manuel, what happened on such an important Sunday morning, at the final round in Valencia?
The rider in front of me braked without warning and I could not avoid him. It hurt, it hurt a lot and my hip was really painful throughout the race. When the collision happened, I said to myself, "that's it, it's not my lucky weekend. Already you've come to the track with a fever, which hasn't happened for the past five years."

"I dedicate the title to dad"

What did you think at the time of the crash?
I did not really have time to think about it. The doctors in the mobile clinic took care of me straight away

V for victory, for a quiet sort of guy.

Manuel Poggiali

and they really did a good job, as I was able to start the race and finish it, even if I was not in the best condition. At the same time, I knew that my mechanics had done everything needed to get my bike ready and set-up for the race.

The title came as a relief, but it was also a time to say thank you, was it not?

Yes, and I would like to dedicate this world title to my poor father, who sadly is no longer with us.

You are now world champion in only your first year in the 250 class. That's something even Valentino Rossi did not manage...

This evening, I can let you into a secret. Even though I was leading the championship from the first race, I never spoke about the title at any time during the year, so as not to put myself under too much pressure. But right from the third

race at Jerez de la Frontera, I started to think it was on the cards. Of the front runners, I was the only one to always get to the finish, always scoring the big points. The consequence of that was that, as others were not so reliable, my closest rival in the series often had a different name. With each race, I got a bit closer to the crown.

Champion in the 250 class, having been champion in the 125s. Can you make a comparison?

In terms of the incredible rush of emotion, they were similar. But it's true that the racing was much closer in the 125, with around ten of us always fighting for the win. In the 250 cc class, it is easier to make a break.

You seem very calm despite your historic achievement. No champagne, no party?

I'm drinking mineral water, because I

feel very weak because of this fever. And I've got a headache. The party will come in a few days time, when I am back in San Marino with all my family and friends.

Are you aware of what you have achieved? Before you, only Tetsuya Harada and Freddie Spencer have won the 250 title at their first attempt.

It's true that this season has been incredible. When I switched to the 250 over the winter, I never thought I could be in the running for the title, especially the way I did it. Because if you look at the figures, I was leading the classification almost all the way, from the first to the last race. So, yes it's true, maybe I have done something historic.

On route to the title in the saddle of the best bike of the field.

Poggiali the champion, as seen by...

Antonella, his mother...
"All's well that ends well. This has been a terrible weekend, with his fever and two falls. I tend to be very excitable, so you can understand this was all very difficult. But deep down, I always believed that Manuel would be able to deal with this final part of the challenge that he faced."

Rossano Brazzi, his chief engineer, who also took this title with Valentino Rossi and Marco Melandri...
"This time, I would like to dedicate the title to the men in my team, who were fantastic. After the fall in the warm-up, the bike was destroyed. In two hours they managed to rebuild it. They did a great job, just like Manuel, who was fantastic."

Ivano Beggio, owner of Aprilia...
"22, we have now won 22 world championship titles! Manuel did very well to stand the stress of a season where he was always leading the series. We did not expect him to be so perfect in his first season in the category. In our opinion, Poggiali can become the big champion of the future. We have him under contract and we will do all we can to keep him."

Jan Witteveen, the father of the racing Aprilia...
"This is a historic result. Poggiali is one of the greats. Even when we went through really difficult moments, he withstood all the pressure. He is very young, but he has just proved that he is already very strong mentally. I predict a great future for him."

The lucky number 54 worn by the double world champion.

BUSINESS CARD

Name:	Poggiali
First name:	Manuel
Born:	14th February 1983
At:	Chiesa Nuova (San Marino)
First race:	1994
First GP:	Imola, 1998 (125)
Number of GP wins:	11 (7/125; 4/250)
First GP win:	France, 2001 (125)

Track record
1994:	5th Italian minibike championship Junior B (Polini)
1995:	2nd du Italian minibike championship (Pasini)
1996:	11th Italian minibike championship (Pasini)
1997:	Italian Champion minibike (Pasini)
1998:	5th European championship 125, Italian champion 125, Winner Italian Cup Honda 125 (Honda)
1999:	17th World Championship 125 (Aprilia)
2000:	16th World Championship 125 (Derbi)
2001:	World Champion 125 (Gilera)
2002:	2th World Championship 125 (Gilera)
2003:	World Champion 250 (Aprilia)

Dani Pedrosa

Pedrosa in full flight: the Spaniard dominated the 2003 season.

Champagne for a first title: it came at Sepang in Malaysia.

Dani Pedrosa, the martyred champion

He set foot in Phillip Island a free spirit, having absorbed the strongest emotions: a week earlier, in winning the Malaysian GP, Daniel Pedrosa had become the second youngest world champion in GP history, at the age of 18 years and 13 days. At the time he had cried, cried real tears of emotion, tears of joy and relief. So what was going through his mind as he walked into the Australian paddock? "The last two important races. But also about going home to Spain to finally celebrate the title with those who are close to me." Alberto Puig's protégé had plenty to think about. It was the eve of the first practice day of the penultimate race of the year. It was the eve of a fall which would put him out of action for several months. He had hoped to spend the winter working on a new challenge of making the transition to the 250 cc class and now he was condemned to an enforced rest.

A triumphal return to the pits after the Malaysian GP: two hours before Valentino Rossi, Pedrosa became a world champion.

The day after he took the title, prior to the Phillip Island accident therefore, Josep Viaplana from the "Sport" newspaper in Barcelona had a long interview with the world champion.

Will your life change as a result of this championship?
On a personal level, I don't know. As far as the sport is concerned, I feel total satisfaction, especially if I look back at the last few races before taking the title. We all worked very well, giving 100% both in practice and the race. I don't know exactly what could have changed in me this year, but I seem to have matured quite a bit and have got to know more people. And to know them better too.

Was the title always a childhood dream?
Ever since I can remember I wanted to be a race rider. When I took part in my first GP in the world championship, I immediately dreamed of victory and of the title. Now, it's done and I have won, but to realise what I have done will take a bit more time.

"My team helped me to grow wings"

What lesson do you draw from this season and this first world title?

Dani Pedrosa

I managed to take the title thanks to a training programme which dates back to 1999 and which involved riding for Alberto Puig's team. It is a complex programme, complete with well known sponsors (Telefonica,) technical ones (Honda,) but also some unusual partners like Dorna, the company which owns the rights to the GPs and realised the importance of helping young riders move up the ladder.) Without them, I would never have succeeded. Today, I would be at home, watching the races on television. They deserve much of the credit because for sure in this environment, if you don't have someone to help you, you will not go far. On the other hand, I have always had a fantastic technical team around me, which right from Day 1 always gave me everything, even

without me deserving it. My backers always believed in me. They have helped me to grow wings. Then it was down to me to prove they were right.

What would you say to kids who watch the races on television and regard you as their idol?
That, if they are really determined, they should give it a try. If I have got to where I am now, it's because it's possible. For them too...

Now, there can be no excuses and it's a step up to 250 cc.
My dream was first to win the championship, then to switch categories. Now I can therefore tackle this new challenge in a calmer frame of mind.

If the 2003 champion had to pick his successor, who would it be?
Lorenzo was very quick in the late

stages of the championship, so he is one likely candidate. He has an experienced team, his machine is not bad and he learns very quickly. But he will not be alone: Barbera seems to get stronger each time out and there are a lot of foreign riders who are progressing like Dovizioso, Kallio, Luthi and all the Aprilia bunch.

Do you still remember your arrival on the GP scene, when Alberto Puig was like a mother hen with his three chicks – Pedrosa, Elias and Olive?
To be honest, when I started it all seemed overwhelming. I can remember my first GP start in Japan. It was total panic. I was towards the back of the field and coming to the first corner, I told myself I had to be very careful. Then, as you get more kilometres under your belt, confidence increases on the track and the respect I had for the others diminished a bit. In the paddock, it was different. I didn't know anything or anyone apart from my team and my people.

Tell us about the first time you met Alberto Puig...
I remember it as if it was yesterday. It was at the Jarama circuit at six in the morning. It was very cold and it was still pitch dark. I was with my father and he walked past us. The first time I met him face to face, I was sitting on the pit wall just before getting on my bike. He gave me a serious look and I think it frightened me.

And today, he can be proud of his young lads...
With him I don't think it is a question of pride, but rather of satisfaction from the work achieved. I know him very well now and I like his attitude, which is similar to mine. I have spent my youth in his company and I learnt a lot from him. When he needs to be very serious he is and he tells me things without pulling any punches. If there are problems, he goes straight to the source and I think that is the best way to solve them. At the races, he is pretty much my best friend.

Pedrosa, Ui, Dovizioso, Jenkner, Nieto: it is the South African GP and the Honda number 3 is in the lead.

Daniel Pedrosa gets a grilling

Your favourite circuits?
Assen and Motegi.

The worst and the best thing about racing?
The best race are those you have against yourself. The worst thing is being away from home for such a long time.

Your best friend in the paddock?
No one in particular.

Who do you admire?
Alberto Puig.

And outside racing?
My parents.

Your hobbies?
Cycling and music.

What kind of music? Who is your favourite band?
I like all sorts of music and I'm particularly keen on Dire Straights, U2 and Mike and the Mechanics.

A girlfriend?
Not at the moment.

Your favourite actress?
Charlize Theron.

What was the last crazy thing you did?
I bought a video camera and an MP3 player.

The last gift you bought?
A complete windsurfing kit for my father for his birthday.

Your ideal holiday?
On the beach with friends, a windsurfer and a bicycle.

BUSINESS CARD

Name:	Pedrosa
First name:	Daniel
Born:	29th September 1985
At:	Castellar del Vallés (Spain)
First race:	1993
First GP:	Japanese GP, 2001 (125)
Number of GP wins:	8 (125)
First GP win:	Dutch GP, 2002 (125)

Track record
1996: 2nd Spanish minibike championship
1997: 3rd Spanish minibike championship
1998: Spanish minibike champion
1999: 8th in the Spanish "Joven" Cup (Honda)
2000: 4th Spanish 125 championship
2001: 8th 125 World championship (Honda)
2002: 3rd 125 World championship (Honda)
2003: 125 World Champion (Honda)

Dani Pedrosa's fan club:
an ever growing band.

JAPAN
Suzuka

World Superbike champion, Colin Edwards, follows World MotoGP champion, Valentino Rossi in qualifying for the Japanese GP. The 2003 season looks like being a stunner. No one yet knows that the race will be marred by a terrible accident which takes the life of Daijiro Kato (opposite) and totally overwhelms the paddock. For everyone else, including Stefano Perugini (above) in the 125 class, the joy of victory had a bitter taste.

Crashes are part and parcel of racing, but fortunately, serious injuries are a rarity.

Japanese Grand Prix
6 April 2003 / Suzuka - 5,824 m

STARTING GRID

1.	46 V. Rossi	Honda	2'06.838
2.	3 M. Biaggi	Honda	2'07.092
3.	11 T. Ukawa	Honda	2'07.298
4.	7 C. Checa	Yamaha	2'07.426
5.	6 M. Tamada	Honda	2'08.103
6.	15 S. Gibernau	Honda	2'08.251
7.	10 K. Roberts	Suzuki	2'08.389
8.	4 A. Barros	Yamaha	2'08.670
9.	45 C. Edwards	Aprilia	2'08.785
10.	56 S. Nakano	Yamaha	2'08.930
11.	74 D. Kato	Honda	2'09.104
12.	21 J. Hopkins	Suzuki	2'09.141
13.	12 T. Bayliss	Ducati	2'09.147
14.	17 N. Abé	Yamaha	2'09.162
15.	65 L. Capirossi	Ducati	2'09.325
16.	25 T. Serizawa	MD211VF	2'09.416
17.	41 N. Haga	Aprilia	2'09.690
18.	48 A. Yanagawa	Kawasaki	2'09.934
19.	9 N. Aoki	Proton 2T	2'10.120
20.	8 G. McCoy	Kawasaki	2'11.514
21.	19 O. Jacque	Yamaha	2'11.924
22.	35 C. Burns	Harris-WCM	2'13.074
23.	69 N. Hayden	Honda	2'13.588
24.	88 A. Pitt	Kawasaki	2'13.871
25.	99 J. McWilliams	Proton 2T	2'14.011

RACE: 21 LAPS = 122.304 KM

1.	Valentino Rossi	44'13.182 (165.949)
2.	Massimiliano Biaggi	+ 6"445
3.	Loris Capirossi	+ 8"209
4.	Sete Gibernau	+ 13"209
5.	Troy Bayliss	+ 23"099
6.	Colin Edwards	+ 29"040
7.	Nicky Hayden	+ 29"126
8.	Alex Barros	+ 30"526
9.	Shinya Nakano	+ 33"447
10.	Carlos Checa	+ 40"200
11.	Norifumi Abé	+ 44"790
12.	Noriyuki Haga	+ 1'03.358
13.	John Hopkins	+ 1'03.950
14.	Kenny Roberts	+ 1'04.085
15.	Olivier Jacque	+ 1'09.990
16.	Garry McCoy	+ 1'16.572
17.	Andrew Pitt	+ 1'17.380
18.	Akira Yanagawa	+ 1'23.605
19.	Tamaki Serizawa	+ 1'35.459
20.	Tohru Ukawa	+ 1'57.128

Fastest lap: Rossi, in 2'04.970
(167,771 km/h. New record/modified track).
Outright fastest lap: Capirossi, in 2'04.604
(168.264 km/h/2003).

CHAMPIONSHIP

1.	V. Rossi	25 (1 win)
2.	M. Biaggi	20
3.	L. Capirossi	16
4.	S. Gibernau	13
5.	T. Bayliss	11
6.	C. Edwards	10
7.	N. Hayden	9
8.	A. Barros	8
9.	S. Nakano	7
10.	C. Checa	6

Runners and riders:
There is an abundance of talent: ten world champions, new faces – Edwards, Hayden, Pitt – an increase in works Hondas, the arrival of Ducati and Kawasaki with only the new KR5 not ready. A surprise, Moriwaki enters his MD211VF prototype, powered by a V5 Honda. In the WCM camp, the four engines brought to Japan all break in practice and Burns has to pull out.

Qualifying:
Attack of the reds on Friday as the Ducati is quickest on the dry track. In the afternoon, in the damp, reigning champion Rossi is first on track and takes the first pole of the season, as it rained on Saturday. It was not the main talking point as the first big crash of the season occurred on Friday morning. Melandri piled into the barrier, which was too close to the track, at around 200 km/h. He suffered several fractures, including nose, femur and tibia. For Saturday, the 250 champion was replaced by Norifume Abe, who had started the weekend as a wildcard. On Sunday morning, Barros fell at the same spot as Melandri, injuring his left knee.

Start:
Checa makes the best getaway, ahead of Biaggi, Bayliss and Rossi. Max takes the lead but is surprised by Capirossi and the Ducati Desmosedici finishes its first ever lap in the lead!

Lap 3:
The three Italians lead, Capirossi 0"270 ahead of Rossi and Biaggi. At the same time, Daijiro Kato has a terrible crash.

Lap 5:
Ukawa falls and Rossi takes the lead down the main straight. Behind the lead trio, Bayliss is already 4 seconds down.

Lap 6:
Rossi steps up the pace, Biaggi hangs on, but not Capirossi who makes a mistake at the chicane. Kato is taken to the medical centre.

Lap 8:
Rossi is lapping in 2'04 with a 1"686 lead over Biaggi, while Capirossi is alone in third, three seconds down on Max. Further back, Gibernau is confirming Honda's faith in him.

Half distance (lap 10):
Rossi continues with his demonstration, leading Biaggi by 2"902 and Capirossi by 5"081. Gibernau is fourth at 9"835. Haga falls at the chicane but keeps going.

Lap 13:
Tamada falls.

Finish (21 laps):
While all sorts of scenarios had seemed possible, world champion Rossi was back on the top step of the podium. But everyone's thoughts are with Kato, who would fight for his life for another ten days.

This is the view most riders had of world champion, Valentino Rossi.

Kato: the little guy rests in peace

He had made his name here at Suzuka back in April 1996. He was the unknown who had finished third, a little guy with eyes which seemed permanently closed. He was the typical Japanese rider who never had much to say in front of a microphone, but whose talent shone on the machine. It seemed as though a great future lay ahead of him and he became a world champion. When attempts were made to dig into his personality during the year when he totally dominated the 250 championship, he had bluffed his way through. He was like an extra-terrestrial who had landed on the GP planet. He would sleep whenever he could and once, before a very important qualifying session, his team even had to wake him up when he fell asleep at the back of the garage! He had won four times at home at Suzuka, where his career ended at 14h08 on Sunday 6th April 2003 on the third lap of the big race of the day.

The accident: "It occurred in circumstances which are still not clear, in the braking area before the double chicane," said race director Paul Butler. "We have looked at all available footage from the television and from the fixed cameras at the marshal posts. What we can say this evening is that this accident could have happened at any circuit." In the immediate aftermath of the accident: "We were immediately told it was serious, as Daijiro Kato was in a coma," explained Doctor Claudio Macchiagodena, the chief medical officer for the grands prix. "He was taken on a stretcher to the ambulance where the first attempts at cardio-respiratory resuscitation were carried out. In the medical centre, the Japanese doctors in the mobile clinic ascertained that only very prompt action had allowed the unfortunate rider's heart to keep beating. His breathing was also maintained

Daijiro Kato on the grid for his last GP. The little Japanese rider suffered a fatal accident in the race.

before he was taken by helicopter to the Mie hospital at Yokkaichi. The scanner revealed the extent of the head injuries with dislocated first and second vertebrae and brain damage. At this time (Sunday evening at 18h15 Japan time) Daijiro Kato is fighting for his life." The fight lasted two weeks. "In my opinion, Daijiro has only a 15% of surviving and even then, it would be in difficult conditions," warned Claudio Costa, every rider's guardian angel. Costa knew there would be no miracle. Kato died on Saturday 19th April, without regaining consciousness, from "heart failure." He leaves a wife and two children, including a little girl

born on 26th March. Her father had promised to chose her name after the first GP of the 2003 season.

After quite a difficult start to the race, Kato tries to catch the leaders, until disaster strikes on lap three.

250cc

Japanese Grand Prix
6 April 2003 / Suzuka - 5,824 m

STARTING GRID

1.	92	H. Aoyama	Honda	2'17.930
2.	71	K. Nakasuga	Yamaha	2'18.105
3.	6	A. Debon	Honda	2'18.274
4.	3	R. Rolfo	Honda	2'19.990
5.	8	N. Matsudo	Yamaha	2'20.018
6.	5	S. Porto	Honda	2'20.285
7.	72	Y. Takahashi	Honda	2'20.998
8.	50	S. Guintoli	Aprilia	2'22.111
9.	10	F. Gonzales-Nieto	Aprilia	2'22.457
10.	96	J. Smrz	Honda	2'22.464
11.	26	A. Baldolini	Aprilia	2'22.811
12.	68	T. Kayo	Yamaha	2'22.869
13.	16	J. Stigefelt	Aprilia	2'23.476
14.	9	H. Marchand	Aprilia	2'23.717
15.	13	J. Hules	Yamaha	2'24.348
16.	21	F. Battaini	Aprilia	2'24.692
17.	14	A. West	Aprilia	2'25.134
18.	33	H. Faubel	Aprilia	2'25.496
19.	28	D. Heidolf	Aprilia	2'26.008
20.	7	R. De Puniet	Aprilia	2'26.613
21.	36	E. Nigon	Aprilia	2'26.613
22.	67	T. Koyama	Yamaha	2'26.730
23.	54	M. Poggiali	Aprilia	2'26.748
24.	15	C. Gemmel	Honda	2'27.509

Not qualified on time, but allowed to race

18.	H. vd Lagemaat	Honda	2'28.804
98.	K. Poensgen	Honda	2'28.988
24.	T. Elias	Aprilia	2'29.111
34.	E. Bataille	Honda	2'31.048
57.	C. Davies	Aprilia	2'32.767
11.	J. Olive	Aprilia	2'33.222

RACE: 19 LAPS = 110.656 KM

1.	Manuel Poggiali	41'36.284 (159.581)
2.	Hiroshi Aoyama	+ 1"373
3.	Yuki Takahashi	+ 1"496
4.	Sebastian Porto	+ 1"700
5.	Franco Battaini	+ 11"771
6.	Alfonso Gonzales-Nieto	+ 13"220
7.	Roberto Rolfo	+ 13"497
8.	Naoki Matsudo	+ 14"027
9.	Tekkyu Kayo	+ 24"546
10.	Sylvain Guintoli	+ 42"722
11.	Alex Debon	+ 43"246
12.	Erwan Nigon	+ 47"871
13.	Joan Olive	+ 1'09.405
14.	Johan Stigefelt	+ 1'09.779
15.	Jakub Smrz	+ 1'21.048
16.	Eric Bataille	+ 1'21.788
17.	Jaroslav Hules	+ 1'35.538
18.	Chaz Davies	+ 1'38.489
19.	Henk vd Lagemaat	+ 1'41.507
20.	Katja Poensgen	+ 1 lap

Fastest lap: Aoyama, in 2'09.839
(161.479 km/h. New record/modified track).
Outright fastest lap: Elias, in 2'09"120
(162.379 km/h/2003).

CHAMPIONSHIP

1.	M. Poggiali	25 (1 win)
2.	H. Aoyama	20
3.	Y. Takahashi	16
4.	S. Porto	13
5.	F. Battaini	11
6.	A. Gonzales-Nieto	10
7.	R. Rolfo	9
8.	N. Matsudo	8
9.	T. Kayo	7
10.	S. Guintoli	6

Runners and riders:

Reigning champion Marco Melandri had moved up a category. His place at Aprilia was taken by former 125 champion, Manuel Poggiali. Alongside him were three other top class riders; Spain's Elias and Gonzales-Nieto and France's De Puniet. For Honda, it is the post-NSR era with the customer RS250W. The same situation applied at Yamaha, where there were no more official YZR, these replaced by the latest TZ. As was the case in 2001, a woman, the German Katja Poensgen was trying her hand in this category which looked like its days were numbered, given that 250 road bikes are scarce, as are two strokes and less and less national championships are run for this discipline.

Qualifying:

With this category invariably being the last to take to the track, it usually picked up the worst of what the weather had to offer. This was the case at Suzuka, starting on Friday afternoon, when the track was covered with dark damp patches. The wildcard riders fared best,

Traffic jam in front of the crowd at the chicane: a typical image from Suzuka.

with Aoyama ahead of Nakasuga, while some of the stars fell: Manuel Poggiali and Toni Elias failed to qualify on the first day and then it poured on Saturday. Poggiali somehow managed to qualify within 107% of the pole time before falling. In the end, everyone was allowed to race.

Start:

Porto gets the best start, ahead of Rolfo, who has a scare on the opening lap and Matsudo. The Argentinian leads by 1"100 from Matsudo. Starting at the back, Elias is already twelfth, just ahead of Poggiali and behind De Puniet, who had been quickest in the morning warm-up.

Lap 4:

De Puniet retires (spark plugs.) Porto now leads West and Nieto by 3"927. Poggiali is up to eighth.

Half distance (lap 10):

Still Porto, but his lead is down to 0"945 over a small group of West, Takhashi, Poggiali (what a comeback!) and Aoyama. Now sixth, Elias is the quickest man on track.

Lap 12:

Nothing can stop Poggiali who takes the lead and immediately pulls out a handy gap.

Lap 14:

Elias retires from sixth (seized.)

Lap 16:

West falls.

Finish (19 laps):

Poggiali wins his first 250 cc race, as did Freddie Spencer in 1985, Kobayashi in 1987 and John Kockinski in 1988.

First time out in a 250 GP, first win: not bad Manuel Poggiali!

A world champion still very confident about the coming challenge: Arnaud Vincent rides the new KTM at Suzuka.

Runners and riders:
KTM presented its impressive looking team the day before practice. Reigning champion Arnaud Vincent did not hide the fact that he was not expecting miracles for the first race as he was still suffering from an Injury picked up over the winter. "It was a silly accident on a supermotard bike when I was only going at 40 km/h." The Frenchman had an operation on his left ankle just two weeks before the Japanese GP. It was also the first event for the original looking Malagutis.

Qualifying:
Friday's qualifying session was effectively over in fifteen minutes or six laps before the rain came. Aprilia nearly made a clean sweep of it taking six of the top seven places, including De Angelis on pole. Vincent was 16th on row 4 with the new KTM. One little piece of history: in Saturday's wet session, Fabrizio Lai put the Malaguti name on top of a time sheet for the first time.

Start:
A great start from Pedrosa, ahead of Casey Stoner and Dovizioso. Arnaud Vincent is tenth.
At the end of the opening lap, the Spaniard leads Dovizioso by 0"256 and Stoner by 0"633.

Lap 2:
Hector Barbera falls.

Lap 3:
Alzazmora retires (cylinder) and Vincent (piston.)

Lap 7:
De Angelis and Dovizioso touch, with the former retiring and the latter dropping to ninth.

Half distance (lap 9):
Bianco and Stoner fall. Pedrosa still leads by 0"571 from Giansanti. Cecchinello, Jenkner and Perugini stay in touch with the top five all within 1"019.

Lap 11:
Giansanti takes the lead.

Lap 12:
It is Perugini's turn to lead.

Lap 14:
Cecchinello now heads Perugini and Giansanti with the top five in 0"591.

Lap 15:
Pedrosa drives through a gravel trap but keeps upright to lie eighth.

Finish (lap 18):
It is a mad dash between the Italians. Lucio Cecchinello goes off at high speed, putting his bike down before slamming into the barrier. He rejoins fourth, missing his braking at the chicane, cutting across it. He crosses the finish line in the lead, but is penalised 30 seconds (article 1.19) which drops him to eighth, before eventually being classified fourth, where he was before the crash. Stefano Perugini wins, just 37 thousandths ahead of Giansanti.

Perugini (7) and Jenkner elbow to elbow. Cecchinello (4) about to go straight on after a coming together with the future winner: exciting stuff!

Japanese Grand Prix
6 April 2003 / Suzuka - 5,824 m

STARTING GRID

1.	15	A. De Angelis	Aprilia	2'15.417
2.	3	D. Pedrosa	Honda	2'15.881
3.	4	L. Cecchinello	Aprilia	2'16.732
4.	6	M. Giansanti	Aprilia	2'16.884
5.	7	S. Perugini	Aprilia	2'16.918
6.	11	M. Sabbatani	Aprilia	2'16.959
7.	27	C. Stoner	Aprilia	2'16.961
8.	34	A. Dovizioso	Honda	2'16.975
9.	80	H. Barbera	Aprilia	2'17.224
10.	33	S. Bianco	Gilera	2'17.349
11.	22	P. Nieto	Aprilia	2'17.569
12.	66	S. Aoyama	Honda	2'17.804
13.	17	S. Jenkner	Aprilia	2'17.990
14.	26	E. Alzamora	Derbi	2'18.126
15.	58	M. Simoncelli	Aprilia	2'18.428
16.	1	A. Vincent	KTM	2'18.710
17.	12	T. Lüthi	Honda	2'19.062
18.	41	Y. Ui	Aprilia	2'19.308
19.	19	A. Bautista	Aprilia	2'19.646
20.	23	G. Borsoi	Aprilia	2'19.711
21.	32	F. Lai	Malaguti	2'19.766
22.	42	G. Pellino	Aprilia	2'20.130
23.	79	G. Talmacsi	Aprilia	2'20.253
24.	31	J. Simon	Malaguti	2'20.298
25.	65	T. Kuzuhara	Honda	2'20.452
26.	68	S. Suma	Honda	2'20.487
27.	10	R. Locatelli	KTM	2'20.572
28.	24	S. Corsi	Honda	2'21.133
29.	48	J. Lorenzo	Derbi	2'21.361
30.	8	M. Azuma	Honda	2'21.446
31.	25	I. Toth	Honda	2'21.730
32.	14	C. Martin	Aprilia	2'21.920
33.	63	M. Di Meglio	Aprilia	2'22.906
34.	36	M. Kallio	Honda	2'23.591
35.	78	P. Lenart	Honda	2'24.088
36.	27	L. Camier	Honda	2'24.229

RACE: 18 LAPS = 104.832 KM

1. Stefano Perugini — 40'53.083 (153.845)
2. Mirko Giansanti — + 0"037
3. Steve Jenkner — + 1"033
4. Lucio Cecchinello — + 6"701
5. Andrea Dovizioso — + 8"594
6. Youichi Ui — + 8"940
7. Pablo Nieto — + 9"083
8. Daniel Pedrosa — + 22"993
9. Thomas Lüthi — + 33"708
10. Gino Borsoi — + 34"234
11. Mika Kallio — + 34"280
12. Simone Corsi — + 35"245
13. Max Sabbatani — + 35"818
14. Gabor Talmacsi — + 35"945
15. Gioele Pellino — + 36"307
16. Fabrizio Lai — + 42"964
17. Masao Azuma — + 43"063
18. Alvaro Bautista — + 51"526
19. Julian Simon — + 57"880
20. Toshihisa Kuzuhara — + 58"129
21. Marco Simoncelli — + 58"412
22. Mike Di Meglio — + 1'16.078
23. Roberto Locatelli — + 1'17.164
24. Imre Toth — + 1'21.140
25. Christopher Martin — + 1'21.384
26. Leon Camier — + 1'56.001
27. Akio Tanaka — + 1 lap

Fastest lap: Perugini, in 2'14.282 (156.137 km/h. New record/modified track. Outright fastest lap).

CHAMPIONSHIP

1. S. Perugini — 25 (1 win)
2. M. Giansanti — 20
3. S. Jenkner — 16
4. L. Cecchinello — 13
5. A. Dovizioso — 11
6. Y. Ui — 10
7. P. Nieto — 9
8. D. Pedrosa — 8
9. T. Lüthi — 7
10. G. Borsoi — 6

SOUTH AFRICA
Welkom

He's done it: Sete Gibernau has just taken the most important win of his career.
Before the start (opposite) all the paddock had gathered to honour Daijiro Kato.
Standing on the top step of the podium (above) the emotion was all too much for the hero of the day.

South African Grand Prix
27 April 2003 / Welkom - 4.242 m

STARTING GRID

1.	15	S. Gibernau	Honda	1'33.174
2.	46	V. Rossi	Honda	1'33.370
3.	3	M. Biaggi	Honda	1'33.386
4.	65	L. Capirossi	Ducati	1'33.408
5.	56	S. Nakano	Yamaha	1'33.548
6.	11	T. Ukawa	Honda	1'33.586
7.	7	C. Checa	Yamaha	1'33.662
8.	45	C. Edwards	Aprilia	1'33.697
9.	12	T. Bayliss	Ducati	1'33.756
10.	4	A. Barros	Yamaha	1'33.765
11.	69	N. Hayden	Honda	1'33.917
12.	19	O. Jacque	Yamaha	1'33.917
13.	99	J. McWilliams	Proton 2T	1'33.938
14.	17	N. Abé	Yamaha	1'34.152
15.	9	N. Aoki	Proton 2T	1'34.269
16.	21	J. Hopkins	Suzuki	1'34.306
17.	10	K. Roberts	Suzuki	1'34.646
18.	6	M. Tamada	Honda	1'34.670
19.	41	N. Haga	Aprilia	1'34.731
20.	88	A. Pitt	Kawasaki	1'35.128
21.	8	G. McCoy	Kawasaki	1'35.566

RACE: 28 LAPS = 118.776 KM

1.	Sete Gibernau	44'10.398 (161.331)
2.	Valentino Rossi	+ 0"363
3.	Massimiliano Biaggi	+ 5"073
4.	Troy Bayliss	+ 12"606
5.	Alex Barros	+ 18"930
6.	Tohru Ukawa	+ 19"113
7.	Nicky Hayden	+ 20"156
8.	Norifumi Abé	+ 20"870
9.	Carlos Checa	+ 22"125
10.	Olivier Jacque	+ 25"218
11.	Shinya Nakano	+ 35"903
12.	Nobuatsu Aoki	+ 39"258
13.	John Hopkins	+ 50"230
14.	Makoto Tamada	+ 1'01.441
15.	Kenny Roberts	+ 1'04.142
16.	Andrew Pitt	+ 1'23.083
17.	Garry McCoy	+ 1 lap

Fastest lap: Rossi, in 1'33.851
(162.851 km/h. New record).
Previous best: Ukawa, in 1'34.834 (161.030/2002).
Outright fastest lap: Gibernau, in 1'33.174 (163.174 km/h/2003).

CHAMPIONSHIP

1.	V. Rossi	45 (1 win)
2.	S. Gibernau	38 (1 win)
3.	M. Biaggi	36
4.	T. Bayliss	24
5.	A. Barros	19
6.	N. Hayden	18
7.	L. Capirossi	16
8.	N. Abé	13
9.	C. Checa	13
10.	S. Nakano	12

A rush of adrenaline at the start: Colin Edwards falls in the middle of the pack and Jeremy McWilliams only just avoids him.

Runners and riders:
The Telefonica team has just one rider, Gibernau. Melandri is replaced by Abe. The FIM stewards do not allow the Harris WCM to take part, maintaining that both bikes, including that of Spaniard David De Gea, due to make his debut, are excluded as they contravene article 2.2.1 of the regulations. This forbids the use in MotoGP of machines derived from production machinery – in this case, the WCM engine, based on that of the R1 Yamaha.

Qualifying:
There were black armbands for the HRC riders, with a number 74 stuck on fairings and some sewn onto leathers as Daijiro Kato cast his shadow over Welkom. Sete Gibernau, the departed rider's team-mate, managed to clear his mind and take pole. "Daijiro was with me on the bike. He was shouting, go on go on…" Rossi was beaten, but he was the most consistent of the front runners. Biaggi and Capirossi, the latter falling with ten minutes to go, round off the front row. Sensation in the Yamaha camp, as Nakano was the best of their runners in 5th place.

Start:
Roberts' engine breaks on the formation lap and leaves oil on the track. The race director

More scary than serious.

calls everyone into the pits while the surface is cleaned, with a new start taking place 50 minutes later. Bayliss is best off the mark, ahead of Gibernau. Nakano is stranded on the grid. Edwards, who gets it sideways as he accelerates, is hit by Jacque. He falls, taking McWilliams with him and Haga runs off into a gravel trap.

Lap 3:
Bayliss leads Gibernau by 0"645. Biaggi is 1"005 down, then comes Rossi at 1"909.

Lap9:
Capirossi pits, having gone off twice. Fantastic duels between Bayliss and Gibernau and Biaggi and Rossi.

Lap 11:
Gibernau takes the lead.

Lap 13:
Haga retires. Biaggi and Rossi have caught Bayliss. Gibernau leads by 1"542.

Half distance (lap 14):
Gibernau leads by 1"940 from Biaggi who is now second. The Bayliss-Rossi tussle thrills the crowd.

Lap 22:
Gibernau now leads Biaggi by 2"229. Then the Roman gets it wrong, letting Rossi through to second.

Finish (lap 28):
Rossi closes up dramatically on the leader, but Gibernau will not be beaten and it is a highly charged moment of emotion as he takes the flag and that much dreamed of win.

Championship:
Rossi keeps the lead, while Sete Gibernau is now second, with three Hondas leading the field.

Gibernau: a perfect race and a moving tale.

Sete, Kato's special envoy

Since the start of a weekend marked by the general realisation for the riders that sadly, death was part of life, the outcome of this South African Grand Prix seemed too poignant. In a cathartic moment for the entire sport, Sete Gibernau delivered the ultimate result, mastering his role as the earthly representative of his team-mate, Daijiro Kato, taken too early from us.

An angel watched over South Africa: Sete Gibernau was keener than anyone to thank his mate Daijiro Kati, who had died a few days earlier.

As a true believer, Gibernau made the sign of the cross on the grid, lingering longer on the left side of his chest, on the precise point where he had stuck a yellow number 74, which was so beloved of his departed colleague.
At the end of his perfect race, which included a fantastic tussle with Bayliss and a great job of fighting off the advances of Rossi, he stood on his footpegs and, like Christ on the cross, he spread his arms wide. Then, after a brief moment of solitude – "what happened then I will keep to myself," he was back in

the arms of his team, a team which had been so badly hit a few days earlier. Team manager, Fausto Gresini, a small sensitive man had only come back from Tokyo two days earlier, having attended his number one rider's funeral. When Gibernau brought his Honda to a stop, he held his head in his hands. His dark visor was his ally in prolonging his moment of isolation, as he finally let his emotions take over as he broke into tears.

Sete Gibernau is a 31 year old Spaniard, based in Chatel St. Denis in Switzerland. Sete Gibernau? As far as the pundits were concerned at the start of the year, his role was clearly that of Daijiro Kato's understudy. Honda dreamed of seeing Kato finally bring home the championship and the title in the blue riband discipline. But Daijio was no longer with us and, in some small way, Sete had become his representative on earth. "It's not me who has won, but the entire family which is the family of racing. Maybe I was in the saddle, but the win was for all of us who wanted to say thank you to someone who was not with us here, but will always live in our hearts."

Sete is an unlikely racer; a well educated young man from a good family, polite and naturally classy. Yet, put him on a bike and he is transformed into an out and out racer. At Welkom, he was under immense pressure, but Gibernau mastered it. "Pole position and the win: who could ask for more? Everything that happened this weekend cannot be bought with money and that's what makes it so wonderful."
Indeed Mr. Gibernau, especially when it was done with such style and talent.

Team manager, Fausto Gresini and rider Sete Gibernau: they decided to race for Daijiro.

250cc

South African Grand Prix
27 April 2003 / Welkom – 4.242 m

STARTING GRID

1.	7	R. De Puniet	Aprilia	1'36.247
2.	54	M. Poggiali	Aprilia	1'36.344
3.	21	F. Battaini	Aprilia	1'36.523
4.	10	F. Gonzales-Nieto	Aprilia	1'36.770
5.	5	S. Porto	Honda	1'37.063
6.	24	T. Elias	Aprilia	1'37.231
7.	14	A. West	Aprilia	1'37.398
8.	3	R. Rolfo	Honda	1'37.426
9.	8	N. Matsudo	Yamaha	1'37.675
10.	33	H. Faubel	Aprilia	1'37.822
11.	50	S. Guintoli	Aprilia	1'37.864
12.	6	A. Debon	Honda	1'37.934
13.	34	E. Bataille	Honda	1'37.999
14.	16	J. Stigefelt	Aprilia	1'38.010
15.	26	A. Baldolini	Aprilia	1'38.086
16.	96	J. Smrz	Honda	1'38.357
17.	9	H. Marchand	Aprilia	1'38.514
18.	36	E. Nigon	Aprilia	1'38.528
19.	28	D. Heidolf	Aprilia	1'38.614
20.	57	C. Davies	Aprilia	1'38.627
21.	11	J. Olive	Aprilia	1'38.751
22.	15	C. Gemmel	Honda	1'39.341
23.	13	J. Hules	Yamaha	1'39.584
24.	18	H. vd Lagemaat	Honda	1'41.087
25.	98	K. Poensgen	Honda	1'42.759

RACE: 26 LAPS = 110.292 KM

1.	Manuel Poggiali	42'14.305 (156.670)
2.	Randy De Puniet	+ 0"615
3.	Franco Battaini	+ 5"641
4.	Sebastian Porto	+ 12"147
5.	Roberto Rolfo	+ 12"967
6.	Anthony West	+ 19"569
7.	Alfonso Gonzales-Nieto	+ 23"080
8.	Toni Elias	+ 27"296
9.	Sylvain Guintoli	+ 30"187
10.	Naoki Matsudo	+ 31"447
11.	Hector Faubel	+ 31"511
12.	Alex Baldolini	+ 39"311
13.	Eric Bataille	+ 40"209
14.	Johan Stigefelt	+ 46"756
15.	Chaz Davies	+ 54"833
16.	Jaroslav Hules	+ 1'02.623
17.	Erwan Nigon	+ 1'09.165
18.	Christian Gemmel	+ 1'16.891
19.	Henk vd Lagemaat	+ lap

Fastest lap: Poggiali, in 1'36.649
(158.006 km/h. New record.
Previous best: Melandri, in 1'36.828 (2001).
Outright fastest lap: De Puniet, in 1'36"247
(158.666 km/h/2003).

CHAMPIONSHIP

1.	M. Poggiali	50 (2 wins)
2.	F. Battaini	27
3.	S. Porto	26
4.	H. Aoyama	20
5.	R. De Puniet	20
6.	R. Rolfo	20
7.	A. Gonzales-Nieto	19
8.	Y. Takahashi	16
9.	N. Matsudo	14
10.	S. Guintoli	13

The battle of the day: Randy De Puniet harried Manuel Poggiali from start to finish.

Runners and riders:
Once again, no surprises. As in the 125 class, everyone is present and there are no invited riders.

Qualifying:
After retiring in Suzuka with plug trouble, France's Randy De Puniet is hungry and the man who had dominated IRTA testing at the start of the year, takes his second world championship pole. But only just, beating Suzuka winner Manuel Poggiali by 97 thousandths. Tony Elias fell on Friday afternoon, sustaining a broken left thumb.

Start:
De Puniet charges into the lead ahead of Fonsi Nieto, who tries to pass, but the Frenchman counter attacks. Elias is third as they cross the line for the first time, ahead of Battaini and Poggiali. De Puniet's lead is 0"486. Debon stalls his Aprilia on the grid and is given a stop-go penalty for push starting over his grid position line.

Lap 4:
two Spaniards, Gonzales-Nieto and Elias, follow 8 tenths behind.

Lap 6:
Poggiali takes charge.

Lap 9:
Debon has failed to come in for his stop-go and is black-flagged. He pulls in furious with life in general.

Half distance (lap 13):
The three top guys are still in front in the order, championship leader Poggiali, with 0"205 over De Puniet, who seems to be waiting, while Battaini is 0"961 down and struggling to keep up. Gonzales-Nieto is over 3 seconds behind. Rolfo is now fifth.

Lap 17:
Rolfo, Porto and West have passed Fonsi in a great dice. Elias finds himself eighth.

Lap 18:
Poggiali sets the fastest race lap which previously belonged to De Puniet, but the Frenchman gets it back one lap later. This little game goes on for several laps.

Finish (lap 26):
0"187 separates the two leaders on the final lap. De Puniet tries his luck on the long straight, where he was faster than Poggiali, but the rider who is a little bit more official than the others in the Aprilia camp fights him off. Battaini is third and Porto wins the Honda duel for fourth place.

Championship:
Two races, 50 points is an ideal start to the season for Aprilia's Manuel Poggiali, a newcomer to the 250 class. He already has a 23 point lead over his nearest rival and fellow countryman, Franco Battaini.

A smiling pole position man, Randy De Puniet.

Runners and riders:

A full house in all categories, with everyone on parade, even if some of the riders arrive in South Africa crippled with a 'flu bug. One of those suffering is one of the revelations of the Japanese GP, the young Swiss, Thomas Luthi. On the technical side, the Derbi company, Gilera decided to bring last year's bikes to do comparison tests after several problems at the start of the season.

Qualifying:

On the Welkom circuit, Japan's Youichi Ui is the main weapon in the Aprilia armoury, dominating both days of qualifying, taking pole by 74 thousandths from Pablo Nieto. The rest are all 6 tenths back. Andrea Dovizioso confirms his potential with third place, while KTM has reliability problems. The latest marque to join the ranks keeps breaking pistons. World Champion, Arnaud Vincent is fourteenth, despite lack of track time because of failures.

Start:

Ui shows the quickest reaction time, leading Dovizioso, Nieto and Perugini. The much feared first corner passes without incident. The Hungarian Talmacsi starts from the pits. Ui ends the

Victory and the upper hand as Daniel Pedrosa is already leading the championship.

first lap with a 0"245 second lead. Series leader Perugini retires (seized).

Lap 3:

The top five – Ui, Dovizioso, Nieto, Jenkner and Pedrosa are nose to tail, with 0"910 between them. De Angelis tries to close on the group.

Lap 7:

Ui still leads with Pedrosa now second. De Angelis has caught the lead group with the top six within 1"554.

Half distance (lap 12) :

Ui leads a brilliant Dovizioso by 0"227 and Pedrosa by 0"392. Jenkner, Nieto and De Angelis follow on.

Lap 21:

Jenkner now leads the chase for Ui with a fight on the cards after several laps of maintaining station.

Welkom kisses.

The young Swiss rider, Thomas Luthi, discovers Africa and its artisans.

Finish (lap 24) :

Dani Pedrosa has timed it to perfection, making a decisive move on the final lap. Dovizisio goes for it as well to take second place. Ui loses all his chances at the last corner as he goes off in the gravel. With Arnaud Vincent twelfth, KTM picks up its first world championship points at only the Austrian marque's second attempt.

Championship:

With the first winner of the season, Perugini, forced to retire, Pedrosa takes the lead on 33 points ahead of Jenkner on 32 after two third places and the revelation of the early part of the year, the young Italian Andrea Dovizioso on 31.

South African Grand Prix
27 April 2003 / Welkom - 4.242 m

STARTING GRID

1.	41	Y. Ui	Aprilia	1'40.834
2.	22	P. Nieto	Aprilia	1'40.908
3.	34	A. Dovizioso	Honda	1'41.449
4.	15	A. De Angelis	Aprilia	1'41.655
5.	7	S. Perugini	Aprilia	1'41.658
6.	17	S. Jenkner	Aprilia	1'41.699
7.	3	D. Pedrosa	Honda	1'41.793
8.	36	M. Kallio	Honda	1'41.813
9.	6	M. Giansanti	Aprilia	1'41.849
10.	79	G. Talmacsi	Aprilia	1'41.973
11.	4	L. Cecchinello	Aprilia	1'42.290
12.	8	M. Azuma	Honda	1'42.348
13.	80	H. Barbera	Aprilia	1'42.501
14.	1	A. Vincent	KTM	1'42.634
15.	23	G. Borsoi	Aprilia	1'42.639
16.	24	S. Corsi	Honda	1'42.654
17.	33	S. Bianco	Gilera	1'42.700
18.	58	M. Simoncelli	Aprilia	1'42.766
19.	27	C. Stoner	Aprilia	1'42.773
20.	48	J. Lorenzo	Derbi	1'42.775
21.	26	E. Alzamora	Derbi	1'42.980
22.	12	T. Lüthi	Honda	1'43.043
23.	11	M. Sabbatani	Aprilia	1'43.121
24.	42	G. Pellino	Aprilia	1'43.277
25.	32	F. Lai	Malaguti	1'43.524
26.	19	A. Bautista	Aprilia	1'43.556
27.	31	J. Simon	Malaguti	1'43.646
28.	14	C. Martin	Aprilia	1'43.697
29.	10	R. Locatelli	KTM	1'43.819
30.	63	M. Di Meglio	Aprilia	1'44.024
31.	25	I. Toth	Honda	1'44.772
32.	27	L. Camier	Honda	1'44.884
33.	78	P. Lenart	Honda	1'46.204

RACE: 24 LAPS = 101.808 KM

1.	Daniel Pedrosa	40'46.694
2.	Andrea Dovizioso	+ 0"356
3.	Steve Jenkner	+ 0"548
4.	Youichi Ui	+ 0"754
5.	Pablo Nieto	+ 0'839
6.	Alex De Angelis	+ 1"965
7.	Mika Kallio	+ 13"997
8.	Lucio Cecchinello	+ 14"790
9.	Masao Azuma	+ 16"790
10.	Casey Stoner	+ 20"649
11.	Gino Borsoi	+ 21"809
12.	Arnaud Vincent	+ 22"015
13.	Hector Barbera	+ 23"814
14.	Simone Corsi	+ 23"871
15.	Mirko Giansanti	+ 24"786
16.	Gioele Pellino	+ 39"565
17.	Thomas Lüthi	+ 42"280
18.	Fabrizio Lai	+ 42"379
19.	Gabor Talmacsi	+ 51"145
20.	Marco Simoncelli	+ 51"186
21.	Stefano Bianco	+ 53"316
22.	Mike Di Meglio	+ 55"253
23.	Emilio Alzamora	+ 56"952
24.	Jorge Lorenzo	+ 57"035
25.	Alvaro Bautista	+ 58"109
26.	Christopher Martin	+ 58"622
27.	Julian Simon	+ 1'05.036
28.	Roberto Locatelli	+ 1'11.674
29.	Peter Lenart	+ 1'35.808

Fastest lap: Pedrosa, in 1'41.006 (151.191 km/h. New record.
Previous best: Poggiali, in 1'42.605 (2002).
Outright fastest time: Ui, in 1'40.834 (151.448 km/h/2003).

CHAMPIONSHIP

1.	D. Pedrosa	33 (1 win)
2.	S. Jenkner	32
3.	A. Dovizioso	31
4.	S. Perugini	25 (1 win)
5.	Y. Ui	23
6.	M. Giansanti	21
7.	L. Cecchinello	21
8.	P. Nieto	20
9.	M. Kallio	14
10.	G. Borsoi	11

SPAIN
Jerez

Back in Europe it's a return to the old habits, both good and bad. Thanks to John Hopkins, Suzuki seems to be returning to form. Randy De Puniet (above) is happy in the Andalusian sun, while Valentino Rossi (opposite) had returned to his favourite role of race winner.

MOTOGP

Spanish Grand Prix
11 May 2003
Jerez de la Frontera - 4.423 m

STARTING GRID

1.	65	L. Capirossi	Ducati	1'41.983
2.	12	T. Bayliss	Ducati	1'41.993
3.	3	M. Biaggi	Honda	1'42.124
4.	11	T. Ukawa	Honda	1'42.258
5.	46	V. Rossi	Honda	1'42.276
6.	15	S. Gibernau	Honda	1'42.285
7.	21	J. Hopkins	Suzuki	1'42.579
8.	9	N. Aoki	Proton 2T	1'42.609
9.	19	O. Jacque	Yamaha	1'42.643
10.	7	C. Checa	Yamaha	1'42.711
11.	45	C. Edwards	Aprilia	1'42.761
12.	6	M. Tamada	Honda	1'42.827
13.	56	S. Nakano	Yamaha	1'42.906
14.	99	J. McWilliams	Proton 2T	1'42.985
15.	4	A. Barros	Yamaha	1'42.988
16.	33	M. Melandri	Yamaha	1'43.020
17.	10	K. Roberts	Suzuki	1'43.026
18.	41	N. Haga	Aprilia	1'43.269
19.	69	N. Hayden	Honda	1'43.474
20.	88	A. Pitt	Kawasaki	1'43.889
21.	66	A. Hofmann	Kawasaki	1'44.702
22.	8	G. McCoy	Kawasaki	1'44.945

RACE: 27 LAPS = 119.421 KM

1.	Valentino Rossi	4'50.345 (152.976)
2.	Massimiliano Biaggi	+ 6"333
3.	Troy Bayliss	+ 12"077
4.	Tohru Ukawa	+ 16"186
5.	Alex Barros	+ 18"630
6.	Makoto Tamada	+ 24"153
7.	John Hopkins	+ 30"959
8.	Shinya Nakano	+ 31"218
9.	Nobuatsu Aoki	+ 36"002
10.	Olivier Jacque	+ 37"566
11.	Noriyuki Haga	+ 43"753
12.	Jeremy McWilliams	+ 43"894
13.	Kenny Roberts	+ 48"891
14.	Colin Edwards	+ 52"128
15.	Andrew Pitt	+ 1'08.179
16.	Alex Hofmann	+ 1'08.372
17.	Marco Melandri	+ 1'31.010
18.	Garry McCoy	+ 1 lap

Fastest lap: Rossi, in 1'42.788
(154.909 km/h. New record).
Previous best: Rossi, in 1'42.920 (154.710/2002).
Outright fastest lap: Rossi, in 1'41.900 (156.259 km/h/2003).

CHAMPIONSHIP

1.	V. Rossi	70 (2 wins)
2.	M. Biaggi	56
3.	T. Bayliss	40
4.	S. Gibernau	38 (1 win)
5.	A. Barros	30
6.	T. Ukawa	23
7.	S. Nakano	20
8.	N. Hayden	18
9.	L. Capirossi	16
10.	J. Hopkins	15

Runners and riders:
With testing of the Proton KR5 delayed, McWilliams and Aoki use the two stroke KR3. The Telefonica Movistar team provides Gibernau with the works 2003 RC221V. Reigning Japanese supersport champion Ryuichi Kiyonari (20 years old) is taken on by Fausto Gresini. Although present in Jerez, the Japanese rider would make his debut at Le Mans. As at Welkom, the Harris-WCM do not get through scrutineering. Melandri is back. In the Kawasaki camp, test rider Hoffman gets his first GP start of the season.

Qualifying:
While Giberneau sets the pace on the first day, the final minutes of the Saturday afternoon session are crazy. Rossi had been quickest in the morning but he was beaten by the yellow, in the form of Biaggi, best of the Hondas ahead of Ukawa and especially the red, as Capirossi sets pole by ten thousandths ahead of Bayliss. There were several fallers during qualifying: Bayliss, Biaggi, Ukawa, Gibernau, Jacque, Barros twice and Melandri, amongst others.

Jerez is the Aprilia track. But Colin Edwards has to settle for a meagre fourteenth place.

Start:
Ducati's launch control does the job, with Bayliss leading from Capirossi, Hopkins, Biaggi and Gibernau. First time past the pits and Capirossi leads Gibernau by 0"648. Bayliss is third ahead of Hopkins, Biaggi, Checa and Rossi.

Lap 2:
In the space of a lap, Rossi has moved up to second, 0"523 behind Capirossi.

Lap 4:
Checa is out with electrical problems. Capirossi puts on a slide show and Rossi takes the lead.

Lap 5:
Capirossi gets it wrong at the final hairpin, so three Hondas lead; Rossi, Gibernau at 1"292 and Biaggi at 1"349.

Lap 7:
Gibernau falls.

Lap 9:
Hayden falls.

Half distance (lap 13):
Capirossi falls. Rossi now leads Biaggi by 3"739, with Bayliss third at 4"724. The

Troy Bayliss in qualifying and about to take a front row position.

surprise of the race is Tamada on his Bridgestone-shod Honda, who has caught up with Barros and is about to pass the Brazilian.

Lap 16:
Melandri, thirteenth, goes straight on.

Finish (lap 27):
Rossi is not troubled and crosses the line pulling a wheelie while standing on the pegs. Ukawa finally won the battle for fourth. Hats off to Tamada and therefore to Bridgestone and also to Hopkins with an excellent performance all weekend.

Championship:
70 points for Rossi, 56 for Biaggi, but now an on-form Bayliss is third, ahead of Gibernau and Barros.

The Doctor anaethetises his rivals!

Jerez de la Frontera, 5h30 on Sunday 11th May 2003. The traffic is already building up on the road from the town to the track. It takes forty minutes to cover a distance of a few kilometres. All night long, the traffic flowed. This mecca of motor sport had not seen such crowds since the glory days of Alex Criville, with 128,423 spectators turning up on the Sunday alone. 128,423 people all as one with their new national hero, Sete Gibernau. A winner at Welkom a fortnight earlier, on provisional pole at the end of the first day, he now had the best equipment available; the Honda 2003 works RC211 V. Jerez de la Frontera, 14h12 on this same boiling hot day. One Spaniard, Carlos Checa, has already parked his Yamaha with electrical problems up against a pile of old tyres. Gibernau has just fallen, when he had Valentino Rossi where he wanted him. It is too much to bear and the fans start to leave the giant grandstands. They are as disappointed as they

were hopeful, after Tony Elias had reigned supreme in the 250 race. It would only make the disappointment harder to deal with. How did this happen? All too easily. It did not take long in this Spanish GP for Valentino Rossi to show all the other riders the rear view of

the formation lap when, at over 300 km/h he ran into his team-mate, Troy Bayliss. Alexandre Barros? Not in top form, the Brazilian had to settle for being the best of the Yamaha riders, the tuning fork marque already in crisis. Troy Bayliss? The Australian

The turning point of the race as Sete Gibernau (background) has just lost control of his Honda. Valentino Rossi charges on to another win.

An acrobat in action:
Valentino Rossi of course!

his saddle and the six coloured letters pasted onto the back of the world champion's leathers: D.O.C.T.O.R.
The Doc was well aware he had to calm his potential rivals after the first two GPs and he dished out some severe medication, upping the pace seemingly at will. Massimiliano Biaggi had come from nowhere after a difficult qualifying, not helped by a public spat with team boss Sito Pons, but Rossi's main rival never really troubled him. Loris Capirossi? Fell after a series of slides, fell after a big fright on

was excellent, taking his first GP podium. But his Ducati Desmosedici, so efficient over a single lap, is still a bit raw to beat the best Hondas on a regular basis.
The others? Far, far behind. They were all knocked out by Doctor Rossi's speed injection, as the Italian looks more and more like a certain Michael Doohan when it comes to teaching his rivals a lesson. Rossi had shown his strong arm tactics and it might well be the theme of the summer months to come.

250cc

Spanish Grand Prix
11 May 2003
Jerez de la Frontera – 4.423 m

STARTING GRID

1.	7	R. De Puniet	Aprilia	1'44.723
2.	54	M. Poggiali	Aprilia	1'44.897
3.	21	F. Battaini	Aprilia	1'44.889
4.	3	R. Rolfo	Honda	1'45.688
5.	10	F. Gonzales-Nieto	Aprilia	1'45.836
6.	24	T. Elias	Aprilia	1'45.968
7.	14	A. West	Aprilia	1'46.119
8.	5	S. Porto	Honda	1'46.122
9.	50	S. Guintoli	Aprilia	1'46.246
10.	8	N. Matsudo	Yamaha	1'46.307
11.	34	E. Bataille	Honda	1'46.364
12.	16	J. Stigefelt	Aprilia	1'46.404
13.	9	H. Marchand	Aprilia	1'46.586
14.	36	E. Nigon	Aprilia	1'46.622
15.	15	C. Gemmel	Honda	1'46.758
16.	6	A. Debon	Honda	1'47.021
17.	33	H. Faubel	Aprilia	1'47.096
18.	57	C. Davies	Aprilia	1'47.358
19.	11	J. Olive	Aprilia	1'47.571
20.	28	D. Heidolf	Aprilia	1'47.669
21.	13	J. Hules	Yamaha	1'48.102
22.	96	J. Smrz	Honda	1'48.117
23.	26	A. Baldolini	Aprilia	1'48.191
24.	40	A. Molina	Aprilia	1'48.667
25.	18	H. vd Lagemaat	Honda	1'49.063
26.	42	G. Leblanc	Honda	1'49.917
27.	39	L. Castro	Yamaha	1'49.917

Not qualified

	98	K. Poensgen	Honda	1'52.287

RACE: 26 LAPS = 114.998 KM

1.	Toni Elias	46'10.793 (149.413 km/h)
2.	Roberto Rolfo	+ 0"521
3.	Randy De Puniet	+ 0"539
4.	Manuel Poggiali	+ 0"607
5.	Anthony West	+ 12"048
6.	Sebastian Porto	+ 14"204
7.	Alfonso Gonzales-Nieto	+ 22"463
8.	Naoki Matsudo	+ 37"840
9.	Alex Debon	+ 42"820
10.	Joan Olive	+ 48"821
11.	Franco Battaini	+ 52"185
12.	Alex Baldolini	+ 54"704
13.	Eric Bataille	+ 56"089
14.	Christian Gemmel	+ 57"708
15.	Dirk Heidolf	+ 1'03.433
16.	Jaroslav Hules	+ 1'08.944
17.	Jakub Smrz	+ 1'18.200
18.	Chaz Davies	+ 1'18.401
19.	Alvaro Molina	+ 1'25.198
20.	Henk vd Lagemaat	+ 1 lap
21.	Luis Castro	+ 1 lap

Fastest lap: Poggiali, in 1'45.350 (151.141 km/h).
Record: Kato, in 1'44.444 (152.452 km/h/2001).
Outright fastest lap: Kato, in 1'43.959 (153.164 km/h/2001).

CHAMPIONSHIP

1.	M. Poggiali	63 (2 wins)
2.	R. Rolfo	40
3.	R. De Puniet	36
4.	S. Porto	36
5.	T. Elias	33 (1 win)
6.	F. Battaini	32
7.	A. Gonzales-Nieto	28
8.	N. Matsudo	22
9.	A. West	21
10.	H. Aoyama	20

The battle between the kings of the category: De Puniet (7), eventual winner Toni Elias (24), Manuel Poggiali (on the outside) and Roberto Rolfo (3).

Runners and riders:
After his fall in the South African GP, Elias quickly went back to Spain, where he had an operation on the double fracture to his left thumb.

Qualifying:
De Puniet confirms he is the man to beat at the moment, by dominating Friday's practice, despite a spectacular fall which left him with some bruises. He did it again on Saturday, falling again with 7 minutes remaining, but he got back on to steal pole back from Poggiali.

Start:
De Puniet demonstrates super reflexes, but not enough to deal with Rolfo who takes the lead from the inside, before being passed by Battaini and Fonsi Nieto. Battaini leads the first lap by 301 thousandths from Gonzales-Nieto, who heads De Puniet by 0"205. Poggiali, the only winner so far this season is fifth.

Lap 3:
Gonzales-Nieto now leads the Aprilia charge, ahead of De Puniet and Poggiali. One lap later, De Puniet makes the most of an error from Fonsi to snatch the lead, but a few hundred metres later, he too makes a mistake, while Poggiali leads at the end of lap 4.

Lap 6:
Poggiali has a 1"326 lead over De Puniet, who has finally managed to pass Gonzales-Nieto.

Lap 10:
0"374 separates Poggiali from De Puniet, with the Frenchman having closed up again. In third place, 0"999 down is a brilliant West, who has Rolfo hanging on. Gonzales-Nieto is slipping back in sixth.

Lap 11:
Battaini had been fifth, but his chain comes off.

Half distance (lap 13):
Poggiali still leads, but only by 0"187 over De Puniet. Rolfo is momentarily the quickest man on the track and is third, 0"660 behind the Frenchman. West is fourth, Elias fifth, while Fonsi Nieto has dropped to seventh.

Lap 15:
Ninth placed Guintoli crashes, De Puniet takes the lead.

Lap 20:
Elias has closed to 1"171 of the lead trio, still with De Puniet in front.

Lap 22:
Elias is with the leaders and passes Rolfo at the end of the straight.

Lap 23:
Stigefelt has a bad fall after his engine seizes.

Finish (lap 26):
The last lap is completely crazy, with all contenders making mistakes. Elias has the last word and the atmosphere was explosive.

Championship:
Poggiali is fourth to keep his championship lead. The consistent Rolfo is now 23 points behind with his Honda. De Puniet is third.

Elias is carried in triumph and it's party time in Andalusia.

Runners and riders:

Everyone is on parade. The mood is tense in the DRD camp, the crew running the Gileras and Derbis, with no points scored this season. The boss Giampiero Sacchi has engineer Harald Bartol in his sights, as the father of the bikes until recently called "the red bullets" has moved to KTM over the winter and a legal action against him is underway. With their national championship starting in a week's time, four Spaniards are entered as wildcards.

Qualifying:

Pablo Nieto sets a very high standard on Friday afternoon. Although his time would be beaten by Dani Pedrosa on Saturday morning, when

The Spain of the future: Pablo Nieto and Hector Barbera.

temperatures are much lower than at 13h15 on Friday. It was good enough to take pole for the first of three GPs to be run on Spanish soil.

Start:

Dovizioso gets the best start off the second row, but Pedrosa is back in charge before the end of the opening lap. As they cross the line, the Spaniard leads Dovizioso by 0"489. Nieto is third, ahead of De Angelis, Barbera and Cecchinello.

Lap 4:

Stefano Bianco falls.

Rider-manager Lucio Cecchinello loves Jerez.

Lap 6:

There are five in the lead group, covered by 1"156. Perugini sets the race fastest lap as the order reads, Pedrosa, Nieto, De Angelis, Cecchinello and Perugini.

Lap 10:

Pablo Nieto retires (gearbox.) Cecchinello leads De Angelis, Perugini and Pedrosa.

Half distance (lap 12):

Four riders are wheel to wheel (Cecchinello, De Angelis, Perugini and Pedrosa.) Jenkner is a lonely fifth, 2"297 ahead of another quartet (Stoner, Ui, Barbera and Dovizioso.)

Lap 14:

Locatelli retires (bent exhaust).

Lap 17:

For the past few laps, Jenkner has been the

quickest man on track with the result that he has caught the lead group.

Lap 20:

De Angelis takes the lead, with Jenkner now second, chased by Cecchinello, while Perugini and Pedrosa are dropped.

Finish (lap 23):

Jenkner will have to wait for his first GP win, as stuck behind the experienced Cecchinello, the German is unable to surprise the Italian at the final corner and Lucio wins another Jerez race by just 88 thousandths.

Championship:

With Pedrosa "only" fourth, Jenkner leads the championship thanks to his consistency, with three podiums from three races. He has a six point lead over the Pedrosa, Cecchinello duo.

Champagne for a veteran of the category, Lucio Cecchinello.

Spanish Grand Prix
11 May 2003
Jerez de la Frontera - 4.423 m

STARTING GRID

1.	22 P. Nieto	Aprilia	1'47.711
2.	4 L. Cecchinello	Aprilia	1'48.059
3.	15 A. De Angelis	Aprilia	1'48.269
4.	3 D. Pedrosa	Honda	1'48.319
5.	17 S. Jenkner	Aprilia	1'48.482
6.	41 Y. Ui	Aprilia	1'48.655
7.	80 H. Barbera	Aprilia	1'48.904
8.	34 A. Dovizioso	Honda	1'48.909
9.	6 M. Giansanti	Aprilia	1'48.942
10.	58 M. Simoncelli	Aprilia	1'49.075
11.	27 C. Stoner	Aprilia	1'49.079
12.	7 S. Perugini	Aprilia	1'49.082
13.	79 G. Talmacsi	Aprilia	1'49.175
14.	36 M. Kallio	Honda	1'49.267
15.	23 G. Borsoi	Aprilia	1'49.279
16.	19 A. Bautista	Aprilia	1'49.535
17.	8 M. Azuma	Honda	1'49.583
18.	11 M. Sabbatani	Aprilia	1'49.600
19.	1 A. Vincent	KTM	1'49.743
20.	12 T. Lüthi	Honda	1'49.756
21.	24 S. Corsi	Honda	1'49.832
22.	48 J. Lorenzo	Derbi	1'50.017
23.	26 E. Alzamora	Derbi	1'50.071
24.	33 S. Bianco	Gilera	1'50.201
25.	42 G. Pellino	Aprilia	1'50.662
26.	32 F. Lai	Malaguti	1'50.688
27.	14 C. Martin	Aprilia	1'51.001
28.	25 I. Toth	Honda	1'51.147
29.	31 J. Simon	Malaguti	1'51.198
30.	10 R. Locatelli	KTM	1'51.296
31.	81 I. Ortega	Aprilia	1'51.372
32.	63 M. Di Meglio	Aprilia	1'51.379
33.	70 S. Gadea	Aprilia	1'51.854
34.	71 R. Catalan	Aprilia	1'53.234
35.	69 D. Bonache	TSR-Honda	1'53.346
36.	27 L. Camier	Honda	1'53.710
37.	78 P. Lenart	Honda	1'54.196

RACE: 23 LAPS = 101.729 KM

1.	Lucio Cecchinello	41'52.177 (145.779 km/h)
2.	Steve Jenkner	+ 0"088
3.	Alex De Angelis	+ 0"378
4.	Daniel Pedrosa	+ 1"385
5.	Stefano Perugini	+ 1"507
6.	Casey Stoner	+ 11"402
7.	Hector Barbera	+ 11"496
8.	Youichi Ui	+ 15"577
9.	Andrea Dovizioso	+ 18"604
10.	Mirko Giansanti	+ 18"897
11.	Masao Azuma	+ 23"532
12.	Thomas Lüthi	+ 23"600
13.	Gino Borsoi	+ 23"810
14.	Marco Simoncelli	+ 24"208
15.	Jorge Lorenzo	+ 25"139
16.	Mika Kallio	+ 25"230
17.	Alvaro Bautista	+ 27"742
18.	Emilio Alzamora	+ 28"511
19.	Gabor Talmacsi	+ 29"036
20.	Gioele Pellino	+ 59"993
21.	Simone Corsi	+ 1'02.499
22.	Arnaud Vincent	+ 1'02.545
23.	Fabrizio Lai	+ 1'02.841
24.	Max Sabbatani	+ 1'03.046
25.	Sergio Gadea	+ 1'11.364
26.	Imre Toth	+ 1'11.453
27.	Ismael Ortega	+ 1'11.693
28.	Mike Di Meglio	+ 1'20.298
29.	Ruben Catalan	+ 1'34.875
30.	Leon Camier	+ 1'34.935

Fastest lap: Perugini, in 1'47.766 (147.753 km/h. New record).
Previous best: Azuma, in 1'48.385 (2001).

CHAMPIONSHIP

1.	S. Jenkner	52
2.	D. Pedrosa	46 (1 win)
3.	L. Cecchinello	46 (1 win)
4.	A. Dovizioso	38
5.	S. Perugini	36 (1 win)
6.	Y. Ui	31
7.	M. Giansanti	27
8.	A. De Angelis	26
9.	P. Nieto	20
10.	C. Stoner	16

FRANCE
Le Mans

The Bugatti Le Mans circuit and its major moments: a big fright for Anthony West (above) in the rain, while the winner in the blue riband category, Sete Gibernau, points a finger at the number 74, worn by his friend Daijiro Kato.

French Grand Prix
25 May 2003 / Le Mans - 4,180 m

STARTING GRID

1.	46	V. Rossi	Honda	1'35.208
2.	4	A. Barros	Yamaha	1'35.985
3.	65	L. Capirossi	Ducati	1'36.019
4.	33	M. Melandri	Yamaha	1'36.161
5.	3	M. Biaggi	Honda	1'36.169
6.	7	C. Checa	Yamaha	1'36.240
7.	15	S. Gibernau	Honda	1'36.314
8.	11	T. Ukawa	Honda	1'36.402
9.	56	S. Nakano	Yamaha	1'36.512
10.	17	N. Abé	Yamaha	1'36.617
11.	21	J. Hopkins	Suzuki	1'36.673
12.	99	J. McWilliams	Proton 2T	1'36.720
13.	69	N. Hayden	Honda	1'36.773
14.	12	T. Bayliss	Ducati	1'36.782
15.	6	M. Tamada	Honda	1'36.868
16.	19	O. Jacque	Yamaha	1'36.962
17.	10	K. Roberts	Suzuki	1'37.033
18.	41	N. Haga	Aprilia	1'37.122
19.	45	C. Edwards	Aprilia	1'37.239
20.	9	N. Aoki	Proton 2T	1'37.515
21.	88	A. Pitt	Kawasaki	1'37.647
22.	8	G. McCoy	Kawasaki	1'38.956
23.	23	R. Kiyonari	Honda	1'39.263

RACE: 13 LAPS = 54.340 KM (*)

1.	Sete Gibernau	24'29.665 (133.107 km/h)
2.	Valentino Rossi	+ 0"165
3.	Alex Barros	+ 1"793
4.	Olivier Jacque	+ 29"912
5.	Massimiliano Biaggi	+ 31"493
6.	Jeremy McWilliams	+ 33"946
7.	Tohru Ukawa	+ 35"447
8.	Noriyuki Haga	+ 36"231
9.	Garry McCoy	+ 51"254
10.	Colin Edwards	+ 1'01.802
11.	Norifumi Abé	+ 1 lap
12.	Nicky Hayden	+ 1 lap
13.	Ryuichi Kiyonari	+ 1 lap
14.	Shinya Nakano	+ 2 laps
15.	Marco Melandri	+ 2 laps
16.	Kenny Roberts	+ 2 laps

Fastest lap: Gibernau, in 1'50.358 (136.356 km/h).
Record: Rossi, in 1'36.846 (155.380/2002).
Outright fastest lap: Rossi, in 1'35.208 (158.053 km/h/2003).

(*): For the first time ever, the race result was decided solely on the order in the second part. The results of the first part – until the rain came – only served to decide the grid positions for the second start.

CHAMPIONSHIP

1.	V. Rossi	90 (2 wins)
2.	M. Biaggi	67
3.	S. Gibernau	63 (2 wins)
4.	A. Barros	46
5.	T. Bayliss	40
6.	T. Ukawa	32
7.	O. Jacque	26
8.	N. Hayden	22
9.	S. Nakano	22
10.	C. Edwards	18

A proud and happy father: Kenny Roberts Senior unveils his Proton KR5.

Runners and riders:
On Friday morning, Kenny Roberts Snr. presents his Proton KR5 four stroke, which McWilliams and Aoki will use in free practice. The machine had come straight from a shakedown test on an airport runway and is the result of work by John Barnard, famous for designing the first carbon fibre F1 car, the McLaren MP4. Other news, the departed Daijiro Kato is replaced by his compatriot, Ryuichi Kiyonara, who had first tested his RC211V the previous week at Michelin's test track. The Harris machines fail scrutineering.

Qualifying:
On a track where, a year earlier, Yamaha had staged its return to form, everyone was waiting to see what the tuning fork marque could do. While Rossi was clearly still the dominant force, Barros was second, the excellent Melandri fourth and Checa sixth. It was clear that the previous week's work at Mugello had born fruit.

Start:
A few drops of rain fell 17 minutes before the start which Capirossi masters better than the rest. He soon comes under attack from Barros. The Brazilian leads across the line on the opening lap.

Lap 3:
Checa falls.

Lap 6:
Capirossi stops with gear selector problems. Aoki and Bayliss fall as Rossi takes the lead.

Half distance (lap 14):
Rossi leads Barros by 3"088, with the Brazilian 0"205 in front of Ukawa. Behind the Japanese rider by 0"322 came a great dice between Biaggi and Gibernau.

Lap 17:
Drizzle descends on the track, Rossi lifts an arm and the race is stopped. The grid is based on positions on lap 15 and it's off again for 13 laps.

Second start:
Ukawa starts from the pits, joined by Biaggi and Jacque, who work out during their two sighting laps that they have made the wrong tyre choice. Barros displays the quickest reflexes and from the end of the first lap, Barros, Gibernau and Rossi are locked in mortal combat, separated by just 0"165. It is chaos further back and Tamada, Hopkins and Pitt will go no further.

Finish (lap 13):
Barros realises there is nothing he could up against the two Hondas. Rossi and Gibernau pass and retake one another in a breathtaking last lap. The Spaniard has the last word, to take his second win.

Championship:
Although beaten, Rossi increases his lead in the championship.

Like so many others, Andrew Pitt discovers that the Le Mans tarmac can be slippery.

Sete: courage and panache!

Gibernau's crucial attack on Rossi, at the final corner. It is absolutely on the limit.

In the past, Grands Prix would be interrupted by rain and the riders would set off on the second leg, armed with a calculator, with victory decided by adding up times from both legs. Those days are gone and now it's a simple case of first man across the line wins, even if he was way back in the first leg. "For sure, for the spectators, it is much easier to understand," explained the first beneficiary of this new system, Spain's Sete Gibernau. "Before it was just a question of doing the sums, with the order not the important thing. All you had to do in the second leg was calculate your effort according to where you finished the first leg and that was quite complicated, " added the Paulista, Alexandre Barros. "Sure, maybe I was the loser today, but you have to say from the point of view of the show, it is much better," concluded Valentino Rossi, second across the line of this historic French GP. The six hundredth race in this blue riband category on two wheels was the first to be run under this rule, which had been demanded by race promoters, precisely to make the result easier

to understand. It had been accepted by the riders, although Rossi added the rider that he hoped this would see the drivers point of view listened to when it came to matters of safety. At Le Mans, the Dunlop chicane was due to be modified and the whole track resurfaced.

This race in two acts also had two completely different scenarios. At two o'clock, when the red lights went out on the Bugatti circuit, the sky was menacing. Barros made the best start, with Rossi taking the lead on lap seven. He had a lead of just 3"088 when the first drops of rain fell. The leader raised his arm, everyone stopped and the positions at this point decided the grid for the second leg. It was to the detriment of the world champion, who was just beginning to pull away. Forty minutes later, the trip meter went back to zero. Some took a risk which did not pay off, in choosing cut slicks on the rear, while Barros, Rossi and Gibernau would leave the rest for dead. In the final stages, the Brazilian suffered from the more brutal power delivery of his Yamaha and had to let the two

Rossi turns round at the end of the first leg: "where are the others?"

Hondas go, on a track where the track was dry in parts, notably at the Raccordement corner and the pit straight. The last lap was fantastic, with Gibernau having the final word. "I might have won, but I must congratulate Barros and Rossi. Like me, they managed to stay upright. And believe me, today that was not easy. The track surface is so worn, that at some places I think we would have been quicker on a moped."

250cc

STARTING GRID

1.	54	M. Poggiali	Aprilia	1'39.229
2.	21	F. Battaini	Aprilia	1'39.324
3.	7	R. De Puniet	Aprilia	1'39.341
4.	10	F. Gonzales-Nieto	Aprilia	1'39.570
5.	24	T. Elias	Aprilia	1'39.802
6.	5	S. Porto	Honda	1'39.936
7.	50	S. Guintoli	Aprilia	1'40.835
8.	8	N. Matsudo	Yamaha	1'40.948
9.	3	R. Rolfo	Honda	1'41.073
10.	14	A. West	Aprilia	1'41.168
11.	36	E. Nigon	Aprilia	1'41.275
12.	9	H. Marchand	Aprilia	1'41.447
13.	11	J. Olive	Aprilia	1'41.609
14.	16	J. Stigefelt	Aprilia	1'41.642
15.	33	H. Faubel	Aprilia	1'41.767
16.	57	C. Davies	Aprilia	1'41.890
17.	6	A. Debon	Honda	1'41.934
18.	34	E. Bataille	Honda	1'41.942
19.	28	D. Heidolf	Aprilia	1'41.980
20.	96	J. Smrz	Honda	1'42.109
21.	13	J. Hules	Yamaha	1'42.199
22.	15	C. Gemmel	Honda	1'42.355
23.	26	A. Baldolini	Aprilia	1'42.827
24.	18	H. vd Lagemaat	Honda	1'44.180
25.	45	S. Aubry	Honda	1'45.613

Not qualified

44	V. Eisen	Honda	1'46.396
98	K. Poensgen	Honda	1'46.421

RACE: 26 LAPS = 108.680 KM

1.	Toni Elias	43'55.538 (148.450 km/h)
2.	Randy De Puniet	+ 3"740
3.	Roberto Rolfo	+ 4"562
4.	Alfonso Gonzales-Nieto	+ 4"972
5.	Naoki Matsudo	+ 5"122
6.	Sylvain Guintoli	+ 6"100
7.	Anthony West	+ 29"672
8.	Alex Debon	+ 34"885
9.	Christian Gemmel	+ 35"013
10.	Joan Olive	+ 35"559
11.	Hector Faubel	+ 45"562
12.	Johan Stigefelt	+ 54"955
13.	Alex Baldolini	+ 55"049
14.	Hugo Marchand	+ 55"794
15.	Eric Bataille	+ 56"183
16.	Jaroslav Hules	+ 57"386
17.	Erwan Nigon	+ 1'27.351
18.	Franco Battaini	+ 1'36.597
19.	Jakub Smrz	+ 1 lap
20.	Henk vd Lagemaat	+ 1 lap

Fastest lap: De Puniet, in 1'40.356 (149.946 km/h).
Record: Melandri, in 1'39.648 (151.011 km/h/2002).
Outright fastest lap: Gonzales-Nieto, in 1'38.903 (152.149 km/h/2002).

CHAMPIONSHIP

1.	M. Poggiali	63 (2 wins)
2.	T. Elias	58 (2 wins)
3.	R. De Puniet	56
4.	R. Rolfo	56
5.	A. Gonzales-Nieto	41
6.	S. Porto	36
7.	N. Matsudo	33
8.	F. Battaini	32
9.	A. West	30
10.	S. Guintoli	23

Randy de Puniet has yet to take his first GP win. In front of his home crowd, he had to give best to Toni Elias.

Runners and riders:
A full house from all the riders registered for the world championship. With the French national 250 championship dying, just as the category had disappeared in England, Italy and Spain, there were only two requests for wildcards, Vincent Eisen, who failed to qualify and Samuel Aubry.

Qualifying:
As in the other categories, the grid positions were decided in one session on Friday. It turned into a fascinating battle between the top three riders of the moment, Manuel Poggiali, Franco Battaini and Randy de Puniet. Jerez winner Elias was fifth.

Start:
Tony Elias made a super start, rushing through from row two on the grid. The Spaniard took the lead at the first chicane, bringing De Puniet with him. Following on are Gonzales-Nieto and Porto. Poggiali is sixth and Battaini is further back.

Lap 4:
De Puniet takes the lead in front of a cheering grandstand. The top eight are within 1"953, the order being, De Puniet, Elias, Porto, Gonzales-Nieto, Poggiali, Rolfo, Battaini and a surprising Guintoli.

Lap 6:
Poggiali harpoons Porto and both men are out. De Puniet has just set the race fastest lap and leads Elias by 0"437.

Half distance (lap 13):
De Puniet still leads Elias by 0"854. Four seconds behind the Spanish rider is a second duo consisting of the Campetella team-mates Battaini and Guintoli. Following, but already 8 seconds down on the leader, are Rolfo, Gonzales-Nieto and Matsudo.

Lap 15:
De Puniet's Aprilia seems very twitchy, because of a bad choice of rear tyre, which allows Elias to pass him.

Lap 16:
Battaini ends up in the gravel trap while Guintoli runs in a podium position.

Lap 25:
Under pressure from Fonsi Nieto, the chasing group has caught Guintoli, who gets it wrong at the Raccordement corner, losing three places. It did not matter as at least the Frenchman had confirmed his promise.

Finish (lap 26):
In a last infernal lap, with third place up for grabs, Gonzales-Nieto makes a slight mistake and Rolfo makes the most of it to get onto the podium, alongside Elias and De Puniet.

Championship:
Despite his mistake, Poggiali keeps the lead, but the title has been blown wide open with four riders covered by just 7 points (Poggiali, 63; Elias 58; De Puniet and Rolfo 56.)

A superb performance from Sylvain Guintoli (50) who, with his standard Aprilia, will fight tooth and nail with Fonsi Gonzales-Nieto.

World Champion Arnaud Vincent went well in qualifying to go 8th on the grid for KTM.

**French Grand Prix
25 May 2003 / Le Mans - 4,180 m**

STARTING GRID

1.	34	A. Dovizioso	Honda	1'43.565
2.	41	Y. Ui	Aprilia	1'43.743
3.	48	J. Lorenzo	Derbi	1'43.947
4.	27	C. Stoner	Aprilia	1'44.203
5.	15	A. De Angelis	Aprilia	1'44.315
6.	3	D. Pedrosa	Honda	1'44.437
7.	4	L. Cecchinello	Aprilia	1'44.510
8.	1	A. Vincent	KTM	1'44.522
9.	80	H. Barbera	Aprilia	1'44.570
10.	12	T. Lüthi	Honda	1'44.638
11.	33	S. Bianco	Gilera	1'44.883
12.	6	M. Giansanti	Aprilia	1'44.891
13.	23	G. Borsoi	Aprilia	1'44.945
14.	36	M. Kallio	Honda	1'44.963
15.	8	M. Azuma	Honda	1'45.031
16.	7	S. Perugini	Aprilia	1'45.326
17.	79	G. Talmacsi	Aprilia	1'45.480
18.	22	P. Nieto	Aprilia	1'45.541
19.	17	S. Jenkner	Aprilia	1'45.554
20.	24	S. Corsi	Honda	1'45.576
21.	11	M. Sabbatani	Aprilia	1'45.700
22.	26	E. Alzamora	Derbi	1'46.007
23.	32	F. Lai	Malaguti	1'46.229
24.	19	A. Bautista	Aprilia	1'46.363
25.	42	G. Pellino	Aprilia	1'46.503
26.	58	M. Simoncelli	Aprilia	1'46.624
27.	31	J. Simon	Malaguti	1'46.929
28.	63	M. Di Meglio	Aprilia	1'46.973
29.	10	R. Locatelli	KTM	1'46.994
30.	72	A. Masbou	Honda	1'47.588
31.	74	J. Petit	Honda	1'47.616
32.	25	I. Toth	Honda	1'47.709
33.	73	W. Gautier	Honda	1'48.321
34.	14	C. Martin	Aprilia	1'48.478
35.	86	G. Lefort	Aprilia	1'48.500
36.	78	P. Lenart	Honda	1'49.165
37.	85	X. Hérouin	Honda	1'49.522
38.	27	L. Camier	Honda	1'50.678

RACE: 24 LAPS = 100.320 KM

1.	Daniel Pedrosa	41'58.500 (143.399 km/h)
2.	Lucio Cecchinello	+ 2"337
3.	Andrea Dovizioso	+ 2"427
4.	Casey Stoner	+ 11"278
5.	Pablo Nieto	+ 11"814
6.	Youichi Ui	+ 12"592
7.	Stefano Perugini	+ 18"930
8.	Steve Jenkner	+ 25"206
9.	Thomas Lüthi	+ 29"471
10.	Masao Azuma	+ 33"910
11.	Hector Barbera	+ 44"379
12.	Mirko Giansanti	+ 44"537
13.	Gino Borsoi	+ 55"218
14.	Simone Corsi	+ 58"773
15.	Roberto Locatelli	+ 58"962
16.	Gabor Talmacsi	+ 1'07.803
17.	Mike Di Meglio	+ 1'17.604
18.	Max Sabbatani	+ 1'20.140
19.	Emilio Alzamora	+ 1'40.757
20.	Julian Simon	+ 1'43.908
21.	Christopher Martin	+ 1'49.778
22.	Peter Lenart	+ 1 lap
23.	Imre Toth	+ 1 lap
24.	Leon Camier	+ 1 lap
25.	Jimmy Petit	+ 1 lap

Fastest lap: Pedrosa, in 1'43.837
(144.919 km/h. New record.)
Previous best: Azuma, in 1'44.259 (2002).
Outright fastest lap: Dovizioso, in 1'43.565
(145.300 km/h/2003).

CHAMPIONSHIP

1.	D. Pedrosa	71 (2 wins)
2.	L. Cecchinello	66 (1 win)
3.	S. Jenkner	60
4.	A. Dovizioso	54
5.	S. Perugini	45 (1 win)
6.	Y. Ui	41
7.	M. Giansanti	31
8.	P. Nieto	31
9.	C. Stoner	29
10.	A. De Angelis	26

Runners and riders:
All contracted riders are present, including Gino Borsoi, who had a funny little adventure shortly after the Spanish Grand Prix. The Italian was playing football in the paddock, broke an ankle and needed an operation. There are five French wildcards, including Masbou and Gautier from the Equipe de France.

Qualifying:
As the teams arrive at the Bugatti circuit, there is unanimity when it comes to predicting the weather: rain will arrive on Saturday and everyone realised that Friday's 30 minutes of qualifying would be decisive. It was the ever more promising Andrea Dovizioso who thus took his first pole, ahead of Ui, the young Spaniard Lorenzo and Australia's Stoner. Championship leader, Germany's Steve Jenkner, was only nineteenth. There were several fallers in the rain on Saturday and again during Sunday's warm-up. Bianco broke his right scaphoid and had to pull out.

Start:
Dovizioso pulls the holeshot ahead of Ui. Lorenzo and Vincent are fallers. Ui finishes the first lap leading Pedrosa by 0"124. Stoner is third. Kallio retires and a group of seven riders lead the way.

Lap 2:
Pedrosa takes the lead.

Lap 5:
Pellino falls. Pedrosa now has a 1"790 lead over a group made up of Dovizioso, Cecchinello and Ui. Perugini, De Angelis and Stoner are a bit further back.

Lap 9:
Cecchinello passes Dovizioso for second place and sets off in pursuit of Pedrosa, who is 4"019 ahead.

Half distance (lap 12):
Pedrosa is operating on another planet and he now leads second placed Dovizioso by 5"342. Cecchinello is still hanging on to his young rival and De Angelis is not far behind. Championship leader Jenkner is back up to ninth.

Finish (lap 24):
As soon as Pedrosa took the lead, it was evident that the main battle would be for second place. Three of them are wheel to wheel for the last two places on the podium. Alex De Angelis makes a spectacular error with a crash that left him limping.

Championship:
Second win from four races, Dani Pedrosa leads the title chase, ahead of the veteran of the category, Cecchinello and Jenkner. The first three are within 11 points of one another, which looks promising for the rest of the season.

The baby of the French bunch, Mike di Meglio.

ITALY
Mugello

The much awaited Italian war was fought out between Massimiliano Biaggi, Valentino Rossi and Loris Capirossi. But around the Mugello track, there were also a few local specialities and a VIP was involved in the shape of footballer Clarence Seedorf (above) who sponsored a 125 cc team this year.

MOTOGP

Rossi, Capirossi and Biaggi as seen by their rivals.

Italian Grand Prix
8 June 2003 / Mugello - 5.245 m

STARTING GRID

1.	46	V. Rossi	Honda	1'51.927
2.	65	L. Capirossi	Ducati	1'51.954
3.	56	S. Nakano	Yamaha	1'51.986
4.	3	M. Biaggi	Honda	1'52.021
5.	11	T. Ukawa	Honda	1'52.027
6.	15	S. Gibernau	Honda	1'52.153
7.	7	C. Checa	Yamaha	1'52.290
8.	19	O. Jacque	Yamaha	1'52.333
9.	4	A. Barros	Yamaha	1'52.439
10.	6	M. Tamada	Honda	1'52.513
11.	12	T. Bayliss	Ducati	1'52.644
12.	33	M. Melandri	Yamaha	1'52.687
13.	45	C. Edwards	Aprilia	1'52.767
14.	21	J. Hopkins	Suzuki	1'52.969
15.	66	A. Hofmann	Kawasaki	1'53.146
16.	41	N. Haga	Aprilia	1'53.149
17.	69	N. Hayden	Honda	1'53.190
18.	10	K. Roberts	Suzuki	1'53.399
19.	99	J. McWilliams	Proton 4T	1'53.813
20.	8	G. McCoy	Kawasaki	1'54.052
21.	88	A. Pitt	Kawasaki	1'54.345
22.	23	R. Kiyonari	Honda	1'55.315
23.	9	N. Aoki	Proton 4T	1'56.394

RACE: 23 LAPS = 120.635 KM

1.	Valentino Rossi	43'28.008 (166.520 km/h)
2.	Loris Capirossi	+ 1"416
3.	Massimiliano Biaggi	+ 4"576
4.	Makoto Tamada	+ 13"210
5.	Shinya Nakano	+ 13"411
6.	Tohru Ukawa	+ 13"666
7.	Sete Gibernau	+ 14"253
8.	Carlos Checa	+ 22"811
9.	Colin Edwards	+ 33"056
10.	Olivier Jacque	+ 38"882
11.	Marco Melandri	+ 38"977
12.	Nicky Hayden	+ 48"639
13.	Ryuichi Kiyonari	+ 50"183
14.	Alex Hofmann	+ 54"213
15.	Garry McCoy	+ 1'23.281
16.	Andrew Pitt	+ 1'37.284

Fastest lap: Capirossi, in 1'52.623 (167,656 km/h).
Record: Ukawa, in 1'52.601 (167.689/2002).
Outright fastest lap: Rossi, in 1'51.258 (169.713 km/h/2002).

CHAMPIONSHIP

1.	V. Rossi	115 (3 wins)
2.	M. Biaggi	83
3.	S. Gibernau	72 (2 wins)
4.	A. Barros	46
5.	T. Ukawa	42
6.	T. Bayliss	40
7.	L. Capirossi	36
8.	S. Nakano	33
9.	O. Jacque	32
10.	N. Hayden	26

Runners and riders:

The Harris-WCM saga rumbles along. The Stewards agreed with the decision taken at the last GP and once again the British bikes are excluded. In the Proton camp, its time for the four strokes and they run the KR5.

Qualifying:

The heat and tension are intense with the three Italian kings going hammer and tongs. On Friday, Capirossi sets an all time top speed record of 328.9 km/h, beating the previous record by 0.7 km/h. On Saturday, Bayliss does better still with 311.1 km/h. On provisional pole on Friday, Capirossi is beaten by Rossi by Rossi on Saturday. Valentino is the most consistent of the riders and Nakano and his Yamaha M1 is the surprise of the day, taking third.

Start:

Once again, the Ducati makes the best start and Capirossi leads from Biaggi, Nakano, Gibernau, Checa and Rossi. The reigning world champion passes the two Spaniards before the end of the first lap, to go fourth.

Lap 3:

Barros has been struggling all weekend and falls. Further back, Hopkins and Roberts collide, putting out both Suzukis and making Kenny Junior very angry as he suffers a shoulder injury in the fall.

Lap 5:

The three Italians are already on another planet. Nakano drops back. Capirossi makes a slight mistake, sliding the Ducati and letting Biaggi lead.

Lap 8:

Haga falls yet again.

Half distance (lap 12):

Biaggi heads Rossi by 0"120 and Capirossi is still there, 0"359 behind, followed a long way back by Ukawa, Tamada and Edwards.

Lap 13:

Fastest race lap for Rossi who takes the lead under braking at the end of the main straight.

Lap 16:

The Rossi-Biaggi duo now leads by 0"397. Capirossi fights back and passes Max when a tiny gap opens up, but the bikes touch.

Lap 20:

Fastest lap for Capirossi who is now 1"287 behind Rossi. Biaggi decides to settle for third.

Finish (lap 23):

Rossi hangs on until the flag with the red devil, Loris Capirossi and his Ducati, in hot pursuit.

Championship:

Rossi now leads by 32 points and can already pace himself. Biaggi is still second.

Carlo Pernat and Loris Capirossi: a solid pairing!

Rossi leads the Italian squadron

The "Frecce Tricolori," the Italian airforce display team would have appreciated the show. Maximum tension all weekend long. On the Tuesday before the Italian Grand Prix, the President of the Republic, Carlo Azeglio Ciampi met every single world champion his country had produced, in the Quirinale Palace, from Carlo Ubbiali to Marco Melandri, including Valentino Rossi, whose entourage snubbed the event. Back at the track, the heat was intense with an air temperature of 34 degrees and more than 50 on the track. The huge multicoloured crowd divided in its rider loyalty was united in its love of racing. The 2003 GP at Mugello will remain in the memory for a long time for the three heroes, Massimiliano Biaggi, Loris Capirossi and the master, Valentino Rossi. "The people might have thought we were mad, but you know, we had a great time. I think we put on a nice show and we were thanked in the best way possible, seeing the crowd in the stands, hearing them cheer and feeling them vibrate and finally singing the national anthem while we were on the podium. It was something unique," said the winner.
The crowd was indeed special. But

what to say about the spectacle put on by the Italian squadron, on two wheels. The perfect controlled slides from Rossi, who wins again, still perfect. What about the dangerous looking style shown by Capirossi, a heroic second? What about Biaggi giving best? The images and figures say it all. The speed of the MotoGP machines is being pushed ever upward by the Ducatis, with Loris Capirossi hitting 33204 km/h at the end of the

straight on the penultimate lap. The duel between the red Ducati and Biaggi's yellow Honda involved several comings-together, as Biaggi never takes defeat lightly.
The entire weekend was a showcase for masters at work, displaying panache, but also total and mutual respect, which they put aside for the 42 minutes of the race when they fight it out in front of the noisy tifosi and the backdrop of the Tuscan hills and an azure

King Valentino Rossi alone at court with the Italian public.

A duel for second place in which Loris Capirossi (65) would come off best.

sky. Words cannot describe it any better than the general ovation which greeted their performance. 72,901 spectators were there to witness the show, along with millions of TV viewers. Valentino proved to be an exceptional champion, while Loris is to be respected for his heart and immense courage and to Massimiliano, respect for a man who still dreams of obtaining revenge- to be king instead of the king.

250cc

STARTING GRID

1.	7	R. De Puniet	Aprilia	1'53.586
2.	54	M. Poggiali	Aprilia	1'53.832
3.	10	F. Gonzales-Nieto	Aprilia	1'54.676
4.	21	F. Battaini	Aprilia	1'54.984
5.	24	T. Elias	Aprilia	1'55.639
6.	3	R. Rolfo	Honda	1'55.969
7.	5	S. Porto	Honda	1'56.163
8.	50	S. Guintoli	Aprilia	1'56.452
9.	8	N. Matsudo	Yamaha	1'56.585
10.	36	E. Nigon	Aprilia	1'56.939
11.	16	J. Stigefelt	Aprilia	1'57.112
12.	11	J. Olive	Aprilia	1'57.117
13.	14	A. West	Aprilia	1'57.252
14.	33	H. Faubel	Aprilia	1'57.352
15.	6	A. Debon	Honda	1'57.646
16.	9	H. Marchand	Aprilia	1'57.657
17.	57	C. Davies	Aprilia	1'58.225
18.	15	C. Gemmel	Honda	1'58.576
19.	34	E. Bataille	Honda	1'58.582
20.	26	A. Baldolini	Aprilia	1'58.677
21.	96	J. Smrz	Honda	1'59.503
22.	13	J. Hules	Yamaha	2'00.025
23.	18	H. vd Lagemaat	Honda	2'01.161
24.	29	C. Pistoni	Aprilia	2'01.203

Not qualified

	98	K. Poensgen	Honda	2'03.163

RACE: 20 LAPS = 108.680 KM

1.	Manuel Poggiali	38'40.038 (162.773 km/h)
2.	Alfonso Gonzales-Nieto	+ 22"445
3.	Franco Battaini	+ 23"446
4.	Roberto Rolfo	+ 24"432
5.	Sylvain Guintoli	+ 31"679
6.	Toni Elias	+ 39"837
7.	Naoki Matsudo	+ 44"832
8.	Sebastian Porto	+ 44"905
9.	Anthony West	+ 1'02.385
10.	Joan Olive	+ 1'06.020
11.	Hugo Marchand	+ 1'11.197
12.	Alex Debon	+ 1'11.257
13.	Chaz Davies	+ 1'17.964
14.	Jakub Smrz	+ 1'21.573
15.	Hector Faubel	+ 1'25.294
16.	Christian Gemmel	+ 1'26.780
17.	Erwan Nigon	+ 1'35.206
18.	Henk vd Lagemaat	+ 1 lap
19.	Christian Pistoni	+ 1 lap

Fastest lap: De Puniet, in 1'54.994 (164.199 km/h).
Record: Nakano, in 1'54.462 (164.963 km/h/2000).
Outright fastest lap: De Puniet, in 1'53.586
(166.235 km/h/2003).

CHAMPIONSHIP

1.	M. Poggiali	88 (3 wins)
2.	R. Rolfo	69
3.	T. Elias	68 (2 wins)
4.	A. Gonzales-Nieto	61
5.	R. De Puniet	56
6.	F. Battaini	48
7.	S. Porto	44
8.	N. Matsudo	42
9.	A. West	37
10.	S. Guintoli	34

Runners and riders:
No wildcards, but one new name: Christian Pistoni replaces the injured Dirk Heidolf in the Aprilia Germany team.

Qualifying:
It's the expected Aprilia-fest. The only question is will pole go to Randy de Puniet or Manuel Poggiali, the two quickest riders since the start of the season. It's the young Frenchman once again, who survived a fall on Friday, as he headed back to the pits to fit the softest tyre at the end of the session. Hules does not start, the Czech having injured both wrists. Katja Poensgen has a spectacular fall, destroying her Honda and fails yet again to make the 107% of pole time required to qualify.

Start:
The first one is aborted, as there was a problem on the front row with Gonzales-Nieto and the lights failed to go out. Fifteen minutes and they are off again for a race distance shortened by one lap. This time, all goes well, especially for Elias who comes through from the second row and for Poggiali. De Puniet makes a slight mistake before the end of the first lap and as they cross the line, Poggiali leads from Elias, Gonzales-Nieto and De Puniet.

Lap 4:
Poggiali shakes off De Puniet down the straight and the more favoured Aprilia rider has just made a point.

Lap 7:
De Puniet hangs onto Poggiali just 0"360 down. Fonsi is already 2"006 down and 5 seconds behind him there is a great scrap between Rolfo, Battaini and the excellent Guintoli.

Half distance (lap 10):
The positions remain the same amongst the lead group.

Lap 14:
Rolfo slides off his machine, but recovers. A

A third win for Manuel Poggiali, an on-form 250 cc new-boy.

bit later, De Puniet falls with brake problems, rejoining fifth. Poggiali leads comfortably, ahead of Gonzales-Nieto (15 seconds down) and Guintoli.

Lap 17:
De Puniet, who has just relieved Battaini of third place, falls again and this time he goes no further.

Finish (lap 20):
It had been an exciting race to the end. The Poggiali-Aprilia RSW-R combo is really too strong for the opposition which, apart from de Puniet, seems to have thrown in the towel.

Championship:
Poggiali is streaking away. Second is the very consistent Rolfo, who is seriously handicapped by his equipment.

De Puniet bites the dust, caught out with brake problems.

In the early stages, the Frenchman was the only one to hold off Poggiali. We know how it ended...

STARTING GRID

1.	27 C. Stoner	Aprilia	1'58.914
2.	7 S. Perugini	Aprilia	1'58.977
3.	15 A. De Angelis	Aprilia	1'59.012
4.	22 P. Nieto	Aprilia	1'59.043
5.	17 S. Jenkner	Aprilia	1'59.115
6.	4 L. Cecchinello	Aprilia	1'59.143
7.	34 A. Dovizioso	Honda	1'59.251
8.	41 Y. Ui	Aprilia	1'59.406
9.	23 G. Borsoi	Aprilia	1'59.433
10.	3 D. Pedrosa	Honda	1'59.608
11.	1 A. Vincent	KTM	1'59.790
12.	80 H. Barbera	Aprilia	1'59.934
13.	42 G. Pellino	Aprilia	2'00.044
14.	79 G. Talmacsi	Aprilia	2'00.140
15.	58 M. Simoncelli	Aprilia	2'00.155
16.	6 M. Giansanti	Aprilia	2'00.303
17.	24 S. Corsi	Honda	2'00.404
18.	48 J. Lorenzo	Derbi	2'00.617
19.	11 M. Sabbatani	Aprilia	2'00.739
20.	10 R. Locatelli	KTM	2'00.949
21.	12 T. Lüthi	Honda	2'00.970
22.	8 M. Azuma	Honda	2'01.042
23.	26 E. Alzamora	Derbi	2'01.236
24.	36 M. Kallio	Honda	2'01.334
25.	25 I. Toth	Honda	2'01.377
26.	87 M. Conti	Honda	2'01.443
27.	50 A. Ballerini	Gilera	2'01.575
28.	60 M. Angeloni	Honda	2'01.681
29.	62 A. Aldrovandi	Malaguti	2'01.699
30.	63 M. Di Meglio	Aprilia	2'01.815
31.	88 R. Harms	Aprilia	2'02.077
32.	32 F. Lai	Malaguti	2'02.482
33.	61 M. Pirro	Aprilia	2'02.728
34.	31 J. Simon	Malaguti	2'03.129
35.	19 A. Bautista	Aprilia	2'03.285
36.	14 C. Martin	Aprilia	2'04.082
37.	27 L. Camier	Honda	2'04.142
38.	78 P. Lenart	Honda	2'05.490

RACE: 20 LAPS = 104.900 KM

1.	Lucio Cecchinello	40'01.738 (157.236 km/h)
2.	Daniel Pedrosa	+ 0"730
3.	Pablo Nieto	+ 0"801
4.	Andrea Dovizioso	+ 0"810
5.	Alex De Angelis	+ 1"454
6.	Youichi Ui	+ 7"656
7.	Stefano Perugini	+ 7"702
8.	Gino Borsoi	+ 7"708
9.	Hector Barbera	+ 21"704
10.	Gioele Pellino	+ 22"132
11.	Mirko Giansanti	+ 22"208
12.	Simone Corsi	+ 34"326
13.	Mika Kallio	+ 34"434
14.	Masao Azuma	+ 34"493
15.	Thomas Lüthi	+ 34"879
16.	Gabor Talmacsi	+ 35"035
17.	Marco Simoncelli	+ 45"352
18.	Casey Stoner	+ 46"072
19.	Andrea Ballerini	+ 46"428
20.	Roberto Locatelli	+ 46"436
21.	Arnaud Vincent	+ 46"615
22.	Michele Conti	+ 52"953
23.	Max Sabbatani	+ 53"338
24.	Mattia Angeloni	+ 1'04.110
25.	Robbin Harms	+ 1'04.186
26.	Alessio Aldrovandi	+ 1'11.059
27.	Imre Toth	+ 1'16.722
28.	Alvaro Bautista	+ 1'16.830
29.	Michaele Pirro	+ 1'22.815
30.	Leon Camier	+ 1 lap
31.	Peter Lenart	+ 1 lap

Fastest lap: Borsoi, in 1'58.969 (158.713 km/h. New record.)
Previous best: Cecchinello, in 1'59.184 (2002).
Outright fastest lap: Nieto, in 1'58.726 (159.038 km/h/2003).

CHAMPIONSHIP

1.	D. Pedrosa	91 (2 wins)
2.	L. Cecchinello	91 (2 wins)
3.	A. Dovizioso	67
4.	S. Jenkner	60
5.	S. Perugini	54 (1 win)
6.	Y. Ui	51
7.	P. Nieto	47
8.	A. De Angelis	37
9.	M. Giansanti	36
10.	C. Stoner	29

Cecchinello heads the pack in front of Pablo Nieto and his own team-mate, the young and fiery Australian, Casey Stoner.

Runners and riders:
Stefano Bianco, who had hurt his shoulder and scaphoid in France is being treated by Dr. Costa and has to scratch from his home race. Gilera team boss, Giampiero Sacchi reckons that some extra rest would be good for his young charge and replaces him with Andrea Ballerini. There are five wildcard riders, including the Dane, Robbin Harms and Michele Conti, who the previous week had won the Croatian round of the European championship in Rijeka.

Qualifying:
Aprilia has long used Mugello as its test and development track and the Italian bikes conclusively dominate qualifying, with only two Hondas in the top ten, those of Dovizioso, in mechanical bother and a long way back on Friday and championship leader, Daniel Pedrosa. Vincent put the ever improving KTM on the 11th slot on the grid. Pedrosa has a major fall in the warm-up.

Start:
Stoner shows the best reflexes, ahead of Perugini and Pablo Nieto. Cecchinello and Dovizioso are not far off. As they cross the line for the first time, the Australian leads from Nieto. The young Frenchman, Di Meglio falls.

Lap 2:
Cecchinello takes matters in hand.

Lap 7:
Eight of them are wheel to wheel and Jenkner briefly leads them round.

Half distance (lap 10):
The 125 category is home of the brave, with ten of them now within 1"275: Cecchinello, Perugini, Nieto, Jenkner, Stoner, Dovizioso, De Angelis, Borsoi, Pedrosa and Ui.

Lap 13:
Pablo Nieto takes the lead and tries to make a break.

Finish (lap 20):
Cecchinello takes the lead with one lap to go and manages to pull out a slight lead to finish ahead of the pack, free of the risk of a collision. The final lap was action packed with a great tussle for the other podium places. Steve Jenkner touches Casey Stoner and both men end up in the gravel. While the young Australian was the hero of the weekend and manages to get going again to finish eighteenth, the German's race is over.

Championship:
Two wins, a second place, a fourth and an eighth each: it's a case of perfect equality between Pedrosa the young Spaniard and his Honda and Cecchinello, the old Italian and lead rider for Aprilia. Dovizioso also scores points for a fifth time in five races to go third.

A kiss for a win for Lucio Cecchinello.

CATALUNYA
Catalunya

A historic moment: Loris Capirossi takes the Ducati Desmosedici to its first GP win. A first also for Randy De Puniet (opposite) who wins in the 250 class, while Marco Melandri's expression (above) says all there is to say about the atmosphere in the Yamaha camp.

MOTOGP

Catalunyan Grand Prix
15 June 2003 / Catalunya - 4,727 m

STARTING GRID

1.	46	V. Rossi	Honda	1'43.927
2.	65	L. Capirossi	Ducati	1'44.333
3.	19	O. Jacque	Yamaha	1'44.358
4.	15	S. Gibernau	Honda	1'44.366
5.	4	A. Barros	Yamaha	1'44.642
6.	56	S. Nakano	Yamaha	1'44.672
7.	45	C. Edwards	Aprilia	1'44.708
8.	7	C. Checa	Yamaha	1'44.790
9.	3	M. Biaggi	Honda	1'44.848
10.	6	M. Tamada	Honda	1'44.922
11.	11	T. Ukawa	Honda	1'45.039
12.	12	T. Bayliss	Ducati	1'45.128
13.	21	J. Hopkins	Suzuki	1'45.516
14.	33	M. Melandri	Yamaha	1'45.804
15.	41	N. Haga	Aprilia	1'46.108
16.	48	A. Yanagawa	Kawasaki	1'46.170
17.	99	J. McWilliams	Proton 4T	1'46.173
18.	69	N. Hayden	Honda	1'46.216
19.	8	G. McCoy	Kawasaki	1'46.647
20.	23	R. Kiyonari	Honda	1'46.950
21.	9	N. Aoki	Proton 4T	1'47.037
22.	88	A. Pitt	Kawasaki	1'47.473

RACE: 25 LAPS = 118.175 KM

1.	Loris Capirossi	44'21.758 (159.830 km/h)
2.	Valentino Rossi	+ 3"075
3.	Sete Gibernau	+ 4"344
4.	Carlos Checa	+ 4"935
5.	Shinya Nakano	+ 5"003
6.	Tohru Ukawa	+ 20"587
7.	Makoto Tamada	+ 22"982
8.	Alex Barros	+ 24"989
12.	Nicky Hayden	+ 27"159
10.	Troy Bayliss	+ 30"376
11.	Ryuichi Kiyonari	+ 33"193
12.	Noriyuki Haga	+ 40"443
13.	Marco Melandri	+ 40"445
14.	Massimiliano Biaggi	+ 42"325
15.	John Hopkins	+ 48"659
16.	Nobuatsu Aoki	+ 1'04.721
17.	Garry McCoy	+ 1'36.914

Fastest lap: Rossi, in 1'45.472 (161.343 km/h).
New record.
Previous best: Rossi, in 1'45.594 (161.156/2002).
Outright fastest lap: Rossi, in 1'43.927 (163.741 km/h/2003).

CHAMPIONSHIP

1.	V. Rossi	135 (3 wins)
2.	S. Gibernau	88 (2 wins)
3.	M. Biaggi	85
4.	L. Capirossi	61 (1 win)
5.	A. Barros	54
6.	T. Ukawa	52
7.	T. Bayliss	46
8.	S. Nakano	44
9.	M. Tamada	34
10.	C. Checa	34

Runners and riders:
As one could have guessed in Mugello, Kenny Roberts misses out on the Catalunya GP with chest pains. So there is only one Suzuki on track, for John Hopkins. Kawasaki holds the wildcard for the constructors, but it is the Japanese test driver, Yanagawa, who gets the ride, rather than the European tester, Hoffmann.

Qualifying:
Rossi sets a very high standard on Friday and is not displeased with his work, as it is hotter still on Saturday afternoon. The session was notable for a great performance from Olivier Jacque, who took the best Yamaha to third on the grid. Capirossi is second with Gibernau completing the front row. Biaggi got the long-awaited new bodywork, but he still complains about his equipment and is only ninth.

Start:
Jacque has the quickest reflexes, but it is Capirossi who powers into the lead ahead of Rossi and Gibernau. Yanagawa, McWilliams and Pitt all collide on the opening lap. Rossi leads across the line with 0"287 over Capirossi and 0"453 over Gibernau. Biaggi is already fourth.

Lap 3:
Biaggi passes Gibernau, who counters by running into him.

Lap 7:
Edwards retires. Rossi still leads Capirossi, Biaggi and Gibernau.

Half distance (lap 12):
Rossi has just stepped up the pace and now leads Capirossi by 0"407, who heads Biaggi by 0"612. Gibernau is fourth.

Lap 13:
Olivier Jacque falls.

Sete Gibernau and his friend Juan Carlos Ferrero, the world tennis number 1.

Lap 16:
Capirossi takes the lead, making the most of Rossi's first mistake. The gap is 0"215. Further back, Gibernau has closed on Biaggi.

Lap 17:
A second mistake from Rossi, who runs across the gravel trap. Bayliss takes a trip over the grass. Capirossi leads Biaggi and Gibernau and Rossi is back in sixth.

Lap 18:
A new lap record, from Rossi!

Lap 21:
Still Capirossi, who now leads the Gibernau-Biaggi duo by 1"501. Rossi is lapping 1"3 quicker than the leader in sixth place, 4"102 down.

Lap 23:
The crowd is on its feet to watch the show as Rossi is now third, before passing Gibernau at the end of the straight.

Lap 24:
Biaggi falls, Rossi is now just 2"705 behind Capirossi.

Finish (lap 25):
A superb Capirossi gives Ducati its first win at its sixth attempt.

Championship:
Rossi is beaten, but his championship chances are helped by Biaggi's fall.

Ducati: making history

There were 96,054 spectators this Sunday 15th June, sitting around the Catalunya circuit in the boiling sun. Most of them were naturally waving the blue colours for Gibernau, who is the new Spanish hero. Of course, there was plenty of yellow for Valentino Rossi, as his fan clubs are, year by year, getting ever more international. Then there was the red of Ducati, whose fans until now had ignored grand prix racing in favour of the World Superbike series. These passionate fans worshipped the Italian technology and were Ducatisti through and through.

Although new to the Continental Circus, the fans knew that one day, the Demosedici, which a week earlier had become the quickest bike in the world, would one day beat the world. Capirossi also knew that by accepting to ride the latest prototype, he was facing a brave challenge. But he also knew he had an entire race team behind him. He knew he would win one day. But even this brave lad, who had so often been unlucky, had not expected victory to come so soon, in the sixth GP of the Desmosedici's career. "The bike is making progress, but we are still in the middle of its development programme and there is still a lot to do," he said the day before what would be an historic race. Historic? Yes, indeed, because not since the days of Giacomo Agostini and his innumerable wins on an MV-Agusta, had an Italian rider won on an Italian bike in the blue riband category of two wheeled racing. In fact, since John Kocinski on a Cagiva had won on a Sunday back in 1993, on a day when everyone's thoughts were with Wayne Rainey back home in a Los Angeles hospital, Japanese bikes had won every single 500 GP and this year's MotoGP events.

So, 15th June 2003 was indeed an historic day. Sure, there was a mistake from Valentino Rossi, who took the opportunity to slag off his employers. "All I will say is that I've

Loris Capirossi is on his knees crying. Thanks to his efforts, Ducati takes its first win in MotoGP.

noticed that when I have a little problem, a Honda doesn't win." But above all, it will be remembered as a day when Capirossi never gave up putting the reigning champion under pressure in the unbearable heat.

On the podium, Loris Capirossi dropped to his knees when the Italian national anthem rung out. He looked up to the sky, singing along and crying at the same time. Underneath the podium, representatives of several major Japanese constructors who were coming up against the wall that is Honda, must have asked themselves how a "little" constructor like Ducati had just dished out a lesson to Yamaha first of all, but also Suzuki and Kawasaki.

250cc

STARTING GRID

1.	7	R. De Puniet	Aprilia	1'47.117
2.	54	M. Poggiali	Aprilia	1'47.284
3.	24	T. Elias	Aprilia	1'47.551
4.	21	F. Battaini	Aprilia	1'47.904
5.	5	S. Porto	Honda	1'48.022
6.	10	F. Gonzales-Nieto	Aprilia	1'48.122
7.	8	N. Matsudo	Yamaha	1'48.133
8.	3	R. Rolfo	Honda	1'48.891
9.	14	A. West	Aprilia	1'48.892
10.	50	S. Guintoli	Aprilia	1'49.126
11.	9	H. Marchand	Aprilia	1'49.294
12.	30	K. Nöhles	Aprilia	1'49.404
13.	16	J. Stigefelt	Aprilia	1'49.442
14.	11	J. Olive	Aprilia	1'49.708
15.	36	E. Nigon	Aprilia	1'49.713
16.	33	H. Faubel	Aprilia	1'49.824
17.	6	A. Debon	Honda	1'49.832
18.	34	E. Bataille	Honda	1'49.906
19.	15	C. Gemmel	Honda	1'50.546
20.	57	C. Davies	Aprilia	1'50.712
21.	96	J. Smrz	Honda	1'50.787
22.	52	L. Pesek	Yamaha	1'50.974
23.	26	A. Baldolini	Aprilia	1'51.534
24.	18	H. vd Lagemaat	Honda	1'52.995
25.	40	A. Molina	Aprilia	1'53.169
26.	98	K. Poensgen	Honda	1'53.222
27.	31	C. Rastel	Honda	1'53.927

RACE: 23 LAPS = 108.721 KM

1.	Randy De Puniet	41'59.893 (155.322 km/h)
2.	Alfonso Gonzales-Nieto	+ 0"244
3.	Anthony West	+ 2"641
4.	Toni Elias	+ 4"329
5.	Naoki Matsudo	+ 7"896
6.	Franco Battaini	+ 11"432
7.	Sebastian Porto	+ 11"883
8.	Sylvain Guintoli	+ 15"761
9.	Roberto Rolfo	+ 24"270
10.	Joan Olive	+ 29"370
11.	Alex Debon	+ 32"091
12.	Klaus Nöhles	+ 34"948
13.	Johan Stigefelt	+ 44"259
14.	Erwan Nigon	+ 46"384
15.	Christian Gemmel	+ 59"767
16.	Lukas Pesek	+ 1'36.297
17.	Katja Poensgen	+ 1 lap
18.	Henk vd Lagemaat	+ 1 lap

Fastest lap: Poggiali, in 1'48.483 (156.865 km/h).
Record: Rossi, in 1'47.585 (158.174 km/h/1998).
Outright fastest lap: De Puniet, in 1'47.117 (158.865 km/h/2003).

CHAMPIONSHIP

1.	M. Poggiali	88 (3 wins)
2.	T. Elias	81 (2 wins)
3.	R. De Puniet	81 (1 win)
4.	A. Gonzales-Nieto	81
5.	R. Rolfo	76
6.	F. Battaini	58
7.	A. West	53
8.	S. Porto	53
9.	N. Matsudo	53
10.	S. Guintoli	42

Runners and riders:

With Hules injured in Italy, he is replaced in the Kurz Yamaha team by fellow countryman, Lukas Pesek. A surprise in the Aprilia Germany camp, as the injured Dirk Heidolf's 250 RSW is entrusted to returnee, Klaus Nohles, the 1999 European 125 champion, who had switched to working in telemetry since the start of this season.

Qualifying:

It was the Super-Randy Show as the Frenchman dominated all four sessions, as well as being quickest in the warm-up. Poggiali is not far behind. Elias was third, ahead of Battaini and Gonzales-Nieto. For the first time since the Continental Circus hit Europe, the German Katja Poensgen lapped quick enough to qualify.

Start:

For once, Elias gets it wrong. Not the Argentine Porto, who ends the first lap in second place, behind Randy de Puniet and head of the series leader, Manuel Poggiali, who is followed by Fonsi Gonzales-Nieto, who took the lead on lap 2.

Lap 3:

De Puniet continues to harry Gonzales-Nieto, the Frenchman 50 thousandths behind the Spaniard. Poggiali is three tenths back.

Lap 4:

The three on-form men this weekend, De Puniet, Fonsi and Poggiali, are covered by just 336 thousandths. Behind them comes the pack, led by Battaini and West, but already 2 seconds down.

Half distance (lap 11):

Poggiali is quickest down the main straight, but De Puniet will not be beaten. At half distance, the Frenchman leads the San Marinese by 0"184, with Gonzales-Nieto a further 1"005 seconds back. West is now fourth, while Tony Elias is working his way back up the order.

De Puniet still leads, Poggiali still glued to his back wheel: the duel would not go the distance.

Finally, the Frenchman takes his first GP win.

Lap 13:

Manuel Poggiali retires at the side of the track with a seized engine. De Puniet leads Gonzales-Nieto by 0"767 and begins to think this is his day.

Lap 20:

The Catalunya circuit comes to life as Gonzales-Nieto takes the lead on the pit straight, but not for long.

Finish (lap 23):

It's done. Randy De Puniet finally wins a world championship event on the same track where his fellow countryman and mate Arnaud Vincent also recorded his first victory.

Championship:

The bets are open again, as things are going less well for Poggiali. The Aprilia number 1 rider is still leading the championship, but there are now three riders in joint second place, 7 points down – Elias, De Puniet and Gonzales-Nieto.

Runners and riders:
Stefano Bianco is still convalescing and as a week earlier at Mugello, he is replaced by his fellow countryman, Andrea Ballerini on the Gilera. Four Spanish riders have wildcard entries.

Qualifying:
For wildcard Ismael Ortega, the GP ends on Friday

morning with a broken foot. It's hot, very hot for the two qualifying days and Daniel Pedrosa becomes the quickest man ever in the history of the 125 cc category on Saturday morning. But it's Nieto who takes pole in the afternoon, after Cecchinello had dominated the first day. The top ten are all in the same second. Young Frenchman Mike Di Meglio is a creditable 15th.

Start:
Barbera gets the best start, ahead of Divizioso, Cecchinello and Ui. Crossing the line for the first time, Dovizioso leads Barbera by 0"269 and Cecchinello by 0"318.

Lap 5:
Cecchinello leads. The top twelve are covered by 2"853.

Lap 10:
Stoner falls.

Half distance (lap 11):
Ui falls and Cecchinello still

leads, 0"038 ahead of De Angelis and Pedrosa (at 0"236.) Following along come Dovizioso, Nieto and the Swiss Luthi.

Lap 12:
Cecchinello takes a trip through the gravel.

Lap 13:
Luthi leads. In the press office, people are asking who he is. There would be more to come. Lucio Cecchinello pits having gone off, because of a faulty front tyre. As they cross the line, Luthi leads Dovizioso by 0"073.

Lap 16:
Barbera and Dovizioso fall, while De Angelis and Luthi have pulled out a slight lead over Pedrosa.

Lap 19:
A handkerchief covers the top four: De Angelis, Pedrosa, who is about to take the lead, Luthi and Nieto.

Youichi Ui: ouch!

Ride of the day came from Thomas Luthi, as the young Swiss rider finishes on the podium for the first time.

Lap 21:
Pablo Nieto falls, getting back in the saddle but failing to finish in the points.

Finish (lap 22):
Incredible but true, it's the young Swiss, Thomas Luthi in his first full GP season, who fights Pedrosa for the lead, attacking him twice on the final lap. In the end he has to give best for the sake of 137 thousandths of a second.

Championship:
Pedrosa does very well out of the weekend as he now has a 25 point lead – one race win's worth – over Cecchinello. Jenkner is back up to third and Luthi makes it into the top ten, while the very young Frenchman, Mike Di Meglio scores his first world championship points.

Pedrosa, Luthi and De Angelis wheel to wheel.

Catalunyan Grand Prix
15 June 2003 / Catalunya - 4,727 m

STARTING GRID

1.	22	P. Nieto	Aprilia	1'51.043
2.	34	A. Dovizioso	Honda	1'51.220
3.	4	L. Cecchinello	Aprilia	1'51.281
4.	80	H. Barbera	Aprilia	1'51.349
5.	15	A. De Angelis	Aprilia	1'51.417
6.	3	D. Pedrosa	Honda	1'51.453
7.	41	Y. Ui	Aprilia	1'51.686
8.	17	S. Jenkner	Aprilia	1'51.977
9.	7	S. Perugini	Aprilia	1'52.011
10.	27	C. Stoner	Aprilia	1'52.076
11.	48	J. Lorenzo	Derbi	1'52.295
12.	79	G. Talmacsi	Aprilia	1'52.386
13.	42	G. Pellino	Aprilia	1'52.954
14.	12	T. Lüthi	Honda	1'52.994
15.	63	M. Di Meglio	Aprilia	1'53.052
16.	24	S. Corsi	Honda	1'53.111
17.	1	A. Vincent	KTM	1'53.122
18.	23	G. Borsoi	Aprilia	1'53.148
19.	36	M. Kallio	Honda	1'53.160
20.	6	M. Giansanti	Aprilia	1'53.168
21.	32	F. Lai	Malaguti	1'53.387
22.	58	M. Simoncelli	Aprilia	1'53.464
23.	10	R. Locatelli	KTM	1'53.494
24.	8	M. Azuma	Honda	1'53.511
25.	26	E. Alzamora	Derbi	1'53.600
26.	50	A. Ballerini	Gilera	1'53.648
27.	70	S. Gadea	Aprilia	1'53.744
28.	31	J. Simon	Malaguti	1'53.875
29.	19	A. Bautista	Aprilia	1'54.044
30.	25	I. Toth	Honda	1'54.246
31.	69	D. Bonache	Honda	1'55.148
32.	27	L. Camier	Honda	1'55.493
33.	11	M. Sabbatani	Aprilia	1'56.270
34.	14	C. Martin	Aprilia	1'56.835
35.	82	J. Carchano	Honda	1'56.934
36.	78	P. Lenart	Honda	1'57.152

RACE: 22 LAPS = 103.994 KM

1.	Daniel Pedrosa	41'16.672 (151.161 km/h)
2.	Thomas Lüthi	+ 0"137
3.	Alex De Angelis	+ 0"315
4.	Steve Jenkner	+ 1"589
5.	Stefano Perugini	+ 19"874
6.	Jorge Lorenzo	+ 22"560
7.	Mika Kallio	+ 22"647
8.	Gino Borsoi	+ 22"856
9.	Gabor Talmacsi	+ 22"916
10.	Roberto Locatelli	+ 23"415
11.	Gioele Pellino	+ 31"815
12.	Mirko Giansanti	+ 34"948
13.	Mike Di Meglio	+ 40"938
14.	Arnaud Vincent	+ 41"163
15.	Simone Corsi	+ 41"405
16.	Marco Simoncelli	+ 41"888
17.	Pablo Nieto	+ 51"330
18.	Andrea Ballerini	+ 51"993
19.	Fabrizio Lai	+ 52"289
20.	Imre Toth	+ 54"364
21.	Max Sabbatani	+ 1'08.127
22.	Masao Azuma	+ 1'09.768
23.	Sergio Gadea	+ 1'22.794
24.	Julian Simon	+ 1'32.672
25.	Jordi Carchano	+ 1'40.507
26.	Peter Lenart	+ 1'40.604
27.	Leon Camier	+ 1'40.730
28.	Alvaro Bautista	+ 5 tours

Fastest lap: Stoner, in 1'51.190 (153.046 km/h. New record.)
Previous best: Ui, in 1'51.443 (2002).
Outright fastest lap: Pedrosa, in 1'50.178 (154.451 km/h/2003).

CHAMPIONSHIP

1.	D. Pedrosa	116 (3 wins)
2.	L. Cecchinello	91 (2 wins)
3.	S. Jenkner	73
4.	A. Dovizioso	67
5.	S. Perugini	65 (1 win)
6.	A. De Angelis	53
7.	Y. Ui	51
8.	P. Nieto	47
9.	M. Giansanti	40
10.	T. Lüthi	39

THE NETHERLANDS
Assen

Not exactly smiling Dutchmen weather. In this Mecca of racing that is Assen, Sete Gibernau would once again produce a faultless performance in infernal conditions. In the 250 class, it is Anthony West (opposite) who produces the ride of his life.

MOTOGP

Dutch Grand Prix
28 June 2003 / Assen - 6.027 m

STARTING GRID

1.	65	L. Capirossi	Ducati	1'59.770
2.	3	M. Biaggi	Honda	1'59.941
3.	46	V. Rossi	Honda	1'59.964
4.	7	C. Checa	Yamaha	2'00.169
5.	19	O. Jacque	Yamaha	2'00.294
6.	4	A. Barros	Yamaha	2'00.501
7.	15	S. Gibernau	Honda	2'00.553
8.	33	M. Melandri	Yamaha	2'00.553
9.	45	C. Edwards	Aprilia	2'00.579
10.	56	S. Nakano	Yamaha	2'00.693
11.	11	T. Ukawa	Honda	2'00.929
12.	69	N. Hayden	Honda	2'00.998
13.	12	T. Bayliss	Ducati	2'01.147
14.	41	N. Haga	Aprilia	2'01.188
15.	71	Y. Kagayama	Suzuki	2'01.601
16.	21	J. Hopkins	Suzuki	2'01.715
17.	66	A. Hofmann	Kawasaki	2'02.172
18.	6	M. Tamada	Honda	2'02.351
19.	99	J. McWilliams	Proton 4T	2'02.996
20.	88	A. Pitt	Kawasaki	2'03.371
21.	8	G. McCoy	Kawasaki	2'03.407
22.	23	R. Kiyonari	Honda	2'03.707
23.	9	N. Aoki	Proton 4T	2'06.172

RACE: 19 LAPS = 114.513 KM

1.	Sete Gibernau	42'39.006 (161.096 km/h)
2.	Massimiliano Biaggi	+ 10"111
3.	Valentino Rossi	+ 13"875
4.	Carlos Checa	+ 36"978
5.	Olivier Jacque	+ 40"345
6.	Loris Capirossi	+ 42"177
7.	Colin Edwards	+ 50"518
8.	Alex Barros	+ 59"023
9.	Troy Bayliss	+ 1'33.536
10.	Alex Hofmann	+ 1'36.403
11.	Nicky Hayden	+ 1'39.033
12.	Tohru Ukawa	+ 1'42.398
13.	Shinya Nakano	+ 1'43.690
14.	Andrew Pitt	+ 1 lap
15.	John Hopkins	+ 1 lap
16.	Makoto Tamada	+ 1 lap
17.	Ryuichi Kiyonari	+ 1 lap
18.	Garry McCoy	+ 1 lap

Fastest lap: Gibernau, in 2'11.805 (164.615 km/h).
Record: Rossi, in 2'00.973 (179.355 km/h/2002).
Outright fastest lap: Capirossi, in 1'59.770 (181.157 km/h/2003).

CHAMPIONSHIP

1.	V. Rossi	151 (3 wins)
2.	S. Gibernau	113 (3 wins)
3.	M. Biaggi	105
4.	L. Capirossi	71 (1 win)
5.	A. Barros	62
6.	T. Ukawa	56
7.	T. Bayliss	53
8.	C. Checa	47
9.	S. Nakano	47
10.	O. Jacque	43

Runners and riders:
Roberts is absent, having returned to the States to be treated for his injuries sustained in the Italian GP. He is replaced by Yukio Kagayama. The technological novelty of the weekend is in Rossi's hands, in the shape of an "evolution" RC211V, which he first tried the day after the Catalunya GP.

Qualifying:
Rossi is quickest on Friday, but on Saturday, Capirossi becomes the first man to break the two minute barrier round Assen. The Yamahas are together behind the infernal Italian trio and there are serious concerns in the Proton camp, especially for poor Nobuatsu Aoki, whose KR5 engine blew up on Friday afternoon. The bike caught fire at the end of the pit straight!

Start:
The rain eases off. The racing line is dry, but there are several wet patches. The race is declared "dry" which means it will be stopped if it rains again, which happens right from the warm-up lap. Everyone pits and a new start is given, with all the bikes on rain tyres this time. Rossi shows the quickest reflexes, but Gibernau takes the lead at the first corner, with Biaggi glued to his back wheel, the gap being 0"147 at the end of the opening lap. Jacque is third, ahead of Rossi, Bayliss, Barros and Edwards.

Lap 2:
Biaggi is now leading. Jacque drops three places in one go.

Lap 4:
Gibernau leads Biaggi by 0"259. Rossi is third, but already 2"115 down and he is about to get caught out by Bayliss in no uncertain terms!

Biaggi and Gibernau put on a display of aquatic equilibrium.

Lap 6:
Bayliss falls but continues.

Half distance (lap 10):
Gibernau has made the break (0"912) ahead of Biaggi and McCoy, one lap down for blocking the Roman. Rossi is a lonely third, nine seconds behind Sete. Jacque is fourth and is being caught by a pumped up Haga. McWilliams falls.

Lap 12:
Aoki falls and Barros only just avoids hitting him.

Lap 14:
Gibernau is a solitary leader, Biaggi trailing by 5"726. Haga continues to put on a show and is now fourth ahead of Checa and Jacque.

Lap 18:
Haga falls.

Finish (lap 19):
Gibernau has ridden a faultless race to take his third win of the season. Biaggi is second ahead of Rossi.

Championship:
Rossi is still solidly in the lead, even though he has lost 9 points to the day's winner, who is second in the classification. Looking at the scores we see that Rossi is on 151, Gibernau 113 and Biaggi 105.

Sete Gibernau is in a hurry!

Seventh of sixteen rounds of the 2003 world championship. Saturday morning, the 28th June. Under darkening skies, Sete Gibernau's Swiss manager, Leo de Graffenried is anxiously pacing up and down the paddock of the Van Drenthe circuit at Assen. It's the place everyone considers the mecca of motorcycle sport, After two sunny days of practice, the dreaded bad weather, which was predicted earlier in the week, is rolling in. It is getting stressful for those who don't like mixed conditions and do not fancy racing on a wet track without having done a single lap in "wet" set-up. "The Dutch weather forecasters were right and it's right for us," says de Graffenreid, confident in his prediction.

Sete Gibernau strolls up. He smiles, looks to the ever darkening sky and grins. The Spaniard had a difficult time in Italy and was unable to give his best in Catalunya as his Honda RC211V engine was down on power, but now he thinks a third win is on the cards, after those in South Africa and France. He knows he has no time to waste this Saturday, which is the traditional race day in the Netherlands. A helicopter will be waiting for him at 5 o'clock to whisk him to Amsterdam's Schipol Airport. He is flying to Barcelona for a few days holiday on the beaches of Girona before the British GP.

His day would go according to plan, or almost. The pack formed up on the grid with the engineers spying on one another as usual. Some riders have gambled on tyres suited to a drying track, while others play safe with rain tyres. Who is right? Will the race turn into an incredible game of poker? No.

The engines fire up for the warm-up lap, but the celestial gods choose this exact moment to deliver the long awaited rain. Everyone heads back for the pits to prepare for a wet race. The soaked track makes

Knees and elbows at the first corner: Rossi is still leading from Biaggi and Gibernau.

acrobats of the riders, while the conditions are the same for everyone. Gibernau is peerless in these conditions, enjoying a great duel with Biaggi before making the break for a perfect race. No one can match him; not Biaggi, nor Valentino Rossi, who finishes third with serious misting problems in his visor. "It fogged up and I could not see anything. I was trying to follow the bike in front of me, but I never knew where I was on the track," smiled the reigning world champion. He could afford to smile, at a time when Honda was trying to persuade him to extend his contract for another two years and he was still solidly in the lead of the championship.

Another perfect race from the revelation of the season.

"Sorry lads, but the helicopter's waiting!"

250cc

Dutch Grand Prix
28 June 2003 / Assen – 6.027 m

STARTING GRID

1.	54	M. Poggiali	Aprilia	2'04.050
2.	7	R. De Puniet	Aprilia	2'04.586
3.	24	T. Elias	Aprilia	2'04.712
4.	10	F. Gonzales-Nieto	Aprilia	2'04.866
5.	5	S. Porto	Honda	2'04.920
6.	50	S. Guintoli	Aprilia	2'05.190
7.	21	F. Battaini	Aprilia	2'05.190
8.	3	R. Rolfo	Honda	2'05.547
9.	14	A. West	Aprilia	2'05.755
10.	8	N. Matsudo	Yamaha	2'05.755
11.	34	E. Bataille	Honda	2'06.330
12.	36	E. Nigon	Aprilia	2'06.417
13.	11	J. Olive	Aprilia	2'06.585
14.	30	K. Nöhles	Aprilia	2'06.957
15.	33	H. Faubel	Aprilia	2'07.040
16.	16	J. Stigefelt	Aprilia	2'07.400
17.	9	H. Marchand	Aprilia	2'07.529
18.	6	A. Debon	Honda	2'07.545
19.	57	C. Davies	Aprilia	2'07.719
20.	15	C. Gemmel	Honda	2'08.125
21.	96	J. Smrz	Honda	2'08.128
22.	26	A. Baldolini	Aprilia	2'08.828
23.	47	A. Vos	Yamaha	2'09.700
24.	18	H. vd Lagemaat	Honda	2'09.713
25.	29	C. Pistoni	Yamaha	2'11.106
26.	48	H. Smees	Honda	2'11.845
27.	46	J. Blok	Honda	2'12.104
28.	98	K. Poensgen	Honda	2'12.716

Not qualified

	49	R. Gevers	Honda	2'13.743

RACE: 18 LAPS = 108.486 KM

1.	Anthony West	41'57.413 (155.139 km/h)
2.	Franco Battaini	+ 2'987
3.	Sylvain Guintoli	+ 10"661
4.	Manuel Poggiali	+ 14"160
5.	Sebastian Porto	+ 26"617
6.	Roberto Rolfo	+ 31"948
7.	Erwan Nigon	+ 1'14.197
8.	Christian Gemmel	+ 1'24.658
9.	Hugo Marchand	+ 1'36.159
10.	Johan Stigefelt	+ 1'36.270
11.	Alex Debon	+ 1'56.249
12.	Jakub Smrz	+ 1'56.979
13.	Toni Elias	+ 2'03.227
14.	Alex Baldolini	+ 2'03.521
15.	Klaus Nöhles	+ 1 lap
16.	Henk vd Lagemaat	+ 1 lap
17.	Hector Faubel	+ 1 lap
18.	Katja Poensgen	+ 1 lap
19.	Jan Blok	+ 1 lap
20.	Christian Pistoni	+ 1 lap
21.	Arie Vos	+ 1 lap
22.	Hans Smees	+ 1 lap
23.	Joan Olive	+ 2 laps
24.	Chaz Davies	+ 2 laps

Fastest lap: Battaini, in 2'16.926 (158.459 km/h).
Record: Rolfo, in 2'04.824 (173.822 km/h/2002).
Outright fastest lap: Poggiali, in 2'04.050 (174.906 km/h/2003).

CHAMPIONSHIP

1.	M. Poggiali	101 (3 wins)
2.	R. Rolfo	86
3.	T. Elias	84 (2 wins)
4.	R. De Puniet	81 (1 win)
5.	A. Gonzales-Nieto	81
6.	A. West	78 (1 win)
7.	F. Battaini	78
8.	S. Porto	64
9.	S. Guintoli	58
10.	N. Matsudo	53

A first podium for Sylvain Guintoli.

Runners and riders:
The same field as in Catalunya line up once again. The Czech, Jaroslav Hules and the German, Dirk Heidolf are still on the sick list and are replaced by Christian Pistoni and Klaus Nohles respectively. There are four wildcard requests from the Dutch riders.

Qualifying:
On the first day, Tony Elias basks in the memory that it is here, at Assen, that he took his first world championship win, but Manuel Poggiali dominates the decisive day, becoming the quickest 250 rider ever at the Dutch track. Randy De Puniet, who won two weeks earlier in Catalunya, falls in the final moments of Friday morning free practice and has to dig deep in the afternoon, with serious pains in his right shoulder, on his way to second place. Once again the front row is all-Aprilia. As in Barcelona two weeks earlier, the charming German Katja Poensgen manages to make the qualifying cut.

Start:
Elias and Gonzales-Nieto are first away, but Poggiali moves into the lead, before handing it to West who leads the first lap by 0"348 from Poggiali. Then come Rolfo, the impressive Sylvain Guintoli and Franco Battaini. Bataille falls at the chicane when lying eighth.

Lap 2:
Guintoli is doing a fantastic job and is second, 3"449 down on West. Randy De Puniet falls, having been off form all weekend.

Lap 6:
Matsudo falls. West leads Battaini by 5"491, the latter having a great duel with team-mate Guintoli.

Lap 7:
Gonzales-Nieto stops on the track when

the chain falls off, forcing his retirement.

Half distance (lap 9):
West has just set the fastest race lap and has a comfortable 4"628 in hand over Battaini and 8"375 over Guintoli. Poggiali is fourth with Porto in his wheel tracks.

Lap 12:
Nohles cuts the chicane and almost hits two bikes.

Lap 16:
Battaini closes to within 3"458 of West.

Finish (lap 18):
It's a day of firsts, as Australia's Anthony West takes his first GP win. It is also the first podium finish for Guintoli, which means that three Aprilia privateers share the podium, while a sensible Poggiali does well in terms of the title.

Championship:
With Elias only thirteenth and De Puniet and Gonzales-Nieto out, Poggiali extends his lead to 15 points over the consistent Rolfo.

The battle behind Anthony West. Guintoli, Rolfo and Battaini are wheel to wheel.

Steve Jenkner shot off after the first few metres of racing, never to be seen again.

Runners and riders:

They have been working hard in the Derbi-Gilera camp. Belgian technical boss, Olivier Liegeois had made the chassis more rigid, contributing to Lorenzo being quickest the previous Sunday in the Spanish championship at Jarama. Bianco is back on parade. On the other hand, its divorce between Chris Martin and Seedorf Racing. The team boss, a Dutch international footballer, is present to see his bike ridden by the Dane, Robbin Harms. There are four Dutch wildcards.

Qualifying:

De Angelis is on great form, dominating three of the four practice sessions, but in the end, he is beaten by 53 thousandths by championship leader, Pedrosa. Cecchinello has tyre worries and is only twelfth. Thomas Luthi shines again, with fifth place, his best ever qualifying position. Tension runs through the KTM squad, where technical director, Harald Bartol is now openly complaining about his two riders: "Locatelli doesn't understand anything and

Vincent thinks he knows everything, but he knows nothing!"

Start:

The rain arrives half an hour before the start and De Angelis slides on the reconnaissance lap. Jenkner is prompt away ahead of Stoner and Ui and leads Stoner by 1"245 at the end of the opening lap, while the chasing pack is already 4"981 adrift, with Kallio leading the charge. Bianco falls.

Lap 3:

Stoner falls. Jenkner has a colossal 13"615 advantage over Pablo Nieto, who is now second.

Lap 6:

Robin Harms had jumped the start, failed to stop for a penalty and is black flagged.

Lap 8:

Vincent retires.

Half distance (lap 9):

Still Jenkner, with a 10"148 lead over Nieto. Barbera is third, 18 seconds down. Then come Ui, Perugini, Pedrosa, Kallio, Talmacsi and Luthi.

Lap 13:

Azuma falls.

Finish (lap 17):

Steve Jenkner finally records his first win, along with the honour of giving Aprilia its 150th GP victory. Indeed, Aprilia makes a clean sweep of the top six places, while Thomas Luthi, rookie of the year, takes his Honda into seventh spot.

Championship:

With Cecchinello out of the points, it's a case of damage limitation for Pedrosa. His lead over Jenkner, who is now second, is 26 points, the equivalent of one race. Cecchinello is third with Perugini back in fourth.

Finally, Germany's Jenkner stands on the top step of the podium.

Pedrosa pulls a face, but limited the damage in the championship.

Dutch Grand Prix
28 June 2003 / Assen - 6.027 m

STARTING GRID

1.	3	D. Pedrosa	Honda	2'10.724
2.	15	A. De Angelis	Aprilia	2'10.777
3.	17	S. Jenkner	Aprilia	2'10.814
4.	7	S. Perugini	Aprilia	2'11.052
5.	12	T. Lüthi	Honda	2'11.545
6.	27	C. Stoner	Aprilia	2'11.632
7.	41	Y. Ui	Aprilia	2'11.700
8.	48	J. Lorenzo	Derbi	2'11.714
9.	80	H. Barbera	Aprilia	2.11.741
10.	36	M. Kallio	Honda	2'11.957
11.	22	P. Nieto	Aprilia	2'12.000
12.	4	L. Cecchinello	Aprilia	2'12.043
13.	23	G. Borsoi	Aprilia	2'12.203
14.	32	F. Lai	Malaguti	2'12.204
15.	58	M. Simoncelli	Aprilia	2'12.267
16.	34	A. Dovizioso	Honda	2'12.398
17.	79	G. Talmacsi	Aprilia	2'12.467
18.	24	S. Corsi	Honda	2'12.608
19.	6	M. Giansanti	Aprilia	2'12.799
20.	19	A. Bautista	Aprilia	2'13.007
21.	1	A. Vincent	KTM	2'13.168
22.	8	M. Azuma	Honda	2'13.420
23.	88	R. Harms	Aprilia	2'13.505
24.	11	M. Sabbatani	Aprilia	2'13.690
25.	63	M. Di Meglio	Aprilia	2'14.095
26.	25	I. Toth	Honda	2'14.185
27.	33	S. Bianco	Gilera	2'14.345
28.	42	G. Pellino	Aprilia	2'14.404
29.	31	J. Simon	Malaguti	2'14.521
30.	10	R. Locatelli	KTM	2'14.621
31.	77	R. Schouten	Honda	2'14.715
32.	26	E. Alzamora	Derbi	2'14.912
33.	76	J. vd Marel	Honda	2'15.604
34.	27	L. Camier	Honda	2'16.036
35.	78	P. Lenart	Honda	2'17.939
36.	75	A. Den Bekker	Honda	2'18.672
37.	89	M. Van Kreij	Honda	2'19.791

RACE: 17 LAPS = 102.459 KM

1.	Steve Jenkner	42'25.609 (144.897 km/h)
2.	Pablo Nieto	+ 11"189
3.	Hector Barbera	+ 24'683
4.	Youichi Ui	+ 30'420
5.	Stefano Perugini	+ 46'439
6.	Alex De Angelis	+ 1'01.726
7.	Thomas Lüthi	+ 1'01.855
8.	Daniel Pedrosa	+ 1'04.598
9.	Gabor Talmacsi	+ 1'05.176
10.	Andrea Dovizioso	+ 1'06.020
11.	Mika Kallio	+ 1'06.075
12.	Simone Corsi	+ 1'06.419
13.	Gino Borsoi	+ 1'06.874
14.	Fabrizio Lai	+ 1'08.301
15.	Mirko Giansanti	+ 1'08.303
16.	Lucio Cecchinello	+ 1'18.978
17.	Julian Simon	+ 1'45.750
18.	Adri Den Bekker	+ 1'51.673
19.	Mike Di Meglio	+ 1'52.001
20.	Marco Simoncelli	+ 2'05.902
21.	Emilio Alzamora	+ 2'07.510
22.	Max Sabbatani	+ 2'31.939
23.	Imre Toth	+ 1 lap
24.	Jarno vd Marel	+ 1 lap

Fastest lap: Barbera, in 2'26.247 (148.359 km/h).
Record: Olive, in 2'11.209 (165.363 km/h/2002).
Outright fastest lap: De Angelis, in 2'10.634 (166.091 km/h/2003).

CHAMPIONSHIP

1.	D. Pedrosa	124 (3 wins)
2.	S. Jenkner	98 (1 win)
3.	L. Cecchinello	91 (2 wins)
4.	S. Perugini	76 (1 win)
5.	A. Dovizioso	73
6.	P. Nieto	67
7.	Y. Ui	64
8.	A. De Angelis	63
9.	T. Lüthi	48
10.	M. Giansanti	41

GREAT BRITAIN
Donington

Biaggi ahead of Rossi on the track (main photo), Rossi raises a finger as a sign of victory (opposite) but he would end up third. Hard to follow. Things were more straightforward in the 250 class for Fonsi Nieto and Poggiali.

British Grand Prix
13 July 2003 / Donington - 4,023 m

STARTING GRID

1.	3	M. Biaggi	Honda	1'30.740
2.	15	S. Gibernau	Honda	1'30.862
3.	33	M. Melandri	Yamaha	1'30.926
4.	46	V. Rossi	Honda	1'30.938
5.	7	C. Checa	Yamaha	1'31.035
6.	12	T. Bayliss	Ducati	1'31.036
7.	65	L. Capirossi	Ducati	1'31.067
8.	19	O. Jacque	Yamaha	1'31.241
9.	45	C. Edwards	Aprilia	1'31.354
10.	11	T. Ukawa	Honda	1'31.385
11.	56	S. Nakano	Yamaha	1'31.614
12.	4	A. Barros	Yamaha	1'31.776
13.	69	N. Hayden	Honda	1'31.779
14.	41	N. Haga	Aprilia	1'31.877
15.	21	J. Hopkins	Suzuki	1'31.962
16.	6	M. Tamada	Honda	1'32.526
17.	71	Y. Kagayama	Suzuki	1'32.573
18.	8	G. McCoy	Kawasaki	1'32.793
19.	99	J. McWilliams	Proton 4T	1'32.802
20.	23	R. Kiyonari	Honda	1'33.288
21.	88	A. Pitt	Kawasaki	1'33.705
22.	9	N. Aoki	Proton 4T	1'34.364
23.	35	C. Burns	ROC Yamaha 2T	1'34.400
24.	52	D. De Gea	Sabre V4 2T	1'36.851

RACE: 30 LAPS = 120.690 KM

1.	Massimiliano Biaggi	46'06.688 (157.041 km/h)
2.	Sete Gibernau	+ 7"138
3.	Valentino Rossi	+ 8"794 (*)
4.	Loris Capirossi	+ 13"041
5.	Troy Bayliss	+ 16"269
6.	Carlos Checa	+ 27"085
7.	Noriyuki Haga	+ 27"662
8.	Nicky Hayden	+ 32"012
9.	Shinya Nakano	+ 34"799
10.	Colin Edwards	+ 35"001
11.	John Hopkins	+ 48"165
12.	Yukio Kagayama	+ 1'00.423
13.	Makoto Tamada	+ 1'06.160
14.	Ryuichi Kiyonari	+ 1'14.866
15.	Nobuatsu Aoki	+ 1'30.291
16.	Garry McCoy	+ 1 lap
17.	Andrew Pitt	+ 1 lap

(*): Valentino Rossi was first past the chequered flag, but was penalised 10" for having passed Loris Capirossi under the yellow flag.

Fastest lap: Rossi, in 1'31.023
(159.111 km/h/new record).
Previous best: Rossi, in 1'32.247 (157.000/2002).
Outright fastest lap: Biaggi, in 1'30.740 (159.607 km/h/2003).

CHAMPIONSHIP

1.	V. Rossi	167 (3 wins)
2.	S. Gibernau	133 (3 wins)
3.	M. Biaggi	130 (1 win)
4.	L. Capirossi	84 (1 win)
5.	T. Bayliss	64
6.	A. Barros	62
7.	C. Checa	57
8.	T. Ukawa	56
9.	S. Nakano	54
10.	N. Hayden	46

Runners and riders:
Roberts is still officially "injured," while it seems that his heart has not been in it for a while now. Yet again he is replaced by Japan's Kagayama. Something new in the WCM camp, as Peter Clifford has been to the museum to dig out an ROC-Yamaha and the Sabre V4 for his two riders, Burns and De Gea.

Qualifying:
Rossi suffers a front wheel rim problem on his Honda in the final minutes of qualifying. Biaggi is having fun now that he has the 2003 chassis for the RC211V. Gibernau wants to show he can also be very quick in the dry. Melandri takes his first front row position in MotoGP. The Ducatis are not far behind. It is one big festival of speed with the top 13 covered by just 1"039. There are three fallers in the warm-up, Ukawa, Barros and Kagayama and the Brazilian has to pull out with a broken right hand.

Start:
Biaggi makes a super getaway, while Rossi is trapped. Ukawa falls at the first corner. As they cross the line, Max has a lead of 0"293 over Gibernau. Melandri is third ahead of Capirossi and Rossi, who is working his way to the front.

Lap 3:
Burns falls and Rossi is already second: the long awaited duel between the Roman and the world champion is on. Hard to guess what will happen later...

Lap 5:
Melandri falls at the chicane and Capirossi only just misses hitting the Yamaha. It allows the lead trio of Biaggi, Rossi and Gibernau to break away by 0"517.

Lap 8:
202 thousandths separate Biaggi and Rossi, with Gibernau 1"190 down on Valentino.

Lap 13:
Biaggi makes a mistake braking for the chicane, so Rossi leads by 1"672, while Gibernau is a lonely third. Half distance (lap 15): Rossi leads, Biaggi is 1"842 down and Gibernau 4"677. Capirossi is fourth and Bayliss has just passed Checa.

Lap 20:
Jacque falls at the chicane.

Finish (lap 30):
Rossi is the class of the field, controlling the final stages of the race, with Biaggi incapable of challenging his "favourite" rival. Gibernau has ridden a sensible race, with the Ducatis filling the next two places. An hour later, the results are changed as Rossi is deemed guilty of passing Capirossi under yellow flags. He is given a ten second penalty, which drops him to third.

Championship:
It should have been a case of Rossi stringing out his lead, but it was not to be and things are getting closer, even if Valentino still has a 34 point lead over Gibernau, who heads Biaggi by three.

Fausto Gresini and Sete Gibernau and a cake for a hundredth GP.

Biaggi heads the pack.

Rossi: but yellow is his favourite colour!

Standing on the top step of the podium, well known Londoner, Mr. Valentino Rossi was enjoying his status as King of the Road, smiling but red faced with the effort, in front of a huge good natured crowd. Around his neck is a yellow flag bearing his lucky number 46, as the king is waving to his subjects: 72,000 of them on this sunny day, which is an outright record for Donington Park. On the giant screen, Rossi and his fans can relive the highlights of those 46 minutes of flair and skill and his duel with Biaggi, which lasted until the Roman made a mistake. It looks just as good on the replay as Rossi gives a lesson in control and balance. Who could guess that the man who loves the colour yellow would soon be turning red with rage. He was about to be demoted to third, the victim of a cruel set of circumstances.

How did it happen? Ukawa fell at Redgate corner, the first turn of this British Grand Prix. Biaggi's Japanese team-mate Tohru Ukawa fell off his yellow Honda, injuring his left shoulder.

The yellow flag is shown ninety seconds later, while marshals drag away the crashed bike. Yellow flags are waved by the marshals to indicate the danger ahead to the riders. A waved yellow flag always means that overtaking is forbidden. Rossi made his mistake while staging a meteoric climb through the field, having been boxed in at the start. He passed Loris Capirossi at the end of the pit straight at the precise point where, amongst other things going on, a marshal was waving the yellow flag.

There could have been a choice of consequences in terms of action from the four race stewards. If the error is spotted immediately, then a stop-go penalty can be imposed, requiring the rider to rumble down pit lane. If the fault is only spotted after the finish, then a time penalty is imposed; in this case ten seconds, although exclusion from the results is also a possibility. There is room to manoeuvre, in that every competitor has the right to appeal against a stewards' decision, within an hour of it being taken. There was no appeal on this hot July Sunday, as the cameras clearly showed the infringement.

"I race on the track, not in the office," said Valentino Rossi. The Italian should have left Donington after the British Grand Prix with a 47 point lead over Gibernau and 51 points ahead of Biaggi. Now, he only

Valentino Rossi has won on the track and he wants people to know about it.

had a 34 point advantage over the Spaniard, who was clearly the revelation of the season. He was still 37 clear of Biaggi, the eventual winner. Max had the decency to sympathise with the loser, remembering that he too, in Barcelona in 1998, had suffered a similar fate. However, Biaggi chose to remind everyone that it been more serious in his case, as it had cost him the championship title! As usual, Max had the last word.

On the second lap and Rossi has just caught out Capirossi, but he did not see the waved yellow flag, indicating that marshals were on the track.

250cc

British Grand Prix
13 July 2003 / Donington – 4,023 m

STARTING GRID

1.	10.	F. Gonzales-Nieto	Aprilia	1'33.859
2.	54	M. Poggiali	Aprilia	1'34.215
3.	24	T. Elias	Aprilia	1'34.386
4.	8	N. Matsudo	Yamaha	1'34.398
5.	7	R. De Puniet	Aprilia	1'34.572
6.	21	F. Battaini	Aprilia	1'34.743
7.	3	R. Rolfo	Honda	1'34.781
8.	5	S. Porto	Honda	1'34.856
9.	50	S. Guintoli	Aprilia	1'34.995
10.	14	A. West	Aprilia	1'35.182
11.	23	J. Vincent	Aprilia	1'35.591
12.	6	A. Debon	Honda	1'35.730
13.	34	E. Bataille	Honda	1'35.833
14.	16	J. Stigefelt	Aprilia	1'35.937
15.	36	E. Nigon	Aprilia	1'36.193
16.	33	H. Faubel	Aprilia	1'36.249
17.	57	C. Davies	Aprilia	1'36.290
18.	11	J. Olive	Aprilia	1'36.390
19.	9	H. Marchand	Aprilia	1'36.411
20.	26	A. Baldolini	Aprilia	1'37.000
21.	96	J. Smrz	Honda	1'37.021
22.	15	C. Gemmel	Honda	1'37.083
23.	28	D. Heidolf	Aprilia	1'37.105
24.	18	H. vd Lagemaat	Honda	1'38.700
25.	60	P. Desborough	Yamaha	1'39.587
26.	58	L. Dickinson	Yamaha	1'39.718
27.	98	K. Poensgen	Honda	1'40.088

Not qualified

	59	A. Sawford	Honda	1'40.664

RACE: 27 LAPS = 108.621 KM

1.	Alfonso Gonzales-Nieto	42'58.011 (151.681 km/h)
2.	Manuel Poggiali	+ 0"269
3.	Anthony West	+ 2"558
4.	Toni Elias	+ 2"933
5.	Roberto Rolfo	+ 2"934
6.	Sebastian Porto	+ 25"030
7.	Franco Battaini	+ 27"663
8.	Randy De Puniet	+ 31"591
9.	Naoki Matsudo	+ 50"348
10.	Alex Debon	+ 53"337
11.	Jason Vincent	+ 58"098
12.	Hector Faubel	+ 1'00.050
13.	Chaz Davies	+ 1'00.250
14.	Jakub Smrz	+ 1'10.355
15.	Dirk Heidolf	+ 1'11.666
16.	Hugo Marchand	+ 1'15.036
17.	Alex Baldolini	+ 1'23.682
18.	Henk vd Lagemaat	+ 1 lap
19.	Katja Poensgen	+ 1 lap

Fastest lap: Poggiali, in 1'34.558 (153.163 km/h).
Record: Kato, in 1'34.096 (153.915 km/h/2001).
Outright fastest lap: Gonzales-Nieto, in 1'33.558 (154.800 km/h/2002).

CHAMPIONSHIP

1.	M. Poggiali	121 (3 wins)
2.	A. Gonzales-Nieto	106 (1 win)
3.	T. Elias	97 (2 wins)
4.	R. Rolfo	97
5.	A. West	94 (1 win)
6.	R. De Puniet	89 (1 win)
7.	F. Battaini	87
8.	S. Porto	74
9.	N. Matsudo	60
10.	S. Guintoli	58

Runners and riders:
Heidolf is back in the saddle for Aprilia Germany, allowing Nohles to return to the telemetry screens. In the Kurz Yamaha squad, Hules is replaced by Italy's Teresio Isola, who will be black flagged on Saturday for riding excessively slowly. After his fall in Assen, Randy De Puniet has been to see a specialist. The Frenchman has a broken left ankle but he can still ride.

Qualifying:
Fonsi Nieto puts everyone in their place on Friday. Manuel Poggiali has a few problems, including three falls and two trips through the gravel and grass over the four sessions. De Puniet grits his teeth and Naoki Matsudo invites himself onto the front row alongside Toni Elias. It all seems to be happening in the 250 class.

Start:
As usual, Elias does it best when the red lights go out. Unfortunately, Matsudo stays glued to the grid. Across the line for the first time, Elias has a 1"115 lead over team-mate Fonsi Gonzales-Nieto and Rolfo is third, a further half second down. Then come Poggiali and De Puniet.

Lap 2:
Guintoli falls. Elias leads Poggiali by 1"285.

Lap 5:
Poggiali takes the lead.

Fonsi Gonzales Nieto and Manuel Poggiali were the two main players on the day and they seemed to come out of nowhere.

Lap 10:
Elias retakes the lead. The Nieto-De Puniet duel has closed to 1"888 of Poggiali.

Lap 12:
Randy De Puniet goes straight on with front brake problems and drops to eighth.

Half distance (lap 13):
Poggiali heads Elias by 0"323, while Nieto is the quickest man on the track, in third place, at 1"249 from Poggiali. Rolfo and West are around two seconds behind.

Lap 17:
Elias tries a daring move, gets it wrong, goes through the gravel and drops to third place. Poggiali now has to fend off the advances of Nieto, who has closed to within 0"461.

Lap 20:
Fonsi mounts his first attack and goes into the lead. West surprises Rolfo as they duel for fourth spot.

Lap 24:
It's still Nieto and Poggiali out in front, while an on-form West battles it out with Elias.

Finish (lap 27):
Gonzales-Nieto does not put a foot wrong and wins from Poggiali. Braking at the final hairpin, Elias tries another risky move and gets it wrong, but Anthony West manages to get the better of Rolfo for third place. It takes a photo finish to decide that Elias is fourth.

Championship:
Poggiali still heads the classification, but his lead over Gonzales-Nieto has dropped to fifteen points. Elias deposes Rolfo for third, while in sixth place, Randy De Puniet is dropping back.

A gallant Doctor Claudio Costa kisses the hand of Miss Katja Poensgen.

Runners and riders:

The Dane, Harms, is suspended for one race, as he was black flagged in Assen for failing to come in for a stop-go penalty for jumping the start, but chose to ignore the flag! He is replaced by Spain's Ismael Ortega. Five Brits have wild cards.

Qualifying:

The Donington circuit, with its spiralling drops and blind corners is a difficult track for newcomers and is very unforgiving. There were several falls during qualifying, including a spectacular one from Alex de Angelis in the final moments of the last session. He broke three toes on his right foot. Japan's Ui fell a few moments later. Eight years after his last pole, Perugini finally took another, ahead of Pedrosa, Dovizioso and his team-mate Simone Corsi, who had never done so well.

Start:

Dovizioso, Pedrosa and Barbera make the best starts, while Jenkner and Corsi fall on the opening lap, which sees Dovizioso leading by 0"577 from Barbera and 1"332 from Pedrosa.

Lap 2:

A fall from Lorenzo takes Luthi with him, although the Swiss rider continues, as well as Sabbatani and Lai.

Lap 5:

Barbera now leads the dance, from Dovizioso, Perugini, Cecchinello and Pedrosa.

Lap 6:

Ui falls, as does Borsoi, who manages to get going again.

Half distance (lap 12):

Cecchinello leads by 0"461 from Perugini who is fighting Barbera. Dovizioso and Pedrosa are still in touch.

Lap 14:

Cecchinello falls and rejoins twelfth. That leaves just four to fight for the win.

A new GP winner: Hector Barbera, 16 years and 253 days.

Lap 19:

Barbera and Perugini manage to pull out a lead of 7 tenths over their two pursuers, Pedrosa and Dovizioso.

Lap 23:

The top four are now wheel to wheel again: Barbera, Perugini, Dovizioso and Pedrosa separated by just 0"806 as they cross the line. Locatelli retires.

Finish (lap 25):

Perugini makes his first mistake and drops to fourth as they come to the hairpin and the Italian collides with Pedrosa, who had run too wide and falls. It is Hector Barbera's first win and, at the age of 16 years and 253 days, he is the third youngest winner in the sport, behind Melandri and Goi.

Championship:

With Pedrosa and Jenkner out and Cecchinello picking up the points for tenth place, Dovizioso and Perugini close up in the order.

Cecchinello falls while leading, but got going again.

British Grand Prix
13 July 2003 / Donington - 4,023 m

STARTING GRID

1.	7	S. Perugini	Aprilia	1'37.984
2.	3	D. Pedrosa	Honda	1'38.078
3.	34	A. Dovizioso	Honda	1'38.143
4.	24	S. Corsi	Honda	1'38.370
5.	36	M. Kallio	Honda	1'38.386
6.	80	H. Barbera	Aprilia	1'38.417
7.	17	S. Jenkner	Aprilia	1'38.609
8.	4	L. Cecchinello	Aprilia	1'38.652
9.	27	C. Stoner	Aprilia	1'38.680
10.	15	A. De Angelis	Aprilia	1'38.752
11.	22	P. Nieto	Aprilia	1'38.754
12.	23	G. Borsoi	Aprilia	1'38.792
13.	12	T. Lüthi	Honda	1'38.845
14.	41	Y. Ui	Aprilia	1'38.889
15.	79	G. Talmacsi	Aprilia	1'38.960
16.	42	G. Pellino	Aprilia	1'38.999
17.	1	A. Vincent	KTM	1'39.012
18.	19	A. Bautista	Aprilia	1'39.037
19.	48	J. Lorenzo	Derbi	1'39.053
20.	6	M. Giansanti	Aprilia	1'39.100
21.	11	M. Sabbatani	Aprilia	1'39.118
22.	8	M. Azuma	Honda	1'39.400
23.	32	F. Lai	Malaguti	1'39.519
24.	58	M. Simoncelli	Aprilia	1'39.879
25.	25	I. Toth	Honda	1'40.009
26.	63	M. Di Meglio	Aprilia	1'40.120
27.	10	R. Locatelli	KTM	1'40.396
28.	26	E. Alzamora	Derbi	1'40.783
29.	33	S. Bianco	Gilera	1'40.867
30.	31	J. Simon	Malaguti	1'41.110
31.	27	L. Camier	Honda	1'41.415
32.	82	I. Ortega	Aprilia	1'41.736
33.	78	P. Lenart	Honda	1'41.975
34.	84	P. Veazey	Honda	1'42.634
35.	51	K. Weston	Honda	1'42.956
36.	50	M. Smart	Honda	1'43.809
37.	49	L. Longden	Honda	1'43.835
38.	83	C. Lusk	Honda	1'44.156

RACE: 25 LAPS = 100.575 KM

1.	Hector Barbera	41'25.907 (145.649 km/h)
2.	Andrea Dovizioso	+ 0"605
3.	Stefano Perugini	+ 2"597
4.	Alex De Angelis	+ 9"170
5.	Casey Stoner	+ 11"692
6.	Pablo Nieto	+ 15"898
7.	Mika Kallio	+ 21"004
8.	Arnaud Vincent	+ 21"756
9.	Gabor Talmacsi	+ 22"212
10.	Lucio Cecchinello	+ 23"642
11.	Mirko Giansanti	+ 23"812
12.	Gioele Pellino	+ 34"153
13.	Masao Azuma	+ 35"552
14.	Alvaro Bautista	+ 35"873
15.	Mike Di Meglio	+ 36"203
16.	Marco Simoncelli	+ 44"343
17.	Imre Toth	+ 51"520
18.	Julian Simon	+ 1'06.379
19.	Gino Borsoi	+ 1'06.972
20.	Peter Lenart	+ 1'11.783
21.	Ismael Ortega	+ 1'12.473
22.	Thomas Lüthi	+ 1'26.143
23.	Paul Veazey	+ 1 lap
24.	Midge Smart	+ 1 lap
25.	Lee Longden	+ 1 lap
26.	Chester Lusk	+ 1 lap

Fastest lap: Cecchinello, in 1'38.463 (147.088 km/h).
Record: Cecchinello, in 1'38.312 (147.314 km/h/2002).
Outright fastest lap: Perugini, in 1'37.984 (147.807 km/h/2003).

CHAMPIONSHIP

1.	D. Pedrosa	124 (3 wins)
2.	S. Jenkner	98 (1 win)
3.	L. Cecchinello	97 (2 wins)
4.	A. Dovizioso	93
5.	S. Perugini	92 (1 win)
6.	P. Nieto	77
7.	A. De Angelis	76
8.	H. Barbera	65 (1 win)
9.	Y. Ui	64
10.	T. Lüthi	48

GERMANY
Sachsenring

Duelling was the order of the day at the Sachsenring, with the best of the battles being fought for the win between Valentino Rossi and Sete Gibernau. The one between Bayliss and Biaggi (opposite) was not bad either. In the 125s (above) Hector Barbera (80) lost his chance when he jumped the start.

MOTOGP

"What have I done?"
Valentino Rossi
asks himself.

German Grand Prix
27 July 2003
Sachsenring - 3,671 m

STARTING GRID

1.	3	M. Biaggi	Honda	1'23.734
2.	99	J. McWilliams	Proton 2T	1'23.736
3.	65	L. Capirossi	Ducati	1'24.058
4.	46	V. Rossi	Honda	1'24.253
5.	15	S. Gibernau	Honda	1'24.287
6.	12	T. Bayliss	Ducati	1'24.405
7.	7	C. Checa	Yamaha	1'24.423
8.	11	T. Ukawa	Honda	1'24.492
9.	9	N. Aoki	Proton 2T	1'24.574
10.	56	S. Nakano	Yamaha	1'24.592
11.	4	A. Barros	Yamaha	1'24.745
12.	33	M. Melandri	Yamaha	1'24.781
13.	45	C. Edwards	Aprilia	1'24.794
14.	10	K. Roberts	Suzuki	1'24.913
15.	69	N. Hayden	Honda	1'24.961
16.	17	N. Abé	Yamaha	1'24.981
17.	41	N. Haga	Aprilia	1'25.008
18.	19	O. Jacque	Yamaha	1'25.038
19.	6	M. Tamada	Honda	1'25.360
20.	8	G. McCoy	Kawasaki	1'25.563
21.	66	A. Hofmann	Kawasaki	1'26.003
22.	21	J. Hopkins	Suzuki	1'26.247
23.	23	R. Kiyonari	Honda	1'26.296
24.	88	A. Pitt	Kawasaki	1'26.302
25.	52	D. De Gea	Sabre V4 2T	1'26.717

RACE: 30 LAPS = 110.130 KM

1.	Sete Gibernau	42'41.180 (154.798 km/h)
2.	Valentino Rossi	+ 0"060
3.	Troy Bayliss	+ 13"207
4.	Loris Capirossi	+ 16"521
5.	Nicky Hayden	+ 16"563
6.	Tohru Ukawa	+ 18"743
7.	Shinya Nakano	+ 18"885
8.	Carlos Checa	+ 26"165
9.	Olivier Jacque	+ 28"281
10.	Norifumi Abé	+ 29"159
11.	Nobuatsu Aoki	+ 29"316
12.	Jeremy McWilliams	+ 30"427
13.	Makoto Tamada	+ 49"580
14.	Colin Edwards	+ 53"444
15.	Kenny Roberts	+ 57"512
16.	Garry McCoy	+ 59"580
17.	Alex Hofmann	+ 1'05.240
18.	Ryuichi Kiyonari	+ 1'05.348
19.	Andrew Pitt	+ 1 lap
20.	David De Gea	+ 1 lap

Fastest lap: Biaggi, in 1'24.630 (156.157 km/h).
New record (modified track).
Outright fastest lap: Biaggi, in 1'23.734 (157.828 km/h/2003).

CHAMPIONSHIP

1.	V. Rossi	187 (3 wins)
2.	S. Gibernau	158 (4 wins)
3.	M. Biaggi	130 (1 win)
4.	L. Capirossi	97 (1 win)
5.	T. Bayliss	80
6.	T. Ukawa	66
7.	C. Checa	65
8.	S. Nakano	63
9.	A. Barros	62
10.	N. Hayden	57

Runners and riders:

Kenny Roberts Junior is back. McWilliams and Aoki turn up at the Sachsenring with two-stroke KR3 500s. Barros has had an operation on his right hand in Barcelona and grits his teeth. There are two wildcards: Abe for Yamaha and Hofmann for Kawasaki.

Qualifying:

"Fire!" Edwards is transformed into a human torch on Friday morning, when his Aprilia RS "Cube" catches fire, as the fuel filler cap had not been closed properly. Fuel spilt out and fell on the exhaust pipes. On track there is a great fight, led by Biaggi and McWilliams who, on the agile Proton KR3 and Bridgestone's qualifying tyres, just misses out on pole, two thousandths slower than Max. There is more excitement to come during the warm-up on race morning; Capirossi falls and his Ducati catches fire as the marshals try to get it back on its wheels. The beautiful Desmosedeci is destroyed.

Start:

A super start from Rossi and the two Ducatis, with Gibernau fourth and Biaggi only ninth. As they cross the line for the first time, Rossi has a 0"458 lead over Capirossi, on his spare machine and almost a second in hand over Gibernau. Biaggi is down in tenth place.

Lap 3:

Rossi is now trailed by Gibernau, 2"175 behind and fighting with Melandri. Biaggi is eighth.

Lap 6:

Gibernau closes on Rossi; the gap now just 1"941. Bayliss is a brilliant third, while Biaggi has climbed up to fifth.

"... a simple mistake" seems to be Sete Gibernau's reply.

Lap 8:

Biaggi is fourth and has just set the fastest race lap. He is 3"028 down on Rossi. Haga falls.

Lap 14:

Biaggi falls, having closed to within 3 seconds of Rossi.

Half-distance (lap 15):

The championship leader is still ahead, but only by 0"873 on Gibernau.

Lap 16:

Barros falls.

Lap 19:

Gibernau has just posted his best lap time and closes to within 364 thousandths of Rossi.

Lap 21:

Gibernau takes the lead and a superb duel ensues.

Lap 24:

Melandri falls, having been fourth and Hopkins retires with a broken engine on his Suzuki.

Finish (lap 30):

The two Honda riders are separated by just 230 thousandths on the penultimate lap, with Gibernau still leading. Rossi mounts a great attacking move in the penultimate corner, but he makes a mistake at the final one. Sete takes his fourth win of 2003 by 60 thousandths of a second.

Championship:

Rossi's lead continues to evaporate, with only 29 points separating him from Gibernau.

"Me, this good?"

They were the best of friends, usually together in the evenings over a GP weekend, happy to share a joke, often spending time together in between the races, when they went to Ibiza to recharge their batteries. They wore the mantle of the architects of some of the best duels the sport had witnessed. One of them, a world champion who had known nothing but success throughout his career, the other, a well bred young man from a good family who was for too long considered as a nice guy who was there to make up the numbers. Rossi and Gibernau were best mates and since this last Sunday in July, they were also the greatest rivals on the track. By taking his fourth win of the season, one more than Rossi, to bring the gap down to 29 points, the Spaniard had climbed another step on ladder of his career.

In April, back in Suzuka, a few hours before the first grand prix of the season, Sete had smiled when he heard predictions that he could well be the big surprise of the season. He had simply replied: "It's nice to think that, but I will never accept that remark as a rider can never be surprised by his own achievements. If that was the case, it would mean he did not believe in himself up to that point."

At the Sachsenring, after a bravura performance up against Rossi, when he came from a long way back and then held off the champion, Sete remembered that earlier conversation. "At the start of the year, I knew I was good. But maybe not to this extent," he said with a smile.

Four wins from nine races, a strengthened second place in the championship was worth a comment. "Beating a rider as legendary as Valentino four times, when he is the best rider in the modern era, is really something." Gibernau has no intentions of stopping there, although he maintains he will not change. "I will

Valentino Rossi stuck to Gibernau's back wheel as the world champion was in for a surprise.

get on with my job in the same serious way I have always done. I will take the races one at a time, without thinking too much about the title. I am having the best season of my career and one thing makes me really happy. From now on, with this success, I know I can pay back with my riding, all those who have helped me along the way; my parents, my close friends and those who have believed in me since the beginning." His mate Rossi, although beaten, is clear as to what went wrong. "I made a mistake, a serious and stupid mistake. Why did I have to absolutely shut the door on Sete in the last corner? If I had tackled this difficulty in the normal way, I would have won. But there you go, when I realised my mistake, I was too quick and had to widen my line." Gibernau listened attentively to Rossi's

comments before replying with a grin: "I never have a game plan for the final metres. I would be too scared not to be able to pull it off.

Smiles all round for Fausto Gresini, Sete Gibernau and Leo De Graffenried on Sunday morning, a few hours before another win!

250cc

Seen here fighting with Randy De Puniet, Roberto Rolfo (3) took his first GP win.

German Grand Prix
27 July 2003
Sachsenring – 3,671 m

STARTING GRID

1.	5	S. Porto	Honda	1'25.728
2.	3	R. Rolfo	Honda	1'25.891
3.	21	F. Battaini	Aprilia	1'25.944
4.	10	F. Gonzales-Nieto	Aprilia	1'25.963
5.	7	R. De Puniet	Aprilia	1'26.032
6.	54	M. Poggiali	Aprilia	1'26.104
7.	8	N. Matsudo	Yamaha	1'26.116
8.	50	S. Guintoli	Aprilia	1'26.381
9.	24	T. Elias	Aprilia	1'26.517
10.	14	A. West	Aprilia	1'26.878
11.	11	J. Olive	Aprilia	1'27.099
12.	26	A. Baldolini	Aprilia	1'27.212
13.	6	A. Debon	Honda	1'27.241
14.	36	E. Nigon	Aprilia	1'27.281
15.	33	H. Faubel	Aprilia	1'27.409
16.	9	H. Marchand	Aprilia	1'27.482
17.	57	C. Davies	Aprilia	1'27.512
18.	28	D. Heidolf	Aprilia	1'27.568
19.	96	J. Smrz	Honda	1'27.656
20.	16	J. Stigefelt	Aprilia	1'27.768
21.	34	E. Bataille	Honda	1'28.057
22.	62	M. Neukirchner	Honda	1'28.458
23.	52	L. Pesek	Yamaha	1'28.563
24.	15	C. Gemmel	Honda	1'28.670
25.	63	T. Palander	Honda	1'29.191
26.	18	H. vd Lagemaat	Honda	1'30.214
27.	66	V. Kallio	Yamaha	1'30.377
28.	65	N. Rank	Honda	1'30.725
29.	98	K. Poensgen	Honda	1'31.103

RACE: 29 LAPS = 106.459 KM

1.	Roberto Rolfo	42'06.199 (151.711 km/h)
2.	Alfonso Gonzales-Nieto	+ 0"150
3.	Randy De Puniet	+ 0"287
4.	Sebastian Porto	+ 5"305
5.	Franco Battaini	+ 13"097
6.	Anthony West	+ 18"289
7.	Toni Elias	+ 20"881
8.	Manuel Poggiali	+ 20"927
9.	Alex Debon	+ 45"171
10.	Alex Baldolini	+ 48"701
11.	Dirk Heidolf	+ 57"078
12.	Chaz Davies	+ 57"268
13.	Jakub Smrz	+ 57"459
14.	Erwan Nigon	+ 1'17.467
15.	Max Neukirchner	+ 1'29.139
16.	Lukas Pesek	+ 1'29.338
17.	Joan Olive	+ 1 lap
18.	Katja Poensgen	+ 1 lap
19.	Vesa Kallio	+ 1 lap

Fastest lap: Gonzales-Nieto, in 1'26.469 (152.836 km/h).
Record. New track.
Outright fastest lap: Porto, in 1'25.728 (154.157 km/h/2003).

CHAMPIONSHIP

1.	M. Poggiali	129 (3 wins)
2.	A. Gonzales-Nieto	126 (1 win)
3.	R. Rolfo	122 (1 win)
4.	T. Elias	106 (2 wins)
5.	R. De Puniet	105 (1 win)
6.	A. West	104 (1 win)
7.	F. Battaini	98
8.	S. Porto	87
9.	N. Matsudo	60
10.	S. Guintoli	58

Runners and riders:
After an abortive run with the Italian, Isola, at Donington the Yamaha Kurz crew try their second rider from the European championship, the young Czech, Lukas Pesek. There are five wildcards.

Qualifying:
On this unusual track, where agility counts for more than power, Porto and Rolfo put two Hondas in the top two places on the grid, ahead of the Aprilias, which had seemed unbeatable in the early part of the season.

Start:
Porto and Rolfo consolidate their grid positions to take the lead from Gonzales-Nieto. Not everyone is as lucky as the first corner sees falls for Matsudo, Marchand, Olive, Gemmel and Faubel. Crossing the line for the first time, Rolfo leads fellow Honda rider Sebastian Porto by 0"254. Fonsi is fourth, ahead of Randy De Puniet. Poggiali is only tenth.

Lap 2:
There are six in the lead group, with Rolfo, Porto, Gonzales-Nieto, De Puniet, Battaini and Guintoli separated by just 1"820.

Lap 5:
Rolfo has a half second lead over Porto with De Puniet now third.

Lap 7:
It's still Rolfo, now 0"280 ahead of De Puniet, with Porto hanging on. Gonzales-Nieto seems to be experiencing some problems and has a spectacular off-track moment and is just ahead of Poggiali.

Half distance (lap 14):
De Puniet has just taken the lead. Rolfo is now 0"126 behind and Guintoli is impressive, now up to third ahead of Porto. Further back, Nieto, Poggiali and Battaini are scrapping. The championship leader falls a bit later and drops to tenth.

Lap 16:
Rolfo is back in the lead.

Lap 20:
The leaders catch the backmarkers. De Puniet is ahead again with Rolfo stuck to his back wheel and Guintoli is still third.

Lap 22:
Guintoli falls.

Lap 24:
Rolfo leads once again with the top three within 0"854.

Finish (lap 29):
As they begin the final lap, 288 thousandths separate Rolfo, De Puniet and Gonzales-Nieto, who passes the Frenchman at the first corner. The Spaniard tries everything he knows and almost comes off, so Roberto Rolfo takes his first GP victory. On the line, Elias passes Poggiali for seventh spot.

Championship:
With Poggiali getting it wrong, the lead group all close up, as Gonzales-Nieto is now just three points adrift, while the winner of the day, Roberto Rolfo is seven behind.

Traffic jam in the gravel trap on the outside of the first corner. Very annoying...

A second win this season for Stefano Perugini.

Runners and riders:

Robbin Harms is back after his one race ban. Alvaro Bautista is on top form after his win in the Spanish championship at Albacete, while Thomas Luthi has come from Brno, where he was the only rider in the category to have tested. There are five invited riders, including Dario Giuseppetti, the leader of the European championship.

Qualifying:

The weather is oppressive with 51% humidity and everyone studies the forecast, which predicts rain for the end of Friday and Saturday. It would never come, at least not when the bikes were on track. As always, the gaps are minimal, with the top sixteen in less than a second. Once again, the Aprilias have the upper hand over the Hondas. Perugini takes pole, ahead of De Angelis, Barbera, Cecchinello and Stoner. Each time local boy Jenkner goes by, the crowd goes wild.

Start:

Barbera makes a very good start and, as at Donington, Lorenzo soon gets it wrong, falling at the first corner. At the end of the opening lap,

Barbera has a 0"329 lead over De Angelis, with Cecchinello, Stoner, Dovizioso, Perugini and Pedrosa in pursuit.

Lap 3:

Di Meglio is a faller.

Lap 4:

It appears that Barbera jumped the start and will have to pit for a stop and go penalty. He comes in on the next lap and Perugini moves into the lead, 0"731 ahead of Stoner, Pedrosa, De Angelis and Cecchinello.

Lap 10:

World Champion Arnaud Vincent comes off. Six fight it out for the win: Stoner, De

Angelis, Perugini, Pedrosa, Dovizioso and Cecchinello.

Half distance (lap 13):

The Aprilias rule the roost. Stoner leads by 0"186 from De Angelis and by 0"436 over Perugini. Championship leader Pedrosa is fourth, hanging onto the trio from Noale.

Lap 15:

Azuma falls.

Lap 19:

Jenkner falls, leaving four fighting for the lead: Stoner, Perugini, De Angelis and Pedrosa. After his stop and go, Barbera is within sight of the points in 16th place.

Lap 24:

Ui falls.

Lap 26:

Luthi falls, while fighting for tenth.

Finish (lap 27):

The first four are covered by 656 thousandths as they start the final lap. Perugini has the last word, ahead of Stoner, De Angelis and Pedrosa.

Dani Pedrosa (3) and his Honda fights it out with a pack of Aprilias – Perugini, Stoner, De Angelis.

Championship:

With Pedrosa beaten by the Aprilias, it's a good day for Perugini as he closes to within 20 points of the leader prior to the short summer break.

125cc

German Grand Prix
27 July 2003
Sachsenring - 3,671 m

STARTING GRID

1.	7	S. Perugini	Aprilia	1'27.717
2.	15	A. De Angelis	Aprilia	1'27.771
3.	80	H. Barbera	Aprilia	1'28.022
4.	4	L. Cecchinello	Aprilia	1'28.097
5.	27	C. Stoner	Aprilia	1'28.223
6.	34	A. Dovizioso	Honda	1'28.291
7.	3	D. Pedrosa	Honda	1'28.355
8.	23	G. Borsoi	Aprilia	1'28.392
9.	17	S. Jenkner	Aprilia	1'28.457
10.	24	S. Corsi	Honda	1'28.459
11.	6	M. Giansanti	Aprilia	1'28.482
12.	36	M. Kallio	Honda	1'28.536
13.	22	P. Nieto	Aprilia	1'28.559
14.	41	Y. Ui	Aprilia	1'28.595
15.	12	T. Lüthi	Honda	1'28.620
16.	42	G. Pellino	Aprilia	1'28.703
17.	79	G. Talmacsi	Aprilia	1'28.766
18.	32	F. Lai	Malaguti	1'28.820
19.	48	J. Lorenzo	Derbi	1'28.951
20.	58	M. Simoncelli	Aprilia	1'29.055
21.	88	R. Harms	Aprilia	1'29.600
22.	10	R. Locatelli	KTM	1'29.657
23.	18	A. Bautista	Aprilia	1'29.691
24.	1	A. Vincent	KTM	1'29.723
25.	11	M. Sabbatani	Aprilia	1'29.732 [*]
26.	31	J. Simon	Malaguti	1'29.742
27.	25	I. Toth	Honda	1'29.966
28.	53	M. Mickan	Honda	1'30.252
29.	26	E. Alzamora	Derbi	1'30.336
30.	91	D. Giuseppetti	Honda	1'30.351
31.	91	J. Büech	Honda	1'30.405
32.	63	M. Di Meglio	Aprilia	1'30.830
33.	8	M. Azuma	Honda	1'30.956
34.	33	S. Bianco	Gilera	1'31.237
35.	52	J. Müller	Honda	1'31.395
36.	54	P. Unger	Honda	1'31.764
37.	27	L. Camier	Honda	1'31.784
38.	78	P. Lenart	Honda	1'32.099

(*): Did not take part – injured.

RACE: 27 LAPS = 99.117 KM

1.	Stefano Perugini	40'11.124 (147.989 km/h)
2.	Casey Stoner	+ 0"212
3.	Alex De Angelis	+ 0"375
4.	Daniel Pedrosa	+ 0"774
5.	Pablo Nieto	+ 5"877
6.	Gabor Talmacsi	+ 11"791
7.	Andrea Dovizioso	+ 12"070
8.	Lucio Cecchinello	+ 12"212
9.	Simone Corsi	+ 12"645
10.	Mika Kallio	+ 16"369
11.	Mirko Giansanti	+ 16"370
12.	Marco Simoncelli	+ 16"825
13.	Gioele Pellino	+ 21"622
14.	Hector Barbera	+ 27"161
15.	Fabrizio Lai	+ 41"028
16.	Robbin Harms	+ 45"131
17.	Gino Borsoi	+ 45"377
18.	Roberto Locatelli	+ 54"576
19.	Dario Giuseppetti	+ 55"177
20.	Julian Simon	+ 1'11.657
21.	Jorge Lorenzo	+ 1'22.753
22.	Peter Lenart	+ 1'36.455
23.	Leon Camier	+ 1 lap

Fastest lap: Nieto, in 1'28.490 (149.345 km/h). Record (new track).
Outright fastest lap: Perugini, in 1'27.717 (150.661 km/h/2003).

CHAMPIONSHIP

1.	D. Pedrosa	137 (3 wins)
2.	S. Perugini	117 (2 wins)
3.	L. Cecchinello	105 (2 wins)
4.	A. Dovizioso	102
5.	S. Jenkner	98 (1 win)
6.	A. De Angelis	92
7.	P. Nieto	88
8.	H. Barbera	67 (1 win)
9.	Y. Ui	64
10.	C. Stoner	60

CZECH
REPUBLIC
Brno

The crowd in the natural bowl of the Masaryk circuit at Brno. And what a spectacle on the track with the battle between Valentino Rossi, Sete Gibernau and the two Ducatisti, Loris Capirossi and Troy Bayliss.
Although beaten, Gibernau takes the opportunity to thank the fans, while below, daddy, Arnaud de Puniet seems even more proud of his son, Randy.

Biaggi concentrates on the start line: Mr. Brno is going to get beaten!

Czech Republic Grand Prix
17 August 2003 / Brno - 5,403 m

STARTING GRID

1.	46	V. Rossi	Honda	1'58.769
2.	15	S. Gibernau	Honda	1'58.899
3.	3	M. Biaggi	Honda	1'58.908
4.	65	L. Capirossi	Ducati	1'58.916
5.	7	C. Checa	Yamaha	1'59.295
6.	12	T. Bayliss	Ducati	1'59.373
7.	69	N. Hayden	Honda	1'59.432
8.	11	T. Ukawa	Honda	1'59.629
9.	4	A. Barros	Yamaha	1'59.765
10.	6	M. Tamada	Honda	2'00.145
11.	19	O. Jacque	Yamaha	2'00.165
12.	45	C. Edwards	Aprilia	2'00.627
13.	21	J. Hopkins	Suzuki	2'00.740
14.	56	S. Nakano	Yamaha	2'00.800
15.	23	R. Kiyonari	Honda	2'00.862
16.	10	K. Roberts	Suzuki	2'00.891
17.	33	M. Melandri	Yamaha	2'00.892
18.	41	N. Haga	Aprilia	2'01.303
19.	8	G. McCoy	Kawasaki	2'01.320
20.	66	A. Hofmann	Kawasaki	2'01.753
21.	99	J. McWilliams	Proton 4T	2'01.809
22.	88	A. Pitt	Kawasaki	2'01.994
23.	9	N. Aoki	Proton 4T	2'02.704
24.	52	D. De Gea	Sabre V4 2T	2'04.638
25.	35	C. Burns	ROC Yamaha 2T	2'05.083

RACE: 22 LAPS = 118.866 KM

1.	Valentino Rossi	44'18.907 (160.937 km/h)
2.	Sete Gibernau	+ 0"042
3.	Troy Bayliss	+ 0"668
4.	Carlos Checa	+ 5"390
5.	Massimiliano Biaggi	+ 8"729
6.	Nicky Hayden	+ 11"043
7.	Alexandre Barros	+ 11"439
8.	Tohru Ukawa	+ 13"574
9.	Makoto Tamada	+ 23"273
10.	Marco Melandri	+ 26"404
11.	Olivier Jacque	+ 26"685
12.	Colin Edwards	+ 30"728
13.	Noriyuki Haga	+ 39"531
14.	Shinya Nakano	+ 41"240
15.	Ryuichi Kiyonari	+ 44"623
16.	Andrew Pitt	+ 55"499
17.	John Hopkins	+ 55"677
18.	Garry McCoy	+ 1'00.700
19.	Alex Hofmann	+ 1'08.130
20.	Kenny Roberts	+ 1'14.524

Fastest lap: Rossi, in 1'59.966 (162.135 km/h).
New record.
Previous best: Kato, in 2'00.605 (161.276 km/h/2002).
Outright fastest lap: Rossi, in 1'58.769 (163.770 km/h/2003).

CHAMPIONSHIP

1.	V. Rossi	212 (4 wins)
2.	S. Gibernau	178 (4 wins)
3.	M. Biaggi	141 (1 win)
4.	L. Capirossi	97 (1 win)
5.	T. Bayliss	96
6.	C. Checa	78
7.	T. Ukawa	74
8.	A. Barros	71
9.	N. Hayden	67
10.	S. Nakano	65

Runners and riders:

Novelties on the technical and tonsorial fronts. The Camel Pramac Pons team has been given the latest HRC updates for Max Biaggi's RC211V, while Rossi has a new image after the break, turning up in Brno with his hair dyed red, after a chance encounter on an Ibizan beach. "I saw a girl with her hair like this and I liked it."

Qualifying:

On Friday, Max Biaggi reminds everyone who the main man is at Brno, having won in the Czech Republic seven times already. He takes provisional pole, but his time would be pulverised by Rossi the following day. The top four – Rossi, Gibernau, Biaggi and Capirossi – go under the 1'59 over a lap and are separated by a mere 147 thousandths of a second. Nakano has a big crash during Saturday morning's free practice and

Two Hondas (Rossi and Gibernau) up against two Ducatis (Bayliss and Capirossi) but where are the other Japanese machines?

has to be taken to hospital for various scans. The next day, he tries his luck in the warm-up and decides to race.

Start:

The Ducatis regularly seem unbeatable when it comes to getting off the line and this time, Bayliss comes through from row two to take the lead. He crosses the line with 0"212 over his pursuers, led by Rossi, Biaggi, Gibernau and Capirossi.

Lap 7:

Bayliss extends his lead to 0"567. Further back, the two championship leaders, Rossi and Gibernau slow one another down as they pass and re-pass each other.

Half distance (lap 11):

The group had closed up two laps earlier and now Rossi leads by half a second from Gibernau, who closes up and takes the lead on lap thirteen.

Lap 20:

It was a fantastic duel, later described by Rossi as

"certainly the best fight in the history of the MotoGP category," as Gibernau never let up the pressure for a single moment. Sadly, Capirossi is forced to retire with electrical woes.

Finish (lap 22):

Gibernau pulls off the move of

Until now, Loris Capirossi's race had been perfection, but he was forced to retire two laps from the flag.

the year on the penultimate lap, but Rossi gets him back to win by 42 thousandths. On the victory lap, the Italian's fan club run onto the track and transform him into a convict, complete with ball and chain.

Championship:

Rossi had not won since the Italian GP and thus extends his lead at the head of the classification, with a 34 point advantage over Gibernau, a solid second in front of Biaggi. Bayliss is now one point behind fourth placed Capirossi.

"It was fun", quotes Rossi!

What to retain from this hot Sunday in August? Dozens of passing moves, breathtaking slides and otherworldly seemingly impossible moves. And the winner, Valentino Rossi turning himself into a convict on his victory lap. The spectacle was definitely grandiose at Brno in the Czech Republic at the height of the summer holiday period.

"There were no tactics, no one was thinking, it was great fun. Maybe it was not always very orthodox, but definitely fun. We took turns to overtake one another, passing again and sliding, constantly defying the laws of gravity. There's not much else to say. It was really enjoyable for us and I guess it was for you too, wasn't it?" It sure was champ! His head tinged with red and covered with a convict's cap, with a ball and chain tied to his ankle, Valentino Rossi had returned to the role of master of ceremonies in the blue riband category of motorcycle racing. It might have been by only 42 thousandths of a second over Sete Gibernau, but it was obvious on the victory lap and the podium, that this win meant something special to the reigning world champion.

"Over the past few weeks, as I had not won for a while, the Italian media were claiming I was going through some sort of crisis. Therefore, this race in the middle of the summer holidays had a special significance. Either I won, or it would be hard labour until my next win. So, on my lap of honour, I made the most of having some of my most loyal supporters on hand to start my new life as a convict." Rossi had become "Vale" once again. He had to dig deep on the track to fend off Sete Gibernau who, yet again, had been magnificent. Rossi had also shown that he is a born entertainer, a media phenomenon who attracts the crowds and galvanises public interest.

As for the Swiss-based Spaniard, Gibernau was now the only man who could trouble Valentino Rossi for the overall title, as Biaggi had engine problems and Capirossi's Ducati suffered an electrical failure. Perfect on track, Sete is also a master in front of the microphone. "Well, if Valentino is going through a crisis, I wonder what will happen to the rest of us when he comes out of it," offered Gibernau looking at his mate Rossi. On the way from the podium to the press conference, the Italian was stung by an aggressive wasp and was treated in front of a captivated crowd by the good Doctor Costa. "What's wrong? A wasp?" enquired Gibernau. "Why didn't it sting you during the race? That would have suited me better today."

The remark was accompanied by a clandestine wink. It seemed that even if there was no quarter given on the track in MotoGP and the media are always looking for an angle, nothing could upset the harmony which existed between the two kings of the 2003 season, the two dominant players...

Valentino Rossi drags his ball and chain around on his lap of honour: "I was condemned to win."

Smiles on the top step of the podium: Gibernau and Bayliss surround the convict, his Majesty, Valentino Rossi!

250cc

Czech Republic Grand Prix
17 August 2003 / Brno – 5,403 m

STARTING GRID

1.	54	M. Poggiali	Aprilia	2'03.872
2.	7	R. De Puniet	Aprilia	2'03.920
3.	10.	F. Gonzales-Nieto	Aprilia	2'04.037
4.	24	T. Elias	Aprilia	2'04.088
5.	21	F. Battaini	Aprilia	2'04.233
6.	3	R. Rolfo	Honda	2'04.413
7.	50	S. Guintoli	Aprilia	2'04.663
8.	14	A. West	Aprilia	2'04.771
9.	8	N. Matsudo	Yamaha	2'04.909
10.	5	S. Porto	Honda	2'05.054
11.	73	R. Rous	Aprilia	2'05.157
12.	9	H. Marchand	Aprilia	2'05.563
13.	6	A. Debon	Honda	2'05.995
14.	33	H. Faubel	Aprilia	2'06.018
15.	34	E. Bataille	Honda	2'06.032
16.	15	C. Gemmel	Honda	2'06.044
17.	28	D. Heidolf	Aprilia	2'06.264
18.	16	J. Stigefelt	Aprilia	2'06.859
19.	36	E. Nigon	Aprilia	2'06.923
20.	57	C. Davies	Aprilia	2'07.038
21.	96	J. Smrz	Honda	2'07.182
22.	11	J. Olive	Aprilia	2'07.493
23.	26	A. Baldolini	Aprilia	2'07.598
24.	52	L. Pesek	Yamaha	2'07.758
25.	66	V. Kallio	Yamaha	2'08.225
26.	74	M. Filla	Yamaha	2'08.960
27.	47	A. Vos	Yamaha	2'09.654
28.	98	K. Poensgen	Honda	2'10.193
29.	75	G. Rizmayer		2'10.236
30.	18	H. vd Lagemaat	Honda	2'10.740

RACE: 20 LAPS = 108.060 KM

1.	Randy De Puniet	41'45.354 (155.273 km/h)
2.	Toni Elias	+ 0"527
3.	Manuel Poggiali	+ 0"951
4.	Roberto Rolfo	+ 5"492
5.	Sebastian Porto	+ 10"407
6.	Alfonso Gonzales-Nieto	+ 10"875
7.	Franco Battaini	+ 15"278
8.	Sylvain Guintoli	+ 15"565
9.	Naoki Matsudo	+ 32"752
10.	Hector Faubel	+ 36"167
11.	Hugo Marchand	+ 36"608
12.	Eric Bataille	+ 50"700
13.	Dirk Heidolf	+ 52"299
14.	Chaz Davies	+ 52"870
15.	Christian Gemmel	+ 53"063
16.	Joan Olive	+ 58"903
17.	Lukas Pesek	+ 1'08.193
18.	Vesa Kallio	+ 1'35.989
19.	Michal Filla	+ 1'44.230
20.	Katja Poensgen	+ 1'59.070
21.	Arie Vos	+ 2'01.799
22.	Gabor Rizmayer	+ 1 lap

Fastest lap: Elias, in 2'03.969 (156.900 km/h).
Record: Melandri, in 2'03.836 (157.069 km/h/2001).
Outright fastest lap: Harada, in 2'02.953 (158.197 km/h/2001).

CHAMPIONSHIP

1.	M. Poggiali	145 (3 wins)
2.	A. Gonzales-Nieto	166 (1 win)
3.	R. Rolfo	135 (1 win)
4.	R. De Puniet	130 (2 wins)
5.	T. Elias	126 (2 wins)
6.	F. Battaini	107
7.	A. West	104 (1 win)
8.	S. Porto	98
9.	N. Matsudo	67
10.	S. Guintoli	66

Runners and riders:

Honda has brought along some new parts for Rolfo and Porto, confirming that it intend to return to winning ways in a category where Aprilia's dominance has ruffled feathers in Tokyo. There are five wildcards, including "foreigners" Arie Vos (Netherlands), Vesa Kallio (Finland, Mika's brother) and Gabor Rizmater (a Hungarian campaigning to see the motorcycle grands prix return to his country).

Qualifying:

Randy De Puniet has fun on Friday, beating Rolfo by around four tenths. On Saturday, the Aprilia armada is back in its favourite racing formation, with five RSW (Poggiali, De Puniet, Gonzales-Nieto, Elias and Battaini) ahead of Rolfo, the best of the Hondas.

Start:

Elias does best on the opening lap, crossing the line fractionally in front of De Puniet, Poggiali and Rolfo. The wildcard rider, Radomil Rous and Frenchman, Nigon do not make it the line.

Lap 4:

De Puniet leads since lap two with a 2 tenths advantage over Poggiali and Elias. The three men would fight tooth and nail to the penultimate lap.

Half distance (lap 10):

Elias is now in the lead from Poggiali and De Puniet. Rolfo has been dropped, as has Gonzales-Nieto who is over three seconds behind the Honda rider.

Finish (lap 20):

The closing stages can be told in the figures that separate the leader from the second placed man: 82 thousandths on lap 14, 79 thousandths one lap later and 55 thousandths on lap 17, with Poggiali always ahead. But we have not heard the last from De Puniet. He takes the lead on the penultimate lap and goes on to record his second win, while Poggiali and Elias get in each other's way. "I knew that if I was with them, I had a big chance. Elias has a talent for attacking in impossible places and

as Poggiali is the sort to fight back, I thought there was a pretty good chance that they ran the risk of making mistakes." Well played Randy. He wins by half a second from Elias.

Championship:

Although beaten, Poggiali does not have such a bad day, as his main rival for the title, Alfonso "Fonsi" Gonzales-Nieto can do no better than sixth. The former 125 world champion leads by nine points. However, they are closing up behind, as Rolfo is now ten points down, De Puniet is 15 behind and Elias at 19.

Daggers drawn in the forest: De Puniet leads the dance.

The second glory day in the career of Randy De Puniet. There is more to come...

Runners and riders:

The first part of the summer break saw some excitement as the reigning world champion, Arnaud Vincent was sacked by KTM. His seat on the 125 orange beast went to Finland's Mika Kallio. This enraged the bosses of the Ajo Motorsports team which had invested heavily in Kallio for several years. His Honda was now entrusted to Hideyuki Kikuchi. Other changes saw Englishman Leon Camier replaced in the Metasystem team by Andrea Ballerini. Finally, amongst the wildcards was Marketa Janakova, a sixteen year old Czech youngster, currently leading his national championship.

Qualifying:

Stoner has all the answers on Friday before suffering a serious fall at the end of the session. He struggles to his feet with a broken left collar bone and wrist. On Saturday, the Aprilias dominate, with De Angelis ahead of Jenkner and Cecchinello. Only two Hondas get onto the front two rows, Pedrosa (4th) and Luthi (7th.)

Start:

Jenkner is quickest as the lights go out, ending the first lap with Pedrosa glued to his rear wheel. A small pack follows, led by Luthi, Talmacsi and Dovizioso.

Lap 3:

Luthi has caught the lead group so that three of them are covered by 166 thousandths.

Lap 6:

Luthi leads what has now become a group of six. The hero of Catalunya is chased by Jenkner, De Angelis, Pedrosa, Cecchinello and Perugini.

Lap 9:

De Angelis' engine tightens up for a moment and he drops several places.

Half distance (lap 10):

Pedrosa is the new leader, with Perugini, Luthi and Pablo Nieto in close attendance.

Lap 11:

Cecchinello falls as his crankshaft breaks and Jenkner cannot avoid him. Out in front, Pedrosa still leads, while fourth placed Luthi seems to be playing a waiting game.

Lap 12:

He felt he could have won, but his dreams went flying literally and figuratively as he hits Pablo Nieto's bike, which had fallen just ahead of him. The Swiss rider's Honda uses the Spaniard's Aprilia like a

It was *the* transfer of the first summer break: Finland's Mika Kallio finds himself at KTM.

springboard and Luthi is taken to the medical centre with a fractured hip and a broken pelvis.

Finish (lap 19):

Pedrosa keeps it together, Perugini does not challenge and De Angelis finds himself third, ahead of Mika Kallio.

Championship:

It was a good day's work for Daniel Pedrosa, who improved his situation vis a vis Stefano Perugini with a 25 point gap, equivalent to one race win. Behind them, it's a very close run thing between Dovizioso, De Angelis, Cecchinello and Jenkner.

Czech Republic Grand Prix
17 August 2003 / Brno - 5,403 m

STARTING GRID

1.	15	A. De Angelis	Aprilia	2'08.100
2.	17	S. Jenkner	Aprilia	2'08.330
3.	4	L. Cecchinello	Aprilia	2'08.421
4.	3	D. Pedrosa	Honda	2'08.562
5.	7	S. Perugini	Aprilia	2'08.755
6.	22	P. Nieto	Aprilia	2'08.817
7.	12	T. Lüthi	Honda	2'08.857
8.	79	G. Talmacsi	Aprilia	2'09.253
9.	80	H. Barbera	Aprilia	2'09.268
10.	34	A. Dovizioso	Honda	2'09.322
11.	27	C. Stoner	Aprilia	2'09.477 (*)
12.	6	M. Giansanti	Aprilia	2'09.532
13.	23	G. Borsoi	Aprilia	2'09.553
14.	48	J. Lorenzo	Derbi	2'09.602
15.	41	Y. Ui	Aprilia	2'09.702
16.	42	G. Pellino	Aprilia	2'10.044
17.	32	F. Lai	Malaguti	2'10.049
18.	36	M. Kallio	KTM	2'10.089
19.	24	S. Corsi	Honda	2'10.112
20.	8	M. Azuma	Honda	2'10.235
21.	39	H. Kikuchi	Honda	2'10.308
22.	33	S. Bianco	Gilera	2'10.836
23.	63	M. Di Meglio	Aprilia	2'10.863
24.	58	M. Simoncelli	Aprilia	2'10.923
25.	31	J. Simon	Malaguti	2'10.928
26.	88	R. Harms	Aprilia	2'10.935
27.	10	R. Locatelli	KTM	2'11.160
28.	26	E. Alzamora	Derbi	2'11.180
29.	11	M. Sabbatani	Aprilia	2'11.213
30.	25	I. Toth	Honda	2'11.270
31.	19	A. Bautista	Aprilia	2'12.753
32.	50	A. Ballerini	Honda	2'12.755
33.	55	I. Kalab	Honda	2'12.792
34.	56	M. Janakova	Honda	2'12.801
35.	92	V. Bittman	Honda	2'13.192
36.	78	P. Lenart	Honda	2'14.256
37.	57	L. Nedog	Honda	2'14.903

(*): Did not take part – injured

RACE: 19 LAPS = 102.657 KM

1.	Daniel Pedrosa	40'59.354 (150.269 km/h)
2.	Stefano Perugini	+ 3'981
3.	Alex De Angelis	+ 10'454
4.	Mika Kallio	+ 11'052
5.	Hector Barbera	+ 12'351
6.	Andrea Dovizioso	+ 12'968
7.	Mirko Giansanti	+ 21'109
8.	Gino Borsoi	+ 21'513
9.	Youichi Ui	+ 24'841
10.	Gioele Pellino	+ 34'942
11.	Gabor Talmacsi	+ 35'213
12.	Jorge Lorenzo	+ 41'042
13.	Masao Azuma	+ 41'362
14.	Marco Simoncelli	+ 41'540
15.	Mike Di Meglio	+ 41'662
16.	Alvaro Bautista	+ 42'513
17.	Roberto Locatelli	+ 43'010
18.	Fabrizio Lai	+ 43'068
19.	Robbin Harms	+ 1'02.481
20.	Stefano Bianco	+ 1'02.611
21.	Emilio Alzamora	+ 1'02.747
22.	Julian Simon	+ 1'10.272
23.	Imre Toth	+ 1'10.398
24.	Igor Kalab	+ 1'20.158
25.	Marketa Janakova	+ 1'31.093
26.	Luka Nedog	+ 1 lap

Fastest lap: Cecchinello, in 2'07.836 (152.154 km/h/New record).
Previous best: Cecchinello, in 2'08.907 (150.894 km/h/2002).
Outright fastest lap: Cecchinello, in 2'07.836 (152.154 km/h/2003).

CHAMPIONSHIP

1.	D. Pedrosa	162 (4 wins)
2.	S. Perugini	137 (2 wins)
3.	A. Dovizioso	112
4.	A. De Angelis	108
5.	L. Cecchinello	105 (2 wins)
6.	S. Jenkner	98 (1 win)
7.	P. Nieto	88
8.	H. Barbera	78 (1 win)
9.	Y. Ui	71
10.	C. Stoner	60

One of the strongest images of the 125 cc season: Switzerland's Thomas Luthi, who had dreams of victory, flies over the Aprilia of Pablo Nieto who fallen just ahead of him.

PORTUGAL
Estoril

What would the first corner look like when the top sixteen in the category qualified within just 1.5 seconds? Like this: De Angelis (number 15) leads the future world champion, Daniel Pedrosa (3). Always a keen student of the opening laps of the 125 race, Loris Capirossi (above) relaxes with his wife, Ingrid. While in the nearby garages it's time for some charm.

MOTOGP

Portuguese Grand Prix
7 September 2003 / Estoril - 4,182 m

STARTING GRID

1.	65	L. Capirossi	Ducati	1'38.412
2.	3	M. Biaggi	Honda	1'38.718
3.	46	V. Rossi	Honda	1'38.744
4.	15	S. Gibernau	Honda	1'38.920
5.	19	O. Jacque	Yamaha	1'39.042
6.	56	S. Nakano	Yamaha	1'39.159
7.	7	C. Checa	Yamaha	1'39.225
8.	12	T. Bayliss	Ducati	1'39.344
9.	6	M. Tamada	Honda	1'39.368
10.	11	T. Ukawa	Honda	1'39.541
11.	33	M. Melandri	Yamaha	1'39.557
12.	4	A. Barros	Yamaha	1'39.571
13.	45	C. Edwards	Aprilia	1'39.837
14.	10	K. Roberts	Suzuki	1'39.839
15.	69	N. Hayden	Honda	1'40.069
16.	99	J. McWilliams	Proton 2T	1'40.325
17.	21	J. Hopkins	Suzuki	1'40.766
18.	41	N. Haga	Aprilia	1'40.779
19.	23	R. Kiyonari	Honda	1'40.883
20.	88	A. Pitt	Kawasaki	1'41.020
21.	52	D. De Gea	Harris WCM	1'41.105
22.	8	G. McCoy	Kawasaki	1'41.485
23.	9	N. Aoki	Proton 4T	1'41.656
24.	35	C. Burns	Harris WCM	1'42.199

RACE: 28 LAPS = 117.096 KM

1.	Valentino Rossi	46'48.005 (150.122 km/h)
2.	Massimiliano Biaggi	+ 2"094
3.	Loris Capirossi	+ 5"254
4.	Sete Gibernau	+ 5"269
5.	Tohru Ukawa	+ 10"581
6.	Troy Bayliss	+ 14"246
7.	Marco Melandri	+ 16"143
8.	Carlos Checa	+ 18"083
9.	Nicky Hayden	+ 18"284
10.	Makoto Tamada	+ 21"815
11.	Alexandre Barros	+ 24"059
12.	Shinya Nakano	+ 27"082
13.	Olivier Jacque	+ 27"651
14.	Colin Edwards	+ 31"505
15.	Noriyuki Haga	+ 57"118
16.	Ryuichi Kiyonari	+ 1'01.412
17.	Kenny Roberts	+ 1'01.542
18.	John Hopkins	+ 1'06.601
19.	Jeremy McWilliams	+ 1'10.958
20.	Nobuatsu Aoki	+ 1'11.523
21.	Andrew Pitt	+ 1'18.550
22.	David De Gea	+ 1 lap

Fastest lap: Rossi, in 1'39.189 (151.782 km/h).
New record.
Previous best: Capirossi, in 1'40.683 (149.530 km/h/2001).
Outright fastest lap: Capirossi, in 1'38.412
(152.981 km/h/2003).

CHAMPIONSHIP

1.	V. Rossi	237 (5 wins)
2.	S. Gibernau	191 (4 wins)
3.	M. Biaggi	161 (1 win)
4.	L. Capirossi	113 (1 win)
5.	T. Bayliss	106
6.	C. Checa	86
7.	T. Ukawa	85
8.	A. Barros	76
9.	N. Hayden	74
10.	S. Nakano	69

Runners and riders:

Rossi is back to his normal hair colour. Barros is still spending a lot of time in Dr. Costa's mobile clinic and, for the first time this season, the WCM four stroke takes to the track, as Peter Clifford's team has finally made enough parts for Burns and De Gea to try their luck.

Qualifying:

Tension is bubbling in the Honda camp, as everyone is waiting for Master Rossi to make up his mind, given that he has still not extended his contract with HRC. Leading on day one, Valentino is beaten by Biaggi on Saturday and also by Capirossi. On the Friday, the Ducati rider had pitted in the final moments, when his intermediate times looked

Finally, the WCM prototype makes its GP debut.

like putting him on pole. The Yamahas appear to be back on form, especially Olivier Jacque who realises his future might be in question.

Start:

The first corner at Estoril is always hotly contested and the order reads Biaggi, Capirossi, Gibernau, Rossi. Crossing the line for the first time, Max leads Capirossi by 641 thousandths.

Lap 2:

Rossi has sensed the danger and is now second, 0"940 behind Biaggi.

Troy Bayliss: close up!

Lap 6:

Biaggi and Rossi are wheel to wheel (130 thousandths.) Capirossi and Gibernau watch the Gods do battle at a distance of just over half a second.

Lap 12:

Capirossi makes a mistake, so Gibernau goes third.

Half distance (lap 14):

Rossi takes the lead at the end of the straight, comfortably throwing his bike through the corners, as he dishes out a second to Biaggi, who is already nothing more than a spectator. Gibernau is third, but 3"437 down. The master has struck yet again.

Lap 23:

It had been a long time since a MotoGP race had been so dull, in terms of Rossi's domination. All eyes are on the battle for third place between Gibernau and Capirossi.

Finish (lap 28):

Capirossi makes his move at the end of the straight, then has a major moment, which gives Gibernau some breathing space and allows him to get ahead at the chicane. But it is not for long, as Capirossi comes through the final turn glued to Sete's back wheel. Once on the straight, the amazing power of the Desmosedici does the necessary and so the podium is an all-Italian affair, with another win for Rossi and a turning point in championship terms.

Championship:

Rossi has a 46 point lead, the equivalent of having almost two races in hand for the reigning world champion.

It's the big Rossi Circus!

After his oh so important win at Brno, Valentino Rossi returned from the break with his morale pumped up to the maximum. As he arrived in the Estoril paddock, his first concern was to stick a note on the bodywork of his Honda RC211V, the bike that everyone wanted...
The world champion had suddenly felt an urgent need to win, after a lean patch which had lasted from the Italian to Czech Republic Grands Prix. He had nevertheless picked up two second places and two thirds including the one which came after being penalised in the British Grand Prix. In Brno, he had celebrated his return to the top step of the podium by dressing up as a convict for his lap of honour. As a memento of this stunt, he placed a sticker on his bike which showed a convict's identity card. It was a sign, just a little sign that the great Rossi Circus was back on the road, both on the track where he had a perfect race and behind the scenes. It was that time of year again as autumn approached. The kings of the track were no longer the sole focal point of interest, as this was the moment when managers and wheeler-dealers stepped up to the mark to talk to the money men and the decision makers.
The talking was all the more frenetic as the lynchpin of the game, Valentino Rossi, had not decided on his berth for next season and had yet to extend his contract with Honda. Hence the arrival in the paddock of the big boss of the marque's competitions department, the honourable Sugura Kanezawa, who held a conference the day before the race.
Speculation was rife, much of it, total invention.
Therefore everyone turned up, keen to hear what Kanezawa had to say, given that he pulled the strings in this show. It was his decision who would be the happy beneficiaries of

the works Honda bikes. The questioning continued throughout the paddock. Had Rossi signed? Was it true Gibernau had still not said yes to his employers? Was Yamaha's sponsor really trying to

Valentino Rossi celebrates another win with a burn-out.

get Rossi? What were all the discussions about?
Nothing much apparently. All that came out of this media show, Japanese-style, was the usual long and totally prepared speech, heard so often in the past. There was one important number in the middle of it all: seven men had got their hands on the RC211V in 2003, the great five cylinder Honda which was dominating the MotoGP category. Next year, there would only be six. As for the rest of the speech, it covered such subjects as combustion chambers and the use

of silicon oil in this great piece of racing kit.
Rossi? Biaggi? Gibernau? "We are not talking about our riders, this is a technical presentation..." That was the end of it, as the Japanese

are experts at keeping quiet and avoiding embarrassing questions.

The duel with Biaggi went on for a few laps!

250cc

Tony Elias hard at work: total domination.

Portuguese Grand Prix
7 September 2003 / Estoril - 4,182 m

STARTING GRID

1.	24	T. Elias	Aprilia	1'42.255
2.	7	R. De Puniet	Aprilia	1'42.458
3.	50	S. Guintoli	Aprilia	1'42.554
4.	54	M. Poggiali	Aprilia	1'42.675
5.	5	S. Porto	Honda	1'42.682
6.	21	F. Battaini	Aprilia	1'42.892
7.	3	R. Rolfo	Honda	1'42.902
8.	10.	F. Gonzales-Nieto	Aprilia	1'43.009
9.	8	N. Matsudo	Yamaha	1'43.149
10.	6	A. Debon	Honda	1'43.340
11.	14	A. West	Aprilia	1'44.001
12.	34	E. Bataille	Honda	1'44.272
13.	9	H. Marchand	Aprilia	1'44.401
14.	57	C. Davies	Aprilia	1'44.835
15.	15	C. Gemmel	Honda	1'44.890
16.	26	A. Baldolini	Aprilia	1'44.924
17.	11	J. Olive	Aprilia	1'44.939
18.	28	D. Heidolf	Aprilia	1'45.016
19.	16	J. Stigefelt	Aprilia	1'45.171
20.	36	E. Nigon	Aprilia	1'45.227
21.	33	H. Faubel	Aprilia	1'45.494
22.	96	J. Smrz	Honda	1'45.889
23.	52	L. Pesek	Yamaha	1'46.021
24.	51	F. Watz	Yamaha	1'46.243
25.	66	V. Kallio	Yamaha	1'47.266
26.	40	A. Molina	Aprilia	1'47.298
27.	41	M. Praia	Yamaha	1'47.884
28.	18	H. vd Lagemaat	Honda	1'48.126
29.	98	K. Poensgen	Honda	1'48.181

RACE: 26 LAPS = 108.732 KM

1.	Toni Elias	44'37.770 (146.179 km/h)
2.	Manuel Poggiali	+ 4"731
3.	Randy De Puniet	+ 5"987
4.	Roberto Rolfo	+ 4"470
5.	Sebastian Porto	+ 25"023
6.	Franco Battaini	+ 25"273
7.	Sylvain Guintoli	+ 27"791
8.	Naoki Matsudo	+ 27"913
9.	Alfonso Gonzales-Nieto	+ 43"047
10.	Anthony West	+ 43"112
11.	Alex Debon	+ 44"796
12.	Eric Bataille	+ 1'10.765
13.	Hector Faubel	+ 1'11.702
14.	Alex Baldolini	+ 1'11.714
15.	Christian Gemmel	+ 1'13.983
16.	Erwan Nigon	+ 1'19.238
17.	Dirk Heidolf	+ 1'36.515
18.	Vesa Kallio	+ 1 lap
19.	Alvaro Molina	+ 1 lap
20.	Chaz Davies	+ 1 lap
21.	Frederik Watz	+ 1 lap
22.	Miguel Praia	+ 1 lap
23.	Henk vd Lagemaat	+ 1 lap

Fastest lap: Poggiali, in 1'42.215 (147.289 km/h). New record.
Previous best: Kato, in 1'42.285 (147.188 km/h/2001).
Outright fastest lap: Porto, in 1'41.708 (148.023 km/h/2002).

CHAMPIONSHIP

1.	M. Poggiali	165 (3 wins)
2.	T. Elias	151 (3 wins)
3.	R. Rolfo	148 (1 win)
4.	R. De Puniet	146 (2 wins)
5.	A. Gonzales-Nieto	143 (1 win)
6.	F. Battaini	117
7.	A. West	110 (1 win)
8.	S. Porto	109
9.	S. Guintoli	75
10.	N. Matsudo	75

Runners and riders:

The 250 scene is calmer than its little 125 sister, with one minor exception – Pesek has now definitively replaced his compatriot, Hules in the Yamaha Kurz team – all the riders who began the season are still on parade. There are four wildcards: Portugal's Miguel Praia, Spain's Alvaro Molina, Sweden's Frederik Watz and Finland's Vesa Kallio.

Qualifying:

Elias secures pole position while sitting out the final session. In great form on the first day, the young Spaniard falls on Saturday after colliding with a wildcard. He suffers a neck injury and serious shock, so misses the second qualifying session, but his time is still good enough, especially as De Puniet was troubled with traffic on his best Saturday afternoon lap. There is a second Frenchman on the front row, as Guintoli is third quickest ahead of Poggiali. The best Honda is Porto in fifth.

Start:

Elias is promptest away, in front of Porto, De Puniet and Debon. Katja Poensgen has a serious fall. Elias crosses the line 0"217 ahead of Porto, Rolfo, who gets a big fright on the next lap and Poggiali.

Lap 4:

Elias makes a mistake allowing Porto to lead, 0"614 in front of De Puniet.

Lap 7:

The top five are covered by 1"228, in the order, Porto, De Puniet, who is about to take the lead, Elias, Poggiali and Rolfo.

Lap 10:

Porto gets level with De Puniet down the straight, forcing the Frenchman to go wide and drop to third. Elias makes the most of it to retake the lead.

Half distance (lap 13):

Still Elias. The Spaniard who was out of action the day before had dominated the warm-up and was now 1"202 ahead of his pursuers: Porto, Poggiali, Rolfo and De Puniet. Then there is a big gap, as sixth placed Battaini is almost 8 seconds behind the lead group.

Lap 16:

Elias is in a different league to the rest and is 2"314 ahead of the small chasing pack.

Lap 19:

Poggiali is second, but over 4 seconds down on the leader.

Finish (lap 26):

Elias was never bothered and all interest on the final lap centred on the battle for second place, with Porto trying a daring move at the uphill chicane. The Argentine collides with Rolfo, falls and De Puniet is the beneficiary, taking third place.

Championship:

Poggiali heads Elias by 14 points. "Fonsi" Nieto is fifth, 22 points down.

A fright, but no harm done for Manuel Poggiali.

Pablo Nieto – Barbera: 22 thousandths separate the two team-mates.

Runners and riders:

The game of musical chairs has begun. Vincent, the Number One man, has found employment again with Aprilia, in the Sterilgarda team, where he replaces Ui. The Japanese rider has popped up at Freesoul, the team owned by the Belgian, Olivier Liegeois who used to run young Frenchman, Di Meglio. Ui has a second Gilera. The Ajo camp confirms it is taking legal action against Kallio and Ballerini has the ride to the end of the season.

Qualifying:

De Angelis is in mourning for one of his supporters, who died

The comeback: Arnaud Vincent finds a ride with Aprilia.

a week earlier in an Italian championship race at Mugello. Nevertheless, he is in top form on Friday and on Saturday he has half a second in hand over the rest of the field; something that has not been seen in this category for a very long time. The surprise of the day comes from Lorenzo, who is third, squeezing his Derbi between Pedrosa's Honda and Perugini's Aprilia. Stoner was

given the green light to ride on the Thursday, falls again on Friday afternoon, after his engine seized. As a result, his collar bone, already broken in Brno, is damaged again and the Australian pulls out.

Start:

De Angelis and Pedrosa make the best getaway, Ui and Simoncelli fall and retire and the race is red flagged.

Second start:

Perugini shows the quickest reflexes, ahead of Talmacsi and Pedrosa, who moves into second place. Cecchinello and Borsoi fall.

Lap 2:

Pedrosa takes the lead, ahead of De Angelis, Perugini and Talmacsi.

Lap 7:

Luthi falls, having been ninth. Pedrosa has 196 thousandths in hand over De Angelis and 382 over Perugini.

Lap 10:

Pedrosa is overwhelmed by a

Constant attention: injured three weeks earlier in Brno, Thomas Luthi insisted on riding in Portugal.

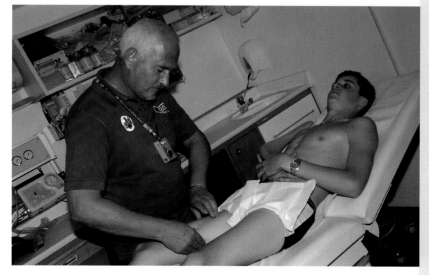

swarm of Aprilias. De Angelis leads from Perugini and Barbera. Jenkner retires.

Half distance (lap 12):

Barbera has taken the lead on the previous lap and now leads by 0"478 from Perugini, who makes a mistake.

Lap 14:

Perugini falls, forcing Dovizioso to cut through the gravel trap. Pedrosa leads Pablo Nieto, Barbera and De Angelis; the four men separated by 282 thousandths.

Lap 19:

Barbera still leads Nieto, De Angelis and Pedrosa. Vincent is fifth.

Finish (lap 23):

Pablo Nieto slipstreams team-mate Barbera to snatch victory on the line. It is his first GP win. The Nieto family thus joins the names Pagani, Graham, Roberts and Rossi in the history books, as families where father and son have won at the highest level.

Championship:

Pedrosa benefits from Perugini's retirement as he now leads by 38 points.

Portuguese Grand Prix
7 September 2003 / Estoril - 4,182 m

STARTING GRID

Pos	No	Rider	Bike	Time
1.	15	A. De Angelis	Aprilia	1'45.580
2.	3	D. Pedrosa	Honda	1'46.106
3.	48	J. Lorenzo	Derbi	1'46.323
4.	7	S. Perugini	Aprilia	1'46.323
5.	22	P. Nieto	Aprilia	1'46.330
6.	58	M. Simoncelli	Aprilia	1'46.414
7.	23	G. Borsoi	Aprilia	1'46.449
8.	34	A. Dovizioso	Honda	1'46.479
9.	17	S. Jenkner	Aprilia	1'46.739
10.	79	G. Talmacsi	Aprilia	1'46.793
11.	4	L. Cecchinello	Aprilia	1'46.800
12.	41	Y. Ui	Gilera	1'46.901
13.	1	A. Vincent	Aprilia	1'46.913
14.	12	T. Lüthi	Honda	1'46.967
15.	8	M. Azuma	Honda	1'47.009
16.	6	M. Giansanti	Aprilia	1'47.055
17.	33	S. Bianco	Gilera	1'47.165
18.	24	S. Corsi	Honda	1'47.186
19.	36	M. Kallio	KTM	1'47.246
20.	31	J. Simon	Malaguti	1'47.303
21.	19	A. Bautista	Aprilia	1'47.386
22.	80	H. Barbera	Aprilia	1'47.392
23.	10	R. Locatelli	KTM	1'47.456
24.	60	M. Angeloni	Honda	1'47.611
25.	32	F. Lai	Malaguti	1'47.656
26.	27	C. Stoner	Aprilia	1'47.805 (*)
27.	42	G. Pellino	Aprilia	1'47.913
28.	50	A. Ballerini	Honda	1'48.915
29.	93	M. Manna	Aprilia	1'48.953
30.	11	M. Sabbatani	Aprilia	1'49.008
31.	88	R. Harms	Aprilia	1'49.149
32.	70	S. Gadea	Aprilia	1'49.207
33.	26	E. Alzamora	Derbi	1'49.287
34.	69	D. Bonache	Honda	1'49.516
35.	78	P. Lenart	Honda	1'49.586
36.	25	I. Toth	Honda	1'49.727
37.	81	I. Ortega	Aprilia	1'50.983

(*): Did not race – injured.

RACE: 23 LAPS = 96.186 KM (*)

Pos	Rider	Time
1.	Pablo Nieto	41'08.307 (140.286 km/h)
2.	Hector Barbera	+ 0"022
3.	Alex De Angelis	+ 0"308
4.	Daniel Pedrosa	+ 0"560
5.	Arnaud Vincent	+ 3"326
6.	Jorge Lorenzo	+ 8"143
7.	Gabor Talmacsi	+ 8"287
8.	Andrea Dovizioso	+ 13"353
9.	Simone Corsi	+ 13"574
10.	Mirko Giansanti	+ 13"869
11.	Roberto Locatelli	+ 24"879
12.	Fabrizio Lai	+ 39"570
13.	Masao Azuma	+ 46"623
14.	Stefano Bianco	+ 46"983
15.	Alvaro Bautista	+ 47"176
16.	Mattia Angeloni	+ 47"278
17.	Manuel Manna	+ 47"614
18.	Sergio Gadea	+ 1'22.395
19.	Emilio Alzamora	+ 1'25.014
20.	Ismael Ortega	+ 1'25.533
21.	Max Sabbatani	+ 1'26.476

(*): Fourteenth across the finish line, Finland's Mika Kallio was disqualified for being under the minimum weight limit.

Fastest lap: Barbera, in 1'46.225 (141.729 km/h/New record).
Previous best: Ui, in 146.329 (141.590 km/h/2001).
Outright fastest lap: De Angelis, in 1'45.580 (142.595 km/h/2003).

CHAMPIONSHIP

Pos	Rider	Points
1.	D. Pedrosa	175 (4 wins)
2.	S. Perugini	137 (2 wins)
3.	A. De Angelis	124
4.	A. Dovizioso	120
5.	P. Nieto	113 (1 win)
6.	L. Cecchinello	105 (1 win)
7.	S. Jenkner	98 (1 win)
8.	H. Barbera	98 (1 win)
9.	Y. Ui	71
10.	M. Giansanti	66

RIO
Jacarepagua

"Sleeping Indian" is the name of this amazing mountain which dominates Jacarepagua, but it is unperturbed by the arrival of two newcomers, in the shape of former Superbike world champions, Troy Bayliss and Colin Edwards.

For his home GP, Alexandre Barros was presented with a new Shark helmet in special colours (above) while Roberto Rolfo (opposite) was unable to do much about the speed of Poggiali's Aprilia.

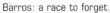
Barros: a race to forget.

Doctor Rossi gives a demonstration.

Rio Grand Prix
20 September 2003
Jacarepaguá - 4,933 m

STARTING GRID

1.	46	V. Rossi	Honda	1'49.038
2.	65	L. Capirossi	Ducati	1'49.340
3.	15	S. Gibernau	Honda	1'49.808
4.	3	M. Biaggi	Honda	1'49.876
5.	12	T. Bayliss	Ducati	1'50.042
6.	56	S. Nakano	Yamaha	1'50.171
7.	69	N. Hayden	Honda	1'50.679
8.	11	T. Ukawa	Honda	1'50.684
9.	6	M. Tamada	Honda	1'50.775
10.	7	C. Checa	Yamaha	1'50.856
11.	4	A. Barros	Yamaha	1'50.876
12.	45	C. Edwards	Aprilia	1'51.007
13.	8	G. McCoy	Kawasaki	1'51.179
14.	19	O. Jacque	Yamaha	1'51.385
15.	23	R. Kiyonari	Honda	1'51.500
16.	33	M. Melandri	Yamaha	1'51.566
17.	9	N. Aoki	Proton 4T	1'51.576
18.	21	J. Hopkins	Suzuki	1'51.802 (*)
19.	10	K. Roberts	Suzuki	1'51.839
20.	41	N. Haga	Aprilia	1'51.870
21.	99	J. McWilliams	Proton 4T	1'52.180
22.	88	A. Pitt	Kawasaki	1'52.715
23.	52	D. De Gea	Harris WCM	1'53.373
24.	35	C. Burns	Harris WCM	1'54.667

(*): Pulls out of race (after qualifying accident on Friday).

RACE: 24 LAPS = 118.392 KM

1.	Valentino Rossi	44'36.633 (159.234 km/h)
2.	Sete Gibernau	+ 3"109
3.	Makoto Tamada	+ 7"298
4.	Massimiliano Biaggi	+ 9"235
5.	Nicky Hayde	+ 11"165
6.	Loris Capirossi	+ 14"826
7.	Tohru Ukawa	+ 17"361
8.	Shinya Nakano	+ 21"239
9.	Carlos Checa	+ 21"522
10.	Troy Bayliss	+ 22"971
11.	Marco Melandri	+ 32"910
12.	Alexandre Barros	+ 40"136
13.	Colin Edwards	+ 54"099
14.	Noriyuki Haga	+ 57"234
15.	Ryuichi Kiyonari	+ 57"678
16.	Jeremy McWilliams	+ 1'06.069
17.	Kenny Roberts	+ 1'09.444
18.	Andrew Pitt	+ 1'22.463
19.	David De Gea	+ 1 lap

Fastest lap: Rossi, in 1'50.453 (160.781 km/h).
New record.
Previous best: Okada, in 1'51.928 (158.662 km/h/1997).
Outright fastest lap: Rossi, in 1'49.038 (162.867 km/h/2003).

CHAMPIONSHIP

1.	V. Rossi	262 (6 wins)
2.	S. Gibernau	211 (4 wins)
3.	M. Biaggi	174 (1 win)
4.	L. Capirossi	123 (1 win)
5.	T. Bayliss	112
6.	T. Ukawa	94
7.	C. Checa	93
8.	N. Hayden	85
9.	A. Barros	80
10.	S. Nakano	77

Runners and Riders:
All present and correct apart from some recurrent fitness concerns for Barros. Back home, the Brazilian has consulted another specialist, who has found a lesion in the tendon of his right shoulder. Normally, it would require an operation. Nevertheless, the Gauloises Yamaha rider decides to ride in his GP and wants to finish the season prior to heading for the operating table. There are long faces in the Yamaha camp: with the exception of Nakano, all the tuning fork marque riders are openly criticising their equipment. Melandri reckons it might even be better for the team to miss a few races to concentrate on fixing the problems!

Qualifying:
Biaggi is quickest on Friday and the atmosphere is electric, but Rossi has it his own way on Saturday. The day is marred by several falls: two for Jacque within seven minutes. Gibernau takes a heavy tumble on the final lap, as does John Hopkins. The Suzuki rider is forced to pull out on Saturday morning with multiple bruising.

Start:
Capirossi's Ducati flies off the line, but Gibernau soon takes the lead ahead of the Desmosedici rider, Rossi, Biaggi and Hayden. At the end of a Wayne Rainey-style opening lap, the Spaniard has a 714 thousandths lead over Rossi and is 855 ahead of Capirossi.

A first podium for Makoto Tamada and a first for Bridgestone in the senior category.

Lap 7:
Gibernau and Rossi, separated by 336 thousands, have pulled out a slight advantage over the chasing pack, which is now led by Biaggi. Capirossi is fourth ahead of Tamada, who sets the fastest race lap up to that point. Jacque pits with pain in an ankle.

Lap 9:
Mr. Rossi obviously feels the pace is not quick enough and takes the lead, crossing the line 762 thousandths in front of Gibernau, setting a lap record in the process.

Half distance (lap 12):
Aoki retires. Thanks to his Bridgestones, Tamada shines in the hot conditions (remember Mugello) and passes Biaggi for third place. Rossi now leads Gibernau by 2"610.

Lap 15:
McCoy retires. Hayden passes Capirossi to go fifth.

Finish (lap 24):
Rossi is enjoying himself, pulling off some incredible slides, out on his own, having demolished the opposition.

Championship:
With a 51 point lead, equivalent to having two races in hand, the reigning champion has made a significant step forward towards keeping his title.

Paths cross in Rio

It was a case of the destinies of men crossing in Rio. Seen as a film, it was not so much a French art house movie of artistic quality, but more of a formulaic type of picture. Rather than being shot in 8 millimetre, it was fought out to the thousandth of a second. It was a love story between two riders and one circuit, between two men and a city, between two champions in a time that would never be forgotten.

A few years ago, the Rio man was Olivier Jacque. The Frenchman had taken his first 250 GP victory at the Jacarepagua circuit, his first win at the highest level. That day back in 1996, he realised he would soon be crowned world champion, but it took him four years to achieve it. Yes, Olivier Jacque was indeed the man of Rio.

"Was," because now that title belonged to Valentino Rossi, who on the eve of this September's race had won six times on this track, not far from the posh parts of this marvellous Brazilian city, far from the misery of the favelas.

Valentino was strong, far too strong for his rivals and too strong for his mate, Sete Gibernau. He also outclassed the surprising Makoto Tamada, the Japanese rider who gave Bridgestone its first podium in the top category. Everyone on the track was powerless to deal with him once Rossi decided to go for it and dash everyone's hopes. He set about picking up the maximum number of points as quickly as possible as he headed for another title, so that he could concentrate on his 2004 future.

In Brazil, just as he had done in Portugal two weeks earlier, he dished it out to the opposition. At Estoril, he taught Max Biaggi a lesson. In Rio, he raised Gibernau's hopes for a moment before attacking when he felt the pace was not quick enough.

Rossi, perfection in riding form.

Then, he just disappeared into the distance, not wishing to hang around for the others to react. In Brazil as in Portugal, he was untouchable, as was the Honda RC211V which filled the top five places. It was as simple as that, although the burning question of the day was not when Valentino would take the title – probably in Malaysia, but what he and his entourage would decide about the future.

It was the question on everyone's lips. As for the former master of Rio, Oliver Jacque limped out of the Jacarepagua circuit, having retired in pain from a practice crash. All Valentino's rivals were getting fed up with making do with the scraps from his table and they really were praying that Rossi would soon decide to try his hand somewhere else.

Rossi has fun, while Melandri and his Yamaha colleagues moan: the 2003 season in one picture.

250cc

STARTING GRID

1.	24	T. Elias	Aprilia	1'53.457
2.	54	M. Poggiali	Aprilia	1'53.589
3.	3	R. Rolfo	Honda	1'53.827
4.	7	R. De Puniet	Aprilia	1'53.832
5.	10	F. Gonzales-Nieto	Aprilia	1'53.872
6.	5	S. Porto	Honda	1'53.876
7.	50	S. Guintoli	Aprilia	1'54.017
8.	21	F. Battaini	Aprilia	1'54.282
9.	8	N. Matsudo	Yamaha	1'55.432
10.	33	H. Faubel	Aprilia	1'55.502
11.	36	E. Nigon	Aprilia	1'55.864
12.	9	H. Marchand	Aprilia	1'55.865
13.	6	A. Debon	Honda	1'56.205
14.	11	J. Olive	Aprilia	1'56.212
15.	57	C. Davies	Aprilia	1'56.227
16.	14	A. West	Aprilia	1'56.305
17.	16	J. Stigefelt	Aprilia	1'56.339
18.	26	A. Baldolini	Aprilia	1'56.524
19.	34	E. Bataille	Honda	1'56.539
20.	28	D. Heidolf	Aprilia	1'56.640
21.	52	L. Pesek	Yamaha	1'57.425
22.	13	J. Hules	Honda	1'57.607
23.	15	C. Gemmel	Honda	1'57.613
24.	18	H. vd Lagemaat	Honda	2'00.061
29.	98	K. Poensgen	Honda	2'00.167 (*)

(*): Pulls out of race: the German was still suffering from his fall in Portugal.

RACE: 22 LAPS = 108.526 KM

1.	Manuel Poggiali	42'09.055 (154.482 km/h)
2.	Roberto Rolfo	+ 12"901
3.	Randy De Puniet	+ 12"965
4.	Sylvain Guintoli	+ 25"317
5.	Naoki Matsudo	+ 47"468
6.	Hector Faubel	+ 55"694
7.	Joan Olive	+ 58"264
8.	Anthony West	+ 58"339
9.	Chaz Davies	+ 1'00.193
10.	Eric Bataille	+ 1'02.606
11.	Alex Debon	+ 1'03.500
12.	Erwan Nigon	+ 1'09.904
13.	Johan Stigefelt	+ 1'14.199
14.	Dirk Heidolf	+ 1'14.370
15.	Jaroslav Hules	+ 1'16.913
16.	Christian Gemmel	+ 1'17.037
17.	Lukas Pesek	+ 1'19.838
18.	Toni Elias	+ 1'27.198
19.	Henk vd Lagemaat	+ 1 lap

Fastest lap: Poggiali, in 1'54.215 (155.485 km/h). New record.
Previous best: Rossi, in 1'54.230 (155.465 km/h/1999).
Outright fastest lap: Elias, in 1'53.457 (156.524 km/h/2003).

CHAMPIONSHIP

1.	M. Poggiali	190 (4 wins)
2.	R. Rolfo	168 (1 win)
3.	R. De Puniet	162 (2 wins)
4.	T. Elias	151 (3 wins)
5.	A. Gonzales-Nieto	143 (1 win)
6.	A. West	118 (1 win)
7.	F. Battaini	117
8.	S. Porto	109
9.	S. Guintoli	88
10.	N. Matsudo	86

Runners and riders:
As boss of the Czech Elit team, Daniel M. Epp has had his patience tried to the limit. Very disappointed with the lack of fire shown by his 250 rider, Jakub Smrz, he decided to dump him the day after the Portuguese GP. Jaroslav Hules is now entrusted with the Honda.

Qualifying:
Toni Elias is on top of his game on Friday and Saturday. Roberto Rolfo, who knows he is on a damage limitation exercise in Rio, prior to getting an evolution Honda in Motegi, qualifies third, with Manuel Poggiali threading between the two of them. The usual first eight (Elias, Poggiali, Rolfo, De Puniet, Gonzales-Nieto, Porto, Guintoli and Battaini) are all within less than 9 tenths. Further back however, there is a big gap, because Matsudo is a second down on Battaini. Suffering with back pains after her

...and it will be Manuel Poggiali, who thus pulls out a considerable lead in the championship.

fall in the Portuguese GP, Katja Poensgen pulls out.

Start:
Rolfo, Porto and Elias do it best, ahead of Fonsi Nieto, Poggiali, De Puniet and Guintoli. At the end of the opening lap, Rolfo leads his Honda team-mate, Sebastian Porto, by 0"122. Elias, Poggiali and Gonzales-Nieto follow.

Lap 2:
Poggiali has taken the lead from Tony Elias.

Lap 3:
Alfonso Gonzales-Nieto has a technical problem

De Puniet, Guintoli and the pack: the Frenchmen finished second and third.

Elias-Poggiali: only one will make it to the finish...

and, at the same time, last year's winner, Porto, falls, as does Battaini. When the dust settles, Poggiali leads Elias by 0"195, Rolfo by 0"880 and De Puniet by 1"820. Fonsi pits.

Lap 9:
De Puniet passes Rolfo. Out in front, Poggiali now leads Elias by 0"412. The third duo, fighting over fifth place, is made up of Guintoli and Matsudo.

Half distance (lap 11):
The gap between Poggiali and Elias is 0"382. The De Puniet – Rolfo duo is six seconds down, with the Italian Honda rider about to take the upper hand, just as Elias takes the lead.

Lap 15:
Poggiali momentarily takes the lead, but Elias passes him when he leaves a tiny door open and the two men touch.

Lap 19:
Poggiali leads again and De Puniet is ahead of Rolfo.

Finish (lap 22):
With just 169 thousandths separating them as they embark on the final lap, Elias tries one last desperate move round the outside at the end of the straight and falls, leaving Poggiali to cruise to a comfortable win.

Championship:
Poggiali has done extremely well out of this weekend as he emerges with a 32 point lead over Rolfo and a further six in hand over De Puniet.

Runners and riders:
Casey Stoner, who had quit at the Portuguese GP, is back. Changes in the Metasystem camp for the Bridgestone-shod Honda, as after Englishman Camier lost the ride, so too does Hungary's Lenart. So, Italy's Michele Danese makes his GP debut and it's a return for France's Di Meglio, the biggest loser from the game of musical chairs kicked off by the divorce between KTM and Vincent.

Qualifying:
Friday morning's practice is run on a damp track. In the afternoon, as usual, De Angelis is quickest. However, when the sun returns on Saturday, Pedrosa has the last word. The top thirteen are all covered by just 893 thousandths of a second and on the slowing down lap at the end of the decisive session, Borsoi crashes heavily into Perugini, fortunately without injury to either party.

Start:
Pedrosa gets it wrong, while Talmacsi pulls off the perfect start, ahead of Barbera and Dovizioso. As they cross the line for the first time, the Hungarian leads De Angelis by 0"822. Then come Barbera, Dovizioso, Stoner, Lorenzo, Perugini, Luthi and Vincent. Pedrosa is twelfth.

Lap 3:
Talmacsi and De Angelis are

A Derbi – Jorge Lorenzo – leads a GP, a sight not seen for quite a while.

wheel to wheel (0"170) and lead the chasing pack by 1.6 seconds, with Barbera leading the chase, but soon to be caught out by Pedrosa.

Lap 5:
Pedrosa is flying and the Spaniard takes the lead ahead of De Angelis and Talmacsi.

Lap 7:
Pedrosa still leads, but Stoner has caught the lead group, with four of them within 0"610. The second group is led by Barbera.

Half distance (lap 10):
De Angelis has just taken the lead, heading Pedrosa by 0"318. Stoner is third, ahead of Talmacsi, Lorenzo, Nieto, Dovizioso and Perugini; all eight of them running in convoy.

Lap 12:
A sight not seen for some time now – a Derbi leads the field, with Jorge Lorenzo on board.

Lap 16:
De Angelis takes control again, but Lorenzo and Stoner

are chasing him down aggressively, with the Australian charging into the lead shortly after. The battle between the top seven is fantastic, while Talmacsi and Barbera have been dropped.

Finish (lap 21):
Jorge Lorenzo had performed extraordinarily all race long to take his first win.

Championship:
Pedrosa might be beaten, but the calculator shows he he continues to extend his lead, as he now heads Perugini by 42 points.

Flat out between a concrete wall and a steel barrier: De Angelis, Stoner and Lorenzo fight it out.

Rio Grand Prix
20 September 2003
Jacarepaguá - 4,933 m

STARTING GRID

1.	3	D. Pedrosa	Honda	1'58.052
2.	15	A. De Angelis	Aprilia	1'58.070
3.	34	A. Dovizioso	Honda	1'58.092
4.	79	G. Talmacsi	Aprilia	1'58.273
5.	48	J. Lorenzo	Derbi	1'58.352
6.	7	S. Perugini	Aprilia	1'58.614
7.	80	H. Barbera	Aprilia	1'58.644
8.	17	S. Jenkner	Aprilia	1'58.675
9.	27	C. Stoner	Aprilia	1'58.687
10.	23	G. Borsoi	Aprilia	1'58.812
11.	1	A. Vincent	Aprilia	1'58.827
12.	12	T. Lüthi	Honda	1'58.944
13.	4	L. Cecchinello	Aprilia	1'58.945
14.	22	P. Nieto	Aprilia	1'59.163
15.	6	M. Giansanti	Aprilia	1'59.213
16.	58	M. Simoncelli	Aprilia	1'59.469
17.	8	M. Azuma	Honda	1'59.488
18.	32	F. Lai	Malaguti	1'59.832
19.	24	S. Corsi	Honda	2'00.101
20.	19	A. Bautista	Aprilia	2'00.165
21.	10	R. Locatelli	KTM	2'00.247
22.	41	Y. Ui	Gilera	2'00.515
23.	36	M. Kallio	KTM	2'00.528
24.	31	J. Simon	Malaguti	2'00.593
25.	26	E. Alzamora	Derbi	2'00.598
26.	33	S. Bianco	Gilera	2'00.605
27.	25	I. Toth	Honda	2'00.819
28.	50	A. Ballerini	Honda	2'00.843
29.	63	M. Di Meglio	Honda	2'01.107
30.	88	R. Harms	Aprilia	2'01.169
31.	42	G. Pellino	Aprilia	2'01.275
32.	28	M. Danese	Honda	2'02.290
33.	11	M. Sabbatani	Aprilia	2'02.656

RACE: 21 LAPS = 103.593 km

1.	Jorge Lorenzo	41'51.624 (148.483 km/h)
2.	Casey Stoner	+ 0"232
3.	Alex De Angelis	+ 0"372
4.	Daniel Pedrosa	+ 0"589
5.	Pablo Nieto	+ 0"771
6.	Andrea Dovizioso	+ 0"899
7.	Stefano Perugini	+ 1"240
8.	Gabor Talmacsi	+ 3"835
9.	Hector Barbera	+ 4"117
10.	Steve Jenkner	+ 15"268
11.	Marco Simoncelli	+ 19"087
12.	Gino Borsoi	+ 19"445
13.	Arnaud Vincent	+ 19"584
14.	Mirko Giansanti	+ 19"673
15.	Thomas Lüthi	+ 20"466
16.	Alvaro Bautista	+ 27"902
17.	Roberto Locatelli	+ 27"992
18.	Lucio Cecchinello	+ 32"727
19.	Mika Kallio	+ 36"138
20.	Stefano Bianco	+ 40"544
21.	Youichi Ui	+ 41"610
22.	Simone Corsi	+ 49"890
23.	Robbin Harms	+ 50"136
24.	Fabrizio Lai	+ 50"179
25.	Julian Simon	+ 55"624
26.	Gioele Pellino	+ 1'00.747
27.	Michele Danese	+ 1'52.184

Fastest lap: Pedrosa, in 1'58.121 (150.344 km/h/New record).
Previous best: Giansanti, in 1'59.368 (148.773 km/h/2000).
Outright fastest lap: Poggiali, in 1'57.888 (150.641 km/h/2002).

CHAMPIONSHIP

1.	D. Pedrosa	188 (4 wins)
2.	S. Perugini	146 (2 wins)
3.	A. De Angelis	140
4.	A. Dovizioso	130
5.	P. Nieto	124 (1 win)
6.	L. Cecchinello	105 (2 wins)
7.	H. Barbera	105 (1 win)
8.	S. Jenkner	104 (1 win)
9.	C. Stoner	80
10.	Y. Ui	71

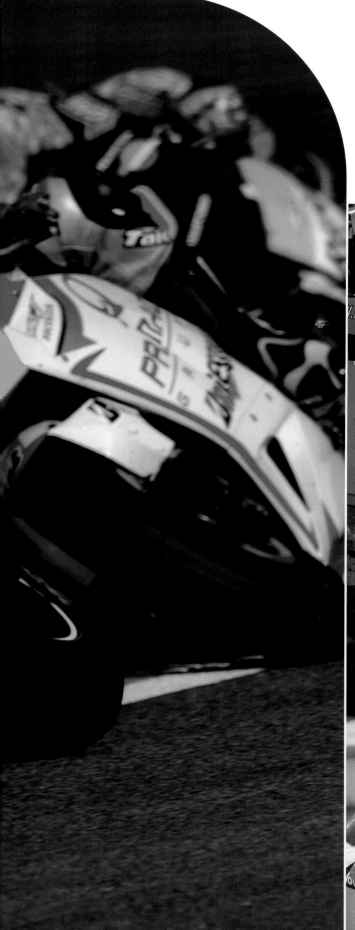

PACIFIC
Motegi

Another festival for the Honda RC211V on the track where it was developed. Although weakened with a fever, Sete Gibernau fought with Tamada for the whole race, with the final cut and thrust proving the downfall of the Japanese rider.

In Japan, the fans range from 1 to 99 years old (opposite) while the machine called 33 is nothing more than the cunning device used to fire Marco Melandri's Yamaha M1 into life.

MOTOGP

Pacific Grand Prix
5 October 2003 / Motegi - 4,801 m

STARTING GRID

1.	3	M. Biaggi	Honda	1'47.696
2.	6	M. Tamada	Honda	1'47.804
3.	46	V. Rossi	Honda	1'48.030
4.	15	S. Gibernau	Honda	1'48.457
5.	69	N. Hayden	Honda	1'48.618
6.	65	L. Capirossi	Ducati	1'48.695
7.	7	C. Checa	Yamaha	1'48.767
8.	4	A. Barros	Yamaha	1'48.780
9.	33	M. Melandri	Yamaha	1'48.882
10.	12	T. Bayliss	Ducati	1'48.964
11.	11	T. Ukawa	Honda	1'49.022
12.	56	S. Nakano	Yamaha	1'49.123
13.	45	C. Edwards	Aprilia	1'49.158
14.	43	A. Ryo	Suzuki	1'49.404
15.	19	O. Jacque	Yamaha	1'49.638
16.	21	J. Hopkins	Suzuki	1'49.650
17.	99	J. McWilliams	Proton 4T	1'50.273
18.	9	N. Aoki	Proton 4T	1'50.421
19.	10	K. Roberts	Suzuki	1'50.436
20.	23	R. Kiyonari	Honda	1'50.480
21.	8	G. McCoy	Kawasaki	1'50.677
22.	88	A. Pitt	Kawasaki	1'51.008
23.	25	T. Seriwaka	Moriwaki	1'51.112
24.	52	D. De Gea	Harris WCM	1'51.429
25.	41	N. Haga	Aprilia	1'51.505
26.	35	C. Burns	Harris WCM	1'53.133

RACE: 24 LAPS = 115.224 KM (*)

1.	Massimiliano Biaggi	43'57.590 (157.267 km/h)
2.	Valentino Rossi	+ 3"754
3.	Nicky Hayden	+ 5"641
4.	Sete Gibernau	+ 19"456
5.	Marco Melandri	+ 19"909
6.	Alexandre Barros	+ 20"938
7.	Tohru Ukawa	+ 22"307
8.	Loris Capirossi	+ 27"887
9.	Shinya Nakano	+ 41"731
10.	Akira Ryo	+ 50"106
11.	Ryuichi Kiyonari	+ 53"214
12.	Noriyuki Haga	+ 53"589
13.	Olivier Jacque	+ 1'05.620
14.	Nobuatsu Aoki	+ 1'07.535
15.	Kenny Roberts	+ 1'09.055
16.	Andrew Pitt	+ 1'11.533
17.	Colin Edwards	+ 1'27.583
18.	Tamaki Serizawa	+ 1'33.001
19.	David De Gea	+ 1 lap

(*): Makato Tamada, third past the chequered flag, was disqualified by the stewards for riding "in an irresponsible manner, putting other riders in danger."

Fastest lap: Rossi, in 1'48.885 (158.732 km/h). New record.
Previous best: Barros, in 1'49.947 (157.199 km/h/2002).
Outright fastest lap: Biaggi, in 1'47.696 (160.485 km/h/2003).

CHAMPIONSHIP

1.	V. Rossi	282 (6 wins)
2.	S. Gibernau	224 (4 wins)
3.	M. Biaggi	199 (2 wins)
4.	L. Capirossi	131 (1 win)
5.	T. Bayliss	112
6.	T. Ukawa	103
7.	N. Hayden	101
8.	C. Checa	93
9.	A. Barros	90
10.	S. Nakano	84

Runners and riders:
A third Suzuki is entered for Akiro Ryo. The bike has special suspension and a different engine configuration with the exhausts coming out the opposite side. Tamaki Serizawa enters the Honda RC211V engined Moriwaki. The two Yamaha M1 machines turn up wth an arty design, the work of Swiss designer, Claudio Colucci.

Qualifying:
Gibernau dominates the first day, but he has to fight off a heavy cold on Saturday. The hero of the day is Tamada: the Bridgestone runner is heading for his first ever pole, but Biaggi pulls out one of his trademark perfect laps to rob him of that achievement, although the prize watch which goes with pole is handed to the Pramac man who is almost his team-mate. Start: Gibernau makes a super start. At the first corner, Hopkins forgets to brake and takes out Bayliss and Checa, while Edwards loses over 30 seconds. Gibernau completes the opening lap just 9 thousandths ahead of Biaggi.

Lap 3:
Biaggi has just taken the lead. Tamada closes on the lead group and is the quickest man on the track. McWilliams falls.

Lap 4:
Rossi sets the quickest lap and is now second.

Lap 7:
Rossi goes through a gravel trap and drops to ninth. Biaggi leads Gibernau by 1"236.

Lap 8:
Tamada has finally got past

Tamada-Gibernau: a little bit further on, the Japanese rider will pull over to the left.

A fright for Biaggi. It would all go much better in the race.

Hayden and the Motegi crowd goes wild. Rossi goes by Melandri.

Lap 10:
Biaggi has now pulled out 2"302 over Gibernau, who is now coming under attack from the heroic Tamada. Rossi is already back to fifth.

Half distance (lap 12):
Biaggi still leads Gibernau by 2"645, followed by Tamada and Hayden. Rossi is the quickest man on track. He is now within three seconds of the group battling for second place.

Lap 16:
Rossi sets another lap record.

Lap 18:
There is now a great scrap between Gibernau, Hayden, Rossi and Tamada, while Biaggi is in control out in front.

Lap 19:
Rossi is third...no make that second, because in the space of two corners, he passes both Hayden and Gibernau!

Finish (lap 24):
Biaggi wins comfortably. Rossi had been magnificent, but he is still not world champion. Tamada finishes third but is disqualified for dangerous riding after his daring move on Gibernau.

Championship:
Rossi has not quite done it yet, even though he leads Gibernau by 58 points. The title (and the news of his move to Yamaha?) should all happen in Malaysia.

My first is a Honda, my second ...

When the new blue riband class of motorcycle racing was created and appropriately named MotoGP, only the most naïve of dreamers and those who never look to the past to find out about the future, would have been unaware that Honda would tackle the new discipline with a sheet of paper that was slightly less blank than that of the opposition. The biggest name in the world of motorcycles had plenty of four stroke experience and adopted a policy of setting up several permanent groups who worked in parallel and in competition with one another within the same company to look at all the various possibilities in terms of engine configurations. All this meant that Honda was the undoubted favourite as the sport embarked on this technical revolution. The rule changes attracted an ever growing number of major manufacturers, with Kawasaki already on board and a strong possibility that a sports technology giant like BMW might even join the fray.

The racing had already confirmed this to be the case last year, with Valentino Rossi proving completely dominant. Now, the giant simply had to increase the number of winning machines, which it did at the end of the 2002 season, with wins for Barros and strong showings from the late lamented Daijiro Kato. It carried on in 2003, with the arrival of Biaggi and Gibernau, the appearance of Tamada and his Bridgestone tyres and the promotion of Nicky Hayden, who had just handed the marque the US Superbike title.

Honda dominated the 2003 championship with Valentino Rossi and Sete Gibernau. It crushed the Japanese competition, as Yamaha had chronic difficulties, Suzuki and Kawazaki were simply no good and the Proton was too young. It also reacted to the startling debut of Ducati, who saw its Desmosedici win in the hands of Loris Capirossi in Barcelona as the red Italian machine proved competitive on a variety of different tracks.

At Motegi, where the RC211V had taken its first serious steps, all the honours went to Max Biaggi, who had ridden a perfect race. It had also been an impressive race for Rossi who staged a great comeback after his initial error and the very spectacular Tamada. He did not deserve to be excluded for his so called risky move on Gibernau on the final lap and Hayden was also there. It was almost a full house for the totally dominant 5 cylinder RC211V project which still shows signs of having plenty of room for improvement.

Biaggi had taken a real win, not like the one handed to him at Donington. As for Rossi, who looked set to take a fifth world title, the only uncertainty on the night of the Pacific GP was to know when the world champions entourage would confirm what everyone thought they had known for the past few days: namely that the best rider in the world would switch to Yamaha. That hopefully meant it would not always be Honda and its fabulous RC211V doing all the winning.

For once, the pupil, (Nicky Hayden) leads the master (Valentino Rossi).

250cc

STARTING GRID

1.	24	T. Elias	Aprilia	1'52.849
2.	21	F. Battaini	Aprilia	1'52.965
3.	7	R. De Puniet	Aprilia	1'53.247
4.	5	S. Porto	Honda	1'53.650
5.	50	S. Guintoli	Aprilia	1'53.713
6.	92	H. Aoyama	Honda	1'53.830
7.	54	M. Poggiali	Aprilia	1'53.868
8.	8	N. Matsudo	Yamaha	1'54.021
9.	67	T. Koyama	Yamaha	1'54.132
10.	55	Y. Takahashi	Honda	1'54.141
11.	3	R. Rolfo	Honda	1'54.385
12.	57	C. Davies	Aprilia	1'54.641
13.	6	A. Debon	Honda	1'54.680
14.	70	C. Kameya	Honda	1'54.714
15.	10	F. Gonzales-Nieto	Aprilia	1'55.095
16.	36	E. Nigon	Aprilia	1'55.164
17.	33	H. Faubel	Aprilia	1'55.300
18.	15	C. Gemmel	Honda	1'55.450
19.	9	H. Marchand	Aprilia	1'55.774
20.	69	M. Tokudome	Yamaha	1'55.811
21.	34	E. Bataille	Honda	1'55.949
22.	26	A. Baldolini	Aprilia	1'56.174
23.	14	A. West	Aprilia	1'56.231
24.	28	D. Heidolf	Aprilia	1'56.343
25.	52	L. Pesek	Yamaha	1'56.361
26.	96	J. Smrz	Honda	1'56.370
27.	16	J. Stigefelt	Aprilia	1'57.112
28.	11	J. Olive	Aprilia	1'57.329
29.	13	J. Hules	Honda	1'57.486
30.	18	H. vd Lagemaat	Honda	1'58.941

RACE: 23 LAPS = 110.423 KM

1.	Toni Elias	43'57.125 (150.740 km/h)
2.	Roberto Rolfo	+ 1"483
3.	Manuel Poggiali	+ 2"159
4.	Yuki Takahashi	+ 6"018
5.	Hiroshi Aoyama	+ 6"163
6.	Randy De Puniet	+ 20"407
7.	Naoki Matsudo	+ 25"938
8.	Alfonso Gonzales-Nieto	+ 28"417
9.	Alex Debon	+ 39"804
10.	Choujun Kameya	+ 39"919
11.	Chaz Davies	+ 49"703
12.	Christian Gemmel	+ 55"921
13.	Alex Baldolini	+ 1'01.015
14.	Dirk Heidolf	+ 1'03.387
15.	Masaki Tokudome	+ 1'03.530
16.	Hugo Marchand	+ 1'04.299
17.	Erwan Nigon	+ 1'04.621
18.	Jakub Smrz	+ 1'21.680
19.	Joan Olive	+ 1'44.192
20.	Henk vd Lagemaat	+ 1 lap

Fastest lap: Elias, in 1'53.612 (152.128 km/h).
Record: Nakano, in 1'52.253 (153.970 km/h/2000).
Outright fastest lap: Nakano, in 1'52.253 (153.970 km/h/2000).

CHAMPIONSHIP

1.	M. Poggiali	206 (4 wins)
2.	R. Rolfo	188 (1 win)
3.	T. Elias	176 (4 wins)
4.	R. De Puniet	172 (2 wins)
5.	A. Gonzales-Nieto	151 (1 win)
6.	A. West	118 (1 win)
7.	F. Battaini	117
8.	S. Porto	109
9.	N. Matsudo	95
10.	S. Guintoli	88

Runners and riders:

The German Katja Poensgen had cracked a bone in her left hand and was replaced by Jacub Smrz. The Hondas of Rolfo and Porto boasted new seat and tank units and there were several wild cards, including last year's hero, Takahashi.

Qualifying:

Poor De Puniet! The Frenchman who set the best time on Friday and repeated the performance on Saturday morning, falls on only the second lap of the afternoon qualifying session. Poggiali is suffering on this track and Gonzales-Nieto is in despair down in 15th place. De Puniet gets up with serious contusions to his left heel and hip, as well as an injured finger. It is Tony Elias, the other on-form man at the moment, who takes pole on his final lap, ahead of Battaini, De Puniet watching the session from the medical centre and Porto.

Start:

De Puniet gets away quickest, but he is too wide at the first turn. Porto, Elias and Rolfo make the most of it. Elias completes the opening lap 0"656 ahead of Porto, 0"954 ahead of Rolfo, while De Puniet is already 1"662 down, with championship leader Poggiali behind him.

Lap 3:

Battaini falls. Elias has a 1"541 lead over Porto, who is followed by Rolfo and the De Puniet-Poggiali duo.

Lap 6:

Elias has just set another fastest lap (but a long way off Nakano's three year old record!) and now has a 2"591 lead over Porto. Poggiali has passed De Puniet, who is gritting his teeth and hanging onto fourth.

Lap 10:

Guintoli falls. His compatriot De Puniet is now under pressure from Aoyama and Takahashi; two invited riders, who will soon get past him.

Poggiali-Rolfo: even on Honda's home turf, Roby was powerless.

Rolfo-like-clockwork: would it be enough faced with the speed of the Aprilias?

Half distance (lap 12):

Elias is now out on his own, 3"802 in hand over Porto and Rolfo who still lead Poggiali, now back in touch with the group. De Puniet is seventh.

Lap 13:

Poggiali has sorted out Porto and Rolfo. He is second, but over 4 seconds behind the leader.

Lap 19:

Porto falls, while Roberto Rolfo is still menacing Poggiali with Elias always out on his own.

Finish (lap 23):

Elias was never troubled. Rolfo took second place on the penultimate lap and kept it to the chequered flag.

Championship:

With Poggiali only third, the order closes up as Rolfo is within 18 points and Elias is 30 points off the leader.

Barbera (80) is not scared of Pedrosa: the young Spaniard takes his second GP win.

Runners and riders:

Five Japanese riders have wild cards: the Hiroaki brothers and Toshihisa Kuzuhara, Aoyama, Suma and Hatano. Masao Azuma (10 GP wins) announces that he will hang up his helmet come the end of the season. "The rules have changed. Today, only the young riders with a big enough budget get the good rides," explained the Japanese man.

Qualifying:

"Here, Dani is working on another planet," let slip the young Swiss rider, Thomas Luthi at the end of qualifying. Although beaten by Dovizioso on Friday, Pedrosa put on a fantastic performance on Saturday to be the only rider to break the 1'58 barrier. Second on the grid was Perugini, 822 thousandths slower.

Start:

Perfect reflexes from Pedrosa, but nevertheless, he is passed by Barbera and then Talmacsi. The championship leader retakes the lead and crosses the line 0"170 ahead of Barbera and Dovizioso is already 0"716 down. Perugini is only sixth.

Lap 4:

Alzamora and Pellino fall.

Pedrosa now leads second placed Dovizioso by 0"888.

Lap 6:

Cecchinello falls, having been fifteenth.

Lap 8:

Di Meglio falls. Dovizioso has closed to within 0"790 of Pedrosa.

Half distance (lap 10):

Pedrosa is in complete control. As Dovizioso appears to be fighting back, the Spaniard counterattacks immediately. At this point in the story, he leads the Italian by 2"467. Stoner is third, ahead of Barbera and Perugini.

Lap 14:

Pedrosa still out on his own, while behind him the others – Stoner, Barbera, Lorenzo and Dovizioso are tripping each other up. Borsoi (11th falls.)

Lap 16:

Technical problems (front fork) for the leader who is passed

by Stoner. Five of them are now in with a chance of victory: Pedrosa, Lorenzo, Stoner, Barbera and Dovizioso.

Lap 17:

Barbera has taken the lead. Pedrosa hangs on in fifth place and sees his title rival Perugini closing on him.

Lap 19:

Lorenzo falls at the chicane.

Lap 20:

Perugini passes Pedrosa.

Finish (lap 21):

Barbera, Stoner and Dovizioso are separated by just 91 thousandths as they embark on the final lap. The young Spaniard gets it right to take his second win of the season.

Championship:

Pedrosa had been heading for a profitable afternoon, given that Perugini was only sixth when the Spaniard was leading. But the Honda rider lost the edge although he still leads by 39 points.

Stoner, Barbera,
Dovizioso: champagne!

Pacific Grand Prix
5 October 2003 / Motegi - 4,801 m

STARTING GRID

1.	3	D. Pedrosa	Honda	1'57.736
2.	7	S. Perugini	Aprilia	1'58.558
3.	48	J. Lorenzo	Derbi	1'58.662
4.	80	H. Barbera	Aprilia	1'58.684
5.	34	A. Dovizioso	Honda	1'58.988
6.	22	P. Nieto	Aprilia	1'59.092
7.	4	L. Cecchinello	Aprilia	1'59.219
8.	15	A. De Angelis	Aprilia	1'59.286
9.	33	S. Bianco	Gilera	1'59.320
10.	27	C. Stoner	Aprilia	1'59.360
11.	23	G. Borsoi	Aprilia	1'59.378
12.	79	G. Talmacsi	Aprilia	1'59.393
13.	36	M. Kallio	KTM	1'59.437
14.	58	M. Simoncelli	Aprilia	1'59.448
15.	12	T. Lüthi	Honda	1'59.520
16.	17	S. Jenkner	Aprilia	1'59.620
17.	24	S. Corsi	Honda	1'59.737
18.	19	A. Bautista	Aprilia	1'59.756
19.	6	M. Giansanti	Aprilia	1'59.866
20.	10	R. Locatelli	KTM	1'59.916
21.	8	M. Azuma	Honda	2'00.076
22.	1	A. Vincent	Aprilia	2'00.381
23.	32	F. Lai	Malaguti	2'00.616
24.	41	Y. Ui	Gilera	2'00.849
25.	31	J. Simon	Malaguti	2'01.198
26.	63	M. Di Meglio	Honda	2'01.340
27.	65	T. Kuzuhara	Honda	2'01.564
28.	26	E. Alzamora	Derbi	2'01.596
29.	66	S. Aoyama	Honda	2'01.614
30.	50	A. Ballerini	Honda	2'01.618
31.	94	S. Suma	Honda	2'02.058
32.	25	I. Toth	Honda	2'02.131
33.	88	R. Harms	Aprilia	2'02.294
34.	42	G. Pellino	Aprilia	2'02.309
35.	11	M. Sabbatani	Aprilia	2'02.495
36.	59	H. Kuzuhara	Honda	2'02.569
37.	95	Y. Hatano	Honda	2'02.771
38.	28	M. Danese	Honda	2'03.345

RACE: 21 LAPS = 100.821 km

1.	Hector Barbera	41'54.483 (144.346 km/h)
2.	Casey Stoner	+ 0"164
3.	Andrea Dovizioso	+ 0"304
4.	Stefano Perugini	+ 2"731
5.	Steve Jenkner	+ 2"970
6.	Daniel Pedrosa	+ 3"215
7.	Mika Kallio	+ 3"264
8.	Pablo Nieto	+ 9"200
9.	Alex De Angelis	+ 13"016
10.	Thomas Lüthi	+ 13"195
11.	Mirko Giansanti	+ 13"353
12.	Alvaro Bautista	+ 19"848
13.	Masao Azuma	+ 20"107
14.	Gabor Talmacsi	+ 20"616
15.	Simone Corsi	+ 23"402
16.	Stefano Bianco	+ 24"840
17.	Youichi Ui	+ 30"548
18.	Fabrizio Lai	+ 47"008
19.	Arnaud Vincent	+ 52"431
20.	Andrea Ballerini	+ 52"675
21.	Shuhei Aoyama	+ 57"467
22.	Robbin Harms	+ 1'11.694
23.	Hiroaki Kuzuhara	+ 1'11.770
24.	Julian Simon	+ 1'13.195
25.	Sadahito Suma	+ 1'16.576
26.	Imre Toth	+ 1'28.964

Fastest lap: Lorenzo, in 1'58.545 (145.797 km/h).
Record: Pedrosa, in 1'58.354 (146.033 km/h/2002).
Outright fastest lap: Pedrosa, in 1'57.736 (146.799 km/h/2003).

CHAMPIONSHIP

1.	D. Pedrosa	198 (4 wins)
2.	S. Perugini	159 (2 wins)
3.	A. De Angelis	147
4.	A. Dovizioso	146
5.	P. Nieto	132 (1 win)
6.	H. Barbera	130 (2 wins)
7.	S. Jenkner	115 (1 win)
8.	L. Cecchinello	105 (2 wins)
9.	C. Stoner	100
10.	M. Giansanti	73

MALAYSIA
Sepang

The Tavullia mob in action on the lap of honour: Valentino Rossi's faithful fans dressed up as convicts and with title in the bag, have delivered him of the need to win. The world champion T-shirt (opposite) is a good reminder of Rossi's ability to totally dominate the opposition.

Malaysian Grand Prix
12 October 2003 / Sepang – 5.548 m

STARTING GRID

1.	46 V. Rossi	Honda	2'02.480
2.	7 C. Checa	Yamaha	2'02.885
3.	6 M. Tamada	Honda	2'03.138
4.	3 M. Biaggi	Honda	2'03.254
5.	56 S. Nakano	Yamaha	2'03.342
6.	65 L. Capirossi	Ducati	2'03.376
7.	15 S. Gibernau	Honda	2'03.381
8.	11 T. Ukawa	Honda	2'03.559
9.	69 N. Hayden	Honda	2'03.564
10.	10 K. Roberts	Suzuki	2'03.936
11.	12 T. Bayliss	Ducati	2'04.000
12.	4 A. Barros	Yamaha	2'04.050
13.	45 C. Edwards	Aprilia	2'04.390
14.	33 M. Melandri	Yamaha	2'04.832
15.	43 A. Ryo	Suzuki	2'05.043
16.	8 G. McCoy	Kawasaki	2'05.084
17.	41 N. Haga	Aprilia	2'05.150
18.	99 J. McWilliams	Proton 4T	2'05.365
19.	9 N. Aoki	Proton 4T	2'05.512
20.	88 A. Pitt	Kawasaki	2'06.112
21.	23 R. Kiyonari	Honda	2'06.819
22.	52 D. De Gea	Harris WCM	2'06.941
23.	19 O. Jacque	Yamaha	2'07.017 (*)
24.	35 C. Burns	Harris WCM	2'08.675

(*): Still suffering from the effects of his concussion in qualifying, the Frenchman withdrew.

RACE: 21 LAPS = 116.508 KM (*)

1.	Valentino Rossi	43'41.457 (159.998 km/h)
2.	Sete Gibernau	+ 2"042
3.	Massimiliano Biaggi	+ 7"644
4.	Nicky Hayden	+ 13"733
5.	Carlos Checa	+ 13"789
6.	Loris Capirossi	+ 20"567
7.	Tohru Ukawa	+ 23"449
8.	Shinya Nakano	+ 26"740
9.	Troy Bayliss	+ 32"149
10.	Makoto Tamada	+ 40"556
11.	Marco Melandri	+ 43"863
12.	Noriyuki Haga	+ 44"613
13.	Colin Edwards	+ 54"667
14.	Kenny Roberts	+ 1'02.687
15.	Alexandre Barros	+ 1'03.006
16.	Andrew Pitt	+ 1'06.128
17.	Jeremy McWilliams	+ 1'10.916
18.	Nobuatsu Aoki	+ 1'11.344
19.	Garry McCoy	+ 1'17.205
20.	Akira Ryo	+ 1'41.315
21.	Ryuichi Kiyonari	+ 1'49.094

Fastest lap: Rossi, in 2'03.822 (161.302 km/h). New record.
Previous best: Biaggi, in 2'04.9254 (159.878 km/h/2002).
Outright fastest lap: Rossi, in 2'02.480 (163.069 km/h/2003).

CHAMPIONSHIP

1.	V. Rossi	307 (7 wins)
2.	S. Gibernau	244 (4 wins)
3.	M. Biaggi	215 (2 wins)
4.	L. Capirossi	141 (1 win)
5.	T. Bayliss	119
6.	N. Hayden	114
7.	T. Ukawa	112
8.	C. Checa	104
9.	S. Nakano	92
10.	A. Barros	91

Runners and riders:
With Hopkins suspended for one GP for "dangerous riding" at Motegi, when he caused a multiple pile up at the first corner, Akira Ryo replaced him. Tamada was also excluded from the race and the riders felt the penalty was too harsh. "Now, you will have to think very carefully before mounting an attack on the final lap," reckoned Rossi.

Qualifying:
Guess who was quickest on Friday? Rossi of course! And on Saturday? Well, for a change, the reigning champion stuck his qualifying tyres on in the middle of the session. The outcome: the Sepang record is beaten by 2"007! Having fallen on Friday, sustaining a heavy blow to the head, Jacque only did a few laps on Saturday before giving up and pulling out of the race.

Start:
Gibernau shows the quickest reflexes, while Capirossi makes the most of the Ducati's launch system and Checa is soon on the pace. Barros is out of luck, falling in the middle of the pack. The Brazilian picks up his Yamaha M1 to pick up the final point for fifteenth place. As they cross the line for the first time, Gibernau leads Checa by 1"113.

Lap 4:
Gibernau's lead peaks at 0"957 on lap 2, but Rossi is already on the back wheel of his only rival for the title.

Lap 8:
Biaggi has passed Checa, Rossi takes the lead and, in the space of two laps, he leads Gibernau by a second.

Half distance (lap 11):
Rossi leads the show from

Gibernau by 1"479. Biaggi is third, 1"707 down on the Spaniard, ahead of a spectacular group made up of Checa, Capirossi and Hayden.

Lap 15:
The gap between Rossi and Gibernau has stabilised at just under two seconds (1"943 at this time.) Hayden is putting on a sliding display, the American having closed to 0"160 of Checa.

Finish (lap 21):
Rossi likes to celebrate winning titles with a victory and he did just that at Sepang. A few metres after the finish line, he leans his RC211V on the pit wall and goes to hug his team. On his lap of honour, his fans, dressed as convicts, in a repeat of Brno, liberate him of his ball and chain. And of his contract with Honda?

Championship:
The top three finishers in the race are also the top three in the championship. There are no changes therefore, except that for Rossi, this is title number five.

Olivier Jacque works out. It was before his fall which would force him to retire.

Valentino Rossi, a free man

Valentino Rossi says it every time: for him racing has to be a game and never become a job like any other. "I need to enjoy myself, to have fun, that's all."

And when Valentino Rossi has fun, it has a profound effect on the already shaky morale of his rivals. Look at this Malaysian weekend, which was a tense affair with everyone asking what this one man would do. "This time, it's not possible, he will make a mistake and will not be able to withstand the pressure he has created for himself," reckoned an old hand on Thursday before qualifying.

The prediction was wide of the mark, as the master dominated his subject and his rivals. To start with, he stood up for John Hopkins, heavily penalised with a one race ban after his attacking move at the first corner of the Pacific GP. Then, he remained mute when asked about his plans for next year. Finally, he was dominant on the track: "because the best way to have fun is to win!" And as that's what he likes best...

The paddock is buzzing with rumour and conjecture, as counter proposal faces counter proposal. The most important sponsor in motor sports,

Champagne shower for the champion: Sete Gibernau drenches Valentino Rossi.

Philip Morris and its lead brand, Marlboro, is beginning to realise that the star of MotoGP could soon be riding for another brand of cigarette, while Rossi's mysterious manager, Gibo Badioli is having a whale of a time in a game in which he is pulling most of the strings. In the meantime, the reigning champ is having fun on the track.

To shuffle the pack a bit, he decides to fit qualifying tyres in the middle of the session on Saturday. The result is hard to swallow for the others, while he just laughs.

The race? It would follow the same pattern. A few laps toying with the others followed by yet another demonstration on the way to a new title. Would the master now tell us that he is planning to step off this bike which he likes so much? He stops to thank his team. Then, he is off again as he has a date with his fans out on the circuit. This time, we are going to find out the truth. Disguised as convicts, the faithful from Tavullia offer him the key to a giant padlock, freeing forever from the ball and chain they had given him at Brno in the height of the summer. Are they freeing him from the obligation of winning which the Italian media placed on his shoulders at one point in the season? Or are they freeing him quite simply from what had been a four year love affair with Honda and with the Repsol team? We were waiting for a definitive answer or some sort of statement. But the situation had now got more complicated with some extra unknown factors.

Rossi is more than ever a free man. A great champion having fun!

A one-man media phenomenon: Rossi at work on yet another glory day.

250cc

Malaysian Grand Prix
12 October 2003 / Sepang – 5.548 m

STARTING GRID

1.	24	T. Elias	Aprilia	2'07.535
2.	54	M. Poggiali	Aprilia	2'08.419
3.	10	F. Gonzales-Nieto	Aprilia	2'08.836
4.	8	N. Matsudo	Yamaha	2'09.278
5.	7	R. De Puniet	Aprilia	2'09.353
6.	21	F. Battaini	Aprilia	2'09.380
7.	5	S. Porto	Honda	2'09.407
8.	50	S. Guintoli	Aprilia	2'09.687
9.	14	A. West	Aprilia	2'09.827
10.	3	R. Rolfo	Honda	2'10.231
11.	6	A. Debon	Honda	2'10.604
12.	26	A. Baldolini	Aprilia	2'10.764
13.	36	E. Nigon	Aprilia	2'10.823
14.	9	H. Marchand	Aprilia	2'10.985
15.	33	H. Faubel	Aprilia	2'11.194
16.	34	E. Bataille	Honda	2'11.316
17.	28	D. Heidolf	Aprilia	2'11.351
18.	11	J. Olive	Aprilia	2'11.412
19.	15	C. Gemmel	Honda	2'11.691
20.	57	C. Davies	Aprilia	2'12.024
21.	13	J. Hules	Honda	2'12.248
22.	52	L. Pesek	Yamaha	2'12.919
23.	16	J. Stigefelt	Aprilia	2'13.210
24.	98	K. Poensgen	Honda	2'15.004
25.	81	S. Huang	Yamaha	2'16.107
26.	18	H. vd Lagemaat	Honda	2'16.377

RACE: 20 LAPS = 110.960 KM

1.	Toni Elias	43'15.925 (153.878 km/h)
2.	Manuel Poggiali	+ 9"931
3.	Alfonso Gonzales-Nieto	+ 9"942
4.	Roberto Rolfo	+ 25"839
5.	Randy De Puniet	+ 34"060
6.	Franco Battaini	+ 36"004
7.	Naoki Matsudo	+ 49"445
8.	Sebastian Porto	+ 53"955
9.	Anthony West	+ 57"165
10.	Alex Baldolini	+ 1'03.700
11.	Dirk Heidolf	+ 1'04.419
12.	Chaz Davies	+ 1'06.349
13.	Hugo Marchand	+ 1'07.487
14.	Joan Olive	+ 1'08.008
15.	Jaroslav Hules	+ 1'18.180
16.	Christian Gemmel	+ 1'21.642
17.	Katja Poensgen	+ 2'08.210
18.	Henk vd Lagemaat	+ 2'13.493
19.	Shi Zhao Huang	+ 1 lap

Fastest lap: Elias, in 2'08.566 (155.350 km/h).
New record.
Previous best: Gonzales-Nieto, in 2'08.858 (154.998 km/h/2002).
Outright fastest lap: Elias, in 2'07.535 (156.606 km/h/2003).

CHAMPIONSHIP

1.	M. Poggiali	226 (4 wins)
2.	T. Elias	201 (5 wins)
3.	R. Rolfo	201 (1 win)
4.	R. De Puniet	183 (2 wins)
5.	A. Gonzales-Nieto	167 (1 win)
6.	F. Battaini	127
7.	A. West	125 (1 win)
8.	S. Porto	117
9.	N. Matsudo	104
10.	S. Guintoli	88

A bit warm in Malaysia, don't you think, Elias father and son?

Runners and riders:
As planned, Katja Poensgen is back with her team in Malaysia. There are two Chinese wild cards in a Yamaha team run by Luis D'Antin. It is an important step for the future as China is bidding to host a grand prix.

Qualifying:
Toni Elias is the man on form this autumn, dominating every session and he will adopt the role of hare for his team-mate, "Fonsi" Gonzales-Nieto on Saturday afternoon in order to ensure he had an ally on the front row. The trick worked as the two Aspar Martinez riders are either side of Poggiali, the championship leader. The surprise on the front row was Matsudo and his Yamaha, while De Puniet was crippled with a bad fever.

Start:
The action begins before the start as Guintoli is complaining about his clutch on the warm-up. He parks his Aprilia at the end of the formation lap, with despair in his soul. Those feelings are completed as Debon charges through from the third row to take the lead. The miracle is too good to be true and in fact, Debon and Porto, just ahead of him on the grid, had both jumped the start and have to come in for a stop-go penalty. Fonsi completes the first lap with a 0"716 lead over the chasing group, led by Rolfo.

Whoops... Hector Faubel leans a bit too far.

Lap 3:
Elias steps up the pace, closing very fast on his team-mate and takes the lead. From then on, no one can match the young Spaniard, so the main point of interest shifts to the fight for second place.

Lap 8:
Because that's where the action is, over six seconds behind Elias. Poggiali is having to contend with Gonzales-Nieto, keen to remind us that racing can sometimes be a team sport. He does all he can, in a very fair manner all the same, to keep Poggiali busy all the time.

An historic moment: two Chinese riders compete in qualifying. Only one would get to race: Shi Zhao Huang (81).

Half distance (lap 10):
Still Elias (8"292 ahead) and still Poggiali-Nieto duelling behind. A further 12 seconds back, Rolfo and De Puniet have not given up, but it is hard to imagine how tough it is for them.

Finish (lap 20):
Elias has ridden the perfect race and, braking for the final corner, Gonzales-Nieto has one last desperate attempt at passing Poggiali, who holds him off to cross the line 11 thousandths ahead of the Spaniard.

Championship:
Manuel Poggiali's race has limited the damage. His lead is now 25 points over both Elias and Rolfo, the Honda no match for the Aprilias in Sepang.

Runners and riders:
In the Derbi-Gilera clan, technical supreme Olivier Liegeois has mixed feelings. On the one hand, Lorenzo's Derbi is making progress, on the other, the Gileras are in a spot of bother. "The bikes are the same, but because of all Bianco's crashes since the start of the season, we are running out of spare parts for the chassis. And this is the area we are working on most."

Qualifying:
Pedrosa reminds everyone on Friday that he intends getting the job done, in other words taking his first world championship title. But Liegeois' optimism is confirmed on Saturday when Lorenzo takes his first pole position. They were also smiling in the "orange" camp as Finland's Kallio puts a KTM on the front row for the first time, with the Harald Bartol designed 125.

Fight for second place between Lorenzo (48) and Kallio.

Start:
Stoner, who completed the front row gets wrong. But not Pedrosa, Kallio and Switzerland's Luthi (6th on the grid) as these three are line abreast in the first corner. Pedrosa comes off best from the usual chaos after the start, leading the opening lap by 1"191. He would never be seen again.

Lap 3:
Pedrosa is closing on the title

with giant steps as he sets the fastest lap and leads by 2"485. Perugini, his only rival for the title stops with engine problems in the pits.

Half distance (lap 10):
Pedrosa is out on his own with a 3"543 lead over the next duo of Lorenzo and Kallio. 1"092 down on the Spaniard and the Finn, another duo features Luthi and the soon to retire Azuma.

Lap 12:
Jenkner retires (the Aprilias were suffering in Sepang). Behind Pedrosa is a gaggle made up of Kallio, Lorenzo, Luthi, Stoner, De Angelis and Azuma, all of them wheel to wheel.

Lap 13:
Stoner falls.

Lap 16:
Cecchinello falls.

Finish (lap 19):
Pedrosa's lead grows to 6"424 on lap 17 before he

It's done: a few hours before Rossi, Daniel Pedrosa became the first man to be crowned world champion in 2003.

eases off to be sure of an unopposed victory. Kallio has the last word for second place, Luthi having lost time on the penultimate lap dealing with Azuma.

Championship:
It's in the bag and Alberto Puig's protégé, Spain's Daniel Pedrosa becomes the second youngest champion in the history of the sport at the age of 18 years and 13 days. Only Capirossi did better, winning at the age of 17 years and 165 days.

Pedrosa out on his own in the lead: the Spaniard totally dominated the season.

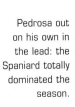

Malaysian Grand Prix
12 October 2003 / Sepang - 5.548 m

STARTING GRID

1.	48	J. Lorenzo	Derbi	2'14.403
2.	3	D. Pedrosa	Honda	2'14.485
3.	36	M. Kallio	KTM	2'14.541
4.	27	C. Stoner	Aprilia	2'14.569
5.	17	S. Jenkner	Aprilia	2'14.655
6.	12	T. Lüthi	Honda	2'14.844
7.	22	P. Nieto	Aprilia	2'14.887
8.	34	A. Dovizioso	Honda	2'14.980
9.	7	S. Perugini	Aprilia	2'15.036
10.	33	S. Bianco	Gilera	2'15.052
11.	6	M. Giansanti	Aprilia	2'15.065
12.	8	M. Azuma	Honda	2'15.088
13.	32	F. Lai	Malaguti	2'15.239
14.	80	H. Barbera	Aprilia	2'15.410
15.	58	M. Simoncelli	Aprilia	2'15.480
16.	15	A. De Angelis	Aprilia	2'15.566
17.	79	G. Talmacsi	Aprilia	2'15.579
18.	1	A. Vincent	Aprilia	2'15.602
19.	10	R. Locatelli	KTM	2'15.720
20.	23	G. Borsoi	Aprilia	2'15.727
21.	19	A. Bautista	Aprilia	2'15.869
22.	4	L. Cecchinello	Aprilia	2'16.091
23.	41	Y. Ui	Gilera	2'16.231
24.	50	A. Ballerini	Honda	2'16.742
25.	42	G. Pellino	Aprilia	2'17.128
26.	63	M. Di Meglio	Honda	2'17.512
27.	88	R. Harms	Aprilia	2'17.851
28.	25	I. Toth	Honda	2'18.055
29.	26	E. Alzamora	Derbi	2'18.064
30.	31	J. Simon	Malaguti	2'18.285
31.	11	M. Sabbatani	Aprilia	2'18.606
32.	28	M. Danese	Honda	2'19.298
33.	24	S. Corsi	Honda	2'19.706 (*)

(*): Injured on the first day of practice, the Italian pulled out of the race.

RACE: 19 LAPS = 105.412 km

1.	Daniel Pedrosa	43'07.647 (146.651 km/h)
2.	Mika Kallio	+ 2"658
3.	Jorge Lorenzo	+ 2"750
4.	Thomas Lüthi	+ 3"006
5.	Masao Azuma	+ 5"032
6.	Alex De Angelis	+ 7"242
7.	Mirko Giansanti	+ 9"549
8.	Hector Barbera	+ 10"908
9.	Pablo Nieto	+ 11"197
10.	Roberto Locatelli	+ 12"874
11.	Marco Simoncelli	+ 14"926
12.	Stefano Bianco	+ 15"443
13.	Andrea Dovizioso	+ 15"576
14.	Gabor Talmacsi	+ 22"889
15.	Alvaro Bautista	+ 24"161
16.	Arnaud Vincent	+ 24"266
17.	Fabrizio Lai	+ 24"860
18.	Youichi Ui	+ 27"972
19.	Andrea Ballerini	+ 47"813
20.	Gino Borsoi	+ 48"612
21.	Robbin Harms	+ 58"448
22.	Mike Di Meglio	+ 58"474
23.	Emilio Alzamora	+ 1'25.522
24.	Imre Toth	+ 1'25.560
25.	Julian Simon	+ 1'25.881
26.	Michele Danese	+ 2'10.497

Fastest lap: Stoner, in 2'14.932 (148.021 km/h).
Record: Cechinello, in 2'13.919 (149.140 km/h/2002).
Outright fastest lap: Pedrosa, in 2'13.310 (149.822 km/h/2002).

CHAMPIONSHIP

1.	D. Pedrosa	223 (5 wins)
2.	S. Perugini	159 (2 wins)
3.	A. De Angelis	157
4.	A. Dovizioso	149
5.	P. Nieto	139 (1 win)
6.	H. Barbera	138 (2 wins)
7.	S. Jenkner	115 (1 win)
8.	L. Cecchinello	105 (2 wins)
9.	C. Stoner	100
10.	M. Kallio	88

AUSTRALIA
Phillip Island

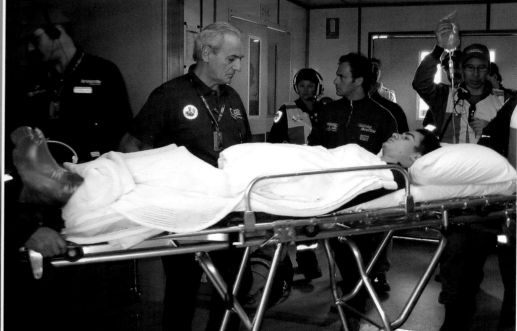

Bayliss-Rossi against a blue sky background: the Phillip Island circuit is paradise for the riders, but it can also turn to hell.
On Friday morning, in the first session, world champion Daniel Pedrosa (above) got it wrong and broke both ankles.
As for the sun, it only reappeared for the MotoGP race, in time to smile on the events of the day.

MOTOGP

STARTING GRID

1.	46 V. Rossi	Honda	1'30.068
2.	65 L. Capirossi	Ducati	1'30.496
3.	15 S. Gibernau	Honda	1'30.676
4.	12 T. Bayliss	Ducati	1'30.683
5.	69 N. Hayden	Honda	1'30.863
6.	3 M. Biaggi	Honda	1'30.993
7.	33 M. Melandri	Yamaha	1'31.227
8.	11 T. Ukawa	Honda	1'31.280
9.	7 C. Checa	Yamaha	1'31.302
10.	99 J. McWilliams	Proton 4T	1'31.367
11.	56 S. Nakano	Yamaha	1'31.444
12.	8 G. McCoy	Kawasaki	1'31.572
13.	21 J. Hopkins	Suzuki	1'31.705
14.	10 K. Roberts	Suzuki	1'31.742
15.	19 O. Jacque	Yamaha	1'31.759
16.	4 A. Barros	Yamaha	1'31.802
17.	6 M. Tamada	Honda	1'31.806
18.	45 C. Edwards	Aprilia	1'31.938
19.	41 N. Haga	Aprilia	1'32.145
20.	9 N. Aoki	Proton 4T	1'32.460
21.	88 A. Pitt	Kawasaki	1'32.555
22.	23 R. Kiyonari	Honda	1'33.900
23.	52 D. De Gea	Harris WCM	1'34.246
24.	35 C. Burns	Harris WCM	1'34.858

RACE: 27 LAPS = 120.096 KM

1.	Valentino Rossi	41'53.543 (172.006 km/h) (*)
2.	Loris Capirossi	+ 5"212
3.	Nicky Hayden	+ 12"039
4.	Sete Gibernau	+ 12"070
5.	Tohru Ukawa	+ 12"294
6.	Olivier Jacque	+ 28"017
7.	Shinya Nakano	+ 28"044
8.	Carlos Checa	+ 40"112
9.	Kenny Roberts	+ 41"410
10.	Makoto Tamada	+ 49"902
11.	Jeremy McWilliams	+ 51"260
12.	John Hopkins	+ 54"101
13.	Garry McCoy	+ 54"779
14.	Noriyuki Haga	+ 1'01.520
15.	Andrew Pitt	+ 1'06.080
16.	Colin Edwards	+ 1'06.630
17.	Massimiliano Biaggi	+ 1'14.003
18.	Nobuatsu Aoki	+ 1 lap
19.	Ryuichi Kiyonari	+ 1 lap
20.	Chris Burns	+ 1 lap

Fastest lap: Rossi, in 1'31.421 (175.154 km/h).
New record.
Previous best: Rossi, in 1'32.233 (173.612 km/h/2002).
Outright fastest lap: Rossi, in 1'30.068 (177.785 km/h/2003).

CHAMPIONSHIP

1.	V. Rossi	332 (8 wins)
2.	S. Gibernau	257 (4 wins)
3.	M. Biaggi	215 (2 wins)
4.	L. Capirossi	161 (1 win)
5.	N. Hayden	130
6.	T. Ukawa	123
7.	T. Bayliss	119
8.	C. Checa	112
9.	S. Nakano	101
10.	A. Barros	91

Runners and riders:
Suspended for one race in Malaysia, Hopkins is back on parade in Phillip Island.

Qualifying:
Liberated now that he has the title in the bag, Rossi arrives in Australia with the intention of having some fun. On Friday, when it looks like being a Ducati one-two, the world champion pulls off an almost perfect last lap, which Loris Capirossi acknowledges with an admiring smile. On Saturday, Rossi steps up the pace, taking another pole position and beating the previous best two-wheeled lap of Phillip Island by over 2 seconds. "If it goes on like this, in five years, we will be quicker than F1 cars."

Start:
Biaggi does it best, but he has to run wide in the first corner, allowing Bayliss, Capirossi and Gibernau to fly by.

Lap 2:
A Yamaha leads – it's Melandri.

Lap 4:
A bad fall for Bayliss, who was hit by Melandri. Hayden takes the lead.

Lap 5:
Rossi takes command. Bayliss is taken to the medical centre.

Lap 7:
Rossi has made his first break (1"308.) Behind him, young lions, Nicky Hayden and Marco Melandri are very entertaining.

Lap 11:
Barros retires. Rossi now leads Melandri by 3"425, with Capirossi and Gibernau next up. Rossi is given a ten second penalty for having passed Melandri under the yellow flags after Bayliss' accident.

A big fright for Troy Bayliss. He only regained consciousness back in the medical centre.

Loris Capirossi did not know he was in the lead!

Half distance (lap 14):
Rossi leads Capirossi by 3"909. So, taking the penalty into account, he is six seconds behind the Ducati.

Lap 15:
Melandri falls.

Lap 16:
Rossi – Capirossi = 4"615. The world champion needs to find 10.001 to be the winner.

Lap 17:
New record, new gap: 5"224.

Lap 18: quicker still: 6"062.

Lap 19: 6"669.

Lap 20: 7"546.

Lap 21: 8"827.

Lap 22: 9"962.

Lap 23:
He's done it! Rossi leads Capirossi by 10"392 and the world champion is now in the lead despite his penalty. Checa goes off the track, losing contact with the group fighting for second place.

Finish (lap 27):
Those important 10 seconds were added to Rossi's last lap time. He is declared the winner with a 5"212 lead over Capirossi. Nicky Hayden takes his first real podium, after a great duel with Sete Gibernau.

Championship:
Gibernau can no longer be beaten for second place in the championship. Hayden takes fifth place.

Valentino is MEGA!

He is young and rich. He has already caught the eye of various famous film starlets. And above all, he loves racing bikes. It is the perpetual challenge and the risk, because he can control it perfectly. He has already won everything, or almost everything: 58 grands prix including this Sunday's, which began in the wet and ended with the sun shining. Since the previous week, he also had five world titles to his name.

He has it all and he is ready to reveal a daring gamble – chopping in his Honda RC211V which he loves so much and is a winner, for a Yamaha YZR-M1, which needs someone of his exceptional talent. He seems to have invented a new category – handicap racing. Of course, we are talking about Valentino Rossi.

The facts. Lap four of this exciting Australian GP. After a coming together with Melandri's Yamaha, Australia's Troy Bayliss (Ducati) falls at high speed. He immediately loses consciousness and his body looks like a rag doll as the marshals rush to the scene. One lap later, at the same spot, Rossi passes Melandri: "Like at Donington, I did not see the yellow flags (waved to indicate an incident, Ed.) I don't know if the other riders saw them, but me, when I'm

Rossi leads already: the world champion has just invented handicap racing.

concentrating, I can never spot them." Three more laps pass. Rossi is now leading when the penalty is announced: a ten second penalty "I went past the pits and I saw a "less 10" sign. I did not have a clue what it meant. On the next lap, I was shown "P8," which meant I had dropped to eighth place. I swore! After Donington, I did not want to lose another race because of a yellow flag that I had not seen!"

The achievement. The world champion now had his

work cut out. He crossed the line with a 3"909 lead over Capirossi's Ducati, but in real terms he was six seconds down on the Desmosedici of his fellow countryman, who has no idea that he is actually leading, as he is second on the road. "As I now had nothing to lose in terms of the championship, I shut my eyes and opened the throttle. Maybe for the first time in my career, I rode at 100% of my ability from start to finish....and it was great. I am sure it was interesting for you to watch, but it was great fun for me as the man with the main interest in this gamble," recounted Valentino. Rossi smiled. He then put together twelve perfect laps. He made up his penalty deficit on Capirossi who seemed almost glad to have been beaten. "In any case, Vale was the strongest. I could see I was being given strange numbers, but I never realised I had briefly led this grand prix."

All that was left was for the master to remember his Australian fans, as he did his lap of honour with a flag bearing the number 7. It was the number worn by the unforgettable Barry Sheene, still a living legend in the land of the kangaroo.

Smiles for Rossi and Hayden (his first podium), while Capirossi finally understands what happened.

250cc

Australian Grand Prix
19 October 2003
Phillip Island – 4.448 m

STARTING GRID

1.	24	T. Elias	Aprilia	1'33.771
2.	5	S. Porto	Honda	1'33.851
3.	21	F. Battaini	Aprilia	1'33.999
4.	7	R. De Puniet	Aprilia	1'34.085
5.	10	F. Gonzales-Nieto	Aprilia	1'34.188
6.	50	S. Guintoli	Aprilia	1'34.446
7.	54	M. Poggiali	Aprilia	1'34.672
8.	3	R. Rolfo	Honda	1'34.703
9.	8	N. Matsudo	Yamaha	1'35.206
10.	13	J. Hules	Honda	1'35.280
11.	14	A. West	Aprilia	1'35.325
12.	36	E. Nigon	Aprilia	1'35.508
13.	6	A. Debon	Honda	1'35.738
14.	34	E. Bataille	Honda	1'35.750
15.	57	C. Davies	Aprilia	1'35.927
16.	33	H. Faubel	Aprilia	1'36.031
17.	28	D. Heidolf	Aprilia	1'36.086
18.	52	L. Pesek	Yamaha	1'36.118
19.	9	H. Marchand	Aprilia	1'36.188
20.	11	J. Olive	Aprilia	1'36.220
21.	26	A. Baldolini	Aprilia	1'36.326
22.	16	J. Stigefelt	Aprilia	1'36.477
23.	15	C. Gemmel	Honda	1'37.038
24.	98	K. Poensgen	Honda	1'39.122
25.	18	H. vd Lagemaat	Honda	1'39.350
26.	79	G. Hardcastle	Yamaha	1'39.985

RACE: 25 LAPS = 111.200 KM

1.	Roberto Rolfo	45'14.993 (147.447 km/h)
2.	Anthony West	+ 14"040
3.	Alfonso Gonzales-Nieto	+ 33"511
4.	Franco Battaini	+ 54"252
5.	Alex Debon	+ 1'06.895
6.	Naoki Matsudo	+ 1'06.943
7.	Erwan Nigon	+ 1'13.421
8.	Jaroslav Hules	+ 1'22.119
9.	Manuel Poggiali	+ 1'22.163
10.	Johan Stigefelt	+ 1'25.303
11.	Toni Elias	+ 1'41.591
12.	Lukas Pesek	+ 2'49.682
13.	Dirk Heidolf	+ 1 lap
14.	Hugo Marchand	+ 1 lap
15.	Chaz Davies	+ 1 lap
16.	Hector Faubel	+ 1 lap
17.	Henk vd Lagemaat	+ 2 laps
18.	Joan Olive	+ 3 laps

Fastest lap: Hules, in 1'45.680 (151.521 km/h).
Record: Rossi, in 1'33.556 (171.157 km/h/1999).
Outright fastest lap: Rossi, in 1'33.521 (171.221 km/h/1999).

CHAMPIONSHIP

1.	M. Poggiali	233 (4 wins)
2.	R. Rolfo	226 (2 wins)
3.	T. Elias	206 (5 wins)
4.	R. De Puniet	183 2 wins)
5.	A. Gonzales-Nieto	183 (1 win)
6.	A. West	145 (1 win)
7.	F. Battaini	140
8.	S. Porto	117
9.	N. Matsudo	114
10.	S. Guintoli	88

Runners and riders:

Randy de Puniet has recovered from his illness, although his stomach is still playing up when he lands in Australia. Five local riders try their luck, including British-born Peter Taplin. Only one will make the qualifying cut-off.

Qualifying:

Tony Elias also had a difficult time, as he fell on Friday, which did not stop him from setting the third quickest time of the day, as Argentina's Porto and his Honda took provisional pole. On Saturday, Elias is back on form and takes yet another pole position. Porto and Battaini confirm their good form on this Phillip Island circuit, while Manuel Poggiali joins the list of fallers and is "only" seventh.

Start:

Even though the rain has eased off, the track is still seriously wet. Roberto Rolfo makes the best start from the third row, Porto goes straight on at the first corner and speeds across the grass. Guintoli falls shortly after. At the end of the opening lap, Rolfo leads Battaini by 0"748, while De Puniet is already 4"264 behind the leader. Poggiali is eighth and Elias tenth.

Lap 2:

Battaini falls, West is tenth. Having gone off the track, Sebastien Porto rejoins the race and is already up to fourteenth.

Lap 4:

Still Rolfo, who now leads West by 8"245. De Puniet is third. The other title contenders are a long way back: Poggiali tenth and Elias, who does not like the rain, eighteenth.

Lap 6:

Katja Poensgen and de Porto are fallers (this time for good, having got back to sixth place).

Half distance (lap 13):

Still Rolfo. West is 6"633 down in second.

The duel of the Grand Prix: De Puniet toughs it out with "Fonsi" Nieto. The Frenchman would end up falling.

Victory for Roberto Rolfo, who throws the title fight wide open.

Behind them, Fonsi Gonzales-Nieto has got to within 1"200 of De Puniet in third. Debon is fifth ahead of Matsudo, Battaini – what a comeback! – Bataille and Poggiali. Elias is fifteenth.

Lap 16:

Fonsi Nieto has passed De Puniet. Rolfo's lead over West drops to 3"697.

Lap 18:

Bataille falls, having been ninth. De Puniet is third again.

Lap 21:

Gemmel falls.

Lap 24:

Randy de Puniet falls.

Finish (lap 25):

Rolfo has ridden a faultless race and wins by over 14 seconds from West. Poggiali is ninth, beaten on the line by a remarkable Jaroslav Hules, who sets the fastest race lap.

Championship:

Elias is now out of the title race. Roberto Rolfo has closed to within seven points of Poggiali. The final in Valencia should be a cracker.

Arnaud Vincent is back on form.

Pedrosa's Honda after his Friday fall: impressive!

125cc

**Australian Grand Prix
19 October 2003
Phillip Island - 4.448 m**

STARTING GRID

1.	7	S. Perugini	Aprilia	1'37.342
2.	15	A. De Angelis	Aprilia	1'37.455
3.	36	M. Kallio	KTM	1'37.644
4.	27	C. Stoner	Aprilia	1'37.787
5.	48	J. Lorenzo	Derbi	1'37.802
6.	80	H. Barbera	Aprilia	1'37.824
7.	6	M. Giansanti	Aprilia	1'37.828
8.	34	A. Dovizioso	Honda	1'37.958
9.	17	S. Jenkner	Aprilia	1'37.967
10.	4	L. Cecchinello	Aprilia	1'38.038
11.	58	M. Simoncelli	Aprilia	1'38.088
12.	12	T. Lüthi	Honda	1'38.125
13.	22	P. Nieto	Aprilia	1'38.190
14.	79	G. Talmacsi	Aprilia	1'38.268
15.	88	R. Harms	Aprilia	1'38.291
16.	19	A. Bautista	Aprilia	1'38.409
17.	8	M. Azuma	Honda	1'38.641
18.	32	F. Lai	Malaguti	1'38.835
19.	10	R. Locatelli	KTM	1'38.919
20.	41	Y. Ui	Gilera	1'39.039
21.	63	M. Di Meglio	Honda	1'39.048
22.	1	A. Vincent	Aprilia	1'39.070
23.	50	A. Ballerini	Honda	1'39.260
24.	23	G. Borsoi	Aprilia	1'39.273
25.	33	S. Bianco	Gilera	1'39.303
26.	11	M. Sabbatani	Aprilia	1'39.432
27.	26	E. Alzamora	Derbi	1'39.651
28.	31	J. Simon	Malaguti	1'39.668
29.	25	I. Toth	Honda	1'40.523
30.	44	J. Waters	Honda	1'40.830
31.	28	M. Danese	Honda	1'41.064
32.	42	G. Pellino	Aprilia	1'41.455
33.	24	S. Corsi	Honda	1'42.184
34.	46	M. Kuhne	Honda	1'43.816

RACE: 23 LAPS = 102.304 km

1. Andrea Ballerini	43'41.886 (140.469 km/h)	
2. Masao Azuma	+ 8"849	
3. Steve Jenkner	+ 14"187	
4. Alvaro Bautista	+ 14"752	
5. Arnaud Vincent	+ 16"387	
6. Hector Barbera	+ 22"852	
7. Alex De Angelis	+ 23"167	
8. Jorge Lorenzo	+ 39"210	
9. Gabor Talmacsi	+ 45"888	
10. Robbin Harms	+ 48"500	
11. Youichi Ui	+ 1'07.473	
12. Julian Simon	+ 1'08.499	
13. Fabrizio Lai	+ 1'25.817	
14. Emilio Alzamora	+ 1'46.395	
15. Stefano Bianco	+ 1 lap	
16. Thomas Lüthi	+ 1 lap	
17. Michele Danese	+ 1 lap	

Fastest lap: Ballerini, in 1'50.518 (144.888 km/h).
Record: Pedrosa, in 1'37.983 (163.424 km/h/2002).
Outright fastest lap: Perugini, in 1'37.342 (164.500 km/h/2003).

CHAMPIONSHIP

1. D. Pedrosa	223	(5 wins)
2. A. De Angelis	166	
3. S. Perugini	159	(2 wins)
4. A. Dovizioso	149	
5. H. Barbera	148	(2 wins)
6. P. Nieto	139	(1 win)
7. S. Jenkner	131	(1 win)
8. L. Cecchinello	105	(2 wins)
9. C. Stoner	100	
10. M. Kallio	88	

Runners and riders:
Forced to pull out in Malaysia after a qualifying accident, Corsi was back, but still in pain he would scratch from the event after the first day.

Qualifying:
While the rays of the sun still shone on the best known of the Australian islands, a storm was raging in the mind and body of the new world champion, Daniel Pedrosa: on Friday morning, due to a technical problem, he had a terrible fall which sent him piling into a barrier made of tyres filled with sand. He ended up with two broken ankles. The Spaniard underwent a four hour operation on Friday evening in a Melbourne hospital. It will take him between three and four months to recover.

Start:
Stoner, Kallio and Perugini get the best start. Tom Luthi (12th on the grid) is caught out under acceleration and only just manages to hang on going down the straight. Dovizioso falls on the opening lap, which Stoner completes in the lead, 0"269 ahead of Perugini.

Lap 3:
Simoncelli falls. Stoner and Perugini are just 612 thousandths apart.

Lap 6:
Stoner falls while leading. Perugini is now out on his own in front with a 7"019 lead over Berbera, who has been caught by Jenkner, Azuma and Ballerini (these last two on Bridgestone tyres.)

Lap 8:
A second fall for Simoncelli. Dovizioso has pitted and Sabbatani retires.

Lap 10:
Kallio falls while scrapping for sixth place with his KTM team-mate, Roberto Locatelli.

Half distance (lap 12):
Still Perugini, with a 2"406 lead over a surprising Ballerini, who heads team-mate Azuma by 3"464.

Lap 13:
Locatelli falls. Ballerini has just set the race fastest lap and closes to 1"419 of Perugini.

Lap 15:
Cecchinello and Pablo Nieto fall.

A Bridgestone festival on the Phillip Island skating rink.

Lap 17:
Ballerini takes the lead. Behind him, Azuma is the quickest man on track and is closing fast on Perugini.

Lap 18:
Perugini falls.

Lap 21:
Giansanti falls, spoiling his record as the only man to have scored points in every race.

Finish (lap 23):
A nice glimpse of the future in the shape of Andrea Ballerini. The Italian, who had replaced Mika Kallio when the Finn moved to KTM, takes his first GP win. Importantly it is also a one-two for Bridgestone.

Championship:
Alex de Angelis, who ended up seventh in the race, takes second place off Stefano Perugini.

VALENCIA
Valencia

A victory burn-out: Valentino Rossi takes his last win with Honda. Randy De Puniet (above) has a perfect end to his 250 season, while the paddock is turned into a beauty pageant.

MOTOGP

STARTING GRID

1.	46	V. Rossi	Honda	1'32.478
2.	15	S. Gibernau	Honda	1'33.148
3.	65	L. Capirossi	Ducati	1'33.275
4.	69	N. Hayden	Honda	1'33.348
5.	7	C. Checa	Yamaha	1'33.454
6.	3	M. Biaggi	Honda	1'33.575
7.	45	C. Edwards	Aprilia	1'33.984
8.	4	A. Barros	Yamaha	1'34.247
9.	11	T. Ukawa	Honda	1'34.286
10.	12	T. Bayliss	Ducati	1'34.398
11.	17	N. Abé	Yamaha	1'34.467
12.	56	S. Nakano	Yamaha	1'34.677
13.	6	M. Tamada	Honda	1'34.742
14.	8	G. McCoy	Kawasaki	1'34.912
15.	99	J. McWilliams	Proton 4T	1'34.975
16.	88	A. Pitt	Kawasaki	1'35.125
17.	21	J. Hopkins	Suzuki	1'35.178
18.	10	K. Roberts	Suzuki	1'35.269
19.	9	N. Aoki	Proton 4T	1'35.439
20.	23	R. Kiyonari	Honda	1'35.572
21.	19	O. Jacque	Yamaha	1'35.816
22.	41	N. Haga	Aprilia	1'36.524
23.	52	D. De Gea	Harris WCM	1'36.604

RACE: 30 LAPS = 120.150 KM

1.	Valentino Rossi	47'13.078 (152.674 km/h)
2.	Sete Gibernau	+ 0"681
3.	Loris Capirossi	+ 11"227
4.	Massimiliano Biaggi	+ 16"293
5.	Carlos Checa	+ 20"868
6.	Alex Barros	+ 30"851
7.	Troy Bayliss	+ 37"770
8.	Colin Edwards	+ 38"922
9.	Norifumi Abé	+ 40"229
10.	Makoto Tamada	+ 46"500
11.	Kenny Roberts	+ 1'01.496
12.	Jeremy McWilliams	+ 1'04.510
13.	John Hopkins	+ 1'05.191
14.	Ryuichi Kiyonari	+ 1'06.012
15.	Noriyuki Haga	+ 1'06.154
16.	Nicky Hayden	+ 1'11.432
17.	Nobuatsu Aoki	+ 1'26.736
18.	Andrew Pitt	+ 1'27.016
19.	Garry McCoy	+ 1'27.450
20.	David De Gea	+ 1 lap

Fastest lap: Rossi, in 1'33.317 (154.505 km/h).
New Record.
Previous best: Barros, in 1'33.873 (153.590 km/h/2002).
Outright fastest lap: Rossi, in 1'32.478 (155.907 km/h/2003).

CHAMPIONSHIP

1.	V. Rossi	357 (9 wins)
2.	S. Gibernau	277 (4 wins)
3.	M. Biaggi	228 (2 wins)
4.	L. Capirossi	177 (1 win)
5.	N. Hayden	130
6.	T. Bayliss	128
7.	C. Checa	123
8.	T. Ukawa	123
9.	A. Barros	101
10.	S. Nakano	101

Runners and riders:
Injured at Phillip Island, Melandri has undergone surgery on his shoulder in Italy and the surgeons made the most of it to treat the collarbone the Italian had broken at Suzuka at the start of the season. He is replaced by Norifume Abe.

Qualifying:
For Chris Burns, the Grand Prix is over during Friday morning's free practice (broken right collarbone.) On this track where he has never won before, Valentino Rossi takes his ninth pole position of the season, with almost 7 tenths of a second in hand over Gibernau. Hayden takes a front row position for the first time in his GP career, while Colin Edwards puts his Aprilia RS Cube on seventh spot.

Start:
Capirossi and Rossi have the quickest reflexes, followed by Hayden, Biaggi and Gibernau. At the end of the opening lap, the Ducati has a 135 thousandths lead over the Honda which Rossi is riding for the final time. Following on are Hayden, Gibernau, Biaggi and Checa.

Lap 2:
Rossi takes the lead.

Lap 4:
Hayden falls, but keeps going. Rossi leads Capirossi by 348 thousandths, with Gibernau next up, having set the fastest race lap.

Lap 5:
Falls for Nakano and Ukawa, as they fight for ninth place. Gibernau is on form on a track where he was first victorious and has moved to second, 351 thousandths behind the world champion.

Lap 9:
Still Rossi, who leads Gibernau by 137 thousandths. Capirossi is third, 819 thousandths behind the leader. Biaggi is now fourth.

Rossi, Gibernau, Capirossi: the top three at the finish.

Lap 11:
Gibernau takes the lead, only to lose it moments later. At the same time, Capirossi and Biaggi have closed on the leaders.

Half distance (lap 15):
Still Rossi-Gibernau, the two main players of the 2003 championship just 0"489 apart. They have stepped up the pace and Capirossi has dropped to 2"678 behind, while Biaggi is around a second adrift of the Ducati.

Lap 23:
The lap record switches from Rossi to Gibernau, who are 0"401 apart. Capirossi is 6 seconds behind.

Lap 25:
The pleasantries had gone on too long for Rossi's liking and in the space of two laps, he pulls out a gap of 1"704 over Gibernau. It's all over.

Lap 27:
Olivier Jacque takes a trip through the gravel trap.

Finish (lap 30):
Rossi has filled the only gap in his fantastic track record by winning at the Ricardo Tormo circuit.

Championship:
Despite falling, Hayden fights back to take fifth and the title of best rookie of the year, at Bayliss' expense.

A hippy look for the championship-winning RC211V: a young Spanish designer produced the livery.

"Maybe I'm mad, but I'll deal with it!"

"I ask you for one last favour. Give me permission to try my new machine before the 31st December, the day our contract expires. Look at all these witnesses, all these people watching us. You cannot refuse me in front of them…" Even at the solemn moment of officialising his divorce from Honda, because he is so keen to take on another challenge, Valentino Rossi is still the crowd-pleasing joker. That is what makes him the outright star of motorcycle racing on a global scale.

It was a bit after six in the evening on Sunday, 2nd November 2003 – a historic day for the short term future of GP racing – in the too small confines of the packed press room at the Ricardo Tormo circuit, at Cheste, near Valencia. Alongside the five times world champion, who only a few hours earlier had taken his 33rd win from 64 starts! in the blue riband category of motorcycle sport, were Carlo Fiorani, sporting director of the Repsol-Honda team and Shoju Tachikawa, the team manager. For their part, they looked a bit more serious. "For several months, we have been in discussion with Rossi's management. We finally realised it was not a question of money, nor a technical choice, but just that Valentino needed a new challenge.

Another perfect weekend and poignant farewells.

Honda understands and accepts this," explained Fiorani, his voice trembling with emotion.

The scenario for this momentous event and the announcement with its inevitable consequences, had been perfectly stage-managed:

-The legal reply. "As I am tied into my Honda contract until 31st December, I will not tell you which colours I will be sporting next year," announced Valentino Rossi. Instead, he spoke of the recent past. "It has been a fantastic time. It has gone on for four years and has brought so much that I

feel as though it has gone on forever. At the same time and especially after the Malaysian GP – when he clinched his latest title – I understood that I had finished my work with this bike. I have won in the dry, in the rain, on tracks I adore and on those, which like Valencia did not suit me that well (until this first Sunday in November.) Maybe it's madness, but I feel the need to try something else."

-The sequel to the soap opera. An hour after this declaration, Yamaha made it known officially that, "now we have learnt that Valentino Rossi is free, we will begin negotiations with him." At the same time, behind the scenes, everything was being tried to untangle the knots which prevented confirmation of the wedding of the year. There was the problem of Rossi's replacement at Honda, Alexandre Barros, getting out of his contract with Yamaha's main sponsor, the Hispano-French Altadis company which still had a year to run. The soap saga of the autumn had not even run its course behind the scenes, but the winter episodes were already about to start. Two days after the final GP of the season, a test schedule had already been drawn up!

Rossi and his shadow…

250cc

Poggiali: champagne for a title.

The crowded paddock at the Riccardo Tormo circuit.

Valencia Grand Prix
2 November 2003
Valencia – 4.005 m

STARTING GRID

1.	7	R. De Puniet	Aprilia	1'36.499
2.	24	T. Elias	Aprilia	1'36.590
3.	50	S. Guintoli	Aprilia	1'36.647
4.	54	M. Poggiali	Aprilia	1'36.735
5.	6	A. Debon	Honda	1'37.221
6.	21	F. Battaini	Aprilia	1'37.327
7.	10	F. Gonzales-Nieto	Aprilia	1'37.711
8.	8	N. Matsudo	Yamaha	1'37.875
9.	5	S. Porto	Honda	1'37.028
10.	3	R. Rolfo	Honda	1'38.110
11.	33	H. Faubel	Aprilia	1'38.313
12.	34	E. Bataille	Honda	1'38.468
13.	14	A. West	Aprilia	1'38.586
14.	13	J. Hules	Honda	1'38.744
15.	57	C. Davies	Aprilia	1'38.850
16.	96	J. Smrz	Honda	1'38.935
17.	36	E. Nigon	Aprilia	1'39.059
18.	28	D. Heidolf	Aprilia	1'39.112
19.	73	R. Rous	Aprilia	1'39.334
20.	15	C. Gemmel	Honda	1'39.382
21.	16	J. Stigefelt	Aprilia	1'39.489
22.	11	J. Olive	Aprilia	1'39.498
23.	9	H. Marchand	Aprilia	1'39.731
24.	26	A. Baldolini	Aprilia	1'39.887
25.	52	L. Pesek	Yamaha	1'40.040
26.	40	A. Molina	Aprilia	1'40.098
27.	18	H. vd Lagemaat	Honda	1'41.656
28.	83	P. Lakerveld	Aprilia	1'42.534

RACE: 27 LAPS = 108.135 KM

1.	Randy De Puniet	44'01.924 (147.349 km/h)
2.	Toni Elias	+ 0"072
3.	Manuel Poggiali	+ 12"810
4.	Sylvain Guintoli	+ 22"496
5.	Alfonso Gonzales-Nieto	+ 30"731
6.	Sebastian Porto	+ 32"381
7.	Roberto Rolfo	+ 35"547
8.	Franco Battaini	+ 36"987
9.	Eric Bataille	+ 38"672
10.	Alex Debon	+ 41"748
11.	Naoki Matsudo	+ 55"156
12.	Dirk Heidolf	+ 1'03.117
13.	Chaz Davies	+ 1'08.018
14.	Jakub Smrz	+ 1'18.041
15.	Radomil Rous	+ 1'24.071
16.	Alvaro Molina	+ 1'29.994
17.	Johan Stigefelt	+ 1'32.471
18.	Henk vd Lagemaat	+ 1 lap
19.	Lukas Pesek	+ 1 lap
20.	Patrick Lakerveld	+ 2 laps

Fastest lap: De Puniet, in 1'36.499 (149.410 km/h).
Record: Nakano, in 1'36.398 (149.567 km/h/2000).
Outright fastest lap: Melandri, in 1'35.885 (150.367 km/h/2002).

CHAMPIONSHIP

1.	M. Poggiali	249 (4 wins)
2.	R. Rolfo	235 (2 wins)
3.	T. Elias	226 (5 wins)
4.	R. De Puniet	208 (3 wins)
5.	A. Gonzales-Nieto	194 (1 win)
6.	F. Battaini	148
7.	A. West	145 (1 win)
8.	S. Porto	127
9.	N. Matsudo	119
10.	S. Guintoli	101

Runners and riders:

Katja Poensgen's season ended prematurely for financial reasons, as the sponsor did not meet its obligations. So, just as in Sepang, it was the Czech, Jakub Smrz who found himself in the saddle of the Dutch Molenaar team Honda. Five riders from five different countries had wild card entries: Spain's Alvaro Molina, France's Gregory Leblanc, the Czech Radomil Rous, Dutchman Patrick Lakerveld and Austria's Yves Polzer.

Qualifying:

Tension was brewing in the Rolfo camp because of technical problems and life was not rosy for Manuel Poggiali, who made two mistakes (on Saturday at the end of qualifying and on Sunday in the morning warm-up.) Randy De Puniet kept his cool and totally dominated qualifying, while fellow countryman Sylvain Guintoli was in the running for pole for quite a while before finishing third.

Start:

A perfect start from Randy De Puniet and the two Spaniards, Toni Elias and Fonsi Gonzales-Nieto. Guintoli makes a hash of his start. At the end of the opening lap, De Puniet leads Nieto by 0"680. Poggiali is fifth, Rolfo eleventh.

Lap 3:

Hules goes missing haven fallen. De Puniet has pulled out a lead of 1"222 over Elias and an on-form Debon.

Lap 7:

Still De Puniet, now leading Elias by 1"777. Poggiali is third, but over four seconds down on the Spaniard. Rolfo, whose bike seized in the morning warm-up, is only tenth.

Half distance (lap 13):

Elias has just set the fastest lap as he closes to within 1"749 of De Puniet. Poggiali is on his own in third.

Lap 15:

De Puniet appears to have bothers with his rear tyre and Elias is only 85 thousandths down.

Lap 21:

De Puniet is in trouble as the engine cuts out for a moment and he momentarily loses the lead to Toni Elias.

Lap 23:

De Puniet gets in front again.

Finish (lap 27):

116 thousandths separate the two men at the start of the final lap. De Puniet is the master of the situation to take his third win of the season. In third place, Poggiali is world champion.

Championship:

Like Tetsuya Harada in 1993 and Freddie Spencer in 1985, Manuel Poggiali takes the 250 title at his first attempt, in a championship where Roberto Rolfo's consistency on the Honda was not enough when faced with Aprilia's dominance. Over the season however, Tony Elias (third in the championship) and Randy De Puniet (fourth) had shown the best turn of speed.

De Puniet-Elias: the Frenchman won the duel between the two quickest men of the 250 season.

Runners and riders:
World Champion, Daniel Pedrosa returned from Australia a week before this Valencia GP. After Masao Azuma in Motegi, it was the turn of two other "old boys" to announce their retirement: Lucio Cecchinello, who was going to concentrate on his management role and former World Champion, Emilio Alzamora.

Qualifying:
It rained on Friday morning and the track was cruelly lacking in grip, on a day when the wind was gusting strongly. Simoncelli was the high flyer at first, but come Saturday, it was De Angelis and Pablo Nieto who were quickest in an all-Aprilia front row.

Emilio Alzamora says his final farewells.

Start:
Barbera makes the best of it, ahead of Stoner and Simoncelli. Luthi had a problem on the warm-up lap and had to retire.

Lap 2:
Alex de Angelis falls, followed by Mika Kallio. Stoner now leads Barbera and Simoncelli, as the three Aprilia riders pull out a gap.

Lap 4:
Corsi and Ballerini fall, as Barbera leads the field.

The final podium of the season: Jenkner (2nd,) Stoner (first win) and Barbera.

Lap 7:
Stoner is now out in front as the lead trio enjoys a three second lead over the first pursuing trio- Dovizioso, Jenkner and Perugini.

Half distance (lap 12):
Barbera is a man possessed in front of his home crowd and heads Stoner by 227 thousandths and Simoncelli by 0"383. Behind them, Jenkner has moved up to fourth, ahead of Perugini and Dovizioso (sixth on his Honda behind five Aprilias.)

Lap 14:
For the past three laps, the Jenkner, Perugini, Dovizioso trio have been lapping quicker than the leaders. The German has closed to 2"110 of Barbera, for the moment back in third place. Arnaud Vincent retires with a broken exhaust.

Lap 18:
The breakaway is over as Jenkner is in Simoncelli's slipstream, the latter struggling to match the pace set by Stoner and Barbera.

Lap 20:
Jenkner is now third behind Stoner and Barbera.

Lap 22:
Still Stoner, but Jenkner is now second ahead of Barbera. Simoncelli has been dropped and is fighting with Perugini.

Finish (lap 24):
Perugini falls on the final lap. Casey Stoner heads for his first GP win, despite coming under attack from Barbera at the final corner. For the Spaniard, it's a case of win or bust and, trying to surprise the Australian round the outside, he runs too wide and ends up third.

Championship:
Despite his mistake, Barbera makes up two places in the championship to finish third.

Pablo Nieto heads Lucio Cecchinello, also in his last GP.

Valencia Grand Prix
2 November 2003
Valencia – 4.005 m

STARTING GRID

1.	15	A. De Angelis	Aprilia	1'40.440
2.	22	P. Nieto	Aprilia	1'40.551
3.	58	M. Simoncelli	Aprilia	1'40.599
4.	80	H. Barbera	Aprilia	1'40.723
5.	34	A. Dovizioso	Honda	1'40.802
6.	7	S. Perugini	Aprilia	1'40.911
7.	19	A. Bautista	Aprilia	1'41.210
8.	27	C. Stoner	Aprilia	1'41.240
9.	23	G. Borsoi	Aprilia	1'41.354
10.	36	M. Kallio	KTM	1'41.457
11.	6	M. Giansanti	Aprilia	1'41.590
12.	1	A. Vincent	Aprilia	1'41.606
13.	17	S. Jenkner	Aprilia	1'41.642
14.	88	R. Harms	Aprilia	1'41.862
15.	4	L. Cecchinello	Aprilia	1'41.875
16.	41	Y. Ui	Gilera	1'41.946
17.	48	J. Lorenzo	Derbi	1'42.056
18.	10	R. Locatelli	KTM	1'42.146
19.	32	F. Lai	Malaguti	1'42.216
20.	12	T. Lüthi	Honda	1'42.286
21.	79	G. Talmacsi	Aprilia	1'42.335
22.	31	J. Simon	Malaguti	1'42.398
23.	33	S. Bianco	Gilera	1'42.430
24.	11	M. Sabbatani	Aprilia	1'42.452
25.	63	M. Di Meglio	Honda	1'42.543
26.	25	I. Toth	Honda	1'42.551
27.	43	M. Hernandez	Aprilia	1'42.827
28.	26	E. Alzamora	Derbi	1'42.996
29.	70	S. Gadea	Aprilia	1'43.098
30.	90	D. Giuseppetti	Honda	1'43.296
31.	8	M. Azuma	Honda	1'43.420
32.	50	A. Ballerini	Honda	1'43.426
33.	24	S. Corsi	Honda	1'43.445
34.	69	D. Bonache	Honda	1'44.590
35.	81	I. Ortega	Aprilia	1'44.745
36.	42	G. Pellino	Aprilia	1'45.123
37.	28	M. Danese	Honda	1'45.780

RACE: 24 LAPS = 96.120 km

1.	Casey Stoner	40'27.662 (142.537 km/h)
2.	Steve Jenkner	+ 0"268
3.	Hector Barbera	+ 1"101
4.	Marco Simoncelli	+ 3"205
5.	Mirko Giansanti	+ 8"760
6.	Alvaro Bautista	+ 8"888
7.	Pablo Nieto	+ 12"265
8.	Andrea Dovizioso	+ 16"738
9.	Lucio Cecchinello	+ 21"089
10.	Gino Borsoi	+ 30"673
11.	Jorge Lorenzo	+ 32"847
12.	Gabor Talmacsi	+ 32"954
13.	Stefano Perugini	+ 33"349
14.	Robbin Harms	+ 34"889
15.	Masao Azuma	+ 34"958
16.	Max Sabbatani	+ 40"633
17.	Roberto Locatelli	+ 45"678
18.	Fabrizio Lai	+ 50"241
19.	Julian Simon	+ 50"313
20.	Sergio Gadea	+ 58"305
21.	Stefano Bianco	+ 58"315
22.	Imre Toth	+ 1'23.309
23.	Ismael Ortega	+ 1'33.631
24.	Emilio Alzamora	+ 1'39.042

Fastest lap: Jenkner, in 1'40.253 (143.816 km/h).
Record: Jenkner, in 1'40.252 (143.817 km/h/2002).
Outright fastest lap: Pedrosa, in 1'39.426 (145.012 km/h/2002).

CHAMPIONSHIP

1.	D. Pedrosa	223 (5 wins)
2.	A. De Angelis	166
3.	H. Barbera	164 (2 wins)
4.	S. Perugini	162 (2 wins)
5.	A. Dovizioso	157
6.	S. Jenkner	151 (1 win)
7.	P. Nieto	148 (1 win)
8.	C. Stoner	125 (1 win)
9.	L. Cecchinello	112 (2 wins)
10.	M. Giansanti	93

(1) RIDER	NATION	(2)	(3)	(4)	(5)	(6)	(7)	(8)	(9)	(10)
1. ROSSI Valentino	ITA	357	16	9	15	9	16	16	1	-
2. GIBERNAU Sete	ESP	277	16	1	9	4	10	15	1	1
3. BIAGGI Max	ITA	228	16	3	12	2	9	14	1	1
4. CAPIROSSI Loris	ITA	177	16	3	12	1	6	12	1	4
5. HAYDEN Nicky	USA	130	16	-	1	-	2	14	3	1
6. BAYLISS Troy	AUS	128	16	-	2	-	3	12	3	4
7. CHECA Carlos	ESP	123	16	-	3	-	-	13	4	3
8. UKAWA Tohru	JAP	123	16	-	2	-	-	13	4	2
9. BARROS Alexandre	BRÉ	101	15	-	1	-	1	12	3	3
10. NAKANO Shinya	JAP	101	16	-	1	-	-	15	5	1
11. TAMADA Tamoko	JAP	87	16	-	2	-	1	12	3	3
12. JACQUE Olivier	FRA	71	15	-	1	-	-	11	4	4
13. EDWARDS Colin	USA	62	16	-	-	-	-	12	6	2
14. HAGA Noriyuki	JAP	47	16	-	-	-	-	12	7	4
15. MELANDRI Marco	ITA	45	13	-	2	-	-	8	5	4
16. ABÉ Norifumi	JAP	31	4	-	-	-	-	4	8	-
17. HOPKINS John	USA	29	14	-	-	-	-	8	7	4
18. MCWILLIAMS Jeremy	GB	27	16	-	1	-	-	5	6	8
19. ROBERTS Kenny	USA	22	13	-	-	-	-	8	9	1
20. KIYONARI Ryuichi	JAP	22	13	-	-	-	-	8	11	-
21. AOKI Nobuatsu	JAP	19	16	-	-	-	-	5	9	6
22. MCCOY Garry	AUS	11	16	-	-	-	-	3	9	3
23. HOFMANN Alex	ALL	8	5	-	-	-	-	2	10	-
24. RYO Akira	JAP	6	2	-	-	-	-	1	10	-
25. KAGAYAMA Yukio	JAP	4	2	-	-	-	-	1	12	-
26. PITT Andrew	AUS	4	16	-	-	-	-	3	14	2

(1) Final Championship Classification   (2) Number of points   (3) Number of qualifications (out of 16 GP)   (4) Number of pole positions   (5) Number of front row starts
(6) Number of victories   (7) Number of podiums   (8) Scored points (top 15)   (9) Best race finish   (10) Number of retirements

FINAL CONSTRUCTOR'S WORLS CHAMPIONSHIP CLASSIFICATION

1.	HONDA	395
2.	DUCATI	225
3.	YAMAHA	175
4.	APRILIA	81
5.	SUZUKI	43
6.	PROTON KR	38
7.	KAWASAKI	19

FINAL TEAMS WORLS CHAMPIONSHIP CLASSIFICATION

1.	Repsol Honda	487
2.	Camel Honda	351
3.	Ducati Marlboro	305
4.	Telefonica Honda	299
5.	Fortuna Yamaha	188
6.	Gauloises Yamaha	172
7.	Alice Aprilia	109
8.	D'Antin Yamaha	101
9.	Pramac Honda	87
10.	Suzuki Grand Prix	55
11.	Proton Team KR	46
12.	Kawasaki Racing	15

ROOKIE OF THE YEAR

1.	HAYDEN Nicky	130
2.	BAYLISS Troy	128
3.	TAMADA Makoto	87
4.	EDWARDS Colin	62
5.	MELANDRI Marco	45
6.	PITT Andrew	4

250cc

(1) RIDER	NATION	(2)	(3)	(4)	(5)	(6)	(7)	(8)	(9)	(10)
1. POGGIALI Manuel	RSM	249	16	3	12	4	10	14	1	2
2. ROLFO Roberto	ITA	235	16	-	4	2	6	16	1	-
3. ELIAS Toni	ESP	226	16	5	10	5	7	14	1	1
4. DE PUNIET Randy	FRA	208	16	5	12	3	9	12	1	4
5. NIETO "Fonsi"	ESP	196	16	1	8	1	6	14	1	2
6. BATTAINI Franco	ITA	148	16	-	8	-	3	14	2	2
7. WEST Anthony	AUS	145	16	-	-	1	4	12	1	4
8. PORTO Sebastian	ARG	127	16	1	3	-	-	12	4	4
9. MATSUDO Naoki	JAP	119	16	-	2	-	-	14	5	2
10. GUINTOLI Sylvain	FRA	101	15	-	2	-	1	10	3	5
11. DEBON Alex	ESP	81	15	-	1	-	-	13	5	2
12. OLIVÉ Joan	ESP	38	16	-	-	-	-	8	7	4
13. FAUBEL Hector	ESP	34	16	-	-	-	-	7	6	7
14. DAVIES Chaz	GB	33	16	-	-	-	-	10	9	2
15. AOYAMA Hiroshi	JAP	31	2	1	1	-	1	2	1	-
16. NIGON Erwan	FRA	30	16	-	-	-	-	6	7	5
17. BALDOLINI Alex	ITA	30	16	-	-	-	-	8	10	7
18. TAKAHASHI Yuki	JAP	29	2	-	-	-	1	2	3	-
19. BATAILLE Eric	FRA	28	15	-	-	-	-	7	9	7
20. STIGEFELT Johan	SUÈ	26	15	-	-	-	-	7	10	7
21. HEIDOLF Dirk	ALL	26	13	-	-	-	-	9	11	3
22. GEMMEL Christian	ALL	24	16	-	-	-	-	7	8	5
23. MARCHAND Hugo	FRA	24	16	-	-	-	-	6	9	8
24. SMRZ Jakub	TCH	14	13	-	-	-	-	6	4	4
25. HULES Jaroslav	TCH	10	9	-	-	-	-	3	8	2
26. KAYO Tekkyu	JAP	7	1	-	-	-	-	1	9	-
27. KAMEYA Choujoun	JAP	6	1	-	-	-	-	1	10	-
28. VINCENT Jason	GB	5	1	-	-	-	-	1	11	-
29. NÖHLES Klaus	ALL	5	2	-	-	-	-	2	12	-
30. PESEK Lukas	TCH	4	9	-	-	-	-	1	12	3
31. NEUKICHNER Max	ALL	1	1	-	-	-	-	1	15	-
32. TOKUDOME Masaki	JAP	1	1	-	-	-	-	1	15	-
33. ROUS Radomil	TCH	1	2	-	-	-	-	1	15	1

(1) Final Championship Classification   (2) Number of points   (3) Number of qualifications (out of 16 GP)   (4) Number of pole positions   (5) Number of front row starts
(6) Number of victories   (7) Number of podiums   (8) Scored points (top 15)   (9) Best race finish   (10) Number of retirements

ROOKIE OF THE YEAR

1. POGGIALI Manuel	249
2. OLIVÉ Joan	38
3. DAVIES Chaz	33
4. BALDOLINI Alex	30
5. BATAILLE Eric	28
6. GEMMEL Christian	24
7. SMRZ Jakub	14

FINAL CONSTRUCTOR'S WORLS CHAMPIONSHIP CLASSIFICATION

1. APRILIA	390
2. HONDA	252
3. YAMAHA	119

125cc

(1) RIDER	NATION	(2)	(3)	(4)	(5)	(6)	(7)	(8)	(9)	(10)
1. PEDROSA Daniel	ESP	223	14	3	9	5	6	13	1	1
2. DE ANGELIS Alex	RSM	166	16	4	11	-	6	13	3	3
3. BARBERA Hector	ESP	164	16	-	4	2	5	14	1	2
4. PERUGINI Stefano	ITA	162	16	3	7	2	4	12	1	4
5. DOVIZIOSO Andrea	ITA	157	16	1	5	-	4	14	2	2
6. JENKNER Steve	ALL	151	16	-	2	1	6	10	1	6
7. NIETO Pablo	ESP	148	16	2	5	1	3	12	1	3
8. STONER Casey	AUS	125	14	1	4	1	4	8	1	5
9. CECCHINELLO Lucio	ITA	112	16	-	5	2	3	8	1	6
10. GIANSANTI Mirko	ITA	93	16	-	1	-	1	15	2	1
11. KALLIO Mika	FIN	88	16	-	2	-	1	10	2	4
12. LORENZO Jorge	ESP	79	16	1	4	1	2	8	1	6
13. UI Youichi	JAP	76	15	1	2	-	-	8	4	4
14. TALMACSI Gabor	HON	70	16	-	1	-	-	12	6	-
15. LÜTHI Thomas	SUI	68	15	-	-	-	1	9	2	3
16. AZUMA Masao	JAP	64	16	-	-	-	1	11	2	3
17. BORSOI Gino	ITA	54	16	-	-	-	-	10	8	3
18. VINCENT Arnaud	FRA	39	15	-	-	-	-	6	5	5
19. CORSI Simone	ITA	32	14	-	1	-	-	9	9	3
20. BAUTISTA Alvaro	ESP	31	16	-	-	-	-	6	4	3
21. SIMONCELLI Marco	ITA	31	15	-	1	-	-	6	4	3
22. BALLERINI Andrea	ITA	25	9	-	-	1	1	1	1	4
23. PELLINO Gioele	ITA	25	16	-	-	-	-	6	10	7
24. LOCATELLI Roberto	ITA	18	16	-	-	-	-	4	10	5
25. LAI Fabrizio	ITA	10	16	-	-	-	-	4	12	3
26. HARMS Robin	DAN	8	10	-	-	-	-	2	10	2
27. BIANCO Stefano	ITA	7	13	-	-	-	-	3	12	5
28. DI MEGLIO Mike	FRA	5	15	-	-	-	-	3	13	6
29. SIMÓN Julian	ESP	4	16	-	-	-	-	1	12	3
30. SABBATANI Max	ITA	3	15	-	-	-	-	1	13	7
31. ALZAMORA Emilio	ESP	2	16	-	-	-	-	1	14	7

(1) Final Championship Classification
(6) Number of victories

(2) Number of points
(7) Number of podiums

(3) Number of qualifications (out of 16 GP)
(8) Scored points (top 15)

(4) Number of pole positions
(9) Best race finish

(5) Number of front row starts
(10) Number of retirements

ROOKIE OF THE YEAR

1. STONER Casey	125
2. LÜTHI Thomas	68
3. CORSI Simone	32
4. BAUTISTA Alvaro	31
5. SIMONCELLI Marco	31
6. PELLINO Gioele	25
7. LAI Fabrizio	10
8. DI MEGLIO Mike	5
9. SIMÓN Julian	4

FINAL CONSTRUCTOR'S WORLS CHAMPIONSHIP CLASSIFICATION

1. APRILIA	343
2. HONDA	286
3. DERBI	79
4. KTM	66
5. GILERA	11
6. MALAGUTI	11

(world, European and national)

Superbike World Championship

2 March - Spain - Valencia

Race I: 1. N. Hodgson (GB, Ducati), 23 laps, 36'56"205 (149,631 km/h); 2. R. Xaus (E, Ducati), 4"700; 3. C. Walker (GB, Ducati), 12"377; 4. J. Toseland (GB, Ducati), 12"682; 5. R. Laconi (F, Ducati), 24"068; 6. S. Martin (AUS, Ducati), 27"006; 7. G. Lavilla (E, Suzuki), 39"792; 8. L. Pedercini (I, Ducati), 49"662; 9. M. Borciani (I, Ducati), 56"200; 10. D. Garcia (E, Ducati), 1'06"328; 11. I. Clementi (I, Kawasaki), 1'09"139; 12. J. Haydon (GB, Foggy FP1), 1'09"541; 13. N. Russo (I, Ducati), 1'14"450; 14. J. Borja (E, Ducati), 1'14"712; 15. S. Fuertes (E, Suzuki), 1'22"845. 16 finishers. **Fastest lap:** N. Hodgson (GB, Ducati), 1'35"557 (150,884 km/h).
Race II: 1. N. Hodgson (GB, Ducati), 23 laps, 36'46"191 (150,311 km/h); 2. R. Xaus (E, Ducati), 2"619; 3. J. Toseland (GB, Ducati), 13"468; 4. C. Walker (GB, Ducati), 23"426; 5. S. Martin (AUS, Ducati), 36"539; 6. G. Lavilla (E, Suzuki), 38"594; 7. T. Corser (AUS, Foggy FP1), 42"969; 8. J. Borja (E, Ducati), 51"625; 9. L. Pedercini (I, Ducati), 52"824; 10. M. Borciani (I, Ducati), 54"721; 11. G. Bussei (I, Yamaha), 1'00"510; 12. D. Garcia (E, Ducati), 1'02"114; 13. M. Sanchini (I, Kawasaki), 1'02"393; 14. I. Clementi (I, Kawasaki), 1'09"885; 15. N. Russo (I, Ducati), 1'17"697. 17 finishers. **Fastest lap:** N. Hodgson (GB, Ducati), 1'35"007 (151,757 km/h).

30 March - Australia - Phillip Island

Race I: 1. N. Hodgson (GB, Ducati), 22 laps, 34'51"974 (168,283 km/h); 2. R. Xaus (E, Ducati), 7"745; 3. G. Lavilla (E, Suzuki), 11"480; 4. S. Martin (AUS, Ducati), 17"968; 5. T. Corser (AUS, Foggy FP1), 18"353; 6. R. Laconi (F, Ducati), 18"647; 7. C. Walker (GB, Ducati), 20"317; 8. D. Garcia (E, Ducati), 29"731; 9. M. Borciani (I, Ducati), 30"113; 10. L. Pedercini (I, Ducati), 30"226; 11. I. Clementi (I, Kawasaki), 30"530; 12. J. Borja (E, Ducati), 43"660; 13. M. Sanchini (I, Kawasaki), 47"605; 14. G. Bussei (I, Yamaha), 47"624; 15. J. Haydon (GB, Foggy FP1), 1'05"711. 19 finishers. **Fastest lap:** N. Hodgson (GB, Ducati), 1'33"895 (170,424 km/h).
Race II: 1. N. Hodgson (GB, Ducati), 22 laps, 34'44"425 (168,893 km/h); 2. R. Xaus (E, Ducati), 0"070; 3. P. Chili (I, Ducati), 6"308; 4. R. Laconi (F, Ducati), 6"409; 5. J. Toseland (GB, Ducati), 14"402; 6. C. Walker (GB, Ducati), 14"409; 7. G. Lavilla (E, Suzuki), 14"426; 8. T. Corser (AUS, Foggy FP1), 14"426; 9. S. Martin (AUS, Ducati), 34"094; 10. M. Borciani (I, Ducati), 34"808; 11. I. Clementi (I, Kawasaki), 34"920; 12. M. Sanchini (I, Kawasaki), 35"667; 13. N. Russo (I, Ducati), 35"773; 14. L. Pedercini (I, Ducati), 55"419; 15. J. Borja (E, Ducati), 1'01"414. 20 finishers. **Fastest lap:** R. Xaus (E, Ducati), 1'33"813 (170,573 km/h).

27 April - Japan - Sugo

Race I: 1. N. Hodgson (GB, Ducati), 25 laps, 37'57"829 (147,654 km/h); 2. R. Laconi (F, Ducati), 7"167; 3. J. Toseland (GB, Ducati), 14"853; 4. R. Xaus (E, Ducati), 28"299; 5. G. Lavilla (E, Suzuki), 32"382; 6. H. Izutsu (J, Honda), 32"584; 7. L. Pedercini (I, Ducati), 1'00"615; 8. A. Watanabe (J, Suzuki), 1'02"154; 9. J. Haydon (GB, Foggy FP1), 1'07"432; 10. J. Borja (E, Ducati), 1'11"446; 11. M. Sanchini (I, Kawasaki), 1'17"354; 12. G. Bussei (I, Yamaha), 1'18"970; 13. M. Borciani (I, Ducati), 1'27"846; 14. K. Nakamura (J, Honda), 1'28"048; 15. S. Martin (AUS, Ducati), 1 Lap. 15 finishers. **Fastest lap:** N. Hodgson (GB, Ducati), 1'29"999 (149,482 km/h).
Race II: 1. N. Hodgson (GB, Ducati), 25 laps, 37'56"499 (147,740 km/h); 2. G. Lavilla (E, Suzuki), 0"818; 3. P. Chili (I, Ducati), 1"470; 4. R. Xaus (E, Ducati), 10"470; 5. J. Toseland (GB, Ducati), 11"133; 6. H. Izutsu (J, Honda), 21"604; 7. R. Laconi (F, Ducati), 21"953; 8. I. Clementi (I, Kawasaki), 48"857; 9. J. Borja (E, Ducati), 1'01"770; 10. M. Sanchini (I, Kawasaki), 1'05"289; 11. G. Bussei (I, Yamaha), 1'09"325; 12. T. Corser (AUS, Foggy FP1), 1'15"284; 13. M. Borciani (I, Ducati), 1 Lap; 14. K. Nakamura (J, Honda); 15. W. Tortoroglio (I, Honda). 15 finishers. **Fastest lap:** P. Chili (I, Ducati), 1'30"146 (149,238 km/h).

18 May - Italy - Monza

Race I: 1. N. Hodgson (GB, Ducati), 18 laps, 32'38"264 (191,893 km/h); 2. R. Laconi (F, Ducati), 0"382; 3. G. Lavilla (E, Suzuki), 0"389; 4. J. Toseland (GB, Ducati), 0"398; 5. P. Chili (I, Ducati), 1"617; 6. C. Walker (GB, Ducati), 24"138; 7. R. Xaus (E, Ducati), 30"889; 8. M. Borciani (I, Ducati), 31"609; 9. S. Martin (AUS, Ducati), 32"877; 10. L. Pedercini (I, Ducati), 35"902; 11. A. Gramigni (I, Yamaha), 41"700; 12. V. Iannuzzo (I, Suzuki), 45"872; 13. T. Corser (AUS, Foggy FP1), 54"204; 14. M. Sanchini (I, Kawasaki), 1'13"406; 15. S. Foti (I, Ducati), 1'27"704. 18 finishers. **Fastest lap:** N. Hodgson (GB, Ducati), 1'47"715 (193,611 km/h).
Race II: 1. N. Hodgson (GB, Ducati), 18 laps, 32'41"366 (191,390 km/h); 2. G. Lavilla (E, Suzuki), 0"044; 3. P. Chili (I, Ducati), 0"657; 4. R. Laconi (F, Ducati), 0"998; 5. J. Toseland (GB, Ducati), 6"379; 6. C. Walker (GB, Ducati), 27"289; 7. S. Martin (AUS, Ducati), 39"585; 8. M. Borciani (I, Ducati), 39"820; 9. V. Iannuzzo (I, Suzuki), 39"881; 10. L. Pedercini (I, Ducati), 43"406; 11. A. Gramigni (I, Yamaha), 51"240; 12. M. Sanchini (I, Kawasaki), 57"491; 13. G. Bussei (I, Yamaha), 57"503; 14. S. Foti (I, Ducati), 1'30"656; 15. W. Tortoroglio (I, Honda), 1'41"410. 17 finishers. **Fastest lap:** R. Laconi (F, Ducati), 1'47"909 (193,263 km/h).

1 June - Germany - Oschersleben

Race I: 1. N. Hodgson (GB, Ducati), 28 laps, 41'29"894 (148,454 km/h); 2. P. Chili (I, Ducati), 0"556; 3. J. Toseland (GB, Ducati), 12"965; 4. R. Laconi (F, Ducati), 16"630; 5. C. Walker (GB, Ducati), 16"754; 6. S. Martin (AUS, Ducati), 38"142; 7. M. Borciani (I, Ducati), 43"496; 8. V. Iannuzzo (I, Suzuki), 45"452; 9. L. Pedercini (I, Ducati), 50"154; 10. G. Bussei (I, Yamaha), 51"218; 11. M. Sanchini (I, Kawasaki), 1'04"353; 12. T. Corser (AUS, Foggy FP1), 1'10"643; 13. N. Russo (I, Ducati), 1 Lap; 14. S. Foti (I, Ducati); 15. J. Mrkyvka (SLO, Ducati). 17 finishers. **Fastest lap:** P. Chili (I, Ducati), 1'27"972 (150,061 km/h).
Race II: 1. J. Toseland (GB, Ducati), 28 laps, 41'20"103 (149,040 km/h); 2. N. Hodgson (GB, Ducati), 7"416; 3. C. Walker (GB, Ducati), 15"314; 4. R. Laconi (F, Ducati), 19"277; 5. R. Xaus (E, Ducati), 24"228; 6. S. Martin (AUS, Ducati), 43"648; 7. J. Borja (E, Ducati), 46"868; 8. V. Iannuzzo (I, Suzuki), 47"807; 9. M. Borciani (I, Ducati), 48"930; 10. L. Pedercini (I, Ducati), 1'02"514; 11. P. Chili (I, Ducati), 1'10"394; 12. M. Sanchini (I, Kawasaki), 1'12"686; 13. I. Clementi (I, Kawasaki), 1'13"019; 14. T. Corser (GB, Foggy FP1), 1'27"387; 15. S. Foti (I, Ducati), 1'14"366. 19 finishers. **Fastest lap:** N. Hodgson (GB, Ducati), 1'27"734 (150,468 km/h).

15 June - Great Britain - Silverstone

Race I: 1. N. Hodgson (GB, Ducati), 20 laps, 38'20"187 (157,362 km/h); 2. J. Toseland (GB, Ducati), 0"440; 3. R. Xaus (E, Ducati), 0"599; 4. R. Laconi (F, Ducati), 0"943; 5. Y. Kagayama (J, Suzuki), 4"779; 6. J. Reynolds (GB, Ducati), 5"085; 7. P. Chili (I, Ducati), 5"942; 8. M. Rutter (GB, Ducati), 6"371; 9. C. Walker (GB, Ducati), 7"229; 10. M. Borciani (I, Ducati), 34"399; 11. L. Pedercini (I, Ducati), 39"260; 12. G. Bussei (I, Yamaha), 43"387; 13. M. Sanchini (I, Kawasaki), 45"266; 14. I. Clementi (I, Kawasaki), 45"628; 15. N. Russo (I, Ducati), 46"388. 17 finishers. **Fastest lap:** G. Lavilla (E, Suzuki), 1'54"105 (158,885 km/h).
Race II: 1. N. Hodgson (GB, Ducati), 20 laps, 38'13"944 (158,065 km/h); 2. G. Lavilla (E, Suzuki), 0"493; 3. R. Xaus (E, Ducati), 0"653; 4. J. Toseland (GB, Ducati), 3"435; 5. Y. Kagayama (J, Suzuki), 4"117; 6. R. Laconi (F, Ducati), 4"220; 7. P. Chili (I, Ducati), 7"246; 8. C. Walker (GB, Ducati), 11"822; 9. M. Rutter (GB, Ducati), 12"399; 10. J. Reynolds (GB, Suzuki), 38"499; 11. L. Pedercini (I, Ducati), 44"491; 12. G. Bussei (I, Yamaha), 48"029; 13. M. Borciani (I, Ducati), 48"803; 14. M. Sanchini (I, Kawasaki), 48"994; 15. V. Iannuzzo (I, Suzuki), 49"432. 18 finishers. **Fastest lap:** G. Lavilla (E, Suzuki), 1'53"629 (159,551 km/h).

22 June - San Marino - Misano

Race I: 1. R. Xaus (E, Ducati), 25 laps, 40'22"423 (150,481 km/h); 2. J. Toseland (GB, Ducati), 0"760; 3. R. Laconi (F, Ducati), 1"711; 4. G. Lavilla (E, Suzuki), 10"933; 5. C. Walker (GB, Ducati), 20"487; 6. S. Martin (AUS, Ducati), 23"234; 7. T. Corser (AUS, Foggy FP1), 27"083; 8. L. Pedercini (I, Ducati), 32"026; 9. M. Sanchini (I, Kawasaki), 36"701; 10. I. Clementi (I, Kawasaki), 48"537; 11. M. Borciani (I, Ducati), 54"636; 12. A. Gramigni (I, Yamaha), 57"320; 13. P. Blora (I, Ducati), 1'01"084; 14. S. Foti (I, Ducati), 1'10"003; 15. S. Fuertes (E, Suzuki), 1'24"423. 17 finishers. **Fastest lap:** R. Xaus (E, Ducati), 1'36"158 (152,000 km/h).
Race II: 1. R. Xaus (E, Ducati), 25 laps, 40'17"321 (151.159 km/h); 2. N. Hodgson (GB, Ducati), 0"244; 3. P. Chili (I, Ducati), 6"896; 4. R. Laconi (F, Ducati), 13"814; 5. G. Lavilla (E, Suzuki), 17"399; 6. L. Pedercini (I, Ducati), 19"345; 7. V. Iannuzzo (I, Suzuki), 24"651; 8. C. Walker (GB, Ducati), 29"164; 9. S. Martin (AUS, Ducati), 32"310; 10. T. Corser (AUS, Foggy FP1), 33"516; 11. M. Sanchini (I, Kawasaki), 44"197; 12. J. Borja (E, Ducati), 52"247; 13. I. Clementi (I, Kawasaki), 52"628; 14. M. Borciani (I, Ducati), 1'01"445; 15. A. Gramigni (I, Yamaha), 1'02"445. 19 finishers. **Fastest lap:** R. Xaus (E, Ducati), 1'35"629 (152,841 km/h).

13 July - United States - Laguna Seca

Race I: 1. P. Chili (I, Ducati), 28 laps, 40'35"653 (149,401 km/h); 2. N. Hodgson (GB, Ducati), 3"068; 3. J. Toseland (GB, Ducati), 6"072; 4. M. Mladin (AUS, Suzuki), 12"322; 5. C. Walker (GB, Ducati), 21"605; 6. A. Yates (USA, Suzuki), 21"891; 7. G. Bussei (I, Ducati), 27"068; 8. T. Corser (AUS, Foggy FP1), 49"287; 9. M. Sanchini (I, Kawasaki), 49"679; 10. M. Borciani (I, Ducati), 50"261; 11. J. Borja (E, Ducati), 1'17"878; 12. W. Tortoroglio (I, Honda), 1 Lap; 13. L. Pedersoli (I, Ducati). 13 finishers. **Fastest lap:** R. Laconi (F, Ducati), 1'26"023 (151,076 km/h).
Race II: 1. R. Xaus (E, Ducati), 28 laps, 40'43"876 (148,898 km/h); 2. N. Hodgson (GB, Ducati), 11"565; 3. C. Walker (GB, Ducati), 13"064; 4. R. Laconi (F, Ducati), 15"560; 5. G. Lavilla (E, Suzuki), 16"354; 6. G. Bussei (I, Ducati), 19"685; 7. J. Borja (E, Ducati), 33"494; 8. M. Sanchini (I, Kawasaki), 35"564; 9. M. Borciani (I, Ducati), 35"859; 10. L. Pedercini (I, Ducati), 39"330. 10 finishers. **Fastest lap:** R. Xaus (E, Ducati), 1'26"451 (150,328 km/h).

27 July - Great Britain - Brands Hatch

Race I: 1. S. Byrne (GB, Ducati), 25 laps, 36'25"400 (172,843 km/h); 2. N. Hodgson (GB, Ducati), 5"799; 3. C. Walker (GB, Ducati), 5"918; 4. R. Laconi (F, Ducati), 6"808; 5. S. Emmett (GB, Ducati), 9"663; 6. J. Toseland (GB, Ducati), 9"926; 7. G. Lavilla (E, Suzuki), 10"370; 8. M. Rutter (GB, Ducati), 32"465; 9. P. Chili (I, Ducati), 32"724; 10. Y. Kagayama (J, Suzuki), 36"218; 11. D. Ellison (GB, Ducati), 45"798; 12. J. Borja (E, Ducati), 52"302; 13. I. Clementi (I, Kawasaki), 53"241; 14. S. Martin (AUS, Ducati), 54"176; 15. M. Sanchini (I, Kawasaki), 1'09"534. 19 finishers. **Fastest lap:** S. Byrne (GB, Ducati), 1'26"755 (174,159 km/h).
Race II: 1. S. Byrne (GB, Ducati), 25 laps, 36'25"639 (172,824 km/h); 2. J. Reynolds (GB, Suzuki), 0"539; 3. J. Toseland (GB, Ducati), 2"891; 4. R. Xaus (E, Ducati), 4"862; 5. N. Hodgson (GB, Ducati), 5"804; 6. G. Lavilla (E, Suzuki), 9"493; 7. P. Chili (I, Ducati), 16"049; 8. R. Laconi (F, Ducati), 17"771; 9. Y. Kagayama (J, Suzuki), 29"290; 10. L. Haslam (GB, Ducati), 31"484; 11. A. Gramigni (I, Yamaha), 1'02"240; 12. D. Ellison (GB, Ducati), 1'02"453; 13. I. Clementi (I, Kawasaki), 1'02"749; 14. M. Borciani (I, Ducati), 1'03"308; 15. M. Sanchini (I, Kawasaki), 1'07"499. 17 finishers. **Fastest lap:** J. Reynolds (GB, Suzuki), 1'26"767 (174,135 km/h).

7 September - The Netherlands - Assen

Race I: 1. R. Xaus (E, Ducati), 16 laps, 33'07"249 (174,691 km/h); 2. N. Hodgson (GB, Ducati), 0"609; 3. P. Chili (I, Ducati), 0"835; 4. J. Toseland (GB, Ducati), 1"062; 5. C. Walker (GB, Ducati), 14"737; 6. T. Corser (AUS, Foggy FP1), 22"981; 7. L. Haslam (GB, Ducati), 23"118; 8. I. Clementi (I, Kawasaki), 23"350; 9. S. Martin (AUS, Ducati), 45"862; 10. M. Sanchini (I, Kawasaki), 54"164; 11. A. Gramigni (I, Yamaha), 1'05"147; 12. L. Pedercini (I, Ducati), 1'39"774; 13. H. Saiger (A, Yamaha), 1'51"449; 14. G. Liverani (I, Yamaha), 1'51"917; 15. J. Mrkyvka (CZ, Ducati), 1'52"416. 17 finishers. **Fastest lap:** G. Lavilla (E, Suzuki), 2'03"081 (176,284 km/h).
Race II: 1. N. Hodgson (GB, Ducati), 16 laps, 32'57"759 (175,530 km/h); 2. R. Xaus (E, Ducati), 0"466; 3. G. Lavilla (E, Suzuki), 7"799; 4. R. Laconi (F, Ducati), 14"884; 5. P. Chili (I, Ducati), 19"868; 6. L. Haslam (GB, Ducati), 27"997; 7. I. Clementi (I, Kawasaki), 39"006; 8. C. Walker (GB, Ducati), 41"568; 9. T. Corser (AUS, Foggy FP1), 43"155; 10. J. Reynolds (GB, Suzuki), 48"883; 11. S. Martin (AUS, Ducati), 57"319; 12. M. Sanchini (I, Kawasaki), 1'06"208; 13. M. Borciani (I, Ducati), 1'08"487; 14. L. Pedercini (I, Ducati), 1'15"103; 15. A. Gramigni (I, Yamaha), 1'27"128. 21 finishers. **Fastest lap:** N. Hodgson (GB, Ducati), 2'02"649 (176,905 km/h).

28 September – Italy – Imola

Race I: 1. R. Xaus (E, Ducati), 21 laps, 38'30"586 (161,403 km/h); 2. N. Hodgson (GB, Ducati), 2"793; 3. R. Laconi (F, Ducati), 8"778; 4. G. Lavilla (E, Suzuki), 32"344; 5. P. Chili (I, Ducati), 37"382; 6. S. Martin (AUS, Ducati), 39"576; 7. T. Corser (AUS, Foggy FP1), 50"840; 8. M. Sanchini (I, Kawasaki), 1'00"616; 9. I. Clementi (I, Kawasaki), 1'01"306; 10. M. Borciani (I, Ducati), 1'09"525; 11. J. Borja (E, Ducati), 1'10"844; 12. D. Garcia (E, Ducati), 1'21"015; 13. A. Gramigni (I, Yamaha), 1'29"975; 14. S. Fuertes (E, Suzuki), 1'33"884; 15. L. Pini (I, Suzuki), 1'44"014. 21 finishers. **Fastest lap:** N. Hodgson (GB, Ducati), 1'49"317 (162,452 km/h).

Race II: 1. R. Xaus (E, Ducati), 21 laps, 38'29"867 (161,453 km/h); 2. R. Laconi (F, Ducati), 12"028; 3. G. Lavilla (E, Suzuki), 15"741; 4. N. Hodgson (GB, Ducati), 24"846; 5. C. Walker (GB, Ducati), 25"952; 6. L. Pedercini (I, Ducati), 51"778; 7. T. Corser (AUS, Foggy FP1), 55"582; 8. M. Sanchini (I, Kawasaki), 1'00"859; 9. J. Borja (E, Ducati), 1'18"737; 10. D. Garcia (E, Ducati), 1'17"924; 11. M. Borciani (I, Ducati), 1'31"807; 12. A. Gramigni (I, Yamaha), 1'34"712; 13. S. Fuertes (E, Suzuki), 1'43"592; 14. H. Saiger (A, Yamaha), 1 Lap; 15. L. Pini (I, Suzuki). 17 finishers. **Fastest lap:** R. Xaus (E, Ducati), 1'49"181 (162,655 km/h).

19 October – France – Magny-Cours

Race I: 1. N. Hodgson (GB, Ducati), 23 laps, 39'03"738 (155,833 km/h); 2. R. Xaus (E, Ducati), 0"348; 3. C. Walker (GB, Ducati), 13"711; 4. G. Lavilla (E, Suzuki), 13"950; 5. J. Toseland (GB, Ducati), 21"480; 6. R. Laconi (F, Ducati), 32"420; 7. S. Martin (AUS, Ducati), 41"098; 8. T. Corser (AUS, Foggy FP1), 41"204; 9. J. Borja (E, Ducati), 1'03"424; 10. M. Sancini (I, Kawasaki), 1'30"317; 11. S. Fuertes (E, Suzuki), 1'46"534; 12. C. Zaiser (A, Suzuki), 1'48"154; 13. B. Stey (F, Honda), 1 Lap; 14. F. Protat (F, Yamaha); 15. H. Saiger (A, Yamaha). 15 finishers. **Fastest lap:** N. Hodgson (GB, Ducati), 1'41"227 (156,871 km/h).

Race II: 1. R. Xaus (E, Ducati), 23 laps, 39'02"453 (155,926 km/h); 2. J. Toseland (GB, Ducati), 10"435; 3. C. Walker (GB, Ducati), 10"582; 4. G. Lavilla (E, Suzuki), 22"253; 5. S. Martin (AUS, Ducati), 35"564; 6. L. Haslam (GB, Ducati), 35"865; 7. J. Borja (E, Ducati), 56"719; 8. S. Gimbert (F, Suzuki), 1'00"813; 9. I. Clementi (I, Kawasaki), 1'02"307; 10. M. Sanchini (I, Kawasaki), 1'03"456; 11. L. Pedercini (I, Ducati), 1'33"537; 12. A. Gramigni (I, Yamaha), 1'41"234; 13. B. Stey (F, Honda), 1 Lap; 14. M. Borciani (I, Ducati); 15. F. Protat (F, Yamaha). 17 finishers. **Fastest lap:** N. Hodgson (GB, Ducati), 1'41"219 (156,884 km/h).

FINAL CLASSIFICATION

1. Neil Hodgson (GB, Ducati)	489
2. Ruben Xaus (E, Ducati)	386
3. James Toseland (GB, Ducati)	271

4. R. Laconi (F, Ducati), 267; 5. G. Lavilla (E, Suzuki), 256; 6. C. Walker (GB, Ducati), 234; 7. P. Chili (I, Ducati), 197; 8. S. Martin (AUS, Ducati), 139; 9. L. Pedercini (I, Ducati), 112; 10. M. Borciani (I, Ducati), 111.

Supersport World Championship

2 March - Spain - Valencia

1. K. Fujiwara (J, Suzuki), 23 Laps, 38'10"992 (144,747 km/h); 2. C. Vermeulen (AUS, Honda), 4"665; 3. A. Corradi (I, Yamaha), 12"889; 4. C. Cogan (F, Honda), 13"125; 5. J. Teuchert (D, Yamaha), 17"513; 6. K. Muggeridge (AUS, Honda), 16"777; 7. B. Parkes (AUS, Honda), 17"193; 8. C. Kellner (D, Yamaha), 17"513; 9. J. Van den Goorbergh (NL, Yamaha), 19"091; 10. W. Daemen (B, Honda), 20"854; 11. P. Riba (E, Kawasaki), 33"937; 12. S. Sanna (I, Yamaha), 34"739; 13. M. Schulten (D, Honda), 37"724; 14. F. Foret (F, Kawasaki), 39"501; 15. M. Lagrive (F, Yamaha), 40"664. 20 finishers. **Fastest lap:** A. Corradi (I, Yamaha), 1'38"874 (145,882 km/h).

30 March – Australia – Phillip Island

1. C. Vermeulen (AUS, Honda), 21 Laps, 34'03"675 (164,430 km/h); 2. K. Fujiwara (J, Suzuki), 9"299; 3. J. Van den Goorbergh (NL, Yamaha), 14"762; 4. S. Chambon (F, Suzuki), 16"008; 5. K. Curtain (AUS, Yamaha), 16"106; 6. J. Teuchert (D, Yamaha), 18"686; 7. K. Muggeridge (AUS, Honda), 18"834; 8. P. Riba (E, Kawasaki), 22"666; 9. A. Corradi (I, Yamaha), 22"685; 10. R. Ulm (A, Honda), 22"791; 11. F. Foret (F, Kawasaki), 22"972; 12. C. Kellner (D, Yamaha), 23"079; 13. C. Cogan (F, Honda), 23"175; 14. W. Daemen (B, Honda), 23"579; 15. S. Sanna (I, Yamaha), 24"666. 22 finishers. **Fastest lap:** K. Fujiwara (J, Suzuki), 1'36"642 (165,580 km/h).

27 April – Japan – Sugo

1. C. Kellner (D, Yamaha), 25 Laps, 39'19"896 (142,519 km/h); 2. R. Kiyonari (J, Honda), 0"243; 3. S. Chambon (F, Suzuki), 3"192; 4. T. Kayo (J, Yamaha), 10"334; 5. C. Vermeulen (AUS, Honda), 14"272; 6. K. Muggeridge (AUS, Honda), 16"377; 7. B. Parkes (AUS, Honda), 16"532; 8. J. Van den Goorbergh (NL, Yamaha), 17"596; 9. P. Riba (E, Kawasaki), 18"516; 10. A. Corradi (I, Yamaha), 28"626; 11. C. Cogan (F, Honda), 30"582; 12. W. Daemen (B, Honda), 37"443; 13. S. Sanna (I, Yamaha), 37"484; 14. G. Nannelli (I, Yamaha), 43"951; 15. K. Fujiwara (J, Suzuki), 45"520. 19 finishers. **Fastest lap:** C. Kellner (D, Yamaha), 1'33"244 (144,280 km/h).

18 May – Italy – Monza

1. C. Vermeulen (AUS, Honda), 16 Laps, 30'16"092 (185,154 km/h); 2. J. Van den Goorbergh (NL, Yamaha), 9"120; 3. I. MacPherson (GB, Honda), 12"236; 4. S. Chambon (F, Suzuki), 12"251; 5. F. Foret (F, Kawasaki), 13"529; 6. S. Charpentier (F, Honda), 13"817; 7. C. Kellner (D, Yamaha), 14"249; 8. A. Corradi (I, Yamaha), 14"562; 9. P. Riba (E, Kawasaki), 15"277; 10. K. Fujiwara (J, Suzuki), 16"066; 11. R. Ulm (A, Honda), 16"962; 12. C. Cogan (F, Honda), 22"557; 13. B. Veneman (NL, Honda), 29"549; 14. S. Sanna (I, Yamaha), 30"447; 15. B. Parkes (AUS, Honda), 38"193. 23 finishers. **Fastest lap:** C. Vermeulen (AUS, Honda), 1'52"635 (185.154 km/h).

1st June – Germany – Oschersleben

1. C. Vermeulen (AUS, Honda), 28 Laps, 42'51"384 (143,749 km/h); 2. S. Chambon (F, Suzuki), 1"775; 3. K. Fujiwara (J, Suzuki), 2"085; 4. J. Van Den Goorbergh (NL, Yamaha), 3"936; 5. B. Parkes (AUS, Honda), 8"438; 6. P. Riba (E, Kawasaki), 8"989; 7. J. Teuchert (D, Yamaha), 14"973; 8. C. Kellner (D, Yamaha), 20"274; 9. S. Charpentier (F, Honda), 24"001; 10. G. Nannelli (I, Yamaha), 29"143; 11. R. Ulm (A, Honda), 29"374; 12. M. Lagrive (F, Yamaha), 29"474; 13. D. Thomas (AUS, Honda), 36"099; 14. B. Veneman (NL, Honda), 41"521; 15. K. Muggeridge (AUS, Honda), 47"448. 20 finishers. **Fastest lap:** K. Fujiwara (J, Suzuki), 1'30"858 (145,295 km/h).

15 June – Great Britain – Silverstone

1. C. Vermeulen (GB, Honda), 19 Laps, 37'21"429 (153,680 km/h); 2. J. Van Den Goorbergh (NL, Yamaha), 12"157; 3. K. Muggeridge (AUS, Honda), 14"223; 4. T. Van Den Bosch (F, Yamaha), 15"462; 5. A. Corradi (I, Yamaha), 16"554; 6. C. Cogan (F, Honda), 22"202; 7. P. Riba (E, Kawasaki), 22"379; 8. K. Fujiwara (J, Suzuki), 24"063; 9. M. Lagrive (F, Yamaha), 27"053; 10. R. Ulm (A, Honda), 27"314; 11. C. Kellner (D, Yamaha), 27"607; 12. T. Tsujimura (J, Honda), 27"891; 13. D. Thomas (AUS, Honda), 32"380; 14. G. Nannelli (I, Yamaha), 35"614; 15. W. Daemen (B, Honda), 45"360. 20 finishers. **Fastest lap:** C. Vermeulen (AUS, Honda), 1'56"459 (155,674 km/h).

22 June – San Marino – Misano

1. F. Foret (F, Kawasaki), 23 Laps, 37'55"497 (147,734 km/h); 2. K. Fujiwara (J, Suzuki), 1"661; 3. B. Parkes (AUS, Honda), 3"953; 4. S. Chambon (F, Suzuki), 8"067; 5. J. Teuchert (D, Yamaha), 10"940; 6. C. Kellner (D, Yamaha), 11"271; 7. A. Corradi (I, Yamaha), 12"391; 8. S. Sanna (I, Yamaha), 17"319; 9. C. Cogan (F, Honda), 24"652; 10. S. Cruciani (I, Kawasaki), 26"136; 11. M. Lagrive (F, Yamaha), 28"189; 12. S. Charpentier (F, Honda), 31"567; 13. A. Polita (I, Yamaha), 33"532; 14. I. MacPherson (AUS, Honda), 42"474; 15. I. Goi (I, Yamaha), 47"125. 19 finishers. **Fastest lap:** K. Fujiwara (J, Suzuki), 1'37"924 (149,259 km/h).

27 July – Great Britain – Brands Hatch

1. S. Chambon (F, Suzuki), 21 Laps, 31'18"121 (168,047 km/h); 2. J. Van Den Goorbergh (NL, Yamaha), 17"045; 3. S. Charpentier (F, Honda), 17"310; 4. K. Muggeridge (AUS, Honda), 20"796; 5. F. Foret (F, Kawasaki), 22"081; 6. C. Vermeulen (AUS, Honda), 24"390; 7. C. Kellner (D, Yamaha), 24"509; 8. J. Teuchert (D, Yamaha), 24"693; 9. K. Fujiwara (J, Suzuki), 25"360; 10. A. Corradi (I, Yamaha), 32"659; 11. I. MacPherson (GB, Honda), 34"199; 12. T. Sykes (GB, Yamaha), 34"381; 13. P. Riba (E, Kawasaki), 36"753; 14. C. Cogan (F, Honda), 37"416; 15. B. Parkes (AUS, Honda), 41"475. 24 finishers. **Fastest lap:** S. Chambon (F, Suzuki), 1'29"149 (169,483 km/h).

7 September – The Netherlands – Assen

1. K. Muggeridge (AUS, Honda), 16 Laps, 34'05"948 (169,679 km/h); 2. C. Vermeulen (AUS, Honda), 0"263; 3. K. Fujiwara (J, Suzuki), 3"959; 4. S. Chambon (F, Suzuki), 4"129; 5. S. Charpentier (F, Honda), 12"102; 6. F. Foret (F, Kawasaki), 19"060; 7. J. Teuchert (D, Yamaha), 30"220; 8. G. Nannelli (I, Yamaha), 30"292; 9. W. Daemen (B, Honda), 30"906; 10. B. Veneman (NL, Honda), 31"047; 11. A. Corradi (I, Yamaha), 31"203; 12. M. Laverty (GB, Honda), 31"231; 13. D. Thomas (AUS, Honda), 31"376; 14. J. Hanson (S, Honda), 31"430; 15. R. Ulm (A, Honda), 31"700. 25 finishers. **Fastest lap:** K. Fujiwara (J, Suzuki), 2'06"922 (170,949 km/h).

28 September – Italy – Imola

1. K. Muggeridge (AUS, Honda), 21 Laps, 39'48"471 (156,140 km/h); 2. C. Vermeulen (AUS, Honda), 0"771; 3. J. Van Den Goorbergh (NL, Yamaha), 7"380; 4. S. Chambon (F, Suzuki), 10"035; 5. S. Charpentier (F, Honda), 10"766; 6. G. Nannelli (I, Yamaha), 13"884; 7. T. Kayo (J, Yamaha), 15"870; 8. I. MacPherson (GB, Honda), 34"341; 9. A. Carlacci (I, Yamaha), 35"085; 10. S. Sanna (I, Yamaha), 35"151; 11. M. Lagrive (F, Yamaha), 35"266; 12. C. Kellner (D, Yamaha), 40"252; 13. R. Ulm (A, Honda), 44"370; 14. J. Teuchert (D, Yamaha), 53"157; 15. A. Polita (I, Yamaha), 53"498. 20 finishers. **Fastest lap:** K. Curtain (AUS, Yamaha), 1'53"122 (156,988 km/h).

19 October – France – Magny-Cours

1. K. Muggeridge (AUS, Honda), 23 Laps, 40'24"892 (150,617 km/h); 2. C. Vermeulen (AUS, Honda), 3"543; 3. J. Van Den Goorbergh (NL, Yamaha), 6"338; 4. S. Charpentier (F, Honda), 5"565; 5. S. Chambon (F, Suzuki), 8"737; 6. P. Riba (E, Kawasaki), 14"446; 7. M. Lagrive (F, Yamaha), 23"042; 8. C. Kellner (D, Yamaha), 23"908; 9. C. Cogan (F, Yamaha), 24"131; 10. W. Daemen (B, Honda), 30"680; 11. S. Sanna (I, Yamaha), 30"977; 12. J. Da Costa (F, Kawasaki), 38"228; 13. G. Nannelli (I, Yamaha), 50"712; 14. M. Schulten (D, Honda), 51"336; 15. L. Holon (F, Yamaha), 52"527. 20 finishers. **Fastest lap:** K. Muggeridge (AUS, Honda), 1'44"643 (151,750 km/h).

FINAL CLASSIFICATION

1. Chris Vermeulen (AUS, Honda)	201
2. Stéphane Chambon (F, Suzuki)	137
3. Jurgen Van Den Goorbergh (NL, Yamaha)	136

4. K. Muggeridge (AUS, Honda), 134; 5. K. Fujiwara (J, Suzuki), 119; 6. C. Kellner (D, Yamaha), 90; 7. S. Charpentier (F, Honda), 72; 8. A. Corradi (I, Yamaha), 68; 9. F. Foret (F, Kawasaki), 64; 10. J. Teuchert (D, Yamaha), 60.

Endurance

MASTERS

14-15 April - Le Mans 24 Hours - France

1. Morrison/Dobé/Vincent (GB/F/F, Suzuki), 817 Laps; 2. Bayle/Gimbert/Dussauge (F, Suzuki), 2 Laps; 3. Donischal/Protat/Gomez (F, Yamaha), 16 Laps; 4. Da Costa/Moreira/Devoyon (F, Kawasaki), 18 Laps; 5. Lerat-Vanstaen/Jond/Cortinovis (F, Suzuki), 20 Laps; 6. Scarnato/Holon/Jerman (F/F/SLO, Yamaha), 33 Laps; 7. Baratin/Thuret/Cheron (F, Suzuki); 8. Boutin/Briere/Loustalet (F, Yamaha), 34 Laps; 9. Jond/Bonhuil/Ulmann (F, Honda), 38 Laps; 10. Dietrich/Tanore/Bouan (F, Suzuki), 39 Laps; 11. Morillon/Cuzin/Haquin (F, Yamaha), 41 Laps; 12. Notte/Bocquet/Gibet (F, Yamaha), 44 Laps; 13. Fabra/Goffinghs/Gabillon (F, Suzuki), 46 Laps; 14. Kedzior/Badziak/Szkopek (POL, Suzuki); 15. Guersillon/Hars/Legname (F, Suzuki).

6-7 July - Liège 24 Hours - Belgium

1. Four/Gimbert/Dussauge (F, Suzuki), 541 Laps; 2. Morrison/Dobé/Vincent (GB/F/F, Suzuki), 2'04"786; 3. Lerat-Vanstaen/Jond/Cortinovis (F, Suzuka), 19 Laps; 4. Cuzin/Nyström/Moreira (F/S/F, Kawasaki), 25 Laps; 5. Baratin/Thuret/Cheron (F, Suzuki), 28 Laps; 6. Seefeld/Schulz/Kitsch (D, Suzuki), 30 Laps; 7. Nickmans/Demeulemeester/Van Landschoot (B, Yamaha); 8. Fabra/Gabillon/Goffinghs (F/F/B, Suzuki); 9. Emonet/Roche/Notte (F, Yamaha), 32 Laps; 10. Balon/Lejeune/Weynand (F, Yamaha), 33 Laps; 11. Carlier/Labussiere/Guerouah (F, Kawasaki), 34 Laps; 12. Vleugels/Buylincks/Bakker (B, Suzuki); 13. Strauch/Röthig/Czyborra (D, Suzuki), 36 Laps; 14. Snickers/Snickers/Hubert (B, Suzuki); 15. Pawelec/Dubelski/Myszkowski (CZ, Yamaha), 37 Laps.

14-15 September - Bol d'Or - France

1. Bayle/Dussauge/Gimbert (F, Suzuki), 788 Laps; 2. Protat/Cogan/Lagrive (F, Yamaha), 9 Laps; 3. Costes/Foti/D. Checa (F/I/E, Suzuki), 15 Laps; 4. Dobé/Morrison/Philippe (F/GB/F, Suzuki), 17 Laps; 5. Haquin/Cuzin/Morillon (F, Yamaha), 25 Laps; 6. Thuret/Cheron/Baratin (F, Suzuki), 35 Laps; 7. Gibet/Roche/Emonet (F, Yamaha); 8. Waldmeier/Monot/Jaggi (F/F/CH,

Suzuki), 39 Laps; 9. Negg/Baker/Monterrat (F/GB/F, Yamaha), 40 Laps; 10. Fourcardet/Bertin/Destoop (F, Honda); 11. Tauziede/Braut/Michel (F, Suzuki), 42 Laps; 12. Giabbani/Diss/Kishida (F/F/J, Suzuki), 43 Laps; 13. Labussierre/Bronec/Guerquah (F, Kawasaki); 14. Dubelski/Pawelek/Myszkowski (POL, Yamaha), 46 Laps; 15. Lejeune/Dos Santos/Sotter (F/F/B, Suzuki), 49 Laps.

WORLD CHAMPIONSHIP

4 May - 200 Miles d'Imola - Italy

1. Nowland/Mertens (AUS/B, Suzuki), 66 Laps (150,972 km/h); 2. Ellison/Four (GB/F, Suzuki), 1'12"386; 3. Saiger/Wilding/Truchsess (A, Yamaha), 1 Lap; 4. Giabbani/Blora (F/I, Suzuki); 5. Kellenberger/Jerzenbeck/Nyström (CH/D/S, Kawasaki); 6. Scarnato/Guyot (F, Yamaha); 7. Tessari/Mauri (I, Ducati); 8. Capriotti/Fabi (I, Suzuki), 2 Laps; 9. Battisti/Bosetti (I, Suzuki); 10. Herber/Bursa (D/CZ, Suzuki); 11. Kedzior/Badziak/Szkopek (POL, Suzuki); 12. Giachino/Marangon (I, Suzuki), 3 Laps; 13. Jaggi/Monot/Waldmeier (CH/F/CH, Suzuki); 14. Spenner/Albrecht/Schmassmann (D/D/CH, Suzuki); 15. Stradi/Caprara/Fecchio (I, Suzuki).

25 May – 200 Miles d'Assen – The Netherlands

1. Jerman/Bonhuil (SLO/F, Suzuki), 83 Laps (161,857 km/h); 2. Ellison/Pridmore (GB/USA, Suzuki), 1"780; 3. Nowland/Mertens (AUS/B, Suzuki), 22"231; 4. Brian/Cuzin/Morillon (F, Yamaha), 1 Lap; 5. Bakker/Batens (NL/B, Suzuki), 2 Laps; 6. Giabbani/Blora/Chauchard (F/I/F, Suzuki); 7. Hutchins/Edwards/Falcke (GB, Suzuki), 2 Laps; 8. Capriotti/Fabi (I, Suzuki), 3 Laps; 9. Fincher/Jessop (GB, Suzuki); 10. Kitsch/Ehrenberger (D, Suzuki), 3 Laps; 11. Tijssen/De Vries/Heindijk (NL, Suzuki), 4 Laps; 12. Meyer/Meyer (D, Suzuki); 13. Carlberg/Notman (S/GB, Yamaha); 14. Platacis/Roth (D, Suzuki); 15. Jaggi/Waldmeier (CH, Suzuki).

15 June – 6 Hours of Brno – Czech Republic

1. Nowland/Mertens (AUS/B, Suzuki), 166 Laps (148,668 km/h); 2. Scarnato/Costes (F, Yamaha), 45"817; 3. Pridmore/Lindström/Four (USA/S/F, Suzuki), 2 Laps; 4. Marchetti/Garcia/Coutelle (I/F/F, Ducati), 3 Laps; 5. Falcke/Hutchins/Edwards (GB, Suzuki), 4 Laps; 6. Giabbani/Blora/Chauchard (F/I/F, Suzuki); 7. Kellenberger/Nyström/Bantli (CH/S/CH, Kawasaki), 5 Laps; 8. Mayer/Mayer (D, Suzuki), 6 Laps; 9. Jaggi/Monot/Pallarith (CH/F/CH, Suzuki); 10. Fincher/Jessop (GB, Suzuki); 11. Roth/Plantius (D, Suzuki), 8 Laps; 12. Bitter/Schmassmann (H/CH, Suzuki); 13. Sikora/Wiczynski (POL, Honda), 9 Laps; 14. Herber/Bursa/Persson (D/CZ/S, Suzuki), 10 Laps; 15. Szkopek/Badziak/Kedzior (POL, Suzuki).

29 June – 12 Hours of Albacete – Spain

1. Nowland/Mertens/Jerman (AUS/B/SLO, Suzuki), 441 Laps (129,940 km/h); 2. Bonhuil/Bontempi/Lerat-Vanstaen (F/I/F, Suzuki), 1 Lap; 3. Fernandez/Tomas/Rodriguez (E, Yamaha); 4. Scarnato/Holon/Foti (F/F/I, Yamaha), 4 Laps; 5. Cazade/Brian/Hacquin/Cuzin (F, Yamaha), 6 Laps; 6. Ellison/Ellison/Lindström (GB/GB/S, Suzuki), 12 Laps; 7. Saiger/Wilding/Truchsess (A, Yamaha), 13 Laps; 8. Kellenberger/Stamm/Nyström (CH/CH/S, Kawasaki), 15 Laps; 9. Jessop/Fincher/Notman (GB, Suzuki), 20 Laps; 10. Hutchins/Falcke/Pilborough (GB, Suzuki), 21 Laps; 11. Spenner/Schmassmann/Albrecht/Reisse (D/CH/D/D, Suzuki), 25 Laps; 12. Reigoto/Da Cunha/Porto (P, Suzuki), 27 Laps; 13. Scheers/Reymenants/Ploemen (B/NL/NL, Yamaha), 28 Laps; 14. P. Meyer/S. Meyer/Peuber (D, Suzuki), 29 Laps; 15. Gil/Lopetegui/Zabaleta/Antillera (E, Suzuki), 30 Laps.

20 July – 6 Hours of A1-Ring – Austria

1. Nowland/Mertens (AUS/B, Suzuki), 225 Laps (161,29 km/h); 2. Jerman/Bonhuil/Bontempi (SLO/F/I, Suzuki), 15"436; 3. Guyot/Foti/Scarnato (F/I/F, Yamaha), 1 Lap; 5. Ellison/Pridmore (GB, Suzuki), 2 Laps; 5. Brian/Morillon/Cuzin (F, Yamaha), 5 Laps; 6. Giabbani/Blora (F/I, Suzuki), 6 Laps; 7. Truchsess/Wilding/Saiger (A, Yamaha), 7 Laps; 8. Marchetti/Garcia/Edwards (I/F/GB, Ducati); 9. Roth/Plantius (D, Suzuki), 10 Laps; 10. Nyström/Kitsch (S/D, Kawasaki); 11. Spenner/Schmassmann/Albrecht (D, Suzuki); 12. P. Meyer/S. Meyer (D, Suzuki), 11 Laps; 13. Ruozi/Codeluppi (I, Suzuki); 14. Monot/Waldmeier (CH, Suzuki), 12 Laps;
15. Clerici/Barluzzi (I, Suzuki), 14 Laps.

3 August – 8 Hours of Suzuka - Japan

1. Nukumi/Kamata (J, Honda), 212 Laps (154,053 km/h); 2. Nakatomi/Yishikawa (J, Yamaha), 1 Lap; 3. Tsujimura/Itoh (J, Honda), 2 Laps; 4. Ellison/Pridmore/Lindholm (GB/GB/S, Suzuki), 4 Laps; 5. Giabbani/Kishida (F/J, Suzuki), 5 Laps; 6. Saito/Fukami (J, Yamaha); 7. Deguchi/H. Aoki (J, Honda); 8. An. Gobert/Ferguson (AUS, Suzuki); 9. Szoke/Young (CAN/GB, Suzuki); 10. Yamaguchi/Takahashi (J, Honda), 6 Laps.

23-24 August – 24 Hours of Oschersleben - Germany

1. Scarnato/Foti/D. Checa (F/I/E, Yamaha), 896 Laps (136,774 km/h);
2. Ellison/Hayes/Lindström (GB/USA/S, Suzuki), 5 Laps; 3. Hacquin/Morillon/Cuzin (F, Yamaha), 7 Laps; 4. Bontempi/Bonhuil/Lerat-Vanstaen (I/F/F, Suzuki), 8 Laps;
5. Kellenberger/Stamm/Nyström (CH/CH/S, Kawasaki), 14 Laps;
6. Giabbani/Blora/Kishida (F/I/J, Suzuki), 20 Laps; 7. Truchsess/Wilding/Saiger (A, Yamaha), 23 Laps; 8. Jaggi/Monot/Waldmeier (CH/CH/F, Suzuki), 26 Laps; 9. P. Meyer/S. Meyer/Wegscheider (D/D/I, Suzuki), 32 Laps; 10. Knöfler/Ludwig/Penzkofer (D, Yamaha), 34 Laps; 11. Cudlin/Fincher/Jessopp (AUS/GB/GB, Suzuki), 38 Laps;
12. Strauch/Röthig/Czyborra (D, Suzuki), 47 Laps; 13. Heiler/Hecker/Gres (D, Ducati), 63 Laps; 14. Carlberg/Varlbark/Andersson (S, Yamaha), 66 Laps; 15. Scheers/Reymenants/Ploemen (B, Yamaha), 67 Laps.

5 October – 200 Miles of Vallelunga - Italy

1. Giabbani/Blora/Moreira (F/I/F, Suzuki), 100 Laps (132,582 km/h); 2. Foti/Scarnato (I/F, Yamaha), 0"068; 3. Marchetti/M. Garcia/M. Edwards (I/F/GB, Ducati), 37"979;
4. Herber/Tode (D, Suzuki), 1 Lap; 5. Nowland/Mertens (GB/B, Suzuki), 2 Laps;
6. Saiger/Wilding/Truchsess (A, Yamaha); 7. Monot/Waldmeier (CH/F, Suzuki);
8. Hutchins/Falcke/Harris (GB, Suzuki); 9. Cudlin/Pilborough/Collins (F/GB/F, ?);
10. Tessari/Mauri (I, Ducati); 11. Haquin/Cuzin (F, Yamaha); 12. Ellison/Lindström/Ellison (GB/S/GB, Suzuki), 3 Laps; 13. Jennings/Sykes (S, Yamaha), 4 Laps;
14. Dionisi/Martinez (I/E, Suzuki); 15. P. Meyer/S. Meyer (D, Suzuki).

FINAL CLASSIFICATION

1. Phase One 143
2. Zonghsen I 127
3. GMT 94 109
4. Police Nationale, 104; 5. Zonghsen II, 91; 6. Moto 38, 72; 7. Yamaha Austria, 62;
8. Bolliger, 56; 9. Jet, 38; 10. Ducati DRE 5, 37.

Side-Cars World Championship

1st March - Spain - Valencia

1. Webster/Woodhead (GB, Suzuki), 18 Laps, 30'55"539 (139,864 km/h);
2. Abbott/Biggs (GB, Yamaha), 11"161; 3. Klaffenböck/Parzer (A, Yamaha), 11"251;
4. Skene/Miller (GB, Suzuki), 1'01"548; 5. Roscher/Heidenreich (D, Suzuki), 1'05"610;
6. Philp/Yendell (GB, Suzuki), 1'25"488; 7. Morrisey/Harper (GB, Yamaha), 1'38"413;
8. Doppler/Wagner (A, Yamaha), 1'43"629; 9. Hendry/Wilson (GB, Suzuki), 1 Lap;
10. Hauzenberger/Simons (A/GB, Suzuki); 11. Pedder/Parnell (GB, Yamaha); 12. Peach/Tomkinson (GB, Suzuki); 13. Minguet/Bidault (F, Suzuki); 14. Fleury/Fleury (NZ, Yamaha). 14 finishers. **Fastest lap:** Webster/Woodhead (GB, Suzuki), 1'41"365 (142,238 km/h).

17 May – Italy – Monza

1. Klaffenböck/Parzer (A, Yamaha), 14 Laps, 27'38"583 (176,034 km/h);
2. Steinhausen/Hopkinson (D/GB, Suzuki), 7"652; 3. Van Gils/Van Gils (NL, Suzuki), 20"391;
4. Roscher/Hänni (D/CH, Suzuki), 49"772; 5. Fisher/Long (GB, Yamaha), 1'09"614;
6. Hauzenberger/Simons (A/GB, Suzuki), 1'19"002; 7. Gällrös/Berglund (S, Suzuki), 1'24"491;
8. Le Bail/Chaigneau (F, Yamaha), 1'30"703; 9. Morrisey/Biggs (GB, Yamaha), 1'31"163;
10. Gatt/Randall (GB, Suzuki), 1'39"109; 11. Pedder/Parnell (GB, Yamaha), 1'4"310;
12. Minguet/Bidault (F, Suzuki), 1'51"016; 13. Founds/Muldoon (GB, Yamaha), 2'00"291;
14. Abbott/Biggs (GB, Yamaha), 1 Lap; 15. Fleury/Fleury (NZ, Yamaha). 17 finishers. **Fastest lap:** Webster/Woodhead (GB, Suzuki), 1'57"251 (177,865 km/h).

31 May – Germany – Oschersleben

1. Webster/Woodhead (GB, Suzuki), 22 Laps, 34'45"872 (139,235 km/h);
2. Klaffenböck/Parzer (A, Yamaha), 13"249; 3. Abbott/Biggs (GB, Yamaha), 17"370;
4. Hanks/Biggs (GB, Yamaha), 18"340; 5. Van Gils/Van Gils (NL, Suzuki), 43"897;
6. Roscher/Hänni (D/CH, Suzuki), 1'21"507; 7. Gällrös/Berglund (S, Suzuki), 1 Lap;
8. Hauzenberger/Simons (A/GB, Suzuki); 9. Philp/Yendell (GB, Suzuki); 10. Doppler/Wagner (A, Yamaha); 11. Founds/Heidenreich (GB/D, Yamaha); 12. Morrisey/Harper (GB, Yamaha);
13. Minguet/Bidault (F, Suzuki); 14. Fleury/Fleury (NZ, Yamaha); 15. Lindström/Riedel (S/D, Yamaha), 3 Laps. 15 finishers. **Fastest lap:** Webster/Woodhead (GB, Suzuki), 1'32"874 (142,141 km/h).

14 June – Great Britain – Silverstone

1. Webster/Woodhead (GB, Suzuki), 16 Laps, 32'19"005 (149,599 km/h);
2. Klaffenböck/Parzer (A, Yamaha), 5"332; 3. Steinhausen/Hopkinson (D/GB, Suzuki), 6"076;
4. Hanks/Biggs (GB, Yamaha), 6"764; 5. Abbott/Biggs (GB, Suzuki), 27"682; 6. Van Gils/Van Gils (NL, Suzuki), 40"360; 7. Roscher/Hänni (D/CH, Suzuki), 1'09"667; 8. Philp/Yendell (GB, Yamaha), 1'10"200; 9. Skene/Miller (GB, Suzuki), 1'11"215; 10. Morrisey/Harper (GB, Yamaha), 1'52"230; 11. Gatt/Randall (GB, Yamaha), 1 Lap; 12. Hendry/Wilson (GB, Suzuki);
13. Woodard/English (GB, Yamaha); 14. Fleury/Fleury (NZ, Yamaha); 15. Gällros/Berglund (S, Suzuki), 4 Laps. 15 finishers. **Fastest lap:** Webster/Woodhead (GB, Suzuki), 1'59"481 (151,736 km/h).

22 June – San Marino – Misano

1. Steinhausen/Hopkinson (D/GB, Suzuki), 20 Laps, 33'50"862 (143,939 km/h);
2. Hanks/Biggs (GB, Yamaha), 0"422; 3. Webster/Woodhead (GB, Suzuki), 4"730;
4. Klaffenböck/Parzer (A, Yamaha), 5"283; 5. Van Gils/Van Gils (NL, Suzuki), 45"569;
6. Roscher/Hänni (D/CH, Suzuki), 1'06"329; 7. Philp/Yendell (GB, Yamaha), 1'13"830;
8. Minguet/Bidault (F, Suzuki), 1'20"380; 9. Gatt/Randall (GB, Yamaha), 1'20"394;
10. Hauzenberger/Simons (A/GB, Yamaha), 1'23"219; 11. Skene/Miller (GB, Suzuki), 1'39"108; 12. Gällros/Berglund (S, Suzuki), 1'40"580; 13. Doppler/Wagner (A, Yamaha), 1 Lap; 14. Founds/Heidenreich (GB/D, Yamaha); 15. Fleury/Fleury (NZ, Yamaha). 16 finishers. **Fastest lap:** Steinhausen/Hopkinson (D/GB, Suzuki), 1'39"739 (146,542 km/h).

27 July – Great Britain – Brands Hatch

1. Webster/Woodhead (GB, Suzuki), 19 Laps, 32'54"191 (145,414 km/h);
2. Steinhausen/Hopkinson (D/GB, Suzuki), 0"440; 3. Klaffenböck/Parzer (A, Yamaha), 27"412;
4. Abbott/Biggs (GB, Suzuki), 34"868; 5. Hanks/Biggs (GB, Yamaha), 35"330; 6. Gatt/Randall (GB, Yamaha), 39"872; 7. Van Gils/Van Gils (NL, Suzuki), 1'00"458; 8. Philp/Yendell (GB, Yamaha), 1'01"693; 9. Hauzenberger/Simons (A/GB, Yamaha), 1'07"972;
10. Lovelock/Holloway (GB, Suzuki), 1'17"314; 11. Roscher/Hänni (D/CH, Suzuki), 1'17"520;
12. Morrisey/Harper (GB, Yamaha), 1'41"226; 13. Gällros/Berglund (S, Suzuki), 1'41"863;
14. Minguet/Bidault (F, Suzuki), 1 Lap; 15. Founds/Founds (GB, Yamaha). 16 finishers. **Fastest lap:** Webster/Woodhead (GB, Suzuki), 1'41"688 (148,584 km/h).

7 September – The Netherlands – Assen

Race I: 1. Webster/Woodhead (GB, Suzuki), 13 Laps, 28'19"356 (165,983 km/h);
2. Steinhausen/Hopkinson (D/GB, Suzuki), 6"865; 3. Klaffenböck/Parzer (A, Yamaha), 19"506;
4. Abbott/Biggs (GB, Suzuki), 19"612; 5. Hanks/Biggs (GB, Yamaha), 57"694; 6. Philp/Yendell (GB, Yamaha), 1'02"167; 7. Skene/Miller (GB, Suzuki), 1'07"477; 8. Gatt/Randall (GB, Yamaha), 1'17"086; 9. Van Gils/Van Gils (NL, Suzuki), 1'19"654; 10. Reeves/Reeves (GB, Yamaha), 1'44"747; 11. Gällros/Berglund (S, Suzuki), 1'45"860; 12. Roscher/Hänni (D/CH, Suzuki), 1'49"249; 13. Steenbergen/Steenbergen (NL, Yamaha), 2'03"178; 14. Fleury/Fleury (NZ, Yamaha), 1 Lap; 15. Stafford/Long (GB, Yamaha). 17 finishers. **Fastest lap:** Webster/Woodhead (GB, Suzuki), 2'08"392 (168,992 km/h).
Race II: 1. Webster/Woodhead (GB, Suzuki), 13 Laps, 28'33"867 (164,577 km/h);
2. Klaffenböck/Parzer (A, Yamaha), 6"413; 3. Abbott/Biggs (GB, Suzuki), 6"679;
4. Hanks/Biggs (GB, Yamaha), 16"377; 5. Van Gils/Van Gils (NL, Suzuki), 16"482;
6. Steinhausen/Hopkinson (D/GB, Suzuki), 41"685; 7. Reeves/Reeves (GB, Yamaha), 1'15"543; 8. Gällros/Berglund (S, Suzuki), 1'18"158; 9. Philp/Yendell (GB, Yamaha), 1'18"955;
10. Founds/Founds (GB, Yamaha), 1'28"826; 11. Morrisey/Harper (GB, Yamaha), 1'55"071;
12. Steenbergen/Steenbergen (NL, Yamaha), 2'11"320; 13. Stafford/Long (GB, Yamaha), 2'17"553; 14. Fleury/Fleury (NZ, Yamaha), 2'18"072; 15. Roscher/Hänni (D/CH, Suzuki), 1 Lap. 16 finishers. **Fastest lap:** Webster/Woodhead (GB, Suzuki), 2'09"925 (166,998 km/h).

27 September – Italy – Imola

1. Steinhausen/Hopkinson (D/GB, Suzuki), 16 Laps, 31'33"153 (150,089 km/h);
2. Webster/Woodhead (GB, Suzuki), 14"433; 3. Klaffenböck/Parzer (A, Yamaha), 31"953;
4. Van Gils/Van Gils (NL, Suzuki), 42"843; 5. Philp/Yendell (GB, Yamaha), 1'31"343;
6. Reeves/Reeves (GB, Yamaha), 1'31"927; 7. Skene/Miller (GB, Suzuki), 1'32"108;
8. Hanks/Biggs (GB, Yamaha), 1'45"556; 9. Gatt/Randall (GB, Yamaha), 1'52"979;
10. Dernoncourt/Lailheugue (F, Suzuki), 1'55"143; 11. Roscher/Hänni (D/CH, Suzuki), 1'58"476; 12. Gällros/Berglund (S, Suzuki), 2'06"350; 13. Founds/Long (GB, Yamaha), 1 Lap;
14. Minguet/Biadault (F, Suzuki); 15. Morrissey/Harper (GB, Yamaha). 18 finishers. **Fastest**

lap: Steinhausen/Hopkinson (D/GB, Suzuki), 1'56"954 (151,844 km/h).

19 October - France - Magny-Cours

1. Steinhausen/Hopkinson (D/GB, Suzuki), 18 Laps, 32'48"255 (145,221 km/h); 2. Abbott/Biggs (GB, Suzuki), 7"261; 3. Klaffenböck/Parzer (A, Yamaha), 12"502; 4. Van Gils/Van Gils (NL, Suzuki), 12"996; 5. Webster/Woodhead (GB, Suzuki), 32"570; 6. Philp/Yandell (GB, Yamaha), 53"316; 7. Dernoncourt/Lailheugue (F, Suzuki), 56"686; 8. Roscher/Hänni (D/CH, Suzuki), 1'02"680; 9. Gatt/Randall (GB, Yamaha), 1'03"004; 10. Minguet/Bidault (F, Suzuki), 1'03"504; 11. Doppler/Wagner (A, Yamaha), 1'19"575; 12. Cameron/Cox (GB, Suzuki), 1'30"350; 13. Skene/Miller (GB, Suzuki), 1'47"017; 14. Le Bail/Chaigneau (F, Yamaha), 1'50"460; 15. Morrisey/Harper (GB, Yamaha), 1'58"220. 20 finishers. **Fastest lap:** Steinhausen/Hopkinson (D/GB, Suzuki), 1'47"674 (147,674 km/h).

FINAL CLASSIFICATION

1. Webster/Woodhead (GB, Suzuki)	197
2. Klaffenböck/Parzer (A, Yamaha)	178
3. Steinhausen/Hopkinson (D/GB, Suzuki)	161

4. Abbott/Biggs (GB, Suzuki), 111; 5. Van Gils/Van Gils (NL, Suzuki), 101; 6. Hans/Biggs (GB, Yamaha), 89; 7. Philp/Yandell (GB, Yamaha), 80; 8. Roscher/Hänni (D/CH, Suzuki), 76; 9. Gatt/Randall (GB, Yamaha), 50; 10. Skene/Miller (GB, Suzuki), 46.

European Championship

125 cmc

27 April - Vallelunga - Italy

1. Di Giuseppe (I, Honda), 19 Laps, 26'06"983 (140,904 km/h); 2. Angeloni (I, Honda), 0"216; 3. Zappa (I, Aprilia), 0"219; 4. Aldrovandi (I, Honda), 1"053; 5. Conti (I, Honda), 1"372; 6. G. Hernandez (E, Aprilia), 2"190; 7. Caffiero (I, Aprilia), 10"059; 8. Giuseppetti (D, Honda), 10"329; 9. Pasini (I, Aprilia), 11"787; 10. Pagnoni (I, Aprilia), 16"005; 11. Narduzzi (I, Honda), 23"625; 12. Suardi (I, Honda), 24"039; 13. Danese (I, Aprilia), 30"449; 14. Kalab (CZ, Honda), 30"543; 15. Gnani (I, Gnani), 34"285.

1st June - Croatia - Rijeka

1. Conti (I, Honda), 16 Laps, 25'20"151 (157,929 km/h); 2. Angeloni (I, Honda), 0"188; 3. Giuseppetti (D, Honda), 1"874; 4. Petrini (I, Aprilia), 3"267; 5. Pasini (I, Aprilia), 3"921; 6. Zappa (I, Aprilia), 4"156; 7. Pagnoni (I, Aprilia), 12"016; 8. Pirro (I, Aprilia), 12"419; 9. Kalab (CZ, Honda), 12"489; 10. Magda (H, Honda), 12"509; 11. Bittman (CZ, Honda), 12"622; 12. Suardi (I, Honda), 20"487; 13. Carchano (E, Honda), 28"408; 14. H. Lauslehto (SF, Honda), 32"619; 15. Nedog (SLO, Honda), 32"863.

27 June - The Netherlands - Assen

1. Giuseppetti (D, Honda), 12 Laps, 28'05"677 (154,458 km/h); 2. Conti (I, Honda), 0"433; 3. Miralles (E, Aprilia), 4"782; 4. Pirro (I, Aprilia), 10"284; 5. Braillard (CH, Honda), 18"193; 6. Hernandez (E, Aprilia), 18"427; 7. Petrini (I, Aprilia), 18"971; 8. Danese (I, Aprilia), 19"648; 9. Kalab (CZ, Honda), 19"719; 10. Angeloni (I, Honda), 29"228; 11. Carchano (E, Honda), 30"908; 12. Masbou (F, Honda), 37"240; 13. Petit (F, Honda), 37"240; 14. Antonelli (I, Honda), 37"922; 15. Zappa (I, Aprilia), 44"474.

13 July - Czech Republic - Most

1. Giuseppetti (D, Honda), 18 Laps, 28'40"373 (156,240 km/h); 2. Angeloni (I, Honda), 2"177; 3. Fröhlich (D, Honda), 13"729; 4. Pagnoni (I, Aprilia), 13"963; 5. Pasini (I, Aprilia), 13"971; 6. Conti (I, Honda), 14"405; 7. Mickan (D, Honda), 22"054; 8. Masbou (F, Honda), 39"730; 9. Suardi (I, Honda), 39"893; 10. Bittman (CZ, Honda), 40"873; 11. Kalab (CZ, Honda), 40"881; 12. D'Amelio (I, Honda), 43"137; 13. Carchano (E, Honda), 43"448; 14. Schouten (NL, Honda), 49"872; 15. Vigilucci (I, Honda), 53"935.

10 August - Anderstorp - Sweden

1. Pasini (I, Aprilia), 17 Laps, 28'33"001 (143,800 km/h); 2. Angeloni (I, Honda), 0"128; 3. Pirro (I, Aprilia), 3"266; 4. Pagnoni (I, Aprilia), 4"569; 5. Braillard (CH, Honda), 22"199; 6. Conti (I, Honda), 22"345; 7. Schouten (NL, Honda), 32"388; 8. Suardi (I, Honda), 37"111; 9. Vigilucci (I, Honda), 37"960; 10. Pianas (E, Honda), 38"269; 11. Gautier (F, Honda), 38"314; 12. D'Amelio (I, Honda), 38"502; 13. Kaulamo (SF, Honda), 38"569; 14. Pekkanen (SF, Honda), 39"116; 15. Srdanov (NL, Aprilia), 39"248.

21 September - Hungaroring - Hungary

1. Giuseppetti (D, Honda), 15 Laps, 28'29"760 (133,676 km/h); 2. Angeloni (I, Honda), 0"210; 3. Pirro (I, Aprilia), 2"120; 4. Magda (H, Honda), 3"380; 5. Pasini (I, Aprilia), 3"980; 6. Ranseder (A, Honda), 12"650; 7. Kalab (CZ, Honda), 15"890; 8. Bittman (CZ, Honda), 16"820; 9. Pagnoni (I, Aprilia), 20"740; 10. Carchano (E, Honda), 22"240; 11. Antonelli (I, Honda), 28"830; 12. Masbou (F, Honda), 32"850; 13. Martin (GB, Honda), 34"490; 14. Nedog (SLO, Honda), 34"690; 15. Vigilucci (I, Honda), 38"180.

5 October - Braga - Portugal

1. Giuseppetti (D, Honda), 21 Laps, 28'43"729 (132,452 km/h); 2. Angeloni (I, Honda), 3"915; 3. Hernandez (E, Aprilia), 15"588; 4. Pagnoni (I, Aprilia), 21"347; 5. Pasini (I, Aprilia), 21"540; 6. Kalab (CZ, Honda), 24"592; 7. Masbou (F, Honda), 31"475; 8. Conti (I, Honda), 31"667; 9. Carchano (E, Honda), 36"185; 10. Magda (CZ, Honda), 41"402; 11. Antonelli (I, Honda), 41"524; 12. De Rosa (I, Aprilia), 41"783; 13. Martin (GB, Aprilia), 51"915; 14. D'Amelio (I, Honda), 56"051; 15. Vigilucci (I, Honda), 57"948.

12 October - Cartagena - Spain

1. Pirro (I, Aprilia), 20 Laps, 33'18"841 (126,250 km/h); 2. Hernandez (E, Aprilia), 1"636; 3. Bonache (E, Honda), 3"044; 4. Angeloni (I, Honda), 11"560; 5. Pasini (I, Aprilia), 11"940; 6. Giuseppetti (D, Honda), 13"449; 7. Pagnoni (I, Aprilia), 15"027; 8. Jerez (E, Honda), 15"586; 9. Gadea (E, Aprilia), 15"823; 10. Kalab (CZ, Honda), 21"959; 11. Magda (CZ, Honda), 36"842; 12. Martin (GB, Honda), 36"883; 13. De Rosa (I, Aprilia), 38"998; 14. Braillard (CH, Honda), 37"048 ; 15. Carchano (E, Honda), 37"539.

FINAL CLASSIFICATION

1. Mattia Anggeloni (I, Honda)	139
2. Dario Giuseppetti (D, Honda)	134
3. Luca Pasini (I, Aprilia)	87

4. Conti (I, Honda), 84; 5. Pirro (I, Aprilia), 78; 6. Pagnoni (I, Aprilia), 70; 7. Hernandez (E, Aprilia), 56; 8. Kalab (CZ, Honda), 41; 9. Magda (CZ, Honda), 30; 10. Zappa (I, Aprilia), 27.

250 cmc

27 April - Vallelunga - Italy

1. Sekiguchi (J, Yamaha), 22 Laps, 29'34"817 (144,047 km/h); 2. Rizmayer (H, Honda), 13"037; 3. Janssen (NL, Yamaha), 15"169; 4. V. Kallio (SF, Yamaha), 20"275; 5. Neikirchner (D, Honda), 20"800; 6. Pesek (CZ, Yamaha), 33"587; 7. Lakerveld (NL, Aprilia), 35"621; 8. Sörensen (DK, Yamaha), 39"351; 9. Rank (D, Honda), 40"279; 10. Rous (CZ, Honda), 40"467; 11. T. Lauslehto (SF, Yamaha), 44"006; 12. Matikainen (SF, Yamaha), 44"023; 13. Filart (NL, Yamaha), 56"843; 14. Anghetti (I, Aprilia), 1'04"853; 15. Sawford (GB, Honda), 1'19"403.

1st June - Croatia - Rijeka

1. Sekiguchi (J, Yamaha), 18 Laps, 27'43"970 (162,314 km/h); 2. Neukirchner (D, Honda), 0"099; 3. Pesek (CZ, Yamaha), 0"568; 4. V. Kallio (SF, Yamaha), 10"756; 5. Janssen (NL, Yamaha), 19"580; 6. T. Lauslehto (SF, Yamaha), 19"634; 7. Rous (CZ, Honda), 19"999; 8. Selmar (DK, Yamaha), 30"320; 9. D. Checa (E, Honda), 30"375; 10. Polzer (A, Honda), 30"408; 11. Anghetti (I, Aprilia), 30"431; 12. Sörensen (DK, Yamaha), 30"563; 13. Aggerholm (DK, Yamaha), 31"123; 14. Filart (NL, Yamaha), 57"994; 15. Heierli (CH, Honda), 58"033.

28 June - The Netherlands - Assen

1. Sekiguchi (J, Yamaha), 13 Laps, 30'34"121 (153,787 km/h); 2. Pesek (CZ, Yamaha), 6"578; 3. Sinke (NL, Aprilia), 26"828; 4. Janssen (NL, Yamaha), 32"739; 5. Sörensen (DK, Yamaha), 36"290; 6. Rous (CZ, Honda), 38"490; 7. Selmar (DK, Yamaha), 40"326; 8. Hoogeveen (NL, Yamaha), 40"744; 9. Rizmayer (H, Honda), 40"810; 10. D. Checa (E, Honda), 46"132; 11. Lakerveld (NL, Aprilia), 46"277; 12. V. Kallio (SF, Yamaha), 46"455; 13. Politiek (NL, Honda), 52"352; 14. Matikainen (SF, Yamaha), 54"923; 15. Polzer (A, Honda), 59"949.

13 July - Czech Republic - Most

1. Sekiguchi (J, Yamaha), 20 Laps, 30'56"036 (160,911 km/h); 2.Pesek (CZ, Yamaha), 3"879; 3. Neukirchner (D, Honda), 7"682; 4. Janssen (NL, Yamaha), 22"290; 5. Rous (CZ, Honda), 22"476; 6. Sörensen (DK, Yamaha), 22"545; 7. Vos (NL, Yamaha), 23"493; 8. Rizmayer (H, Honda), 38"593; 9. Polzer (A, Honda), 49"188; 10. Rank (D, Honda), 49"387; 11. V. Kallio (SF, Yamaha), 55"442; 12. T. Lauslehto (SF, Yamaha), 56"572; 13. Leblanc (F, Honda), 56"670; 14. Cerny (S, Yamaha), 56"780; 15. Heierli (CH, Honda), 1'01"891.

10 August - Anderstorp - Sweden

1. Sekiguchi (J, Yamaha), 19 Laps, 40'48"662 (148,924 km/h); 2. V. Kallio (SF, Yamaha), 0"868; 3. Lakerveld (NL, Aprilia), 7"530; 4. Watz (S, Yamaha), 13"468; 5. Sörensen (DK, Yamaha), 18"407; 6. Rous (CZ, Honda), 29"013; 7. Leblanc (F, Honda), 29"377; 8. Polzer (A, Honda), 29"702; 9. Aggerholm (DK, Yamaha), 45"450; 10. Rizmayer (H, Honda), 45"755; 11. Filla (CZ, Yamaha), 46"233; 12. Matikainen (S, Yamaha), 46"311; 13. Martensson (SF, Yamaha), 1'00"440; 14. Lindfors (S, Aprilia), 1'13"523; 15. Fransson (S, Yamaha), 1'26"099.

21 September - Hungaroring - Hungary

1. Sekiguchi (J, Yamaha), 16 Laps, 30'35"030 (137,516 km/h); 2. V. Kallio (SF, Yamaha), 29"240; 3. Leblanc (F, Honda), 33"400; 4. Sörensen (DK, Yamaha), 33"520; 5. Polzer (A, Honda), 36"000; 6. Filla (SLO, Yamaha), 40"920; 7. Selmar (DK, Yamaha), 41"770; 8. Aggerhorm (DK, Yamaha), 41"910; 9. Rank (D, Honda), 49"210; 10. Anghetti (I, Aprilia), 54"160; 11. T. Lauslehto (SF, Yamaha), 1'01"590; 12. Lindfors (S, Aprilia), 1'12"870; 13. Heierli (CH, Honda), 1'12"99; 14. Sawford (GB, Honda), 1'14"450; 15. Mordgren (S, Honda), 1'42"580.

5 October - Braga - Portugal

1. Sekiguchi (J, Yamaha), 24 Laps, 32'09"387 (135,239 km/h); 2. V. Kallio (SF, Yamaha), 24"878; 3. Neukirchner (D, Honda), 29"754; 4. Janssen (NL, Yamaha), 29"974; 5. Rous (CZ, Honda), 36"303; 6. T. Lauslehto (SF, Yamaha), 42"044; 7. Sörensen (DK, Yamaha), 42"246; 8. Selmar (DK, Yamaha), 42"639; 9. Zanette (I, Yamaha), 58"096; 10. Aggerholm (DK, Yamaha), 1'03"276; 11. Leblanc (F, Honda), 1'07"567; 12. Polzer (A, Honda), 1'08"347; 13. Rank (D, Honda), 1'08"609; 14. Heierli (CH, Honda), 1 Lap; 15. S. Edwards (GB, Honda).

12 October - Cartagena - Spain

1. Sekiguchi (J, Yamaha), 24 Laps, 39'02"933 (129,350 km/h); 2. Molina (E, Aprilia), 1"117; 3. Neukirchner (D, Honda), 27"427; 4. V. Kallio (SF, Yamaha), 33"558; 5. Rous (CZ, Honda), 43"809; 6. Sörensen (DK, Yamaha), 57"939; 7. T. Lauslehto (SF, Yamaha), 49"596; 8. Aggerholm (DK, Yamaha), 1'06"638; 9. Filla (SLO, Yamaha), 1'17"075; 10. Polzer (A, Honda), 1'19"327; 11. Rank (D, Honda), 1'20"263; 12. Zanette (I, Yamaha), 1'26"112; 13. S. Edwards (GB, Honda), 1'32"012; 14. Rizmayer (H, Honda), 1 Lap; 15. Vehniainen (SF, Honda).

FINAL CLASSIFICATION

1. Taro Sekiguchi (J, Yamaha)	200
2. Vesa Kallio (SF, Yamaha)	108
3. Max Neukirchner (D, Honda)	79

4. Sörensen (DK, Yamaha), 76; 5. Rous (CZ, Honda), 66; 6. Pesek (CZ, Yamaha), 66; 7. Janssen (NL, Yamaha), 66; 8. Rizmayer (H, Honda), 43; 9. Polzer (A, Honda), 42; 10. T. Lauslehto (SF, Yamaha), 43.

Supersport

27 April - Vallelunga - Italy

1. Boccolini (I, Honda), 25 Laps, 34'07"447 (141,894 km/h); 2. Baiocco (I, Yamaha), 0"235; 3. Mariottini (I, Yamaha), 5"783; 4. Carlacci (I, Yamaha), 5"871; 5. G. Guareschi (I, Kawasaki), 6"130; 6. Jansson (S, Yamaha), 14"722; 7. Landström (S, Yamaha), 16"157; 8. Tarrizo (I, Yamaha), 38"934; 9. Penna (SF, Yamaha), 39"695; 10. Biagioli (I, Yamaha), 41"894; 11. Anello (I, Yamaha), 1'14"772; 12. Rasmussen (DK, Kawasaki), 1 Lap; 13. Lauridsen (DK, Kawasaki); 14. Hafenegger (D, Yamaha), 2 Laps; 15. D'Agui (I, Yamaha).

1st June - Croatia - Rijeka

1. Hafenegger (D, Yamaha), 20 Laps, 31'25"292 (159,177 km/h); 2. Boccolini (I, Honda), 2"609; 3. Penna (SF, Yamaha), 4"831; 4. Bartolini (I, Honda), 10"059; 5. Emili (I, Kawasaki), 11"103; 6. Mariottini (I, Yamaha), 11"629; 7. Baiocco (I, Yamaha), 16"749; 8. G. Guareschi (I, Kawasaki), 16"956; 9. Giugovaz (I, Honda), 24"156; 10. Tarizzo (I, Yamaha), 30"449; 11. Haarala (SF, Kawasaki), 30"833; 12. Tuden (CRO, Kawasaki), 32"560; 13. Sacchetti (I, Yamaha), 38"027; 14. M. Jerman (SLO, Kawasaki), 57"545; 15. Vida (H, Honda), 1'04"295.

13 July - Czech Republic - Most

1. Boccolini (I, Honda), 21 Laps, 32'44"294 (159,645 km/h); 2. Hafenegger (D, Yamaha), 0"025; 3. Baiocco (I, Yamaha), 4"130; 4. Giugovaz (I, Honda), 10"306; 5. Zaiser (A, Yamaha), 14"589; 6. Tode (D, Yamaha), 19"171; 7. Müller (D, Yamaha), 20"511; 8. Haarala (SF, Kawasaki), 21"231; 9. Penna (SF, Yamaha), 21"841; 10. G. Guareschi (I, Kawasaki), 30"778; 11. Sacchetti (I, Yamaha), 39"095; 12. Kaldovski (POL, Suzuki), 48"551; 13. Kaderabek (CZ, Yamaha), 1'09"720; 14. Urbanec (CZ, Suzuki), 1'18"286; 15. Lauridsen (DK, Kawasaki), 1'23"522.

10 August – Anderstorp – Sweden

1. Hafenegger (D, Yamaha), 22 Laps, 35'58"455 (147,689 km/h); 2. Baiocco (I, Yamaha), 0"255; 3. Boccolini (I, Honda), 0"761; 4. Sacchetti (I, Yamaha), 1"999; 5. Penna (SF, Yamaha), 2"294; 6. Folkesson (S, Honda), 9"294; 7. Solberg (N, Yamaha), 33"816; 8. Giugovaz (I, Honda), 41"905; 9. Rothlaan (EST, Suzuki), 48"999; 10. M. Jerman (SLO, Kawasaki), 52"171; 11. Lilja (S, Honda), 54"707; 12. T. Andersson (S, Yamaha), 1'01"847; 13. Lundgren (S, Yamaha), 1'03"059; 14. J. Andersson (S, Yamaha), 1'03"823; 15. C. Andersson (S, Yamaha), 1'19"345.

7 September – The Netherlands – Assen

1. Hafenegger (D, Yamaha), 14 Laps, 30'32"621 (165,752 km/h); 2. Baiocco (I, Yamaha), 0"095; 3. Folkesson (S, Honda), 0"751; 4. Sacchetti (I, Yamaha), 13"825; 5. Van Steenbergem (NL, Honda), 18"783; 6. Giugovaz (I, Honda), 19"173; 7. G. Guareschi (I, Kawasaki), 31"958; 8. Penna (SF, Yamaha), 32"158; 9. Boccolini (I, Honda), 38"201; 10. Haarala (SF, Kawasaki), 39"276; 11. Vanlandschoot (NL, Yamaha), 40"161; 12. Opheij (NL, Yamaha), 40"304; 13. Turkstra (NL, Honda), 40"502; 14. Ahnendorp (NL, Honda), 46"455; 15. Vos (NL, Kawasaki), 53"676.

21 September – Hungaroring – Hungary

1. Sachetti (I, Yamaha), 20 Laps, 38'41"280 (135,887 km/h); 2. Baiocco (I, Yamaha), 13"700; 3. Hafenegger (D, Yamaha), 13"830; 4. Giugovaz (I, Yamaha), 21"570; 5. Penna (SF, Yamaha), 21"890; 6. Haarala (SF, Kawasaki), 32"600; 7. G. Guareschi (I, Kawasaki), 32"600; 8. M. Jerman (SLO, Kawasaki), 41"540; 9. Szekely (H, Honda), 51"030; 10. Ger. Talmacsi (H, Yamaha), 1'07"340; 11. Fritsche (D, Yamaha), 1'19"950; 12. Lauridsen (DK, Kawasaki), 1'22"230; 13. Boccolini (I, Honda), 1'41"920; 14. Broz (CZ, Kawasaki), 1'44"970; 15. Varga (H, Yamaha), 1 Lap.

5 October – Braga – Portugal

1. Sachetti (I, Yamaha), 27 Laps, 36'42"091 (133,302 km/h); 2. Baiocco (I, Yamaha), 2"117; 3. Penna (SF, Yamaha), 3"679; 4. Hafenegger (D, Yamaha), 6"291; 5. Korpiaho (SF, Yamaha), 6"726; 6. Haarala (SF, Kawasaki), 12"708; 7. G. Guareschi (I, Kawasaki), 37"337; 8. Praia (P, Honda), 38"041; 9. Nunes (P, Honda), 1'02"438; 10. Giugovaz (I, Honda), 1'15"485; 11. Pimenta (P, Honda), 1 Lap; 12. Rasmussen (DK, Kawasaki); 13. Kaderabek (CZ, Yamaha); 14. Oliveira (P, Honda); 15. Lauridsen (DK, Kawasaki), 2 Laps.

12 October – Cartagena – Spain

1. Solberg (N, Yamaha), 24 Laps, 40'01"495 (126,100 km/h); 2. Baiocco (I, Yamaha), 0"328; 3. Penna (SF, Yamaha), 0"653; 4. Giugovaz (I, Honda), 0"653; 5. Folkesson (S, Honda), 0"931; 6. Boccolini (I, Honda), 1"424; 7. Haarala (SF, Kawasaki), 1"616; 8. Korpiaho (SF, Yamaha), 2"113; 9. G. Guareschi (I, Kawasaki), 52"577; 10. Müller (D, Yamaha), 1'03"894; 11. Lauridsen (DK, Kawasaki), 1'06"647; 12. Rasmussen (DK, Kawasaki), 1'07"040; 13. Kaderabek (CZ, Yamaha), 1 Lap. 13 finishers.

FINAL CLASSIFICATION

1. Matteo Baiocco (I, Yamaha) 145
2. Philipp Hafenegger (D, Yamaha) 126
3. Gilles Boccolini (I, Honda) 96

4. Sacchetti (I, Yamaha), 94; 5. Penna (SF, Yamaha), 76; 6. Giugovaz (I, Honda), 70; 7. G. Guareschi (I, Kawasaki), 61; 8. Haarala (SF, Kawasaki), 49; 9. Folkesson (S, Honda), 37; 10. Solberg (N. Yamaha), 34.

Superstock

2 March - Spain - Valencia

1. Lanzi (I, Ducati), 13 Laps, 21'49"017 (143,187 km/h); 2. Rocamora (E, Suzuki), 5"085; 3. Alfonsi (I, Yamaha), 5"802; 4. Dionisi (I, Suzuki), 5"892; 5. Chiarello (I, Ducati), 6"946; 6. A. Martinez (E, Suzuki), 7"468; 7. M. Laverty (GB, Suzuki), 7"837; 8. B. Martinez (E, Suzuki), 12"637; 9. Hurtado (E, Suzuki), 14"880; 10. Velini (I, Yamaha), 15"760; 11. Bisconti (I, Yamaha), 16"494; 12. Vizziello (I, Yamaha), 22"795; 13. W. De Angelis (RSM, Ducati), 22"803; 14. J. Laverty (GB, Suzuki), 24"633; 15. Romanelli (I, Suzuki), 26"674.

18 May – Italy – Monza

1. Fabrizio (I, Suzuki), 11 Laps, 20'45"798 (184,141 km/h); 2. Dionisi (I, Suzuki), 1"066; 3. Lanzi (I, Ducati), 4"311; 4. Alfonsi (I, Yamaha), 4"827; 5. Rocamora (E, Suzuki), 4"945; 6. J. Ellison (GB, Suzuki), 5"398; 7. Chiarello (I, Ducati), 14"077; 8. A. Martinez (E, Suzuki), 15"259; 9. W. De Angelis (RSM, Ducati), 16"225; 10. Hurtado (E, Suzuki), 24"111; 11. Bisconti (I, Yamaha), 25"610; 12. Velini (I, Yamaha), 25"636; 13. Lerat-Vanstaen (F, Suzuki), 34"445; 14. Bottalico (I, Suzuki), 38"913; 15. Brannetti (I, Aprilia), 39"253.

1st June – Germany – Oschersleben

1. Lanzi (I, Ducati), 15 Laps, 22'58"119 (143,687 km/h); 2. Vizziello (I, Yamaha), 6"462; 3. Alfonsi (I, Yamaha), 6"799; 4. A. Martinez (E, Suzuki), 16"979; 5. Chiarello (I, Ducati), 18"590; 6. J. Ellison (GB, Suzuki), 18"668; 7. B. Martinez (E, Suzuki), 23"456; 8. Lerat-Vanstaen (F, Suzuki), 23"622; 9. Hurtado (E, Suzuki), 23"999; 10. W. De Angelis (RSM, Ducati), 41"850; 11. Bisconti (I, Yamaha), 43"787; 12. Dal Corso (I, Ducati), 44"130; 13. Bottalico (I, Suzuki), 57"941; 14. Saelens (B, Honda), 58"247; 15. Brannetti (I, Aprilia), 58"808.

15 June – Great Britain – Silverstone

1. Fabrizio (I, Suzuki), 12 Laps, 23'53"029 (151,815 km/h); 2. Vizziello (I, Yamaha), 0"255; 3. Alfonsi (I, Yamaha), 0"559; 4. B. Martinez (E, Suzuki), 0"759; 5. J. Ellison (GB, Suzuki), 1"091; 6. Brogan (GB, Suzuki), 1"459; 7. W. De Angelis (RSM, Ducati), 1"768; 8. Chiarello (I, Ducati), 2"141; 9. Dionisi (I, Suzuki), 4"857; 10. Quigley (GB, Suzuki), 5"123; 11. Wilson (GB, Suzuki), 14"029; 12. Velini (I, Yamaha), 17"397; 13. Lerat-Vanstaen (F, Suzuki), 17"556; 14. Brannetti (I, Aprilia), 18"247; 15. Romanelli (I, Suzuki), 20"644.

22 June – San Marino – Misano

1. Fabrizio (I, Suzuki), 15 Laps, 24'58"378 (146,318 km/h); 2. Chiarello (I, Ducati), 0"094; 3. Lanzi (I, Ducati), 0"104; 4. Alfonsi (I, Yamaha), 0"209; 5. Dionisi (I, Suzuki), 0"643; 6. B. Martinez (E, Suzuki), 8"480; 7. W. De Angelis (RSM, Ducati), 9"056; 8. Velini (I, Yamaha), 11"016; 9. Rocamora (E, Suzuki), 17"382; 10. J. Ellison (GB, Suzuki), 17"487; 11. Romanelli (I, Suzuki), 19"302; 12. Buzzi (I, Suzuki), 32"405; 13. Brannetti (I, Aprilia), 32"910; 14. Bottalico (I, Suzuki), 38"982; 15. De Marco (I, Yamaha), 39"396.

27 July – Great Britain – Brands Hatch

1. J. Ellison (GB, Suzuki), 15 Laps, 22'55"008 (164,827 km/h); 2. Quigley (GB, Suzuki), 0"157; 3. Alfonsi (I, Yamaha), 2"692; 4. A. Martinez (E, Suzuki), 3"423; 5. Vizziello (I, Yamaha), 9"449; 6. Wilson (GB, Suzuki), 9"740; 7. Wylie (GB, Suzuki), 11"196; 8. Dionisi (I, Suzuki), 11"253; 9. J. Laverty (GB, Suzuki), 12"538; 10. Alfonsi (I, Yamaha), 13"156; 11. Lanzi (I, Ducati), 21"702; 12. Rocamora (E, Suzuki), 23"748; 13. Lerat-Vanstaen (F, Suzuki), 26"410; 14. Reilly (GB, Suzuki), 29"377; 15. B. Martinez (E, Suzuki), 29"807.

7 September – The Netherlands – Assen

1. Lanzi (I, Ducati), 11 Laps, 23'44"074 (167,596 km/h); 2. J. Ellison (GB, Suzuki), 6"172; 3. Vizziello (I, Yamaha), 8"113; 4. Alfonsi (I, Yamaha), 8"113; 5. Fabrizio (I, Suzuki), 14"994; 6. Dionisi (I, Suzuki), 15"562; 7. Quigley (GB, Suzuki), 15"767; 8. B. Martinez (E, Suzuki), 16"010; 9. W. De Angelis (RSM, Ducati), 16"448; 10. Rocamora (E, Suzuki), 23"190; 11. Chiarello (I, Ducati), 23"726; 12. Brannetti (I, Aprilia), 24"710; 13. Velini (I, Yamaha), 28"038; 14. J. Laverty (GB, Suzuki), 28"879; 15. Hurtado (E, Suzuki), 34"344.

28 September – Italy – Imola

1. Fabrizio (I, Suzuki), 13 Laps, 24'50"551 (154,885 km/h); 2. Chiarello (I, Ducati), 9"276; 3. J. Laverty (GB, Suzuki), 16"240; 4. B. Martinez (E, Suzuki), 17"555; 5. Rocamora (E, Suzuki), 18"847; 6. J. Ellison (GB, Suzuki), 22"868; 7. W. De Angelis (RSM, Ducati), 23"263; 8. Vizziello (I, Yamaha), 25"872; 9. Velini (I, Yamaha), 29"092; 10. Lerat-Vanstaen (F, Suzuki), 32"323; 11. A. Martinez (E, Suzuki), 39"239; 12. Pasini (I, Suzuki), 39"976; 13. Badovini (I, Ducati), 41"659; 14. Scillieri (I, Yamaha), 42"814; 15. Tonini (I, Suzuki), 43"112.

19 October – France – Magny-Cours

1. Lanzi (I, Ducati), 14 Laps, 24'38"017 (150,414 km/h); 2. J. Ellison (GB, Suzuki), 0"388; 3. Rocamora (E, Suzuki), 16"076; 4. Fabrizio (I, Suzuki), 17"782; 5. Chiarello (I, Ducati), 18"241; 6. B. Martinez (E, Suzuki), 18"615; 7. Dionisi (I, Suzuki), 18"916; 8. Velini (I, Yamaha), 19"237; 9. Lerat-Vanstaen (F, Suzuki), 22"541; 10. J. Laverty (GB, Suzuki), 26"630; 11. Alfonsi (I, Yamaha), 27"419; 12. Badovini (I, Ducati), 31"946; 13. Cudlin (AUS, Ducati), 34"631; 14. Dietrich (F, Suzuki), 35"043; 15. J. Smrz (CZ, Honda), 35"305.

FINAL CLASSIFICATION

1. Michel Fabrizio (I, Suzuki) 140
2. Lorenzo Lanzi (I, Ducati) 137
3. James Ellison (GB, Suzuki) 112

4. Alfonsi (I, Yamaha), 98; 5. Chiarello (I, Ducati), 95; 6. Vizziello (I, Yamaha), 79; 7. Dionisi (I, Suzuki), 78; 8. Rocamora (E, Suzuki), 75; 9. B. Martinez (E, Suzuki), 72; 10. W. De Angelis (RSM, Ducati), 50.

France

125 cmc

23 March - Le Mans

1. Lefort (Aprilia); 2. Hérouin (Honda); 3. Masbou (Honda); 4. J. Petit (Honda); 5. Gautier (Honda); 6. Michel (Honda); 7. Leleu (Honda); 8. Olagnon (Honda); 9. Burdin (Honda); 10. Lussiana (Honda).

27 April - Carole

1. J. Petit (Honda); 2. Lefort (Aprilia); 3. Masbou (Honda); 4. Hérouin (Honda); 5. Perdriat (Yamaha); 6. Gautier (Honda); 7. Marsac (Honda); 8. Sicard (Honda); 9. Leblanc (Honda); 10. F. Millet (Honda).

1st June - Le Vigeant

1. Masbou (Honda); 2. J. Petit (Honda); 3. Gines (Honda); 4. Hérouin (Honda); 5. F. Millet (Honda); 6. Lussiana (Honda); 7. Servaes (Honda); 8. Violland (Honda); 9. K. Foray (Yamaha); 10. Proutheau (Honda).

27 July – Dijon-Prenois

1. Gautier (Honda); 2. Masbou (Honda); 3. Lefort (Aprilia); 4. J. Petit (Honda); 5. Perdriat (Yamaha); 6. Marsac (Honda); 7. K. Foray (Yamaha); 8. Brestoli (Honda); 9. Servaes (Honda); 10. Burdin (Honda).

24 August – Magny-Cours

1. Gautier (Honda); 2. Lefort (Aprilia); 3. Masbou (Honda); 4. Gines (Honda); 5. Burdin (Honda); 6. Lougassi (Aprilia); 7. Hérouin (Honda); 8. K. Foray (Yamaha); 9. F. Millet (Honda); 10. Larrive (Yamaha).

7 September - Lédenon

1. Lefort (Aprilia); 2. Gautier (Honda); 3. Masbou (Honda); 4. Perdriat (Yamaha); 5. Lougassi (Aprilia); 6. Olagon (Honda); 7. Lussiana (Honda); 8. Hérouin (Honda); 9. Basseville (AVM); 10. Leleu (Honda).

12 October – Carole

1. J. Petit (Honda); 2. Lefort (Aprilia); 3. Masbou (Honda); 4. Gines (Honda); 5. Perdriat (Yamaha); 6. Lougassi (Aprilia); 7. Chevalley (Honda); 8. Proutheau (Honda); 9. Leleu (Honda); 10. Violland (Honda).

FINAL CLASSIFICATION

1. Grégory Lefort Aprilia 126
2. Alexis Masbou Honda 125
3. Jimmy Petit Honda 97

4. Gautier (Honda), 91; 5. Hérouin (Honda), 67; 6. Gines (Honda), 52; 7. Perdriat (Yamaha), 46; 8. Lougassi (Aprilia), 31; 9. F. Millet (Honda), 29; 10. Lussiana (Honda), 28.

250 cmc

23 March - Le Mans

1. Leblanc (Honda); 2. Rastel (Honda); 3. Aubry (Honda); 4. Scaccia (Yamaha); 5. Eisen (Honda); 6. B. Rebuttini (Yamaha); 7. Poulle (Honda); 8. J. Foray (Yamaha); 9. Vecchioni (Yamaha); 10. Balland (Honda).

27 April - Carole

1. Aubry (Honda); 2. Poulle (Honda); 3. Leblanc (Honda); 4. Eisen (Honda); 5. Scaccia (Yamaha); 6. J. Foray (Yamaha); 7. Laurentz (Honda); 8. Balland (Honda); 9. Vecchioni (Yamaha); 10. Prohet (Honda).

1st June - Le Vigeant

1. Nigon (Aprilia); 2. Marchand (Aprilia); 3. Aubry (Honda); 4. B. Rebuttini (Yamaha); 5. Poulle (Honda); 6. Eisen (Honda); 7. J. Foray (Yamaha); 8. Montoya (Honda); 9. Bourgade (Honda); 10. Balland (Honda).

27 July – Dijon-Prenois
1. Poulle (Honda); 2. Eisen (Honda); 3. Leblanc (Honda); 4. B. Rebuttini (Yamaha); 5. Balland (Honda); 6. Aubry (Honda); 7. Bourgade (Honda); 8. Prohet (Honda); 9. Dambrine (Yamaha); 10. Dos Santos (Honda).

24 August – Magny-Cours
1. Leblanc (Honda); 2. Aubry (Honda); 3. Eisen (Honda); 4. Poulle (Honda); 5. B. Rebuttini (Yamaha); 6. Dos Santos (Honda); 7. Balland (Honda); 8. J. Foray (Yamaha); 9. Montoya (Honda); 10. Bourgade (Honda).

7 September - Lédenon
1. Eisen (Honda); 2. Poulle (Honda); 3. B. Rebuttini (Yamaha); 4. Balland (Honda); 5. Leblanc (Honda); 6. Aubry (Honda); 7. J. Foray (Yamaha); 8. Bourgade (Honda); 9. Florin (Aprilia); 10. Pons (Aprilia).

12 October – Carole
1. Aubry (Honda); 2. Eisen (Honda); 3. B. Rebuttini (Yamaha); 4. Poulle (Honda); 5. Detot (Honda); 6. Rastel (Honda); 7. Montoya (Honda); 8. Dos Santos (Honda); 9. Vecchioni (Yamaha); 10. Balland (Honda).

FINAL CLASSIFICATION
1. Samuel Aubry   Honda   122
2. Vincent Eisen   Honda   115
3. Franck Poulle   Honda   111
4. Leblanc (Honda), 97; 5. B. Rebuttini (Yamaha), 79; 6. Balland (Honda), 59; 7. J. Foray (Yamaha), 44; 8. Bourgade (Honda), 36; 9. Scaccia (Yamaha), 31; 10. Rastel (Honda), 30.

Supersport

23 March - Le Mans
1. Holon (Yamaha); 2. Da Costa (Kawasaki); 3. Donischal (Yamaha); 4. Giabbani (Suzuki); 5. D'Orgeix (Yamaha); 6. Diss (Yamaha); 7. Rousseau (Yamaha); 8. Lussiana (Yamaha); 9. Jaulneau (Suzuki); 10. Tiberio (Honda).

27 April - Carole
1. Holon (Yamaha); 2. Da Costa (Kawasaki); 3. Muteau (Yamaha); 4. Duterne (Yamaha); 5. Donischal (Yamaha); 6. Bolley (Honda); 7. Giabbani (Suzuki); 8. Diss (Yamaha); 9. Jaulneau (Suzuki); 10. Guérin (Kawasaki).

1st June - Le Vigeant
1. Da Costa (Kawasaki); 2. Holon (Yamaha); 3. Tiberio (Honda); 4. Diss (Yamaha); 5. Duterne (Yamaha); 6. Rousseau (Yamaha); 7. Fremy (Yamaha); 8. Lussiana (Yamaha); 9. Donischal (Yamaha); 10. Moreira (Kawasaki).

27 July – Dijon-Prenois
1. Da Costa (Kawasaki); 2. Holon (Yamaha); 3. Tiberio (Honda); 4. Stey (Honda); 5. Donischal (Yamaha); 6. Rousseau (Yamaha); 7. Muteau (Yamaha); 8. Diss (Yamaha); 9. Metro (Suzuki); 10. J. Enjolras (?).

24 August – Magny-Cours
1. Charpentier (Honda); 2. Riba (E, Kawasaki); 3. Van Den Bosch (Yamaha); 4. Da Costa (Kawasaki); 5. Tiberio (Honda); 6. Diss (Yamaha); 7. Muteau (Yamaha); 8. Lussiana (Yamaha); 9. Duterne (Yamaha); 10. Rousseau (Yamaha).

7 September - Lédenon
1. Muteau (Yamaha); 2. Fremy (Yamaha); 3. Tiberio (Honda); 4. Diss (Yamaha); 5. Pelesso (Kawasaki); 6. Holon (Yamaha); 7. Duterne (Yamaha); 8. Da Costa (Kawasaki); 9. Lussiana (Yamaha); 10. Donischal (Yamaha).

12 October – Carole
1. Da Costa (Kawasaki); 2. Tiberio (Honda); 3. Frémy (Yamaha); 4. Muteau (Yamaha); 5. Holon (Yamaha); 6. Mounier (Yamaha); 7. Diss (Yamaha); 8. Rousseau (Yamaha); 9. Stey (Honda); 10. Duterne (Yamaha).

FINAL CLASSIFICATION
1. Julien Da Costa   Kawasaki   139
2. Ludovic Holon   Yamaha   111
3. Yoann Tiberio   Honda   87
4. Muteau (Yamaha), 73; 5. Diss (Yamaha), 72; 6. Donischal (Yamaha), 58; 7. Duterne (Yamaha), 52; 8. Rousseau (Yamaha), 48; 9. Frémy (Yamaha), 45; 10. Lussiana (Yamaha), 32.

Superproduction/Stocksport

23 March - Le Mans
1. Gimbert (Suzuki SPP); 2. Philippe (Suzuki SPP); 3. Muscat (Ducati SPP); 4. Dobe (Suzuki SPP); 5. Protat (Ducati SPP); 6. Dietrich (Suzuki STK); 7. Four (Suzuki STK); 8. Stey (Honda SPP); 9. Guersillon (Suzuki STK); 10. Lerat-Vanstaen (Suzuki STK).

27 April - Carole
1. Muscat (Ducati SPP); 2. Gimbert (Suzuki SPP); 3. Philippe (Suzuki SPP); 4. Four (Suzuki STK); 5. Brian (Suzuki SPP); 6. S. Jond (Suzuki STK); 7. Lerat-Vanstaen (Suzuki STK); 8. Guersillon (Suzuki STK); 9. Bouan (Suzuki STK); 10. Bourgau (Yamaha STK).

1st June - Le Vigeant
1. Gimbert (Suzuki SPP); 2. Muscat (Ducati SPP); 3. Four (Suzuki STK); 4. Dietrich (Suzuki STK); 5. Di Foggia (Suzuki STK); 6. Brian (Suzuki SPP); 7. F. Jond (Suzuki STK); 8. Gibet (Yamaha SPP); 9. Fouloi (Suzuki STK); 10. Moisan (Suzuki STK).

27 July – Dijon-Prenois
1. Muscat (Ducati SPP); 2. Four (Suzuki STK); 3. Gimbert (Suzuki SPP); 4. Philippe (Suzuki SPP); 5. Protat (Ducati SPP); 6. F. Jond (Suzuki STK); 7. Bouan (Suzuki STK); 8. Stey (Honda SPP); 9. S. Jond (Suzuki STK); 10. Fouloi (Suzuki STK).

24 August – Magny-Cours
1. Gimbert (Suzuki SPP); 2. Philippe (Suzuki SPP); 3. Muscat (Ducati SPP); 4. Four (Suzuki STK); 5. F. Jond (Suzuki STK); 6. Stey (Honda SPP); 7. Gomez (Suzuki STK); 8. Moisan (Suzuki STK); 9. Guersillon (Suzuki STK); 10. S. Jond (Suzuki STK).

7 September - Lédenon
1. Muscat (Ducati SPP); 2. Gimbert (Suzuki SPP); 3. Four (Suzuki SPP); 4. Protat (Ducati SPP); 5. Leglatin (Suzuki STK); 6. Gibet (Yamaha SPP); 7. F. Jond (Suzuki STK); 8. Bouan (Suzuki STK); 9. Fouloi (Suzuki STK); 10. Hernandez (Suzuki STK).

12 October – Carole
1. Muscat (Ducati SPP); 2. Gimbert (Suzuki SPP); 3. Philippe (Suzuki SPP); 4. Four (Suzuki STK); 5. Protat (Ducati SPP); 6. Moisan (Suzuki STK); 7. F. Jond (Suzuki STK); 8. Gomez (Suzuki STK); 9. Tangre (Suzuki STK); 10. Fouloi (Suzuki STK).

FINAL CLASSIFICATION SUPERPRODUCTION
1. David Muscat   Ducati   152
2. Sébastien Gimbert   Suzuki   151
3. Olivier Four   Suzuki   100
4. Philippe (Suzuki), 85; 5. F. Jond (Suzuki), 52; 6. Protat (Ducati), 46; 7. Bouan (Suzuki), 36; 8. Stey (Honda), 31; 9. S. Jond (Suzuki), 27; 10. Fouloi (Suzuki), 27.

FINAL CLASSIFICATION STOCKSPORT
1. Olivier Four   Suzuki   145
2. Frédéric Jond   Suzuki   100
3. Denis Bouan   Suzuki   68
4. S. Jond (Suzuki), 64; 5. Fouloi (Suzuki), 61; 6. Dietrich (Suzuki), 51; 7. Moisan (Suzuki), 51; 8. Guersillon (Suzuki), 50; 9. Le Glatin (Suzuki), 39; 10. Hernandez (Suzuki), 36.

Side-Cars

23 March - Le Mans
1. Le Bail/Chaigneau (Yamaha); 2. Delannoy/Capon (Suzuki); 3. Niogret/Marais (Suzuki); 4. Baer/Rault (Yamaha); 5. Cluze/Cluze (Motul); 6. Bessy/Bessy (Deglise); 7. Piroutet/Petitjean (Suzuki); 8. Morio/Lebeau (ADS); 9. Fauvelle/Faure (Yamaha); 10. Leblond/Leblond (Yamaha).

27 April - Carole
1. Delannoy/Capon (Suzuki); 2. Cluze/Cluze (Motul); 3. Le Bail/Chaigneau (Yamaha); 4. Piroutet/Petitjean (Suzuki); 5. Morio/Lebeau (ADS); 6. Pirault/Bajus (Suzuki); 7. Hachet/Geffray (JPX); 8. Bourchis/Scellier (Honda); 9. Fauvelle/Faure (Yamaha); 10. Leblond/Leblond (Yamaha).

1st June - Le Vigeant
1. Delannoy/Capon (Suzuki); 2. Le Bail/Chaigneau (Yamaha); 3. Dernoncourt/Lailheuge (Suzuki); 4. Cluze/Cluze (Suzuki); 5. Marzloff/Marzloff (Suzuki); 6. Niogret/Marais (Suzuki); 7. Bessy/Bessy (Deglise); 8. Sylvestre-Baron/Cote (Yamaha); 9. Gallerne/Geffray (Honda); 10. Guigue/Delpeux (Suzuki).

27 July – Dijon-Prenois
1. Delannoy/Capon (Suzuki); 2. Marzloff/Marzloff (Suzuki); 3. Dernoncourt/Lailheuge (Suzuki); 4. Le Bail/Chaigneau (Yamaha); 5. Baquillon/Beydon (?); 6. Morio/Lebeau (ADS); 7. Pilault/Da Costa (Suzuki); 8. Fauvelle/Faure (Yamaha); 9. Sylvestre/Bron (Seymaz); 10. Leblond/Leblond (Yamaha).

24 August – Magny-Cours
1. Hanks/Biggs (GB, Yamaha); 2. Delannoy/Capon (Suzuki); 3. Minguet/Bidault (Suzuki); 4. Dernoncourt/Lailheuge (Suzuki); 5. Le Bail/Chaigneau (Yamaha); 6. Cluze/Cluze (Suzuki); 7. Marzloff/Marzloff (Suzuki); 8. Lacour/Lacour (JPX); 9. Guigue/Delpeux (Suzuki); 10. Gallerne/Lelias (Honda).

7 September - Lédenon
1. Dernoncourt/Lailheuge (Suzuki); 2. Delannoy/Guignard (Suzuki); 3. Cluze/Cluze (Suzuki); 4. Lacour/Lacour (JPX); 5. Fauvelle/Faure (Yamaha); 6. Bourchis/Scellier (Honda); 7. Leblond/Leblond (Honda); 8. Lacroix/Pascut (Suzuki); 9. Gallerne/Lelias (Honda); 10. Pilault/Da Costa (Suzuki).

12 October – Carole
1. Delannoy/Capon (Suzuki); 2. Dernoncourt/Lailheuge (Suzuki); 3. Marzloff/Marzloff (Suzuki); 4. Cluze/Cluze (Suzuki); 5. Baer/Rault (Yamaha); 6. Lacour/Lacour (JPX); 7. Pilault/Da Costa (Suzuki); 8. Bourchis/Scellier (Honda); 9. Hachet/Geffray (Senic); 10. Fauvelle/Faure (Yamaha).

FINAL CLASSIFICATION
1. Delannoy/Capon   Suzuki   152,5
2. Dernoncourt/Lailheuge Suzuki   85
3. Cluze/Cluze   Suzuki   84,5
4. Le Bail/Chaigneau (Suzuki), 80,5; 5. Marzloff/Marzloff (Suzuki), 47; 6. Fauvelle/Faure (Yamaha), 41; 7. Bourchis/Scellier (Honda), 35; 8. Lacour/Lacour (JPX), 34; 9. Pilault/Da Costa (Suzuki), 29,5; 10. Leblond/Leblond (Yamaha), 29.

Italy

125 cmc

13 April – Misano
1. Angeloni (Honda); 2. Lai (Malaguti); 3. Pirro (Aprilia); 4. Zappa (Aprilia); 5. Aldrovandi (Malaguti); 6. Pagnoni (Aprilia); 7. Conti (Honda); 8. Danese (Aprilia); 9. Narduzzi (Honda); 10. Tresoldi (CH, Honda).

6 July – Mugello
1. Conti (Honda); 2. Angeloni (Honda); 3. Lai (Malaguti); 4. Di Giuseppe (Honda); 5. Aldrovandi (Malaguti); 6. Zappa (Aprilia); 7. Pirro (Aprilia); 8. Petrini (Aprilia); 9. Pasini (Aprilia); 10. Vigilucci (Honda).

3 August – Misano
1. Lai (Malaguti); 2. Angeloni (Honda); 3. Pasini (Aprilia); 4. Aldrovandi (Malaguti); 5. Danese (Aprilia); 6. Pagnoni (Aprilia); 7. Bianchi (Honda); 8. Zanetti (Honda); 9. Suardi (Honda); 10. Giorgi (Honda).

31 August – Mugello
1. Lai (Malaguti); 2. Aldrovandi (Malaguti); 3. Pasini (Aprilia); 4. Angeloni (Honda); 5. Pirro

(Aprilia); 6. Danese (Aprilia); 7. Venturi (Honda); 8. Pagnoni (Aprilia); 9. Tresoldi (CH, Honda); 10. Debbia (Honda).

14 September – Vallelunga
1. Lai (Malaguti); 2. Aldrovandi (Malaguti); 3. Angeloni (Honda); 4. Pagnoni (Aprilia); 5. Narduzzi (Honda); 6. Zanetti (Honda); 7. Vigilucci (Honda); 8. Bianchi (Honda); 9. Bosio (Malaguti); 10. Conti (Honda).

FINAL CLASSIFICATION
1. Fabrizio Lai	Malaguti	95
2. Mattia Angeloni	Honda	81
3. Alessio Aldrovandi	Malaguti	64

4. Pasini (Aprilia), 43; 5. Pagnoni (Aprilia), 41; 6. Conti (Honda), 40; 7. Pirro (Aprilia), 36; 8. Danese (Aprilia), 29; 9. Zanetti (Honda), 24; 10. Zappa (Aprilia), 23.

Supersport

13 April – Misano
1. Nannelli (Yamaha); 2. Corradi (Yamaha); 3. Goi (Yamaha); 4. Polita (Yamaha); 5. Cruciani (Kawasaki); 6. Carlacci (Yamaha); 7. Mariottini (Yamaha); 8. Prattichizzo (Honda); 9. Baiocco (Yamaha); 10. Addamo (Yamaha).

6 July – Mugello
1. Corradi (Yamaha); 2. Prattichizzo (Honda); 3. Proietto (Honda); 4. Carlacci (Yamaha); 5. Baiocco (Yamaha); 6. Mariottini (Yamaha); 7. Polita (Yamaha); 8. Migliorati (Kawasaki); 9. Magnani (Yamaha); 10. Malatesta (Kawasaki).

3 August – Misano
1. Corradi (Yamaha); 2. Goi (Yamaha); 3. Migliorati (Kawasaki); 4. Nannelli (Yamaha); 5. Prattichizzo (Honda); 6. Polita (Yamaha); 7. Carlacci (Yamaha); 8. Baiocco (Yamaha); 9. Mariottini (Yamaha); 10. Proietto (Honda).

31 August – Mugello
1. Goi (Yamaha); 2. Nannelli (Yamaha); 3. Prattichizzo (Honda); 4. Polita (Yamaha); 5. Baiocco (Yamaha); 6. Bartolini (Honda); 7. Carlacci (Yamaha); 8. Sacchetti (Yamaha); 9. Migliorati (Kawasaki); 10. Proietto (Honda).

14 September – Vallelunga
1. Proietto (Honda); 2. Carlacci (Yamaha); 3. Nannelli (Yamaha); 4. Cruciani (Kawasaki); 5. Goi (Yamaha); 6. Brignola (Kawasaki); 7. Prattichizzo (Honda); 8. Bartolini (Honda); 9. Mariottini (Yamaha); 10. Polita (Yamaha).

FINAL CLASSIFICATION
1. Mauro Nannelli	Yamaha	74
2. Ivan Goi	Yamaha	72
3. Alessio Corradi	Yamaha	70

4. Prattichizzo (Honda), 56; 5. Proietto (Honda), 53; 6. Carlacci (Yamaha), 52; 7. Polita (Yamaha), 51; 8. Baiocco (Yamaha), 37; 9. Migliorati (Kawasaki), 36; 10. Mariottini (Yamaha), 33.

Superstock

13 April – Misano
1. Lanzi (Ducati); 2. Dionisi (Suzuki); 3. Vizziello (Yamaha); 4. Valia (Ducati); 5. Conforti (Suzuki); 6. Pellizzon (Aprilia); 7. Bisconti (Yamaha); 8. Ricci (Suzuki); 9. Romanelli (Suzuki); 10. Battisti (Suzuki).

6 July – Mugello
1. Lanzi (Ducati); 2. Conforti (Suzuki); 3. Dionisi (Suzuki); 4. Valia (Ducati); 5. Alfonsi (Yamaha); 6. Pellizzon (Aprilia); 7. Buzzi (Suzuki); 8. W. De Angelis (RSM, Ducati); 9. Velini (Yamaha); 10. Romanelli (Suzuki).

3 August – Misano
1. Valia (Ducati); 2. Dionisi (Suzuki); 3. Capriotti (Suzuki); 4. Ricci (Suzuki); 5. W. De Angelis (Ducati); 6. Velini (Yamaha); 7. Chiarello (Ducati); 8. Romanelli (Suzuki); 9. Scillieri (Yamaha); 10. Pontini (Suzuki).

31 August – Mugello
1. Lanzi (Ducati); 2. Dionisi (Suzuki); 3. Rocamora (Suzuki); 4. Conforti (Suzuki); 5. Chiarello (Ducati); 6. Velini (Yamaha); 7. W. De Angelis (RSM, Ducati); 8. Pellizzon (Aprilia); 9. Mauri (Ducati); 10. De Noni (Suzuki).

14 September – Vallelunga
1. Lanzi (Ducati); 2. Conforti (Suzuki); 3. Dionisi (Suzuki); 4. Valia (Ducati); 5. Pellizzon (Aprilia); 6. Chiarello (Ducati); 7. Alfonsi (Yamaha); 8. Velini (Yamaha); 9. Ricci (Suzuki); 10. Mauri (Ducati).

FINAL CLASSIFICATION
1. Lorenzo Lanzi	Ducati	100
2. Ilario Dionisi	Suzuki	76
3. Luca Conforti	Suzuki	67

4. Valia (Ducati), 64; 5. Pellizzon (Aprilia), 40; 6. Velini (Yamaha), 36; 7. Ricci (Suzuki), 34; 8. W. De Angelis (RSM, Ducati), 34; 9. Chiarello (Ducati), 32; 10. Romanelli (Suzuki), 26.

Superbike

13 April – Misano
1. Gramigni (Yamaha); 2. Sanchini (Kawasaki); 3. Borciani (Ducati); 4. Blora (Ducati); 5. Iannuzzo (Suzuki); 6. Mazzali (MV Agusta); 7. Pini (Suzuki); 8. Di Maso (Suzuki); 9. Zannini (Ducati); 10. Grandi (Suzuki).

6 July – Mugello
1. Sanchini (Kawasaki); 2. Borciani (Ducati); 3. Romboni (Ducati); 4. Mazzali (MV Agusta); 5. Pini (Suzuki); 6. Zannini (Ducati); 7. Zacconi (Ducati); 8. Di Maso (Suzuki); 9. Vizziello (Yamaha); 10. Costa (Honda).

3 August – Misano
1. Iannuzzo (Suzuki); 2. Pedercini (Ducati); 3. Borciani (Ducati); 4. Sanchini (Kawasaki);

---

5. Vizziello (Yamaha); 6. Romboni (Ducati); 7. Gugnali (Suzuki); 8. Di Maso (Suzuki); 9. Conti (Suzuki); 10. Scatola (Yamaha).

31 August – Mugello
1. Pedercini (Ducati); 2. Iannuzzo (Suzuki); 3. Borciani (Ducati); 4. Romboni (Ducati); 5. Sanchini (Kawasaki); 6. Vizziello (Yamaha); 7. Blora (Ducati); 8. Mazzali (MV Agusta); 9. Scatola (Suzuki); 10. Di Maso (Suzuki).

14 September – Vallelunga
1. Pedercini (Ducati); 2. Romboni (Ducati); 3. Vizziello (Yamaha); 4. Sanchini (Kawasaki); 5. Mazzali (MV Agusta); 6. Borciani (Ducati); 7. Pini (Suzuki); 8. Blora (Ducati); 9. Conti (Suzuki); 10. Zannini (Ducati).

FINAL CLASSIFICATION
1. Mauro Sanchini	Kawasaki	76
2. Marco Borciani	Ducati	72
3. Lucio Pedercini	Ducati	70

4. Iannuzzo (Suzuki), 58; 5. Vizziello (Yamaha), 44; 6. Mazzali (MV Agusta), 43; 7. Romboni (Ducati), 36; 8. Pini (Suzuki), 35; 9. Blora (Ducati), 33; 10. Di Maso (Suzuki), 31.

Great Britain

125 cmc

30 March – Silverstone
1. Pearson (Honda); 2. Elkin (Honda); 3. Lusk (Honda); 4. Farbrother (*) (Honda); 5. P. Robinson (Honda); 6. Cooper (Honda); 7. Owens (Honda); 8. Bridewell (Honda); 9. Weston (Honda); 10. J. Vincent (Honda).
(*): The young British rider died a week later as a result of a road accident.

13 April – Snetterton
1. Wilcox (Honda); 2. Bridewell (Honda); 3. Coutts (Honda); 4. P. Robinson (Honda); 5. E. Laverty (Honda); 6. Elkin (Honda); 7. Veazey (Honda); 8. Pearson (Honda); 9. Weston (Honda); 10. Lusk (Honda).

20 April – Thruxton
1. Wilcox (Honda); 2. Coutts (Honda); 3. Pearson (Honda); 4. Longden (Honda); 5. Veazey (Honda); 6. Weston (Honda); 7. E. Laverty (Honda); 8. Bridewell (Honda); 9. Owens (Honda); 10. Lusk (Honda).

5 May – Oulton Park
1. M. Smart (Honda); 2. Wilcox (Honda); 3. Weston (Honda); 4. E. Laverty (Honda); 5. Elkin (Honda); 6. Bridewell (Honda); 7. Lusk (Honda); 8. Owens (Honda); 9. Coutts (Honda); 10. Logden (Honda).

18 May – Knockhill
1. Longden (Honda); 2. M. Smart (Honda); 3. Wilcox (Honda); 4. Rea (Honda); 5. Pearson (Honda); 6. Bridewell (Honda); 7. Veazey (Honda); 8. J. Vincent (Honda); 9. Dickinson (Honda); 10. Saxelby (Honda).

22 June – Brands Hatch
1. Wilcox (Honda); 2. Bridewell (Honda); 3. Pearson (Honda); 4. Veazey (Honda); 5. Owens (Honda); 6. M. Smart (Honda); 7. Clark (Honda); 8. Dickinson (Honda); 9. Lusk (Honda); 10. Saxelby (Honda).

6 July – Rockingham
Race cancelled because of safety problems with the track.

20 July – Mondello Park
1. Bridewell (Honda); 2. Pearson (Honda); 3. M. Smart (Honda); 4. Longden (Honda); 5. Guiver (Honda); 6. Owens (Honda); 7. Weston (Honda); 8. O'Connor (Honda); 9. Stott (Honda); 10. Ford (Honda).

10 August – Oulton Park
1. E. Laverty (Honda); 2. Martin (Honda); 3. Bridewell (Honda); 4. Wilcox (Honda); 5. Owens (Honda); 6. Pearson (Honda); 7. Elkin (Honda); 8. Longden (Honda); 9. Veazey (Honda); 10. Saxelby (Honda).

25 August – Cadwell Park
1. Martin (Honda); 2. Pearson (Honda); 3. Wilcox (Honda); 4. M. Smart (Honda); 5. Weston (Honda); 6. E. Laverty (Honda); 7. Bridewell (Honda); 8. Saxelby (Honda); 9. Longden (Honda); 10. Dickinson (Honda).

14 September – Brands Hatch
1. M. Smart (Honda); 2. Neate (Honda); 3. Rea (Honda); 4. Bridewell (Honda); 5. Wilcox (Honda); 6. Longden (Honda); 7. Guiver (Honda); 8. Veazey (Honda); 9. Cooper (Honda); 10. Saxelby (Honda).

28 September – Donington
1. Martin (Honda); 2. Pearson (Honda); 3. Wilcox (Honda); 4. M. Smart (Honda); 5. Owens (Honda); 6. Longden (Honda); 7. Saxelby (Honda); 8. Clark (Honda); 9. Rea (Honda); 10. Veazey (Honda).

FINAL CLASSIFICATION
1. Mark Wilcox	Honda	183
2. Jim Pearson	Honda	159
3. Midge Smart	Honda	145

4. Bridewell (Honda), 139; 5. Martin (Honda) et Longden (Honda), 98; 7. E. Laverty (Honda), 81; 8. Owens (Honda), 77; 9. Weston (Honda), 70; 10. Veazey (Honda), 72.

Supersport

30 March – Silverstone
1. Harris (Honda); 2. Crockford (Honda); 3. Easton (Ducati); 4. Haslam (Ducati); 5. Coates

(Honda); 6. Sykes (Honda); 7. Andrews (Yamaha); 8. M. Laverty (Honda); 9. Jones (Triumph); 10. Murphy (Kawasaki).

13 April – Snetterton
1. M. Laverty (Honda); 2. Harris (Yamaha); 3. Frost (Kawasaki); 4. Coates (Honda); 5. Andrews (Yamaha); 6. McGuiness (Honda); 7. Jones (Triumph); 8. Moodie (Triumph); 9. Tunstall (Yamaha); 10. Ramsay (Honda).

20 April – Thruxton
1. Easton (Ducati); 2. Harris (Honda); 3. Crockford (Honda); 4. Andrews (Yamaha); 5. Sykes (Yamaha); 6. Coates (Honda); 7. Frost (Kawasaki); 8. Murphy (Kawasaki); 9. Tunstall (Yamaha); 10. Norval (SA, Yamaha).

5 May – Oulton Park
1. Harris (Honda); 2. Thomas (Honda); 3. Andrews (Yamaha); 4. L. Haslam (Ducati); 5. M. Laverty (Honda); 6. Easton (Ducati); 7. Coates (Honda); 8. Jones (Triumph); 9. J. Robinson (Yamaha); 10. Murphy (Kawasaki).

18 May – Knockhill
1. Harris (Honda); 2. Haslam (Ducati); 3. Frost (Kawasaki); 4. Easton (Ducati); 5. J. Robinson (Yamaha); 6. Coates (Honda); 7. Jones (Triumph); 8. Sykes (Yamaha); 9. Thomas (Honda); 10. Crockford (Honda).

22 June – Brands Hatch
1. Thomas (Honda); 2. Harris (Honda); 3. Easton (Ducati); 4. Haslam (Ducati); 5. Andrews (Yamaha); 6. Sykes (Yamaha); 7. Tsujimura (J, Honda); 8. J. Robinson (Yamaha); 9. Frost (Kawasaki); 10. Jones (Triumph).

6 July – Rockingham
1. Harris (Honda); 2. Easton (Ducati); 3. Thomas (Honda); 4. Crockford (Honda); 5. Andrews (Yamaha); 6. M. Laverty (Honda); 7. Coates (Honda); 8. Jones (Triumph); 9. J. Robinson (Yamaha); 10. Norval (SA, Yamaha).

20 July – Mondello Park
1. Easton (Ducati); 2. Sykes (Honda); 3. M. Laverty (Honda); 4. Crockford (Honda); 5. Andrews (Yamaha); 6. Jones (Triumph); 7. Murphy (Kawasaki); 8. Frost (Kawasaki); 9. Coates (Honda); 10. J. Robinson (Yamaha).

10 August – Oulton Park
1. Harris (Honda); 2. Easton (Ducati); 3. Andrews (Yamaha); 4. Frost (Kawasaki); 5. Crockford (Honda); 6. Sykes (Yamaha); 7. M. Laverty (Honda); 8. Thomas (Honda); 9. Jones (Triumph); 10. Tunstall (Yamaha).

25 August – Cadwell Park
1. Harris (Honda); 2. M. Laverty (Honda); 3. Andrews (Yamaha); 4. Easton (Ducati); 5. Sykes (Yamaha); 6. Coates (Honda); 7. Frost (Kawasaki); 8. Thomas (Honda); 9. Ashkenazi (Yamaha); 10. Tunstall (Yamaha).

14 September – Brands Hatch
1. Easton (Ducati); 2. Andrews (Yamaha); 3. Thomas (Honda); 4. Crockford (Honda); 5. Ashkenazi (Yamaha); 6. Tunstall (Yamaha); 7. Norval (SA, Yamaha); 8. Jones (Triumph); 9. Crawford (Honda); 10. Beaumont (Kawasaki).

28 September – Donington
1. M. Laverty (Honda); 2. Harris (Honda); 3. Jones (Triumph); 4. Thomas (Honda); 5. Andrews (Yamaha); 6. Sykes (Yamaha); 7. Easton (Ducati); 8. J. Robinson (Yamaha); 9. Ashkenazi (Yamaha); 10. Tunstall (Yamaha).

FINAL CLASSIFICATION
1. Karl Harris   Honda   235
2. Stuart Easton   Ducati   192
3. Scott Andrews   Yamaha   146
4. M. Laverty (Honda), 127; 5. Thomas (Honda), 116; 6. Crockford (Honda), 95; 7. Jones (Triumph) 91; 8. Sykes (Yamaha), 90; 9. Coates (Honda), 79; 10. Frost (Kawasaki), 78.

Superstock

30 March – Silverstone
1. Lanzi (I, Ducati); 2. Jefferies (*) (Suzuki); 3. Tinsley (Suzuki); 4. Quigley (Suzuki); 5. Llewellyn (Suzuki); 6. Palmer (Suzuki); 7. Allan (Kawasaki); 8. Brogan (Suzuki); 9. Johnson (Yamaha); 10. Morley (Suzuki).

13 April – Snetterton
1. Llewellyn (Suzuki); 2. Morley (Suzuki); 3. Brogan (Suzuki); 4. Jefferies (*) (Suzuki); 5. Tinsley (Suzuki); 6. Davis (Suzuki); 7. Quigley (Suzuki); 8. Palmer (Suzuki); 9. J. Laverty (Suzuki); 10. Thompson (Suzuki).

20 April – Thruxton
1. Jefferies (*) (Suzuki); 2. Llewellyn (Suzuki); 3. Brogan (Suzuki); 4. Tinsley (Suzuki); 5. Davis (Suzuki); 6. J. Laverty (Suzuki); 7. Johnson (Yamaha); 8. Wilson (Suzuki); 9. Reilly (Suzuki); 10. Ashley (Ducati).

5 May – Oulton Park
1. Jefferies (*) (Suzuki); 2. Brogan (Suzuki); 3. Tinsley (Suzuki); 4. Morley (Suzuki); 5. Quigley (Suzuki); 6. Llewellyn (Suzuki); 7. Mitchell (Suzuki); 8. Davis (Suzuki); 9. Hobday (Suzuki); 10. Allan (Kawasaki).

18 May – Knockhill
1. Brogan (Suzuki); 2. Allan (Kawasaki); 3. Hobday (Suzuki); 4. MacFadyen (Suzuki); 5. Jefferies (*) (Suzuki); 6. Davis (Suzuki); 7. Johnson (Yamaha); 8. Bennett (Suzuki); 9. Miller (Suzuki); 10. MacLeod (Suzuki).

22 June – Brands Hatch
1. Mitchell (Suzuki); 2. Llewellyn (Suzuki); 3. Tinsley (Suzuki); 4. Quigley (Suzuki); 5. Cowie (Suzuki); 6. Palmer (Suzuki); 7. Brogan (Suzuki); 8. Wilson (Suzuki); 9. Morley (Suzuki); 10. Houston (Suzuki).

6 July – Rockingham
Race annulée en raison de problèmes de sécurité sur la piste.

10 August – Oulton Park
1. Brogan (Suzuki); 2. Tinsley (Suzuki); 3. Quigley (Suzuki); 4. Davis (Suzuki); 5. J. Laverty (Suzuki); 6. Palmer (Suzuki); 7. Johnson (Yamaha); 8. Mitchell (Suzuki); 9. Hutchinson (Suzuki); 10. Hobday (Suzuki).

25 August – Cadwell Park
1. Wilson (Suzuki); 2. Tinsley (Suzuki); 3. Morley (Suzuki); 4. Quigley (Suzuki); 5. Llewellyn (Suzuki); 6. Brogan (Suzuki); 7. Mitchell (Suzuki); 8. Nutt (Suzuki); 9. Palmer (Suzuki); 10. Shand (Suzuki).

14 September – Brands Hatch
1. Quigley (Suzuki); 2. Wilson (Suzuki); 3. Palmer (Suzuki); 4. Morley (Suzuki); 5. Tinsley (Suzuki); 6. Nutt (Suzuki); 7. Mitchell (Suzuki); 8. Thompson (Suzuki); 9. Johnson (Yamaha); 10. Brogan (Suzuki).

28 September – Donington
Race I: 1. Quigley (Suzuki); 2. Tinsley (Suzuki); 3. Wilson (Suzuki); 4. Beaumont (Suzuki); 5. Mitchell (Suzuki); 6. Palmer (Suzuki); 7. Frost (Kawasaki); 8. Johnson (Yamaha); 9. Thompson (Suzuki); 10. Wylie (Suzuki).
Race II: 1. Tinsley (Suzuki); 2. Quigley (Suzuki); 3. Wilson (Suzuki); 4. Mitchell (Suzuki); 5. Beaumont (Suzuki); 6. S. Harris (Suzuki); 7. McGuiness (Suzuki); 8. Nutt (Suzuki); 9. Fitzpatrick (Suzuki); 10. Wylie (Suzuki).

FINAL CLASSIFICATION
1. Andrew Tinsley   Suzuki   178
2. Steve Brogan   Suzuki   161
3. Luke Quigley   Suzuki   153
4. Llewellyn (Suzuki), 120; 5. Wilson (Suzuki), 111; 6. Jefferies (*) (Suzuki), 105; 7. Morley (Suzuki), 89; 8. Palmer (Suzuki), 88; 9. Mitchell (Suzuki), 85; 10. Johnson (Yamaha), 60.

(*): David Jefferies was killed on 29th May 2003 during practice for the Tourist Trophy on the Isle of Man.

Superbike

30 March – Silverstone
Race I: 1. Byrne (Ducati); 2. Kagayama (J, Suzuki); 3. Richards (Kawasaki); 4. Rutter (Ducati); 5. Mason (Yamaha); 6. S. Smart (Kawasaki); 7. Ellison (Ducati); 8. Hislop (*) (Yamaha); 9. Jackson (Kawasaki); 10. Thomas (Yamaha).
Race II: 1. Rutter (Ducati); 2. Byrne (Ducati); 3. Richards (Kawasaki); 4. Kagayama (J, Suzuki); 5. Hislop (*) (Yamaha); 6. Crawford (Ducati); 7. S. Smart (Kawasaki); 8. Mason (Yamaha); 9. Thomas (Yamaha); 10. Plater (Honda).

13 April – Snetterton
Race I: 1. Rutter (Ducati); 2. Byrne (Ducati); 3. Reynolds (Suzuki); 4. Plater (Honda); 5. Richards (Kawasaki); 6. Crawford (Ducati); 7. Young (Yamaha); 8. Mason (Yamaha); 9. S. Smart (Kawasaki); 10. Kirkham (Yamaha).
Race II: 1. Byrne (Ducati); 2. Emmett (Ducati); 3. Reynolds (Suzuki); 4. Mason (Yamaha); 5. Kagayama (J, Suzuki); 6. Crawford (Ducati); 7. Heckles (Honda); 8. Plater (Honda); 9. Young (Yamaha); 10. S. Smart (Kawasaki).

20 April – Thruxton
Race I: 1. Byrne (Ducati); 2. Hislop (*) (Yamaha); 3. Rutter (Ducati); 4. Richards (Kawasaki); 5. Plater (Honda); 6. Emmett (Ducati); 7. Mason (Yamaha); 8. Heckles (Honda); 9. Kagayama (J, Suzuki); 10. Crawford (Ducati).
Race II: 1. Byrne (Ducati); 2. Rutter (Ducati); 3. Richards (Kawasaki); 4. Plater (Honda); 5. Hislop (*) (Yamaha); 6. Mason (Yamaha); 7. Emmett (Ducati); 8. Heckles (Honda); 9. Kagayama (J, Suzuki); 10. Ellison (Ducati).

5 May – Oulton Park
Race I: 1. Byrne (Ducati); 2. Rutter (Ducati); 3. Hislop (*) (Yamaha); 4. Plater (Honda); 5. Kagayama (J, Suzuki); 6. Crawford (Ducati); 7. Mason (Yamaha); 8. Reynolds (Suzuki); 9. Richards (Kawasaki); 10. Heckles (Honda).
Race II: 1. Byrne (Ducati); 2. Reynolds (Suzuki); 3. Rutter (Ducati); 4. Kagayama (J, Suzuki); 5. Hislop (*) (Yamaha); 6. Heckles (Honda); 7. Ellison (Ducati); 8. Richards (Kawasaki); 9. Mason (Yamaha); 10. Crawford (Ducati).

18 May – Knockhill
Race I: 1. Byrne (Ducati); 2. Young (Yamaha); 3. Reynolds (Suzuki); 4. Plater (Honda); 5. Emmett (Ducati); 6. Richards (Kawasaki); 7. Mason (Yamaha); 8. McGuiness (Ducati); 9. Crawford (Ducati); 10. Kagayama (J, Suzuki).
Race II: 1. Byrne (Ducati); 2. Reynolds (Suzuki); 3. Plater (Honda); 4. Richards (Kawasaki); 5. Hislop (*) (Yamaha); 6. Mason (Yamaha); 7. Kagayama (J, Suzuki); 8. Emmett (Ducati); 9. Young (Yamaha); 10. McGuiness (Ducati).

22 June – Brands Hatch
Race I: 1. Byrne (Ducati); 2. Reynolds (Suzuki); 3. Plater (Honda); 4. Mason (Yamaha); 5. Hislop (*) (Yamaha); 6. Richards (Kawasaki); 7. S. Smart (Kawasaki); 8. McGuiness (Ducati); 9. Crawford (Ducati); 10. Jackson (Kawasaki).
Race II: 1. Reynolds (Suzuki); 2. Byrne (Ducati); 3. Rutter (Ducati); 4. Emmett (Ducati); 5. Richards (Kawasaki); 6. Mason (Yamaha); 7. Hislop (*) (Yamaha); 8. Plater (Honda); 9. S. Smart (Kawasaki); 10. Kagayama (J, Suzuki).

6 July – Rockingham
Race I: 1. Kagayama (J, Suzuki); 2. Byrne (Ducati); 3. Plater (Honda); 4. Rutter (Ducati); 5. Reynolds (Suzuki); 6. Richards (Kawasaki); 7. Emmett (Ducati); 8. Haslam (Ducati); 9. S. Smart (Kawasaki); 10. Hislop (*) (Yamaha).
Race II: 1. Kagayama (J, Suzuki); 2. Byrne (Ducati); 3. Rutter (Ducati); 4. Plater (Honda); 5. Reynolds (Suzuki); 6. S. Smart (Kawasaki); 7. Mason (Yamaha); 8. Emmett (Ducati); 9. L. Haslam (Ducati); 10. Heckles (Honda).

20 July – Mondello Park
Race I: 1. Reynolds (Suzuki); 2. Emmett (Ducati); 3. Kagayama (J, Suzuki); 4. Richards (Kawasaki); 5. Rutter (Ducati); 6. Plater (Honda); 7. Mason (Yamaha); 8. S. Smart (Kawasaki); 9. Byrne (Ducati); 10. L. Haslam (Ducati).
Race II: 1. Reynolds (Suzuki); 2. Byrne (Ducati); 3. Richards (Kawasaki); 4. Mason (Yamaha); 5.

Rutter (Ducati); 6. Plater (Honda); 7. L. Haslam (Ducati); 8. S. Emmett (Ducati); 9. Heckles (Honda); 10. Young (Yamaha).

10 August – Oulton Park
Race I: 1. Plater (Honda); 2. Kagayama (J, Suzuki); 3. Emmett (Ducati); 4. Rutter (Ducati); 5. Richards (Kawasaki); 6. S. Smart (Kawasaki); 7. Heckles (Honda); 8. Haslam (Ducati); 9. Wood (Suzuki); 10. Ellison (Ducati).
Race II: 1. Kagayama (J, Suzuki); 2. Reynolds (Suzuki); 3. Emmett (Ducati); 4. Byrne (Ducati); 5. Plater (Honda); 6. Rutter (Ducati); 7. Haslam (Ducati); 8. Richards (Kawasaki); 9. Heckles (Honda); 10. S. Smart (Kawasaki).

25 August – Cadwell Park
Race I: 1. Byrne (Ducati); 2. Reynolds (Suzuki); 3. Rutter (Ducati); 4. Mason (Yamaha); 5. Richards (Kawasaki); 6. S. Smart (Kawasaki); 7. Emmett (Ducati); 8. Hobbs (Suzuki); 9. Jackson (Kawasaki); 10. Medd (Ducati).
Race II: 1. Plater (Honda); 2. Reynolds (Suzuki); 3. Byrne (Ducati); 4. Haslam (Ducati); Mason (Yamaha); 6. Richards (Kawasaki); 7. Emmett (Ducati); 8. Burns (Yamaha); 9. Jackson (Kawasaki); 10. Ellison (Ducati).

14 September – Brands Hatch
Race I: 1. Reynolds (Suzuki); 2. Emmett (Ducati); 3. Byrne (Ducati); 4. Rutter (Ducati); 5. Richards (Kawasaki); 6. Mason (Yamaha); 7. Plater (Honda); 8. S. Smart (Kawasaki); 9. Haslam (Ducati); 10. Burns (Yamaha).
Race II: 1. Emmett (Ducati); 2. Reynolds (Suzuki); 3. Byrne (Ducati); 4. Richards (Kawasaki); 5. Haslam (Ducati); 6. Plater (Honda); 7. Mason (Yamaha); 8. Smart (Kawasaki); 9. Rutter (Ducati); 10. Heckles (Honda).

28 September – Donington
Race I: 1. Byrne (Ducati); 2. Emmett (Ducati); 3. Reynolds (Suzuki); 4. Rutter (Ducati); 5. Richards (Kawasaki); 6. S. Smart (Kawasaki); 7. L. Haslam (Ducati); 8. Mason (Yamaha); 9. Ellison (Ducati); 10. Kirkham (Yamaha).
Race II: 1. Byrne (Ducati); 2. Reynolds (Suzuki); 3. Emmett (Ducati); 4. Rutter (Ducati); 5. L. Haslam (Ducati); 6. Richards (Kawasaki); 7. Mason (Yamaha); 8. Kirkham (Yamaha); 9. Heckles (Honda); 10. Hobbs (Suzuki).

FINAL CLASSIFICATION
1. Shane Byrne   Ducati   488
2. John Reynolds   Suzuki   358
3. Michael Rutter   Ducati   289
4. Richards (Kawasaki), 255; 5. Emmett (Ducati), 247; 6. Plater (Honda), 246; 7. Kagayama (J, Suzuki), 214; 8. Mason (Yamaha), 208; 9. S. Smart (Kawasaki), 154; 10. Hislop (*) (Yamaha), 122.

(*): Steve Hislop was killed in a helicopter accident.

Spain

2002

125 cmc

17 November – Valencia
1. Barbera (Aprilia); 2. Talmacsi (H, Aprilia); 3. Di Meglio (F, Honda); 4. Lüthi (CH, Honda); 5. Bautista (Aprilia); 6. Pesek (CZ, Honda); 7. Lai (I, Engines); 8. Bonache (Honda); 9. A. Aldrovandi (I, Engines); 10. Martin (GB, Honda).

24 November – Jerez de la Frontera
1. Barbera (Aprilia); 2. Dovizioso (I, Honda); 3. Bonache (Honda); 4. Corsi (I, Honda); 5. Gadea (Honda); 6. Lüthi (CH, Honda); 7. Davies (GB, Honda); 8. Bautista (Aprilia); 9. Garrido (Honda); 10. Lai (I. Engines).

FINAL CLASSIFICATION
1. Hector Barbera   Aprilia   158
2. Alvaro Bautista   Aprilia   102
3. Fabrizio Lai (I) Engines   100
4. Simón (Honda), 76; 5. A. Aldrovandi (I, Engines), 54; 6. Catalán (Honda), 45; 7. Bonache (Honda), 44; 8. Tiberio (F, Honda), 34; 9. Miralles (Aprilia), 34; 10. Lüthi (CH, Honda), 23.

2003

18 May – Catalunya
1. Lüthi (CH, Honda); 2. Miralles (Aprilia); 3. Bautista (Aprilia); 4. Gadea (Aprilia); 5. R. Harms (DK, Aprilia); 6. Manna (I, Aprilia); 7. Bonache (TSR-Honda); 8. Ballesteros (Aprilia); 9. Hernandez (Aprilia); 10. Petrini (I, Aprilia).

22 June – Jarama
1. Lorenzo (Derbi); 2. Bautista (Aprilia); 3. Miralles (Aprilia); 4. Gadea (Aprilia); 5. R. Harms (DK, Aprilia); 6. Espargaro (Honda); 7. Rodriguez (Aprilia); 8. Ballesteros (Aprilia); 9. Hernandez (Aprilia); 10. Terol (Aprilia).

20 July – Albacete
1. Bautista (Aprilia); 2. Carchano (Honda); 3. Ortega (Aprilia); 4. Bonache (Honda); 5. Jerez (Honda); 6. Lascorz (Aprilia); 7. Perren (Honda); 8. Catalán (Aprilia); 9. R. Harms (DK, Aprilia); 10. Saez (Aprilia).

14 September – Jerez de la Frontera
1. Bautista (Aprilia); 2. Bonache (Honda); 3. Gadea (Aprilia); 4. Hernandez (Aprilia); 5. Ortega (Aprilia); 6. Carchano (Honda); 7. Catalán (Aprilia); 8. Terol (Aprilia); 9. Lascorz (Aprilia); 10. Ballesteros (Aprilia).

28 September – Albacete
1. Bautista (Aprilia); 2. Hernandez (Aprilia); 3. Gadea (Aprilia); 4. Ortega (Aprilia); 5. Ballesteros (Aprilia); 6. Saez (Aprilia); 7. Espargaro (Honda); 8. Terol (Aprilia); 9. Catalán (Aprilia); 10. Elkin (GB, Honda).

The final two races of the season (Valencia, 16th November and Jerez, 23rd November) took place after publication of this book.

250 cmc

2002

17 November – Valencia
1. Faubel (Aprilia); 2. Bataille (AND, Honda); 3. Molina (Yamaha); 4. Jara (Aprilia); 5. Watz (S, Yamaha); 6. Leblanc (F, Honda); 7. Polzer (A, Honda); 8. Ortega (Honda); 9. Braillard (CH, Honda); 10. Sawford (GB, Honda).

24 November – Jerez de la Frontera
1. Bataille (AND, Honda); 2. Jara (Aprilia); 3. Faubel (Aprilia); 4. Matikainen (SF, Yamaha); 5. Polzer (A, Honda); 6. Sawford (GB, Honda); 7. Braillard (CH, Honda); 8. Fransson (S, Yamaha); 9. Rastel (F, Honda); 10. Aubry (F, Yamaha).

FINAL CLASSIFICATION
1. Hector Faubel   Aprilia   139
2. Eric Bataille (AND) Honda   115
3. Raúl Jara   Aprilia   113
4. Molina (Yamaha), 86; 5. Ortega (Honda), 66; 6. Matikainen (SF, Yamaha), 51; 7. Castro (Yamaha), 40; 8. Garcia Ramos (Aprilia), 38; 9. Forés (Honda), 35; 10. Rastel (F, Honda), 33.

The category was abolished in 2003.

Supersport

2002

17 November – Valencia
1. De Gea (Suzuki); 2. Del Amor (Yamaha); 3. Fernández (Yamaha); 4. Benito (Suzuki); 5. Bonilla (Yamaha); 6. Oliver (Honda); 7. Roda (Honda); 8. B. Martínez (Yamaha); 9. Escobar (Suzuki); 10. F.-J. Oliver (Yamaha).

24 November – Jerez de la Frontera
1. Del Amor (Yamaha); 2. De Gea (Suzuki); 3. Fernández (Yamaha); 4. Cárdenas (Suzuki); 5. Roda (Honda); 6. Bonilla (Yamaha); 7. Piñera (Yamaha); 8. L. Oliver (Honda); 9. Ribalta (Suzuki); 10. Tomás (Honda).

FINAL CLASSIFICATION
1. Javier Del Amor   Yamaha   120
2. Guim Roda   Honda   75
3. Bernat Martínez   Yamaha   73
4. De Gea (Suzuki), 70; 5. Ribalta (Suzuki), 66; 6. Tomás (Honda), 65; 7. Bonilla (Yamaha), 57; 8. Garcia Almansa (Honda), 46; 9. L. Oliver (Honda), 40; 10. F.-J. Oliver (Yamaha), 40.

2003

18 May – Catalunya
1. Jara (Yamaha); 2. Silva (Yamaha); 3. Forés (Honda); 4. Tiberio (F, Honda); 5. Cardenas (Yamaha); 6. Delgado (Yamaha); 7. Sanchez (Kawasaki); 8. J. Enjolras (F, Yamaha); 9. J. Oliver (Honda); 10. Salom (Yamaha).

22 June – Jarama
1. Silva (Yamaha); 2. Delgado (Yamaha); 3. Jara (Yamaha); 4. Carrasco (Honda); 5. Forés (Honda); 6. Tiberio (F, Honda); 7. Piñera (Yamaha); 8. Salom (Yamaha); 9. Moral (Yamaha); 10. Pandilla (Kawasaki).

20 July – Albacete
1. Silva (Yamaha); 2. Jara (Yamaha); 3. Forés (Honda); 4. Carrasco (Honda); 5. Delgado (Yamaha); 6. Piñera (Yamaha); 7. Sanchez (Kawasaki); 8. F.-J. Oliver (Honda); 9. Carazo (Suzuki); 10. Arquer (Yamaha).

14 September – Jerez de la Frontera
1. Silva (Yamaha); 2. Carrasco (Honda); 3. Delgado (Yamaha); 4. Jara (Yamaha); 5. Forés (Honda); 6. Piñera (Yamaha); 7. Carazo (Suzuki); 8. Steenhoudt (NL, Yamaha); 9. Tizon (Yamaha); 10. Pandilla (Kawasaki).

28 September – Albacete
1. Silva (Yamaha); 2. Carrasco (Honda); 3. Tiberio (F, Honda); 4. Forés (Honda); 5. Jara (Yamaha); 6. Piñera (Yamaha); 7. Arquer (Yamaha); 8. Torres (Yamaha); 9. Sanchez (Kawasaki); 10. Perez (Honda).

The final two races of the season (Valencia, 16th November and Jerez, 23rd November) took place after publication of this book.

Formula Extreme

2002

17 November – Valencia
1. Fernández (Yamaha); 2. Cardoso (Yamaha); 3. D. Oliver (Suzuki); 4. Morales (Yamaha); 5. Carrasco (Suzuki); 6. Sánchez (Suzuki); 7. Delgado (Suzuki); 8. Cabana (Yamaha); 9. Hurtado (Suzuki); 10. I. Gavira (Suzuki).

24 November – Jerez de la Frontera
1. Ullastres (Yamaha); 2. Sardá (Yamaha); 3. I. Gavira (Suzuki); 4. Cabana (Yamaha); 5. Morales (Yamaha); 6. Casas (Yamaha); 7. Silva (Honda); 8. D. Oliver (Suzuki); 9. A. Martínez (Suzuki); 10. Moreno (Yamaha).

FINAL CLASSIFICATION
1. Daniel Oliver   Suzuki   115
2. Josep Sardá   Yamaha   101
3. Oriol Fernández   Yamaha   75
4. Ullastres (Yamaha), 66; 5. I. Gavira (Suzuki), 62; 6. A. Martínez (Suzuki), 62; 7. Carrasco (Suzuki), 51; 8. Monge (Yamaha), 46; 9. Cabana (Yamaha), 43; 10. Silva (Honda), 38.

2003

18 May – Catalunya
1. Fernández (Suzuki); 2. De Gea (Suzuki); 3. Tomas (Suzuki); 4. Sarda (Suzuki); 5. Escobar

(Suzuki); 6. Monge (Yamaha); 7. L. Oliver (Suzuki); 8. K. Noyes (Honda); 9. Bonilla (Ducati); 10. Ribalta (Suzuki).

22 June – Jarama
1. De Gea (Suzuki); 2. Sarda (Suzuki); 3. Cardoso (Yamaha); 4. Tomas (Suzuki); 5. Fernández (Suzuki); 6. Monge (Suzuki); 7. L. Oliver (Suzuki); 8. Roda (Honda); 9. Escobar (Suzuki); 10. Ribalta (Suzuki).

20 July – Albacete
1. De Gea (Suzuki); 2. Cardoso (Yamaha); 3. Fernández (Suzuki); 4. Ribalta (Suzuki); 5. L. Oliver (Suzuki); 6. Morales (Suzuki); 7. Tomas (Suzuki); 8. Escobar (Suzuki); 9. Sarda (Suzuki); 10. Ramirez (Suzuki).

14 September – Jerez de la Frontera
1. Morales (Suzuki); 2. Tomas (Suzuki); 3. Fernandez (Suzuki); 4. Ribalta (Suzuki); 5. De Gea (Suzuki); 6. Del Amor (Yamaha); 7. Cardoso (Yamaha); 8. Hervas (Suzuki); 9. Ullastres (Suzuki); 10. Cabana (Suzuki).

28 September – Albacete
1. Cardoso (Yamaha); 2. Amor (Yamaha); 3. Morales (Suzuki); 4. De Gea (Suzuki); 5. Tomas (Suzuki); 6. L. Oliver (Suzuki); 7. F. Oliver (Suzuki); 8. Escobar (Suzuki); 9. Ribalta (Suzuki); 10. Ramirez (Suzuki).

The final two races of the season (Valencia, 16th November and Jerez, 23rd November) took place after publication of this book.

Germany

125 cmc

4 May – Sachsenring
1. Giuseppetti (Honda); 2. Müller (Honda); 3. Seidel (Honda); 4. Büch (Honda); 5. Kalab (CZ, Honda); 6. Magda (H, Honda); 7. Bittman (CZ, Honda); 8. Schwing (Honda); 9. Walter (Honda); 10. Cortese (I, Honda).

18 May – Hockenheim
1. Giuseppetti (Honda); 2. Fröhlich (Honda); 3. Cortese (I, Honda); 4. Büch (Honda); 5. Mickan (Honda); 6. Schwing (Honda); 7. Kalab (CZ, Honda); 8. Bittman (CZ, Honda); 9. Unger (Honda); 10. Ranseder (A, Honda).

15 June – Most – Czech Republic
1. Giuseppetti (Honda); 2. Fröhlich (Honda); 3. Kalab (CZ, Honda); 4. Bittman (CZ, Honda); 5. Mickan (Honda); 6. Unger (Honda); 7. Ranseder (A, Honda); 8. Seidel (Honda); 9. Büch (Honda); 10. Schwing (Honda).

6 July – Salzburgring - Austria
1. Fröhlich (Honda); 2. Giuseppetti (Honda); 3. Seidel (Honda); 4. Kalab (CZ, Honda); 5. Unger (Honda); 6. Mickan (Honda); 7. Schwing (Honda); 8. Büch (Honda); 9. Müller (Honda); 10. Ranseder (A, Honda).

3 August – Nürburgring
1. Fröhlich (Honda); 2. Giuseppetti (Honda); 3. Mickan (Honda); 4. Büch (Honda); 5. Cortese (I, Honda); 6. Seidel (Honda); 7. Magda (H, Honda); 8. Ranseder (A, Honda); 9. Unger (Honda); 10. Bittmann (CZ, Honda).

31 August - Lausitz
1. Fröhlich (Honda); 2. Cortese (I, Honda); 3. Giuseppetti (Honda); 4. Unger (Honda); 5. Seidel (Honda); 6. Kalab (CZ, Honda); 7. Ranseder (A, Honda); 8. Mickan (Honda); 9. Magda (H, Honda); 10. Bittmann (CZ, Honda).

14 September - Oschersleben
1. Fröhlich (Honda); 2. Giuseppetti (Honda); 3. Seidel (Honda); 4. Mickan (Honda); 5. Ranseder (A, Honda); 6. Magda (H, Honda); 7. Unger (Honda); 8. Litjens (NL, Honda); 9. März (Honda); 10. Bittmann (CZ, Honda).

28 September - Hockenheim
1. Ranseder (A, Honda); 2. Cortese (I, Honda); 3. Giuseppetti (Honda); 4. Walther (Honda); 5. Seidel (Honda); 6. Kaulamo (SF, Honda); 7. Unger (Honda); 8. Hesterberg (Honda); 9. Eismann (Honda); 10. Bourdin (F, Honda).

FINAL CLASSIFICATION
1. Dario Giuseppetti   Honda   167
2. Georg Fröhlich   Honda   140
3. Matti Seidel   Honda   88
4. Cortese (I, Honda), 81; 5. Mickan (Honda), 75; 6. Ranseder (A, Honda), 74; 7. Unger (Honda), 67; 8. Kalab (CZ, Honda), 59; 9. Büch (Honda), 54; 10. Bittman (CZ, Honda), 54.

Supersport

4 May – Sachsenring
1. Schulten (Honda); 2. Penzkofer (Yamaha); 3. Sofuoglu (TUR, Yamaha); 4. Kirmeier (Honda); 5. Wachter (Honda); 6. Hafenegger (Yamaha); 7. Bauer (A, Kawasaki); 8. Knöfler (Yamaha); 9. Kaufmann (Suzuki); 10. Neukirchen (Honda).

18 May – Hockenheim
1. Hafenegger (Yamaha); 2. Sofuoglu (TUR, Yamaha); 3. Schulten (Honda); 4. Kaufmann (Suzuki); 5. Stamm (CH, Kawasaki); 6. Kirmeier (Honda); 7. Neukirchen (Honda); 8. Bauer (A, Kawasaki); 9. Penzkofer (Yamaha); 10. Wachter (Honda).

15 June – Most – Czech Republic
1. Schulten (Honda); 2. Sofuoglu (TUR, Yamaha); 3. Hafenegger (Yamaha); 4. Penzkofer (Yamaha); 5. Tode (Yamaha); 6. Kirmeier (Honda); 7. Cudlin (AUS, Kawasaki); 8. Neukirchen (Honda); 9. Kaufmann (Suzuki); 10. Fernandez (F, Suzuki).

6 July – Salzburgring - Austria
1. Schulten (Honda); 2. Hafenegger (Yamaha); 3. Bauer (A, Honda); 4. Kaufmann (Suzuki); 5. Neukirchen (Honda); 6. Andersen (N, Kawasaki); 7. Knöfler (Yamaha); 8. Cudlin (AUS, Kawasaki); 9. Fernandez (F, Suzuki); 10. Gaisbauer (A, Yamaha).

3 August – Nürburgring
1. Teuchert (Yamaha); 2. Kellner (Yamaha); 3. Sofuoglu (TUR, Yamaha); 4. Hafenegger (Yamaha); 5. Schulten (Honda); 6. Tode (Yamaha); 7. Kirmeier (Honda); 8. Kaufmann (Suzuki); 9. Fernandez (F, Suzuki); 10. Andersen (N, Kawasaki).

31 August - Lausitz
1. Kaufmann (Suzuki); 2. Tode (Yamaha); 3. Andersen (N, Kawasaki); 4. Sofuoglu (TUR, Yamaha); 5. Bauer (A, Suzuki); 6. Schulten (Honda); 7. Penzkofer (Yamaha); 8. Linke (Suzuki); 9. Heese (Yamaha); 10. Knöfler (Yamaha).

14 September - Oschersleben
1. Sofuoglu (TUR, Yamaha); 2. Schulten (Honda); 3. Kirmeier (Honda); 4. Fernandez (F, Suzuki); 5. Kaufmann (Suzuki); 6. Tode (Yamaha); 7. Penzkofer (Yamaha); 8. Neukirchen (Honda); 9. Stamm (CH, Kawasaki); 10. Cudlin (AUS, Kawasaki).

28 September - Hockenheim
1. Hafenegger (Yamaha); 2. Sofuoglu (TUR, Yamaha); 3. Schulten (Honda); 4. Andersen (N, Kawasaki); 5. Kirmeier (Honda); 6. Penzkofer (Yamaha); 7. Bauer (A, Suzuki); 8. Gaisbauer (A, Yamaha); 9. Wachter (Honda); 10. Ludwig (Yamaha).

FINAL CLASSIFICATION
1. Michael Schulten   Honda   153
2. Kenan Sofuoglu (TUR)   Yamaha   143
3. Philipp Hafenegger   Yamaha   116
4. Kaufmann (Suzuki), 86; 5. Penzkofer (Yamaha), 74; 6. Kirmeier (Honda), 71; 7. Tode (Yamaha), 62; 8. Bauer (A, Suzuki), 58; 9. Neukirchen (Honda), 54; 10. Andersen (N, Kawasaki), 52.

Superbike

4 May – Sachsenring
Race I: 1. Oelschläger (Honda); 2. Wegscheider (I, Suzuki); 3. Schulten (Honda); 4. Nebel (Suzuki); 5. Scheschowitsch (Suzuki); 6. Kitsch (Suzuki) 7. Fritz (Suzuki); 8. Bähr (Suzuki); 9. Nabert (Suzuki); 10. Sebrich (Suzuki).
Race II: 1. Schulten (Honda); 2. Meklau (A, Ducati); 3. Wegscheider (I, Suzuki); 4. Nebel (Suzuki); 5. Scheschowitsch (Suzuki); 6. Ehrenberger (Suzuki); 7. Fritz (Suzuki); 8. Bähr (Suzuki); 9. Wohner (A, Suzuki); 10. Nabert (Suzuki).

18 May – Hockenheim
Race I: 1. Oelschläger (Honda); 2. Nebel (Suzuki); 3. Meklau (A, Ducati); 4. Schulten (Honda); 5. Scheschowitsch (Suzuki); 6. Ehrenberger (Suzuki); 7. Wegscheider (I, Suzuki); 8. Heidger (Suzuki); 9. Bähr (Suzuki); 10. Fritz (Suzuki).
Race II: 1. Nebel (Suzuki); 2. Oelschläger (Honda); 3. Wegscheider (I, Suzuki); 4. Schulten (Honda); 5. Fritz (Suzuki); 6. Heidger (Suzuki); 7. Meklau (A, Ducati); 8. Leuthard (CH, Yamaha); 9. Wohner (A, Suzuki); 10. Kitsch (Suzuki).

15 June – Most – Czech Republic
Race I: 1. Schulten (Honda); 2. Scheschowitsch (Suzuki); 3. Oelschläger (Honda); 4. Nebel (Suzuki); 5. Wegscheider (I, Suzuki); 6. Bähr (Suzuki); 7. Fritz (Suzuki); 8. Sessler (Yamaha); 9. Nabert (Suzuki); 10. Ehrenberger (Suzuki).
Race II: 1. Meklau (A, Ducati); 2. Nebel (Suzuki); 3. Scheschowitsch (Suzuki); 4. Oelschläger (Honda); 5. Schulten (Honda); 6. Wegscheider (I, Suzuki); 7. Bähr (Suzuki); 8. Fritz (Suzuki); 9. Ehrenberger (Suzuki); 10. Sessler (Yamaha).

6 July – Salzburgring - Austria
Race I: 1. Nebel (Suzuki); 2. Bähr (Suzuki); 3. Wegscheider (I, Suzuki); 4. Scheschowitsch (Suzuki); 5. Meklau (A, Ducati); 6. Wohner (A, Suzuki); 7. Ehrenberger (Suzuki); 8. Nabert (Suzuki); 9. Sebrich (Suzuki); 10. Grammer (A, Yamaha).
Race II: 1. Nebel (Suzuki); 2. Schulten (Honda); 3. Scheschowitsch (Suzuki); 4. Bähr (Suzuki); 5. Meklau (A, Ducati); 6. Wohner (A, Suzuki); 7. Nabert (Suzuki); 8. Grammer (A, Yamaha); 9. Sebrich (Suzuki); 10. Hahn (Suzuki).

3 August – Nürburgring
Race I: 1. Scheschowitsch (Suzuki); 2. Nebel (Suzuki); 3. Meklau (A, Ducati); 4. Schulten (Honda); 5. Sebrich (Suzuki); 6. Ehrenberger (Suzuki); 7. Bähr (Suzuki); 8. Hahn (Suzuki); 9. Fritz (Suzuki); 10. Sessler (Yamaha).
Race II: 1. Wegscheider (I, Suzuki); 2. Scheschowitsch (Suzuki); 3. Nabert (Suzuki); 4. Ehrenberger (Suzuki); 5. Bähr (Suzuki); 6. Sessler (Yamaha); 7. Sebrich (Suzuki); 8. Grammer (A, Yamaha); 9. Wohner (A, Suzuki); 10. Fritz (Suzuki).

31 August - Lausitz
Race I: 1. Sebrich (Suzuki); 2. Wegscheider (I, Suzuki); 3. Wohner (A, Suzuki); 4. Nebel (Suzuki); 5. Fritz (Suzuki); 6. Knobloch (A, Yamaha); 7. Heidger (Suzuki); 8. Leuthard (CH, Yamaha); 9. Grams (Suzuki); 10. Grammer (A, Yamaha).
Race II: 1. Wegscheider (I, Suzuki); 2. Nebel (Suzuki); 3. Schulten (Honda); 4. Oelschläger (Honda); 5. Sebrich (Suzuki); 6. Hahn (Suzuki); 7. Scheschowitsch (Suzuki); 8. Bähr (Suzuki); 9. Ehrenberger (Suzuki); 10. Knobloch (A, Yamaha).

14 September - Oschersleben
Race I: 1. Nebel (Suzuki); 2. Barth (Suzuki); 3. Oelschläger (Honda); 4. Schulten (Honda); 5. Meklau (A, Ducati); 6. Wegscheider (I, Suzuki); 7. Bähr (Suzuki); 8. Heidger (Suzuki); 9. Nabert (Suzuki); 10. Hahn (Suzuki).
Race II: 1. Nebel (Suzuki); 2. Schulten (Honda); 3. Wegscheider (I, Suzuki); 4. Oelschläger (Honda); 5. Scheschowitsch (Suzuki); 6. Bähr (Suzuki); 7. Meklau (A, Ducati); 8. Hecker (Suzuki); 9. Nabert (Suzuki); 10. Hahn (Suzuki).

28 September - Hockenheim
Race I: 1. Oelschläger (Honda); 2. Nebel (Suzuki); 3. Scheschowitsch (Suzuki); 4. Meklau (A, Ducati); 5. Hahn (Suzuki); 6. Bähr (Suzuki); 7. Wegscheider (I, Suzuki); 8. Heidger (Suzuki); 9. Ehrenberger (Suzuki); 10. Sebrich (Suzuki).
Race II: 1. Oelschläger (Honda); 2. Scheschowitsch (Suzuki); 3. Schulten (Honda); 4. Wegscheider (I, Suzuki); 5. Heidger (Suzuki); 6. Sebrich (Suzuki); 7. Grams (Suzuki); 8. Knobloch (A, Yamaha); 9. Heiler (Yamaha); 10. Hahn (Suzuki).

FINAL CLASSIFICATION
1. Stefan Nebel | Suzuki | 282
2. Markus Wegscheider (I) | Suzuki | 220
3. Michael Schulten | Honda | 208

4. Scheschowitsch (Suzuki), 199; 5. Oelschläger (Honda), 195; 6. Meklau (A, Ducati), 143; 7. Bähr (Suzuki), 141; 8. Sebrich (Suzuki), 92; 9. Ehrenberger (Suzuki), 91; 10. Fritz (Suzuki), 86.

Side-Cars

4 May – Sachsenring
1. Steinhausen/Hopkinson (D/GB, Suzuki); 2. Roscher/Heidenreich (Suzuki); 3. Schröder/Wäfler (CH, Suzuki); 4. Centner/Helbig (Suzuki); 5. Doppler/Wagner (A, Yamaha); 6. Göttlich/Koloska (Suzuki); 7. Hainbucher/Wörner (A, Suzuki); 8. Zimmermann/Bührer (LCR); 9. Eilers/Homann (Suzuki); 10. Foukal/Pertlicek (CZ, Yamaha).

18 May – Hockenheim
1. Centner/Helbig (Suzuki); 2. Schröder/Wäfler (CH, Suzuki); 3. Moser/Wechselberger (A, Suzuki); 4. Göttlich/Koloska (Suzuki); 5. Eilers/Homann (Suzuki); 6. Hock/Kasel (Yamaha); 7. Zimmermann/Bührer (LCR); 8. Thalmann/Roth (CH, Suzuki); 9. Hainbucher/Wörner (A, Suzuki); 10. Kohlmann/Höss (Suzuki).

15 June – Most – Czech Republic
1. Centner/Helbig (Suzuki); 2. Doppler/Wagner (A, Yamaha); 3. Göttlich/Koloska (Suzuki); 4. Arabin/Backmann (Honda); 5. Moser/Wechselberger (A, Suzuki); 6. Eilers/Homann (Suzuki); 7. Hainbucher/Wörner (A, Suzuki); 8. Thalmann/Roth (CH, Suzuki); 9. Kiser/Schmied (CH, Kawasaki); 10. Bereuter/Ölmann (CH/D, Swissauto).

6 July – Salzburgring - Austria
1. Klaffenböck/Parzer (A, Yamaha); 2. Steinhausen/Hopkinson (D/GB, Suzuki); 3. Hauzenberger/Simmons (A/GB, Suzuki); 4. Doppler/Wagner (A, Yamaha); 5. Centner/Helbig (Suzuki); 6. Schröder/Wäfler (CH, Suzuki); 7. Moser/Wechselberger (A, Suzuki); 8. Arabin/Backmann (Honda); 9. Göttlich/Koloska (Suzuki); 10. Hainbucher/Wörner (A, Suzuki).

3 August – Nürburgring
1. Steinhausen/Kölsch (Suzuki); 2. Van Gils/Van Gils (NL, Suzuki); 3. Schröder/Wäfler (CH, Suzuki); 4. Doppler/Wagner (A, Yamaha); 5. Roscher/Hänni (D/CH, Suzuki); 6. Moser/Wechselberger (A, Suzuki); 7. Eilers/Homann (Suzuki); 8. Göttlich/Koloska (Suzuki); 9. Hock/Kasel (Yamaha); 10. Hainbucher/Wörner (A, Suzuki).

31 August - Lausitz
1. Steinhausen/Hopkinson (D/GB, Suzuki); 2. Schröder/Wäfler (CH, Suzuki); 3. Doppler/Wagner (A, Yamaha); 4. Centner/Helbig (Suzuki); 5. Eilers/Homann (Suzuki); 6. Hock/Kölsch (Yamaha); 7. Arabin/Backmann (Honda); 8. Thalmann/Roth (CH, Suzuki); 9. Veltjens/Hildebrand (LCR); 10. Kohlmann/Hoss (Suzuki).

14 September - Oschersleben
1. Steinhausen/Hopkinson (D/GB, Suzuki); 2. Schröder/Wäfler (CH, Suzuki); 3. Centner/Helbig (Suzuki); 4. Roscher/Heidenreich (Suzuki); 5. Arabin/Backmann (Honda); 6. Kohlmann/Babtist (Suzuki); 7. Hainbucher/Wörner (A, Suzuki); 8. Kiser/Schmied (CH, Kawasaki); 9. Eilers/Hofmann (Suzuki); 10. Thalmann/Roth (CH, Suzuki).

28 September - Hockenheim
1. Centner/Helbig (Suzuki); 2. Hock/Kasel (Yamaha); 3. Schröder/Wäfler (CH, Suzuki); 4. Eilers/Homann (Suzuki); 5. Arabin/Backmann (Honda); 6. Kiser/Schmied (CH, Kawasaki); 7. Steinhausen/Hopkinson (D/GB, Suzuki); 8. Thalmann/Roth (CH, Suzuki); 9. Moser/Wechselberger (A, Suzuki); 10. Veltjens/Hildebrand (LCR).

FINAL CLASSIFICATION
1. Steinhausen/Hopkinson (D/GB) | Suzuki | 134
2. Centner/Helbig | Suzuki | 133
3. Schröder/Wäfler (CH) | Suzuki | 130

4. Doppler/Wagner (A, Yamaha), 83; 5. Eilers/Homann (Suzuki), 69; 6. Arabin/Backmann (Honda), 60; 7. Göttlich/Koloska (Suzuki), 59; 8. Moser/Wechselberger (A, Suzuki), 56; 9. Hock/Kölsch (Yamaha), 55; 10. Hainbucher/Wörner (A, Suzuki), 49.

USA

250 cmc

9 March - Daytona
1. Oliver (Yamaha); 2. Sorensen (Aprilia); 3. Turner (IRL, Honda); 4. Jensen (Aprilia); 5. Sorbo (Yamaha); 6. Melneciuc (Yamaha); 7. Pyles (Honda); 8. Richardson (Yamaha); 9. Marchini (Yamaha); 10. Hellström (S, Honda).

6 April – Fontana
1. Oliver (Yamaha); 2. Sorensen (Aprilia); 3. Turner (IRL, Honda); 4. Jensen (Aprilia); 5. Melneciuc (Yamaha); 6. Montoya (Yamaha); 7. Fulce (Yamaha); 8. Pyles (Honda); 9. Marchini (Yamaha); 10. Noce (CAN, Yamaha).

4 May – Sonoma
1. Oliver (Yamaha); 2. Sorensen (Aprilia); 3. Turner (IRL, Honda); 4. Sorbo (Yamaha); 5. Marchini (Yamaha); 6. Melneciuc (Yamaha); 7. Pyles (Honda); 8. Fulce (Yamaha); 9. Noce (CAN, Yamaha); 10. Aron (Yamaha).

18 May – Road Atlanta
1. Oliver (Yamaha); 2. Jensen (Aprilia); 3. Sorbo (Yamaha); 4. Pyles (Honda); 5. Melneciuc (Yamaha); 6. Marchini (Yamaha); 7. Esser (Honda); 8. Fulce (Yamaha); 9. Noce (CAN, Yamaha); 10. Long (Yamaha).

1st June – Fountain
1. Oliver (Yamaha); 2. Sorensen (Aprilia); 3. Turner (IRL, Honda); 4. Jensen (Aprilia); 5. Marchini (Yamaha); 6. Melneciuc (Yamaha); 7. Pyles (Honda); 8. Esser (Honda); 9. Noce (Yamaha); 10. Sorbo (Yamaha).

8 June – Elkhart Lake
1. Oliver (Yamaha); 2. Sorensen (Aprilia); 3. Turner (IRL, Honda); 4. Melneciuc (Yamaha); 5. Pyles (Honda); 6. Noce (Yamaha); 7. Esser (Honda); 8. Long (Yamaha); 9. Bonnett (Yamaha); 10. Himmelsbach (Yamaha).

29 June – Brainerd
1. Oliver (Yamaha); 2. Turner (IRL, Honda); 3. Jensen (Aprilia); 4. Melneciuc (Yamaha); 5. Pyles (Honda); 6. Marchini (Yamaha); 7. Noce (Yamaha); 8. Esser (Honda); 9. France (Honda); 10. Wray (Yamaha).

13 July – Laguna Seca
1. Oliver (Yamaha); 2. Sorensen (Aprilia); 3. Melneciuc (Yamaha); 4. Turner (IRL, Honda); 5. Montoya (Yamaha); 6. Sorbo (Yamaha); 7. Jensen (Aprilia); 8. Pyles (Honda); 9. Esser (Honda); 10. Watts (Honda).

27 July – Lexington
1. Oliver (Yamaha); 2. Sorensen (Aprilia); 3. Turner (IRL, Honda); 4. Melneciuc (Yamaha); 5. Pyles (Honda); 6. Marchini (Yamaha); 7. Long (Yamaha); 8. Maloney (Yamaha); 9. Himmelsbach (Yamaha); 10. France (Honda).

31 August – Alton
1. Oliver (Yamaha); 2. Turner (IRL, Honda); 3. Melneciuc (Yamaha); 4. Sorensen (Aprilia); 5. Pyles (Honda); 6. Long (Yamaha); 7. Noce (Yamaha); 8. Sorbo (Yamaha); 9. France (Honda); 10. McNew (Honda).

21 September – Birmingham
1. Oliver (Yamaha); 2. Sorensen (Aprilia); 3. Turner (IRL, Honda); 4. Jensen (Aprilia); 5. Montoya (Yamaha); 6. Melneciuc (Yamaha); 7. Marchini (Yamaha); 8. Long (Yamaha); 9. Sorbo (Yamaha); 10. Noce (CAN, Yamaha).

FINAL CLASSIFICATION
1. Richard H. Oliver | Yamaha | 415
2. Simon Turner (IRL) | Honda | 294
3. Perry Melneciuc | Yamaha | 291

4. Sorensen (Aprilia), 284; 5. Pyles (Honda), 269; 6. Marchini (Yamaha), 230; 7. Noce (CAN, Yamaha), 221; 8. Sorbo (Yamaha), 209; 9. Jensen (Aprilia), 193; 10. France (Honda), 167. 70 finishers.

Supersport

9 March – Daytona
1. Ku. Roberts (Honda); 2. Hacking (Yamaha); 3. Mi. Duhamel (CAN, Honda); 4. Zemke (Honda); 5. Di Salvo (Yamaha); 6. Buckmaster (AUS, Yamaha); 7. Stauffer (Yamaha); 8. Aa. Gobert (AUS, Yamaha); 9. Spies (Suzuki); 10. B. Bostrom (Honda).

6 April – Fontana
1. Hacking (Yamaha); 2. Aa. Gobert (AUS, Yamaha); 3. T. Hayden (Kawasaki); 4. Buckmaster (AUS, Yamaha); 5. Spies (Suzuki); 6. Chandler (Honda); 7. Mi. Duhamel (CAN, Honda); 8. Di Salvo (Yamaha); 9. R.-L. Hayden (Honda); 10. Zemke (Honda).

4 May – Sonoma
1. Hacking (Yamaha); 2. Buckmaster (AUS, Yamaha); 3. Zemke (Honda); 4. Spies (Suzuki); 5. T. Hayden (Kawasaki); 6. Aa. Gobert (AUS, Yamaha); 7. Di Salvo (Yamaha); 8. Al. Gobert (AUS, Honda); 9. Chandler (Honda); 10. Meiring (Kawasaki).

18 May – Road Atlanta
1. Spies (Suzuki); 2. Buckmaster (AUS, Yamaha); 3. Aa. Gobert (AUS, Yamaha); 4. Al. Gobert (AUS, Honda); 5. Di Salvo (Yamaha); 6. Zemke (Honda); 7. T. Hayden (Kawasaki); 8. Meiring (Kawasaki); 9. R.-L. Hayden (Honda); 10. Chandler (Honda).

1st June – Fountain
1. Hacking (Yamaha); 2. Aa. Gobert (AUS, Yamaha); 3. Di Salvo (Yamaha); 4. Buckmaster (AUS, Yamaha); 5. T. Hayden (Kawasaki); 6. Spies (Suzuki); 7. Zemke (Honda); 8. Picotte (Yamaha); 9. Al. Gobert (AUS, Honda); 10. Stauffer (Suzuki).

8 June – Elkhart Lake
1. T. Hayden (Kawasaki); 2. R.-L. Hayden (Honda); 3. Buckmaster (AUS, Yamaha); 4. Al. Gobert (AUS, Honda); 5. Hacking (Yamaha); 6. Curtis (Honda); 7. Mi. Duhamel (CAN, Honda); 8. Meiring (Kawasaki); 9. Zemke (Honda); 10. Rojos (Yamaha).

29 June – Brainerd
1. Mi. Duhamel (CAN, Honda); 2. Hacking (Yamaha); 3. Spies (Suzuki); 4. Di Salvo (Yamaha); 5. Jensen (Yamaha); 6. Buckmaster (AUS, Yamaha); 7. R.-L. Hayden (Honda); 8. Meiring (Kawasaki); 9. Al. Gobert (AUS, Honda); 10. T. Hayden (Kawasaki).

13 July – Laguna Seca
1. Hacking (Yamaha); 2. Zemke (Honda); 3. Spies (Suzuki); 4. Buckmaster (AUS, Yamaha); 5. R.-L. Hayden (Honda); 6. B. Bostrom (Honda); 7. Mi. Duhamel (CAN, Honda); 8. Meiring (Kawasaki); 9. Stauffer (Suzuki); 10. Al. Gobert (AUS, Honda).

27 July – Lexington
1. Zemke (Honda); 2. Hacking (Yamaha); 3. Buckmaster (AUS, Yamaha); 4. Spies (Suzuki); 5. Picotte (Yamaha); 6. Di Salvo (Yamaha); 7. R.-L. Hayden (Honda); 8. Aa. Gobert (AUS, Yamaha); 9. Meiring (Kawasaki); 10. T. Hayden (Kawasaki).

31 August – Alton
1. Buckmaster (AUS, Yamaha); 2. T. Hayden (Kawasaki); 3. Meiring (Kawasaki); 4. Aa. Gobert (AUS, Yamaha); 5. Spies (Suzuki); 6. Di Salvo (Yamaha); 7. Mi. Duhamel (CAN, Honda); 8. Hacking (Yamaha); 9. Zemke (Honda); 10. Craggill (AUS, Honda).

21 September – Birmingham
1. T. Hayden (Kawasaki); 2. Buckmaster (AUS, Yamaha); 3. Mi. Duhamel (CAN, Honda); 4. Aa. Gobert (AUS, Yamaha); 5. Hacking (Yamaha); 6. Zemke (Honda); 7. Al. Gobert (AUS, Honda); 8. R.-L. Hayden (Honda); 9. Meiring (Kawasaki); 10. Young (Honda).

FINAL CLASSIFICATION
1. Jamie A. Hacking | Yamaha | 334
2. Damon Buckmaster (AUS) | Yamaha | 326

3. Tommy Hayden   Kawasaki   250
4. Al. Gobert (AUS, Honda), 241; 5. Zemke (Honda), 240; 6. Aa. Gobert (AUS, Yamaha), 239; 7. Meiring (Kawasaki), 238; 8. R.-L. Hayden (Honda), 230; 9. Spies (Suzuki), 228; 10. Di Salvo (Yamaha), 222. 106 finishers.

Superstock

9 March - Daytona
1. T. Hayden (Kawasaki); 2. Acree (Suzuki); 3. Wood (Suzuki); 4. Rapp (Suzuki); 5. Haskovec (Suzuki); 6. Ciccotto (Suzuki); 7. Fergusson (Suzuki); 8. Meiring (Kawasaki); 9. Di Salvo (Yamaha); 10. Furtek (Suzuki).

6 April - Fontana
1. T. Hayden (Kawasaki); 2. Fergusson (AUS, Suzuki); 3. Meiring (Kawasaki); 4. Caylor (Suzuki); 5. Haskovec (Suzuki); 6. Moore (Suzuki); 7. Stauffer (AUS, Yamaha); 8. Haner (Suzuki); 9. Di Salvo (Yamaha); 10. Hayes (Suzuki).

4 May - Sonoma
1. T. Hayden (Kawasaki); 2. Haskovec (Suzuki); 3. Fergusson (AUS, Suzuki); 4. Di Salvo (Yamaha); 5. Moore (Suzuki); 6. Hayes (Suzuki); 7. Meiring (Kawasaki); 8. Caylor (Suzuki); 9. Szoke (CAN, Suzuki); 10. Haner (Suzuki).

18 May - Road Atlanta
1. Haskovec (Suzuki); 2. Hayes (Suzuki); 3. Caylor (Suzuki); 4. T. Hayden (Kawasaki); 5. Ciccotto (Suzuki); 6. Wood (Suzuki); 7. Fergusson (AUS, Suzuki); 8. Moore (Suzuki); 9. Haner (Suzuki); 10. Di Salvo (Yamaha).

1st June - Fountain
1. Meiring (Kawasaki); 2. Fergusson (Suzuki); 3. Di Salvo (Yamaha); 4. Hayes (Suzuki); 5. T. Hayden (Kawasaki); 6. Moore (Suzuki); 7. Rapp (Suzuki); 8. Haskovec (Suzuki); 9. Szoke (Suzuki); 10. Haner (Suzuki).

8 June - Elkhart Lake
1. Rapp (Suzuki); 2. Haskovec (Suzuki); 3. Hayes (Suzuki); 4. Moore (Suzuki); 5. Caylor (Suzuki); 6. T. Hayden (Kawasaki); 7. Fergusson (Suzuki); 8. Jacobi (Suzuki); 9. Ciccotto (Suzuki); 10. Haner (Suzuki).

29 June - Brainerd
1. Rapp (Suzuki); 2. Hayes (Suzuki); 3. Haskovec (Suzuki); 4. Ciccotto (Suzuki); 5. T. Hayden (Kawasaki); 6. Di Salvo (Yamaha); 7. Caylor (Suzuki); 8. Dugan (Suzuki); 9. Meiring (Kawasaki); 10. Stokes (Suzuki).

13 July - Laguna Seca
1. Hayes (Suzuki); 2. T. Hayden (Kawasaki); 3. Fergusson (Suzuki); 4. Meiring (Kawasaki); 5. Rapp (Suzuki); 6. Toye (Suzuki); 7. Holden (Suzuki); 8. Perez (Yamaha); 9. Haskovec (Suzuki); 10. Ulrich (Suzuki).

27 July - Lexington
1. Hayes (Suzuki); 2. Rapp (Suzuki); 3. Haskovec (Suzuki); 4. Fergusson (Suzuki); 5. T. Hayden (Kawasaki); 6. Haner (Suzuki); 7. Picotte (Yamaha); 8. Stokes (Suzuki); 9. Meiring (Kawasaki); 10. Ulrich (Suzuki).

31 August - Alton
1. T. Hayden (Kawasaki); 2. Hayes (Suzuki); 3. Meiring (Kawasaki); 4. Rapp (Suzuki); 5. Fergusson (Suzuki); 6. Di Salvo (Yamaha); 7. Haskovec (Suzuki); 8. Haner (Suzuki); 9. Wood (Suzuki); 10. Holden (Suzuki).

21 September - Birmingham
1. T. Hayden (Kawasaki); 2. Hayes (Suzuki); 3. Di Salvo (Yamaha); 4. Haskovec (Suzuki); 5. Rapp (Suzuki); 6. Meiring (Kawasaki); 7. Haner (Suzuki); 8. Caylor (Suzuki); 9. Wood (Suzuki); 10. J. Ellison (GB, Suzuki).

FINAL CLASSIFICATION
1. Joshua Kurt Hayes   Suzuki   332
2. Tommy Hayden   Kawasaki   326
3. Vincent Haskovec   Suzuki   306
4. Meiring (Kawasaki), 272; 5. Fergusson (Suzuki), 259; 6. Rapp (Suzuki), 237; 7. Di Salvo (Yamaha), 225; 8. Caylor (Suzuki), 218; 9. Haner (Suzuki), 209; 10. Ciccotto (Suzuki), 200. 93 finishers.

Superbike

11 March - Daytona
1. Mi. Duhamel (CAN, Honda); 2. B. Bostrom (Honda); 3. Ku. Roberts (Honda); 4. Yates (Suzuki); 5. E. Bostrom (Kawasaki); 6. Mladin (AUS, Suzuki); 7. Spies (Suzuki); 8. Barnes (Suzuki); 9. Pridmore (Suzuki); 10. Higbee (Suzuki).

6 April - Fontana
Race I: 1. Mladin (AUS, Suzuki); 2. Yates (Suzuki); 3. B. Bostrom (Honda); 4. E. Bostrom (Kawasaki); 5. Mi. Duhamel (CAN, Honda); 6. Ku. Roberts (Honda); 7. Pegram (Ducati); 8. Pridmore (Suzuki); 9. Crevier (CAN, Suzuki); 10. Higbee (Suzuki).
Race II: 1. Mladin (AUS, Suzuki); 2. E. Bostrom (Kawasaki); 3. Mi. Duhamel (CAN, Honda); 4. Yates (Suzuki); 5. Ku. Roberts (Honda); 6. B. Bostrom (Honda); 7. An. Gobert (AUS, Ducati); 8. Szoke (CAN, Suzuki); 9. Higbee (Suzuki); 10. Deatherage (Suzuki).

4 May - Sonoma
Race I: 1. Mladin (AUS, Suzuki); 2. Yates (Suzuki); 3. Mi. Duhamel (CAN, Honda); 4. E. Bostrom (Kawasaki); 5. B. Bostrom (Honda); 6. Rapp (Suzuki); 7. Ku. Roberts (Honda); 8. Pegram (Ducati); 9. Pridmore (Suzuki); 10. Acree (Suzuki).
Race II: 1. Mladin (AUS, Suzuki); 2. Yates (Suzuki); 3. B. Bostrom (Honda); 4. Ku. Roberts (Honda); 5. E. Bostrom (Kawasaki); 6. Pegram (Ducati); 7. Pridmore (Suzuki); 8. Szoke (CAN, Suzuki); 9. Crevier (CAN, Suzuki); 10. Higbee (Suzuki).

18 May - Road Atlanta
Race I: 1. Yates (Suzuki); 2. E. Bostrom (Kawasaki); 3. Ku. Roberts (Honda); 4. An. Gobert (AUS, Ducati); 5. B. Bostrom (Honda); 6. Pegram (Ducati); 7. Szoke (Suzuki); 8. Barnes (Suzuki); 9. May (Suzuki); 10. Higbee (Suzuki).
Race II: 1. Mladin (AUS, Suzuki); 2. E. Bostrom (Kawasaki); 3. Ku. Roberts (Honda); 4. Yates

---

(Suzuki); 5. B. Bostrom (Honda); 6. Pridmore (Suzuki); 7. Pegram (Ducati); 8. An. Gobert (AUS, Ducati); 9. Mi. Duhamel (CAN, Honda); 10. Higbee (Suzuki).

1st June - Fountain
1. E. Bostrom (Kawasaki); 2. Ku. Roberts (Honda); 3. Yates (Suzuki); 4. B. Bostrom (Honda); 5. An. Gobert (AUS, Ducati); 6. Pridmore (Suzuki); 7. Mi. Duhamel (CAN, Honda); 8. Szoke (Suzuki); 9. Mladin (AUS, Suzuki); 10. Rapp (Suzuki).

8 June - Elkhart Lake
Race I: 1. Mladin (AUS, Suzuki); 2. Mi. Duhamel (CAN, Honda); 3. Ku. Roberts (Honda); 4. B. Bostrom (Honda); 5. An. Gobert (AUS, Ducati); 6. Pridmore (Suzuki); 7. Higbee (Suzuki); 8. Szoke (Suzuki); 9. Ciccotto (Suzuki); 10. May (Suzuki).
Race II: 1. E. Bostrom (Kawasaki); 2. Yates (Suzuki); 3. Pegram (Ducati); 4. Mi. Duhamel (CAN, Honda); 5. B. Bostrom (Honda); 6. Pridmore (Suzuki); 7. Higbee (Suzuki); 8. Barnes (Suzuki); 9. Ku. Roberts (Honda); 10. Mladin (AUS, Suzuki).

29 June - Brainerd
1. Yates (Suzuki); 2. Mi. Duhamel (CAN, Honda); 3. Ku. Roberts (Honda); 4. E. Bostrom (Kawasaki); 5. Bussei (I, Ducati); 6. Pridmore (Suzuki); 7. Mladin (AUS, Suzuki); 8. Szoke (Suzuki); 9. Higbee (Suzuki); 10. Haskovec (Suzuki).

13 July - Laguna Seca
1. Mladin (AUS, Suzuki); 2. Yates (Suzuki); 3. E. Bostrom (Kawasaki); 4. B. Bostrom (Honda); 5. Pridmore (Suzuki); 6. Mi. Duhamel (CAN, Honda); 7. Szoke (Suzuki); 8. Higbee (Suzuki); 9. Barnes (Suzuki); 10. Randolph (Suzuki).

27 July - Lexington
Race I: 1. Mladin (AUS, Suzuki); 2. Pridmore (Suzuki); 3. Mi. Duhamel (CAN, Honda); 4. B. Bostrom (Honda); 5. Yates (Suzuki); 6. Bussei (I, Ducati); 7. Ku. Roberts (Honda); 8. Higbee (Suzuki); 9. May (Suzuki); 10. Cicotto (Suzuki).
Race II: 1. Mladin (AUS, Suzuki); 2. Pridmore (Suzuki); 3. B. Bostrom (Honda); 4. Yates (Suzuki); 5. Szoke (Suzuki); 6. Bussei (I, Ducati); 7. Higbee (Suzuki); 8. May (Suzuki); 9. Haskovec (Suzuki); 10. Cicotto (Suzuki).

31 August - Alton
Race I: 1. Mladin (AUS, Suzuki); 2. Mi. Duhamel (CAN, Honda); 3. B. Bostrom (Honda); 4. Bussei (I, Ducati); 5. Szoke (Suzuki); 6. Yates (Suzuki); 7. Higbee (Suzuki); 8. May (Suzuki); 9. Holden (Suzuki); 10. Cicotto (Suzuki).
Race II: 1. Ku. Roberts (Honda); 2. Yates (Suzuki); 3. Mi. Duhamel (Honda); 4. B. Bostrom (Honda); 5. Mladin (AUS, Suzuki); 6. Bussei (I, Ducati); 7. Pridmore (Suzuki); 8. Higbee (Suzuki); 9. Szoke (Suzuki); 10. Rapp (Suzuki).

21 September - Birmingham
Race I: 1. Yates (Suzuki); 2. Ku. Roberts (Honda); 3. B. Bostrom (Honda); 4. Mladin (AUS, Suzuki); 5. Bussei (I, Ducati); 6. Higbee (Suzuki); 7. Mi. Duhamel (CAN, Honda); 8. Szoke (Suzuki); 9. Kipp (Kawasaki); 10. Haskovec (Suzuki).
Race II: 1. Ku. Roberts (Honda); 2. Bussei (I, Ducati); 3. Mladin (AUS, Suzuki); 4. Yates (Suzuki); 5. Rapp (Suzuki); 6. Higbee (Suzuki); 7. Kipp (Kawasaki); 8. Haskovec (Suzuki); 9. Wood (Suzuki); 10. Barnes (Suzuki).

FINAL CLASSIFICATION
1. Mathew Mladin (AUS)   Suzuki   550
2. Aaron W. Yates   Suzuki   519
3. Kurtis L. Roberts   Honda   474
4. B. Bostrom (Honda), 462; 5. M. Duhamel (CAN, Honda), 417; 6. Higbee (Suzuki), 396; 7. E. Bostrom (Kawasaki), 350; 8. Pridmore (Suzuki), 339; 9. Haskovec (Suzuki), 285; 10. Szoke (Suzuki), 283. 91 finishers.

Switzerland

Promosport

20 April - Lédenon - France
Race I: 1. Rüegg (Suzuki); 2. O. Andenmatten (Suzuki); 3. Schmid (Yamaha); 4. Wildisen (Suzuki); 5. Aufdenblatten (Suzuki); 6. Lehmann (Yamaha); 7. Schröder (Yamaha); 8. Hofer (Honda); 9. Streun (Yamaha); 10. Kroug (Suzuki).
Race II: 1. Grosjean (Suzuki); 2. Schröder (Yamaha); 3. Vuille (Suzuki); 4. Junod (Suzuki); 5. G. Crotta (Honda); 6. Aufdenblatten (Suzuki); 7. Hofer (Honda); 8. Schmid (Yamaha); 9. Wildisen (Suzuki); 10. Balestra (Kawasaki).

22 June - Buochs
Race I: 1. O. Andenmatten (Suzuki); 2. Pahud (Suzuki); 3. Rüegg (Suzuki); 4. Streun (Yamaha); 5. Schröder (Yamaha); 6. Schmid (Yamaha); 7. Grosjean (Suzuki); 8. Hofer (Honda); 9. Chèvre (Suzuki); 10. Peter (Honda).
Race II: 1. Pahud (Suzuki); 2. Aufdenblatten (Suzuki); 3. Schröder (Yamaha); 4. O. Andenmatten (Suzuki); 5. Wildisen (Suzuki); 6. Schmid (Yamaha); 7. Grosjean (Suzuki); 8. Chèvre (Suzuki); 9. Peter (Fauenfeld); 10. Hofer (Honda).

20 July - Dijon - France
Race I: 1. Rüegg (Suzuki); 2. Wildisen (Suzuki); 3. Aufdenblatten (Suzuki); 4. O. Andenmatten (Suzuki); 5. Hofer (Honda); 6. Vuille (Suzuki); 7. Chèvre (Suzuki); 8. Junod (Suzuki); 9. Grosjean (Suzuki); 10. Peter (Honda).
Race II: 1. Wildisen (Suzuki); 2. Chèvre (Suzuki); 3. Grosjean (Suzuki); 4. O. Andenmatten (Suzuki); 5. Peter (Honda); 6. Vuille (Suzuki); 7. Hofer (Honda); 8. Lehmann (Yamaha); 9. Junod (Suzuki); 10. Pahud (Suzuki).

10 August - Magny-Cours - France
Race I: 1. Wildisen (Suzuki); 2. Grosjean (Suzuki); 3. Vuille (Suzuki); 4. Rüegg (Suzuki); 5. Schmid (Yamaha); 6. O. Andenmatten (Suzuki); 7. Hofer (Honda); 8. Lehmann (Yamaha); 9. Aufdenblatten (Suzuki); 10. Graf (Kawasaki).
Race II: 1. Wildisen (Suzuki); 2. Chèvre (Suzuki); 3. Rüegg (Suzuki); 4. Vuille (Suzuki); 5. O. Andenmatten (Suzuki); 6. Schmid (Yamaha); 7. Hofer (Honda); 8. Lehmann (Yamaha); 9. Grosjean (Suzuki); 10. Peter (Honda).

23 August - Lausitzring - Germany
Race I: 1. Wildisen (Suzuki); 2. Aufdenblatten (Suzuki); 3. Schmid (Yamaha); 4. Lehmann (Yamaha); 5. Vuille (Suzuki); 6. Chèvre (Suzuki); 7. Junod (Suzuki); 8. Brönnimann (Yamaha); 9.

9. Kroug (Suzuki); 10. Schröder (Yamaha).
Race II: 1. Grosjean (Suzuki); 2. Wildisen (Suzuki); 3. Aufdenblatten (Suzuki); 4. Schmid (Yamaha); 5. Graf (Kawasaki); 6. Hofer (Honda); 7. Lehmann (Yamaha); 8. O. Andenmatten (Suzuki); 9. Chèvre (Suzuki); 10. Schröder (Yamaha).

5 October – Oschersleben – Germany
Race I: 1. O. Andenmatten (Suzuki); 2. Grosjean (Suzuki); 3. Graf (Kawasaki); 4. Lehmann (Yamaha); 5. Schmid (Yamaha); 6. Rüegg (Suzuki); 7. Balestra (Kawasaki); 8. Peter (Honda); 9. Junod (Suzuki); 10. Aufdenblatten (Suzuki).
Race II: 1. Rüegg (Suzuki); 2. Graf (Kawasaki); 3. Wildisen (Suzuki); 4. Balestra (Kawasaki); 5. Lehmann (Yamaha); 6. Aufdenblatten (Suzuki); 7. Schmid (Yamaha); 8. Grosjean (Suzuki); 9. Peter (Honda); 10. Chèvre (Suzuki).

FINAL CLASSIFICATION
1. Marc Wildisen   Suzuki   187
2. Olivier Andenmatten   Suzuki   148
3. Pascal Grosjean   Suzuki   146
4. Rüegg (Suzuki), 135; 4. Audfenblatten (Suzuki), 121; 5. Schmid (Yamaha), 121; 7. Lehmann (Yamaha), 93; 8. Chèvre (Suzuki), 92; 9. Vuille (Suzuki), 84; 10. Hofer (Honda), 79.

Supersport

20 April – Lédenon – France
Race I: 1. Stamm (Kawasaki); 2. Lang (Suzuki); 3. Portmann (Yamaha); 4. Sonderer (Kawasaki); 5. Raschle (Kawasaki); 6. Gantner (Honda); 7. Leibundgut (Honda); 8. Muff (Kawasaki); 9. Eichmann (Yamaha); 10. Villiger (Yamaha).
Race II: 1. Stamm (Kawasaki); 2. Portmann (Yamaha); 3. Muff (Kawasaki); 4. Villiger (Yamaha); 5. Sonderer (Kawasaki); 6. Leemann (Kawasaki); 7. Lang (Suzuki); 8. Eichmann (Yamaha); 9. Monsch (Honda); 10. Gantner (Honda).

22 June – Buochs
Race I: 1. Stamm (Kawasaki); 2. Raschle (Kawasaki); 3. Keiser (Yamaha); 4. Sonderer (Kawasaki); 5. Eichmann (Yamaha); 6. Leibundgut (Honda); 7. Da Silva (Yamaha); 8. Gantner (Honda); 9. Bachmann (Honda); 10. Leemann (Kawasaki).
Race II: 1. Stamm (Kawasaki); 2. Hagmann (Yamaha); 3. Lang (Suzuki); 4. Raschle (Kawasaki); 5. Sonderer (Kawasaki); 6. Leibundgut (Honda); 7. Eichmann (Yamaha); 8. Villiger (Yamaha); 9. Gantner (Honda); 10. Da Silva (Yamaha).

20 July – Dijon – France
Race I: 1. Stamm (Kawasaki); 2. Leibundgut (Honda); 3. Gantner (Honda); 4. Raschle (Kawasaki); 5. Leemann (Kawasaki); 6. Lang (Suzuki); 7. Da Silva (Yamaha); 8. Keiser (Yamaha); 9. Sonderer (Honda); 10. Eichmann (Yamaha).
Race II: 1. Stamm (Kawasaki); 2. Leibundgut (Honda); 3. Gantner (Honda); 4. Raschle (Kawasaki); 5. Sonderer (Honda); 6. Eichmann (Yamaha); 7. Leemann (Kawasaki); 8. Da Silva (Yamaha); 9. Lang (Suzuki); 10. Villiger (Yamaha).

10 August – Magny-Cours – France
Race I: 1. Muff (Kawasaki); 2. Leemann (Kawasaki); 3. Leibundgut (Honda); 4. Eichmann (Yamaha); 5. Villiger (Yamaha); 6. Lang (Suzuki); 7. Da Silva (Yamaha); 8. Gantner (Honda). 8 finishers.
Race II: 1. Stamm (Kawasaki); 2. Raschle (Kawasaki); 3. Muff (Kawasaki); 4. Gantner (Honda); 5. Eichmann (Yamaha); 6. Lang (Suzuki); 7. Leibundgut (Honda); 8. Da Silva (Yamaha). 8 finishers.

23 August – Lausitzring – Germany
Race I: 1. Raschle (Kawasaki); 2. Gantner (Honda); 3. Leibundgut (Honda); 4. Muff (Kawasaki); 5. Hagmann (Yamaha); 6. Lang (Suzuki); 7. Eichmann (Yamaha); 8. Villiger (Yamaha); 9. Leemann (Kawasaki). 9 finishers.
Race II: 1. Raschle (Kawasaki); 2. Muff (Kawasaki); 3. Hagmann (Yamaha); 4. Leibundgut (Honda); 5. Gantner (Honda); 6. Lang (Suzuki); 7. Eichmann (Yamaha); 8. Villiger (Yamaha); 9. Leemann (Kawasaki). 9 finishers.

5 October – Oschersleben – Germany
Race I: 1. Stamm (Kawasaki); 2. Muff (Kawasaki); 3. Lang (Suzuki); 4. Leibundgut (Honda); 5. Raschle (Kawasaki); 6. Eichmann (Yamaha); 7. Gantner (Honda); 8. Leemann (Kawasaki); 9. Keiser (Yamaha); 10. Villiger (Yamaha).
Race II: 1. Muff (Kawasaki); 2. Lang (Suzuki); 3. Gantner (Honda); 4. Keiser (Yamaha); 5. Raschle (Kawasaki); 6. Leibundgut (Honda); 7. Villiger (Yamaha); 8. Rohner (Suzuki); 9. Sonderer (Kawasaki); 10. Leemann (Kawasaki).

FINAL CLASSIFICATION
1. Roman Stamm   Kawasaki   200
2. Roman Raschle   Kawasaki   165
3. Daniel Leibundgut   Honda   150
4. Gantner (Honda), 144; 5. Muff (Kawasaki), 143; 6. Lang (Suzuki), 137; 7. Eichmann (Yamaha), 100; 8. Leemann (Kawasaki), 78; 9. Sonderer (Kawasaki), 74; 10. Villiger (Yamaha), 72.

Superstock

20 April – Lédenon – France
Race I: 1. Bantli (Yamaha); 2. Künzi (Yamaha); 3. Flückiger (Suzuki); 4. Gyger (Suzuki); 5. Dähler (Yamaha); 6. Häfeli (Yamaha); 7. Geisser (Suzuki); 8. Brodard (Yamaha); 9. A. Andenmatten (Suzuki); 10. Da. Maillard (Ducati).
Race II: 1. Bantli (Yamaha); 2. Künzi (Yamaha); 3. Flückiger (Suzuki); 4. A. Andenmatten (Suzuki); 5. Di. Maillard (Ducati); 6. Häfeli (Yamaha); 7. Brodard (Yamaha); 8. Kernen (Yamaha); 9. Landis (Honda); 10. Kobe (Suzuki).

22 June – Buochs
Race I: 1. Bantli (Yamaha); 2. Dähler (Yamaha); 3. Gyger (Suzuki); 4. Künzi (Yamaha); 5. Jenny (Yamaha); 6. Monney (Suzuki); 7. Brodard (Yamaha); 8. Kernen (Yamaha); 9. A. Andenmatten (Suzuki); 10. Wenger (Yamaha).
Race II: 1. Bantli (Yamaha); 2. Gyger (Suzuki); 3. Monney (Suzuki); 4. Kernen (Yamaha); 5. Dähler (Yamaha); 6. Jenny (Yamaha); 7. Brodard (Yamaha); 8. Parolari (Suzuki); 9. A. Andenmatten (Suzuki); 10. Kobe (Suzuki).

20 July – Dijon – France
Race I: 1. Devoyon (F, Suzuki); 2. Künzi (Yamaha); 3. Alma (Suzuki); 4. Bantli (Yamaha); 5. Monney (Suzuki); 6. A. Andenmatten (Suzuki); 7. Flückiger (Suzuki); 8. Kausch (Suzuki);

---

9. Brodard (Yamaha); 10. Carrard (Yamaha).
Race II: 1. Gyger (Suzuki); 2. Künzi (Yamaha); 3. Bantli (Yamaha); 4. Devoyon (F, Suzuki); 5. Monney (Suzuki); 6. Flückiger (Suzuki); 7. Kausch (Suzuki); 8. A. Andenmatten (Suzuki); 9. Dähler (Yamaha); 10. Carrard (Yamaha).

10 August – Magny-Cours – France
Race I: 1. Devoyon (F, Suzuki); 2. Bantli (Yamaha); 3. Künzi (Yamaha); 4. Flückiger (Suzuki); 5. Gyger (Suzuki); 6. Monney (Suzuki); 7. A. Andenmatten (Suzuki); 8. Carrard (Yamaha); 9. Dähler (Yamaha); 10. Parolari (Suzuki).
Race II: 1. Devoyon (F, Suzuki); 2. Gyger (Suzuki); 3. Bantli (Yamaha); 4. Künzi (Yamaha); 5. Flückiger (Suzuki); 6. A. Andenmatten (Suzuki); 7. Monney (Suzuki); 8. Dähler (Yamaha); 9. Parolari (Suzuki); 10. Carrard (Yamaha).

23 August – Lausitzring – Germany
Race I: 1. Gyger (Suzuki); 2. Bantli (Yamaha); 3. Künzi (Yamaha); 4. Monney (Suzuki); 5. Brodard (Yamaha); 6. Kausch (Suzuki); 7. Flückiger (Suzuki); 8. Dähler (Yamaha); 9. Parolari (Suzuki); 10. A. Andenmatten (Suzuki).
Race II: 1. Bantli (Yamaha); 2. Künzi (Yamaha); 3. A. Andenmatten (Suzuki); 4. Kausch (Suzuki); 5. Parolari (Suzuki); 6. Flückiger (Suzuki); 7. Brodard (Yamaha); 8. Kobe (Suzuki); 9. Kernen (Yamaha); 10. Häfeli (Yamaha).

5 October – Oschersleben – Germany
Race I: 1. Gyger (Suzuki); 2. Künzi (Yamaha); 3. Flückiger (Suzuki); 4. Pollheide (D, Suzuki); 5. A. Andenmatten (Suzuki); 6. Monney (Suzuki); 7. Koch (Yamaha); 8. Carrard (Yamaha); 9. Häfeli (Yamaha); 10. Kobe (Suzuki).
Race II: 1. Gyger (Suzuki); 2. Künzi (Yamaha); 3. Parolari (Suzuki); 4. Flückiger (Suzuki); 5. Koch (Yamaha); 6. A. Andenmatten (Suzuki); 7. Monney (Suzuki); 8. Häfeli (Yamaha); 9. Kernen (Yamaha); 10. Kobe (Suzuki).

FINAL CLASSIFICATION
1. Roger Bantli   Yamaha   210
2. Christian Künzi   Yamaha   198
3. Yann Gyger   Suzuki   185
4. Flückiger (Suzuki), 123; 5. A. Andenmatten (Suzuki), 115; 6. Monney (Suzuki); 7. Devoyon (F, Suzuki), 88; 8. Dähler (Yamaha), 79; 9. Brodard (Yamaha), 62; 10. Kernen (Yamaha), 60.

SUPERMOTARD

Prestige

11 May – Eschenbach
Race I: 1. Götz (KTM); 2. Müller (Yamaha); 3. Gautschi (Husqvarna); 4. Hirschi (KTM); 5. Ferrari (Husqvarna); 6. Messerli (Yamaha); 7. Zachmann (Suzuki); 8. Baumgartner (Yamaha); 9. Rohner (KTM); 10. Gysi (KTM).
Race II: 1. Götz (KTM); 2. Müller (Yamaha); 3. Hirschi (KTM); 4. Wunderlin (Honda); 5. Zachmann (Suzuki); 6. Messerli (Yamaha); 7. Baumgartner (Yamaha); 8. Wehrli (KTM); 9. Rohner (KTM); 10. Gautschi (Husqvarna).

1st June – Büron
Race I: 1. Müller (Yamaha); 2. Götz (KTM); 3. Hirschi (KTM); 4. Wunderlin (Honda); 5. Ferrari (Husqvarna); 6. Wehrli (KTM); 7. Alpstäg (KTM); 8. Scheidegger (Husaberg); 9. Baumgartner (Yamaha); 10. Rohner (KTM).
Race II: 1. Müller (Yamaha); 2. Hirschi (KTM); 3. Messerli (Yamaha); 4. Götz (KTM); 5. Wehrli (KTM); 6. Ferrari (Husqvarna); 7. Alpstäg (KTM); 8. Rohner (KTM); 9. Scheidegger (Husaberg); 10. Murer (Honda).

29 June – Payerne
Event boycotted for safety reasons.

27 July – Buchs
Race I: 1. Götz (KTM); 2. Hirschi (KTM); 3. Zachmann (Suzuki); 4. Wunderlin (Honda); 5. Müller (Yamaha); 6. Ferrari (Husqvarna); 7. Gautschi (Husqvarna); 8. Messerli (Yamaha); 9. Alpstäg (KTM); 10. Baumgartner (Yamaha).
Race II: 1. Götz (KTM); 2. Müller (Yamaha); 3. Zachmann (Suzuki); 4. Gautschi (Husqvarna); 5. Hirschi (KTM); 6. Möri (Yamaha); 7. Wunderlin (Honda); 8. Wehrli (KTM); 9. Alpstäg (KTM); 10. Singele (Yamaha).

14 September – Frauenfeld
Race I: 1. Götz (KTM); 2. Hirschi (KTM); 3. Gautschi (Husqvarna); 4. Müller (Yamaha); 5. Zachmann (Suzuki); 6. Wehrli (KTM); 7. Wunderlin (Honda); 8. Messerli (Yamaha); 9. Möri (Yamaha); 10. Ferrari (Husqvarna).
Race II: 1. Götz (KTM); 2. Müller (Yamaha); 3. Hirschi (KTM); 4. Gautschi (Husqvarna); 5. Zachmann (Suzuki); 6. Wunderlin (Honda); 7. Wehrli (KTM); 8. Möri (Yamaha); 9. Messerli (Yamaha); 10. Ferrari (Husqvarna).

28 September – Aarberg
Race I: 1. Müller (Yamaha); 2. Götz (KTM); 3. Zachmann (Suzuki); 4. Gautschi (Husqvarna); 5. Wunderlin (Honda); 6. Baumgartner (Yamaha); 7. Singele (Yamaha); 8. Rohner (KTM); 9. Oehri (KTM); 10. Marti (Yamaha).
Race II: 1. Gautschi (Husqvarna); 2. Müller (Yamaha); 3. Götz (KTM); 4. Zachmann (Suzuki); 5. Wunderlin (Honda); 6. Wehrli (KTM); 7. Rohner (KTM); 8. Schmid (KTM); 9. Singele (Yamaha); 10. Gysi (KTM).

FINAL CLASSIFICATION
1. Marcel Götz   KTM   232
2. Daniel Müller   Yamaha   219
3. Michael Hirschi   KTM   160
4. Gautschi (Husqvarna), 153; 5. Zachmann (Suzuki), 139; 6. Wunderlin (Honda), 137; 7. Ferrari (Husqvarna), 115; 8. Wehrli (KTM), 109; 9. Baumgartner (Yamaha), 105; 10. Rohner (KTM), 104.

Challenger

11 May – Eschenbach
Race I: 1. Oechslin (KTM); 2. Waeber (Yamaha); 3. Spörri (KTM); 4. Gsell (Husqvarna); 5. Notari (Husqvarna); 6. Gallina (KTM); 7. Lugemwa (Yamaha); 8. Mathez (Husqvarna); 9. Putzi (Husaberg); 10. Griette (Husqvarna).
Race II: 1. Waeber (Yamaha); 2. Spörri (KTM); 3. Gsell (Husqvarna); 4. Oechslin (KTM); 5. Gallina (KTM); 6. Notari (Husqvarna); 7. Pavid (Yamaha); 8. Lugemwa (Yamaha); 9. Dähler (Honda); 10. Studer (Honda).

1st June – Büron
Race I: 1. Zimmermann (Husqvarna); 2. Gsell (Husqvarna); 3. B. Schaufelberger (Yamaha); 4. Berger (KTM); 5. Spörri (KTM); 6. Waeber (Yamaha); 7. Bucher (Husaberg); 8. Notari (Husqvarna); 9. Oechslin (KTM); 10. Schlatter (Husaberg).
Race II: 1. Waeber (Yamaha); 2. Bucher (Husaberg); 3. B. Schaufelberger (Yamaha); 4. Studer (KTM); 5. Berger (KTM); 6. Notari (Husqvarna); 7. Spörri (KTM); 8. Gsell (Husqvarna); 9. Monsch (Honda); 10. Schlatter (Husaberg).

29 June – Payerne
Race I: 1. Bucher (Husaberg); 2. B. Schaufelberger (Yamaha); 3. Waeber (Yamaha); 4. Oechslin (KTM); 5. Gsell (Husqvarna); 6. Gallina (KTM); 7. Studer (KTM); 8. Putzi (Husaberg); 9. Faust (Husaberg); 10. Haag (Yamaha).
Race II: 1. B. Schaufelberger (Yamaha); 2. Bucher (Husaberg); 3. Monsch (Honda); 4. Waeber (Yamaha); 5. Oechslin (KTM); 6. Gsell (Husqvarna); 7. Gallina (KTM); 8. Lugemwa (Yamaha); 9. Zünd (KTM); 10. Spörri (KTM).

27 July – Buchs
Race I: 1. Oechslin (KTM); 2. Gsell (Husqvarna); 3. Chanton (KTM); 4. Waeber (Yamaha); 5. Bucher (Husaberg); 6. Kaufmann (Suzuki); 7. Lugemwa (Yamaha); 8. Terraneo (Yamaha); 9. Schlatter (Husaberg); 10. Studer (KTM).
Race II: 1. Oechslin (KTM); 2. Waeber (Yamaha); 3. B. Schaufelberger (Yamaha); 4. Bucher (Husaberg); 5. Kaufmann (Suzuki); 6. Schlatter (Husaberg); 7. Faust (Husaberg); 8. Lugemwa (Yamaha); 9. Zünd (KTM); 10. Studer (KTM).

14 September – Frauenfeld
Race I: 1. Oechslin (KTM); 2. Bucher (Husaberg); 3. Gsell (Husqvarna); 4. Spörri (KTM); 5. Wirth (KTM); 6. B. Schaufelberger (Yamaha); 7. Putzi (Husaberg); 8. Schlatter (Husaberg); 9. Müller (Suzuki); 10. Faust (Husaberg).
Race II: 1. Gsell (Husqvarna); 2. Wirth (KTM); 3. Spörri (KTM); 4. B. Schaufelberger (Yamaha); 5. Bucher (Husaberg); 6. Oechslin (KTM); 7. Putzi (Husaberg); 8. Zünd (KTM); 9. Studer (KTM); 10. R. Schaufelberger (Yamaha).

28 September – Aarberg
Race I: 1. Bucher (Husaberg); 2. Gsell (Husqvarna); 3. Gallina (KTM); 4. Studer (KTM); 5. Spörri (KTM); 6. Burkhalter (Suzuki); 7. Lugemwa (Yamaha); 8. Barmettler (Husqvarna); 9. Faust (Husaberg); 10. Schlatter (Husaberg).
Race II: 1. Waeber (Yamaha); 2. Gsell (Husqvarna); 3. Gallina (KTM); 4. Bucher (Husaberg); 5. Faust (Husaberg); 6. Burkhalter (Suzuki); 7. Studer (KTM); 8. Oechslin (KTM); 9. R. Schaufelberger (Yamaha); 10. Putzi (Husaberg).

FINAL CLASSIFICATION
1. Frédéric Waeber   Yamaha   215
2. Daniel Gsell   Husqvarna   214
3. Roland Bucher   Husaberg   206
4. Oechslin (KTM), 192; 5. B. Schaufelberger (Yamaha), 150; 6. Gallina (KTM), 141; 7. Spörri (KTM), 140; 8. Studer (KTM), 122; 9. Putzi (Husaberg), 93; 10. Lugemwa (Yamaha), 90.

Rookie

11 May – Eschenbach
Race I: 1. Marti (Yamaha); 2. Schüpbach (Kawasaki); 3. Pouchon (Suzuki); 4. Saxer (KTM); 5. S. Scheiwiller (Yamaha); 6. Blöchliger (KTM); 7. Rè (Honda); 8. Hess (Yamaha); 9. Näscher (KTM); 10. R. Scheiwiller (KTM).
Race II: 1. Marti (Yamaha); 2. Züger (KTM); 3. S. Scheiwiller (Yamaha); 4. Saxer (KTM); 5. Hess (Yamaha); 6. Blöchliger (KTM); 7. Schüpbach (Kawasaki); 8. Näscher (KTM); 9. Von Gunten (Honda); 10. Zani (Husqvarna).

1st June – Büron
Race I: 1. Marti (Yamaha); 2. Züger (KTM); 3. Schüpbach (Kawasaki); 4. S. Scheiwiller (Yamaha); 5. Rè (Honda); 6. Von Gunten (Honda); 7. Zurfluh (Yamaha); 8. Lanz (KTM); 9. R. Scheiwiller (KTM); 10. Vallotton (Honda).
Race II: 1. Marti (Yamaha); 2. Schüpbach (Kawasaki); 3. S. Scheiwiller (Yamaha); 4. Pouchon (Suzuki); 5. Von Gunten (Honda); 6. Zurfluh (Yamaha); 7. Kammermann (Honda); 8. Rè (Honda); 9. Zani (Husqvarna); 10. Blöchliger (KTM).

29 June – Payerne
Race I: 1. Marti (Yamaha); 2. Züger (KTM); 3. Schüpbach (Kawasaki); 4. Pouchon (Suzuki); 5. S. Scheiwiller (Yamaha); 6. Aggeler (Yamaha); 7. Näscher (KTM); 8. Von Gunten (Honda); 9. Lanz (KTM); 10. Zani (Husqvarna).
Race II: 1. Marti (Yamaha); 2. Schüpbach (Kawasaki); 3. Pouchon (Suzuki); 4. Aggeler (Yamaha); 5. Kammermann (Honda); 6. Von Gunten (Honda); 7. R. Scheiwiller (KTM); 8. Zani (Husqvarna); 9. Saxer (KTM); 10. Lanz (KTM).

27 July – Buchs
Race I: 1. Marti (Yamaha); 2. Aggeler (Yamaha); 3. Schüpbach (Kawasaki); 4. Züger (KTM); 5. S. Scheiwiller (Yamaha); 6. Kammermann (Honda); 7. Rè (Honda); 8. Zani (Husqvarna); 9. Calabresi (Yamaha); 10. Burch (Yamaha).
Race II: 1. Marti (Yamaha); 2. Züger (KTM); 3. Schüpbach (Kawasaki); 4. Aggeler (Yamaha); 5. S. Scheiwiller (Yamaha); 6. Kammermann (Honda); 7. Rè (Honda); 8. Zani (Husqvarna); 9. Von Gunten (Honda); 10. Burch (Yamaha).

14 September – Frauenfeld
Race I: 1. Züger (KTM); 2. Marti (Yamaha); 3. S. Scheiwiller (Yamaha); 4. Aggeler (Yamaha); 5. Kammermann (Honda); 6. Von Gunten (Honda); 7. Pouchon (Suzuki); 8. Stoff (KTM); 9. Hess (Yamaha); 10. Zani (Husqvarna).
Race II: 1. Züger (KTM); 2. Aggeler (Yamaha); 3. Marti (Yamaha); 4. Pouchon (Suzuki); 5. S. Scheiwiller (Yamaha); 6. Von Gunten (Honda); 7. Stoff (KTM); 8. Saxer (KTM); 9. Zani (Husqvarna); 10. Hess (Yamaha).

28 September – Aarberg
Race I: 1. Aggeler (Yamaha); 2. S. Scheiwiller (Yamaha); 3. Züger (KTM); 4. Von Gunten (Honda); 5. Kammermann (Honda); 6. Pouchon (Suzuki); 7. Rè (Honda); 8. Zani (Husqvarna); 9. Schüpbach (Kawasaki); 10. Hoffstetter (Vertemati).
Race II: 1. Von Gunten (Honda); 2. Saxer (KTM); 3. Rè (Honda); 4. Aggeler (Yamaha); 5. Kummer (Honda); 6. Kammermann (Honda); 7. Pouchon (Suzuki); 8. Schilliger (Yamaha); 9. Züger (KTM); 10. Blöchliger (KTM).

FINAL CLASSIFICATION
1. André Marti   Yamaha   242
2. Serge Scheiwiller   Yamaha   203
3. Stefan Züger   KTM   185
4. Schüpbach (Kawasaki), 181; 5. Von Gunten (Honda), 159; 6. Aggeler (Yamaha), 151; 7. Pouchon (Suzuki), 149; 8. Kammermann (Honda), 127; 9. Rè (Honda), 126; 10. Saxer (KTM), 125.

Youngster

11 May – Eschenbach
Race I: 1. Aeschbacher (KTM); 2. Imboden (Husqvarna); 3. Tschupp (Husqvarna); 4. Zimmermann (Yamaha); 5. Ricklin (Yamaha); 6. Kalberer (Yamaha); 7. Steiner (Yamaha); 8. Kummer (Husqvarna); 9. Walker (Yamaha); 10. Joos (Yamaha).
Race II: 1. Aeschbacher (KTM); 2. Tschupp (Husqvarna); 3. Kalberer (Yamaha); 4. Imboden (Husqvarna); 5. Zimmermann (Yamaha); 6. Ricklin (KTM); 7. Kummer (Husqvarna); 8. Graf (Sachs); 9. Reinisch (Yamaha); 10. Meyer (Suzuki).

1st June – Büron
Race I: 1. Imboden (Husqvarna); 2. Zimmermann (Yamaha); 3. Tschupp (Husqvarna); 4. Ricklin (KTM); 5. Reinisch (Yamaha); 6. Meyer (Suzuki); 7. Kalberer (Yamaha); 8. Ulrich (KTM); 9. Tanner (Yamaha); 10. Hunkeler (Yamaha).
Race II: 1. Imboden (Husqvarna); 2. Kalberer (Yamaha); 3. Aeschbacher (KTM); 4. Tschupp (Husqvarna); 5. Zimmermann (Yamaha); 6. Meyer (Suzuki); 7. Reinisch (Yamaha); 8. Joos (Yamaha); 9. Ricklin (KTM); 10. Walker (Yamaha).

29 June – Payerne
Race I: 1. Kalberer (Yamaha); 2. Zimmermann (Yamaha); 3. Imboden (Husqvarna); 4. Tschupp (Husqvarna); 5. Reinisch (Yamaha); 6. Aeschbacher (KTM); 7. Tanner (Yamaha); 8. Meyer (Suzuki); 9. Ricklin (KTM); 10. Kummer (Husqvarna).
Race II: 1. Aeschbacher (KTM); 2. Imboden (Husqvarna); 3. Kalberer (Yamaha); 4. Tanner (Yamaha); 5. Zimmermann (Yamaha); 6. Tschupp (Husqvarna); 7. Joos (Yamaha); 8. Ricklin (KTM); 9. Graf (Sachs); 10. Ulrich (KTM).

27 July – Buchs
Race I: 1. Tschupp (Husqvarna); 2. Imboden (Husqvarna); 3. Tanner (Yamaha); 4. Aeschbacher (KTM); 5. Reinisch (Yamaha); 6. Steiner (Yamaha); 7. Meyer (Suzuki); 8. Ricklin (KTM); 9. Schumacher (KTM); 10. Joos (Yamaha).
Race II: 1. Kalberer (Yamaha); 2. Tschupp (Husqvarna); 3. Imboden (Husqvarna); 4. Tanner (Yamaha); 5. Reinisch (Yamaha); 6. Ricklin (KTM); 7. Aeschbacher (KTM); 8. Schumacher (KTM); 9. Steiner (Yamaha); 10. Zimmermann (Yamaha).

14 September – Frauenfeld
Race I: 1. Tschupp (Husqvarna); 2. Aeschbacher (KTM); 3. Zimmermann (Yamaha); 4. Kalberer (Yamaha); 5. Imboden (Husqvarna); 6. Ricklin (KTM); 7. Joos (Yamaha); 8. Würsch (Sachs); 9. Steiner (Yamaha); 10. Reinisch (Yamaha).
Race II: 1. Aeschbacher (KTM); 2. Kalberer (Yamaha); 3. Tschupp (Husqvarna); 4. Zimmermann (Yamaha); 5. Imboden (Husqvarna); 6. Ricklin (KTM); 7. Würsch (Sachs); 8. Steiner (Yamaha); 9. Ulrich (KTM); 10. Richlik (Yamaha).

28 September – Aarberg
Race I: 1. Zimmermann (Yamaha); 2. Imboden (Husqvarna); 3. Kalberer (Yamaha); 4. Aeschbacher (KTM); 5. Tschupp (Husqvarna); 6. Albert (Sachs); 7. Reinisch (Yamaha); 8. Richlik (Yamaha); 9. Ulrich (KTM); 10. Rüdisüli (KTM).
Race II: 1. Zimmermann (Yamaha); 2. Imboden (Husqvarna); 3. Hunkeler (Yamaha); 4. Aeschbacher (KTM); 5. Richlik (Yamaha); 6. Ulrich (KTM); 7. Tschupp (Husqvarna); 8. Kalberer (Yamaha); 9. Reinisch (Yamaha); 10. Ricklin (KTM).

FINAL CLASSIFICATION
1. Manuel Imboden   Husqvarna 250
2. Raoul Tschupp   Husqvarna 235
3. Mike Aeschbacher   KTM   225
4. Kalberer (Yamaha), 221; 5. Zimmermann (Yamaha), 211; 6. Ricklin (KTM), 155; 7. Reinisch (Yamaha), 143; 8. Ulrich (KTM), 107; 9. Joos (Yamaha), 99; 10. Tanner (Yamaha), 95.

SHARE THE POWER

New MotoGP glory for Michelin. Valentino Rossi
is world champion with the Repsol Honda Team.
Our Partners dominate the top 10 finishes.
We've set a world record with 300 MotoGP victories.
We race for tyre perfection. For the track of for you,
every meichelin tyre shares this srip and control.
now you know why michelin races ahead.

Share the Spirit